BAR CODE ON BACK PAGE

KU-877-475

Introduction to Information Systems

organisations, applications, technology and design

David Whiteley

Department of Computing and Mathematics
Manchester Metropolitan University

O.B.M.S.

B05815

© David Whiteley 2004

All rights reserved. No reproduction, copy or transmission of this
publication may be made without written permission.

No paragraph of this publication may be reproduced, copied or transmitted
save with written permission or in accordance with the provisions of the
Copyright, Designs and Patents Act 1988, or under the terms of any licence
permitting limited copying issued by the Copyright Licensing Agency, 90
Tottenham Court Road, London W1T 4LP.

Any person who does any unauthorised act in relation to this publication
may be liable to criminal prosecution and civil claims for damages.

The author has asserted his right to be identified as the author
of this work in accordance with the Copyright, Designs and
Patents Act 1988.

First published 2004 by
PALGRAVE MACMILLAN
Houndmills, Basingstoke, Hampshire RG21 6XS and
175 Fifth Avenue, New York, N.Y. 10010
Companies and representatives throughout the world

PALGRAVE MACMILLAN is the global academic imprint of the Palgrave
Macmillan of St. Martin's Press LLC and of Palgrave Macmillan Ltd. Macmillan® is a
registered trademark in the United States, United Kingdom and other countries.
Palgrave is a registered trademark in the European Union and other countries.

ISBN 0–333–99766–2

This book is printed on paper suitable for recycling and made from fully managed
and sustained forest sources.

A catalogue record for this book is available from the British Library.

10   9   8   7   6   5   4   3   2   1
13 12 11 10 09 08 07 06 05 04

Printed in China

UNIVERSITY
LIBRARY
2 8 JUL 2005
HUDDERSFIELD
SQ 0911935 3

Brief Table of Contents

Contents

Acknowledgements

Firstly my thanks to Rebecca Mashayekh, Helen Bugler and Dave Hatter at Palgrave Macmillan. Dave was in at the inception of the project and has kept faith even when the dates were put back. Somehow his e-Mails asking 'how you doing me boy?' always arrived just when doing was not what was happening. Rebecca has been there in the background but came in with perceptive contributions on scheduling and on the presentation of the material. Helen replaced Rebecca at the end and gently but firmly reminded me of deadlines and pointed out formalities I would have forgotten.

Also my gratitude to Peter Linecar of South Bank University and Pamela Quick at MMU who have reviewed the complete text and given excellent feedback. Others colleagues who have helped, reviewed and encouraged are Keith Miller, Janet Rothwell, Martin Stanton and Nick Whittaker: my thanks to them as well. As all authors say (and it is true), the design errors and the bugs that have got through the testing stages are the responsibility of the author, not the reviewers.

Finally a mention for my family, my partner Lena Dominelli and our son Nic. Lena is an inspirational academic, a prolific author and an example to me. Nic is a voice of reason – he urges both his parents to stop writing books and usually he is ignored.

DaveW

Preface

Information technology (IT) and Information systems (IS) are all-pervasive throughout societies in developed countries. Organisations use IT and IS in their administration systems and IT is an integral part of the production equipment on the factory floor. Many members of the public also have computer equipment at home and IT is built into many consumer durables. The interface between the public and organisations is also mediated by the use of IT: indirectly through call centres or directly by networked systems. Additionally IT is an essential component of many of the services we use, for example, the electronic tills in shops, the information displays at the railway station and the electronics built into the aeroplanes we fly in.

IT, and the IS it supports, do not exist in isolation but are linked using communications technologies together we refer to this as information and communications technologies (ICTs). The use of networked IT integrates the business systems of organisations with those of their supplier and customer organisations. The use of the Internet is part of this and also allows members of the public, with their home computers, to communicate with one another and with organisations across the globe.

For people everywhere, the ability to access and use ICT is a part of their jobs and is becoming essential for everyday life. The need to use IT systems should be accompanied by an understanding of the technologies involved and the uses to which they are put. Governments throughout the world have recognised these imperatives and have promoted IT awareness in schools, in further and higher education and through adult, life-long learning schemes.

This book is intended as part of a general education in IS and IT. It is not aimed at the school market or at general readers (although interested adults would be very welcome customers) but at computing and business students doing an introductory course in IS.

The six main areas of study presented by the book are:

- Information system introduction and case studies.
- An introduction to business.
- The business use of information systems.
- IT for information systems.
- Systems analysis and design.
- Legal, social and ethical implications of IS and IT.

These are presented as Parts I to VI followed by a seventh part which presents the concluding chapter. Each of these parts is outlined below to help the educator using the book as a text to plan his or her course, and to help the reader who wishes to select the topics of interest rather than read the book from cover to cover.

◆ **Part I   Introduction to Information Systems**

❖   Chapter 1   Information Systems

This chapter explains an information system as the interface between the business (the topic of *Part II*) and the information technology (the topic of *Part IV*). Some of the uses of

IS are explained (this is extensively dealt with in **Part III**) and there is reference to their societal implications (the topic of **Part VI**). The nature of information systems is further illustrated by outlining the development process (further developed in **Part V**).

This chapter is intended as a course introduction – not just as an introduction to the text.

❖   Chapter 2   Case Study

The case study is Universal Home Stores (UHS), a large (and fictitious) multiple clothing retailer. The case study is used in subsequent chapters to illustrate aspects of business IS such as the IS infrastructure of a large organisation, order processing, and EDI systems.

The case study serves to demonstrate the size of IS / IT investment that is undertaken by many large organisations and the extent to which those organisations are reliant on their information systems.

◆   **Part II   Business**

❖   Chapter 3   The Business Environment

This chapter introduces a three layer model of business / organisations (derived from Needle's business in context model). The chapter then looks at the organisation's relationship with its environment. One of the environmental factors is IT.

❖   Chapter 4   Business Ownership, Structure and Culture

Organisations have different forms of ownership, structures and cultures. These three aspects of the management layer of the business IS environment model are examined in this chapter.

❖   Chapter 5   Business Strategy

This chapter continues with the management layer but is devoted to the topic of business strategy. Porter's model of competitive forces, SWOT and the Boston Consulting Group matrix are explained and used as tools for strategy development. The chapter also looks at strategy for IS and IT within the organisation.

❖   Chapter 6   Business Activity

This chapter looks at the diverse activities that together make the organisation function. Porter's generic vale chain is used as an illustration of the overall functioning of the organisation and the Universal Home Store case study provides a context with which to illustrate the detail.

Note: Part II is not a full business study course but is intended to provide the background for the use of information systems within an organisation – courses with a separate unit, or units, on business may wish to omit these four chapters. Part II also includes a number of business models with a secondary aim of introducing students to the role of models within academia.

◆   **Part III   Business Use of Information Systems**

❖   Chapter 7   The IS Infrastructure

Students (and others) are familiar with desk top systems but not normally with the extensive and complex IS / IT infrastructure that is typically used by medium and large organisations. This chapter develops a series of system diagrams from the Universal Home Stores case study (presented in *Part I*) to make the point.

❖ Chapter 8   Example Systems

The web of IS / IT provision illustrated in the previous chapter includes a number of large systems which are themselves complex. This chapter outlines a (generic) payroll and an order processing system to illustrate that complexity and a number of other implications. Among the points brought out are the analysis and design decisions that can make an information system function efficiently for, and within, the organisation.

❖ Chapter 9   EDI Systems

EDI has been significant over the last decade or more in linking the information systems in customer and supplier organisations and in automating the supply chain. EDI is described in some detail as a component of information systems and as an example of the business use of information and communications technologies (ICTs).

❖ Chapter 10   e-Commerce Systems

The development of ICTs has enabled the Internet and its use for consumer c Commerce. This chapter looks at the information systems that are used for e-Commerce.

❖ Chapter 11   Expert Systems

Another developing technology in information systems is the use of artificial intelligence (AI). This chapter looks at AI, the workings of expert systems, and the application of AI in information systems.

❖ Chapter 12   Management Information

The basic, essential function of the information systems is the processing of business transactions. Transaction processing accumulates vast stores of data that can then be analysed to inform management decisions at the operational, tactical and strategic level. This chapter looks at the nature of management information, the systems that produce it and its effective presentation.

❖ Chapter 13   From DP to Desk Top

IT and IS systems come in many shapes and sizes. They range from a free-standing PC to corporate networks that span the world. The applications that are used can be bought in or they can be bespoke systems. This chapter surveys the spectrum of IS / IT provision and tries to make sense of what sort of provision might be appropriate, where and for what purpose.

◆ **Part IV**   **Information Technology**

❖ Chapter 14   Computer Systems

'Boxes' come in many shapes and sizes – they range from the ubiquitous PC (which all students must be familiar with) up to large mainframe and super computers (of which many students may be only vaguely aware). This chapter outlines the spectrum of computers that are available and suggests why differing processors and configurations might be appropriate for different applications. It also gives a brief insight into how the computer works. It is not magic and the IS practitioner should have some idea as to what is involved.

❖   Chapter 15   Files and Data Structures

A central part of an information system is the storage of data, and that storage must be appropriately structured if the data is to be readily available and the system is to run efficiently. This chapter looks at the requirement to store data and the three basic file structures that can be used. The chapter leads on to the study of databases – databases rely on the data structures studied in this chapter.

❖   Chapter 16   Databases

The main storage of data, in most information systems, is on a database. This chapter looks at databases, the various types and how they work. The chapter concentrates on the relational model as the most widely used (even if the author is an advocate of network databases!).

❖   Chapter 17   Networks

Most computers are networked and the network is a vital element of most information systems. This chapter looks at networks but the concentration is on the business requirements for networking rather than the technical detail of network implementation.

❖   Chapter 18   Transaction and Distributed Processing

Continuing on the network theme, this chapter looks at transaction processing and distributed processing. Arguably it is the most technical chapter in the book but it is there to illustrate the problems of system integrity and the need to take full account of that in the design of information systems.

◆   **Part V   Systems Analysis and Design**

❖   Chapter 19   System Development Lifecycles

This chapter is an introduction to systems analysis and design (SA&D). It provides an outline of the main approaches: soft, structured, object oriented (OO) and rapid application development (RAD) (although categorising approaches to SA&D is not necessarily that simple). The chapter looks at the lifecycles of the methodologies and the generic activities required in the SA&D process.

The chapter is followed by more detail on structured and OO SA&D. These chapters are seen as alternatives with the tutor deciding which approach to adopt. There is a move to OO approaches and structured approaches are increasingly seen as dated. That said, OO analysis and design sensibly leads onto OO programming and implementation whereas the project work in this book is aimed at using a database package where the structured diagrams are more immediately relevant.

The chapter includes case studies for High Peak Bicycles and Madcaster University, which are used for SA&D examples and exercises throughout *Part V*.

❖   Chapter 20   Structured Systems Analysis and Design

This chapter concentrates on four techniques – the data flow diagram (DFD), entity relationship diagram (ER diagram), relational data analysis and entity life histories (ELH). The chapter uses the bike hire shop case study and there is a further case study for student exercises.

❖   Chapter 21   Object-Oriented System Analysis and Design

This chapter uses UML and concentrates on three techniques – the use case diagram, class diagram and sequence diagram. The chapter includes its own simple lifecycle for the application of UML. The chapter uses the bike hire shop case study and there is a further case study for student exercises.

❖ Chapter 22   Interfaces

The user interface and its appropriate design are crucial to the effective implementation of almost all information systems. This chapter looks at interface design and gives a brief introduction to human–computer interaction (HCI). The bike hire shop case study is again used as a example.

❖ Chapter 23   Projects, Programming and Implementation

Once the system is designed it has to be implemented. Implementation requires project management and it includes programming (or installing a package), testing, going live and then the new system requires maintenance.

❖ Chapter 24   Student Project

The intention is that students will take the design work covered in the earlier chapters of this part and implement the system on an Access database. The students can implement the Madcaster University system or, alternatively, one of the other short case studies given in this chapter (in the latter case they will be more dependent on their own design work). This chapter will outline the implementation steps and greater detail is available on the web page (where it can be amended to take account of new versions of the software).

◆ **Part VI   Legal, Social and Ethical Implications of IS and IT**

❖ Chapter 25   IT and Society

Whilst IS and IT has generally made businesses more efficient and increased the possibilities of accessing information for many people, this has not been without a cost. IT in business has cost jobs and made other jobs somewhat unskilled and soulless. IT in society can make it possible to access, collate and communicate information that is detrimental to individuals and to the proper operation of a free society. This chapter presents an overview of the social and ethical implications of the widespread use of computers in society.

❖ Chapter 26   IS and the Law

Some of the actual and potential abuses and misuses of IT and IS applications are addressed by the law, and organisations and individuals can seek redress through regulators and / or in the courts. The chapter provides a brief introduction to the data protection and computer misuse acts.

◆ **Part VII   Conclusions**

❖ Chapter 27   Conclusions

This chapter attempts to bring together the threads that have run throughout the book. The emphasis is on the range of requirements and the diversity of provisions. The aims of the course are to make the students aware of this diversity and the importance of appropriate design in the provision of information systems facilities.

The book has been divided into chapters of roughly equal length, each intended as a unit of study (chapters 1 and 2 can be taken together as a single unit). The pattern that is envisaged is that the study of each chapter will consist of:

- A lecture – slides are provided on the web site.
- A tutorial – appropriate tutorial topics / exercises are suggested.
- Self study – the student should read the chapter and do the exercises.

The exception to this is the two chapters in *Part V* on SA&D techniques. It is important that students take their time to understand and practise the techniques, and each chapter should be taken as four units of study – one week for each of the techniques presented (and remember it is anticipated that students will concentrate on either structured or OO SA&D).

In addition to the lecture there are topics for assignments associated with each part of the book – these are at the end of the last chapter of each part.

The author and Palgrave the publisher both hope you enjoy the book and find it useful. There is material on the accompanying web site at http://www.palgrave.com/resources, to help both tutors and students. You are invited to make full use of these resources.

DaveW

Part I
Introduction to Information Systems

In this introductory section we define the term information system (IS) and we outline the topics that are included in the study of IS. These points are illustrated by looking at the role of the IS / IT function within the organisation and by looking at a system development lifecycle (the tasks involved in analysing, designing and developing an information system).

This section includes an extensive case study of the use of information systems and information technology in a large, multiple retailer. This illustrates the complexity of the IS provision in a large organisation – it is used in later sections of the book to illustrate further aspects of the study of information systems.

Chapter 1
Information Systems

Summary

An information system can be defined as a 'business application of the computer'. The subject area of information systems (or management information systems as the Americans would have it) includes an understanding of:

- Business / organisations – their aims, management, structures and methods of working.
- Information systems and their use within organisations.
- The information technology used in information systems.
- The process and techniques of analysing and designing an information system.
- The professional, legal, social and ethical issues involved in the application of information systems and information technology.

The information system function within an organisation can be seen as an intermediary between the business and the information technology infrastructure of the organisation. The role of the information system specialist is further illustrated by the system development lifecycle.

1.1   What is an Information System?

An information system is a broad categorisation. The term does not mean quite what it would seem to imply. It can be defined as:

An information system is: *a business application of the computer.*

An information system, or a management information system (MIS) which is the North American term, is not just about providing information but also about processing business transactions. Information systems are also data processing systems (DP) and business transaction processing systems (TP). Examples of commonly used information systems are:

- Payroll. This system starts with details of employees and their rates of pay and processes this data to produce bank transfers, pay slips, etc. The system also provides information on, for example, the payroll cost of staff in the various departments and grades within the organisation.

◆ Order processing: The main input transaction is the customer order which is processed using customer and product data to output the delivery note and invoice transactions. In addition to processing the business transactions the system can produce a wealth of management information on what is selling, who is buying and the overall sales totals for each month and year.

Most organisations will have a small number of information systems that are central to their operation. Examples of this are:

◆ A supermarket with its sales and stock replenishment system.
◆ A manufacturing company with materials requirement planning and production control systems.
◆ A college or university with its student registration and records system.

In addition to these central systems, on which the operations of the organisation depends, there will be a number of further systems for functions such as marketing, accounts, the customer complaints department and so on. Some of these applications will be formal information systems and some will make use of standard desk top packages.

The central business systems of the organisation will be supported by an extensive IT infrastructure. Many organisations, and the large multiple retailers are good examples of this, are totally dependent of their IS / IT infrastructure. In these organisations most or all employees will be interfacing with the core information system. In the supermarket for example:

> The electronic point of sale system (EPOS) reads the barcodes, looks up the prices of the merchandise and calculates the customer bill. As each item is checked through the EPOS system the sales are totalled and that total is then taken from the store's stock total to calculate the replenishment requirement for each product sold by the store. The stock replenishment system then comes into operation to order a delivery from the regional warehouse to the store and, after further calculation, electronic orders are sent to the food processor for stock to be delivered to the warehouse. Details of all transactions are stored and analysed to derive accounts, marketing and management information.

For a large supermarket chain concerned with ensuring good stock availability with minimum stock holding this is a very large and sophisticated IS. The system consists of the EPOS terminals and back office servers in the stores, warehouse systems in the depots and, in all probability, a large data centre at a head office site. The supermarket's IS will be linked to its suppliers' order processing ISs creating an 'inter-organisational information system'. The overall system is illustrated in *figure 1.1*. The overall system costs a large sum of money and many years of effort will have gone into building up and tuning the system. The supermarket can not operate without the system: if, for example, the EPOS infrastructure breaks down the store has to close its doors (and that occasionally does happen despite the efforts of the organisation to make its systems secure).

Not all systems are that large and their operation is not necessarily critical to the organisation. Your college or university does have, as already mentioned, its own information systems but they do not, in general, greatly impinge on the day to day function of teaching and learning – the classes can still go ahead even if the student registration and record system is not available.

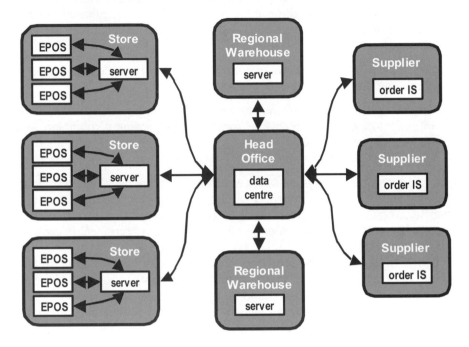

Figure 1.1 Supermarket Chain – IT Infrastructure.

1.2 The Study of Information Systems

The study of information systems has two main strands:

- ◆ The application and effect of information systems within organisations.
- ◆ The analysis, design and implementation of information systems.

To understand the application of information systems within businesses and other organisations the IS student must first have some understanding of the structure and *modus operandi* of those organisations; this is looked at in *Part II*. Following on from that, the reader needs to have some understanding of:

- ◆ The nature of information systems, how they work within organisations and their effect on those organisations; this is looked at in *Part III*.
- ◆ The scope of information technology and how it can be utilised in IS; this is the subject of *Part IV*.

Armed with this background, the IS practitioner is in a position to investigate organisational requirements for IT and design an IS; an introduction to system analysis and design is given on *Part V*. All IS development and application should be legal and within an appropriate ethical framework; this is discussed in *Part VI*.

These areas together constitute the discipline of information systems. This book examines each at an introductory level and should equip students with a comprehensive background understanding of the field of IS. For IS students, and students in related areas of study, the topics in this book will be further developed in subsequent units of study.

The topics outlined above, together, constitute the knowledge and skill base of the system analysis role. It is also information that is useful to all other roles within the IS / IT function and many other functions in organisations, at all levels.

1.3 The IS Function within an Organisation

As indicated above, the primary role in the information systems function is that of the systems analyst. Further roles that require an understanding of the field of IS and the techniques used in IS include project manager, business analyst, analyst programmer and the system integrator. These roles exist within the IS / IT function of an organisation, shown diagrammatically in *figure 1.2*.

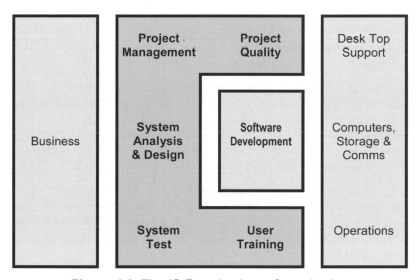

Figure 1.2 The IS Function in an Organisation

The IS function exists as the interface between the business on one hand and the IT infrastructure (computers, storage and communications network) on the other hand.

The business (organisation) performs a number of functions and many of these can be controlled or assisted by the application of IS / IT. It may well be that people within the organisation will have the knowledge and expertise to use IT equipment and information systems but, for large complex requirements that interface with other departments and (possibly) other organisations, they are likely to require the assistance of IS specialists.

IT equipment will be dispersed throughout the organisation with many / most employees having a PC or specialist terminal on their desk or at their work station. All this equipment has to be set up and maintained. The desktop / workstation IT equipment is very probably networked to server / central mainframe facilities and these also need to be operated and maintained.

The IS function is to analyse business operations, suggest how IT can be used to expedite these functions and to design the information systems that will be used in the business. The central role is that of system analysis and design, and this is further broken down in the next section. Further roles in the IS function are:

◆ Project management: Any significant IS development will normally have a project team set up to do the work involved. The project has to be planned and then the activity of the project team must be monitored to ensure that appropriate progress is being made. The role of the project manager is to plan the project, run the project team and ensure that the project is delivered on time and on budget.

◆ Project quality: As well as being on time the project needs to be a quality system; it must be fit for the purpose for which it is intended. To be a quality system it must meet the business objectives that have been set, operate efficiently and be readily maintained and updated. The project manager is responsibly for delivering a quality system (possibly assisted by a separate quality assurance function).

◆ System and acceptance test: Once a system is developed the project team must check that it works. The system needs to cope with all possible inputs, produce the correct results and perform efficiently in the operational environment. After the project team has accepted the system it is the turn of the users. The acceptance test is their opportunity to check that the system does the job that they require.

◆ User training: As well as making sure that the system is ready the users of the system have to be ready. A new system can require radical changes in working practice and it requires careful planning to ensure all goes smoothly and that the users are fully trained when a new, or enhanced, system is introduced.

While the specification and the testing of the system are IS functions, the development of the system is the task of the programmers. The programmers take the technical speciation from the system analyst and translate that into the programming instructions that the computer needs to perform the task. The programmers will also unit test their modules before handing them over for system and acceptance testing.

Traditionally information systems have been developed through the analysis, design, programming and test sequence. The process of building your own information systems can be both time consuming and expensive and more and more systems are bought in as packaged solutions. The analysis, programming and testing functions are still part of the process of adapting and installing a packaged solution but the system development processes and functions need tailoring to the requirements of the installation being undertaken.

The classic IS function started many years ago when computer systems were centralised mainframes and very few people in the business knew anything about IT. The data processing department provided the expertise necessary to create and operate computer application systems for the organisation. Since those days, ICT equipment and some knowledge of IS / IT have become defused throughout the organisation, and the IT department is no longer the central monolith it once was. Nevertheless, most organisations of a significant size will still have an IS department and the diagram is illustrative of the function.

1.4 The System Development Lifecycle

The system development activities outlined above can be represented as stages in a system development lifecycle. Each stage of the lifecycle performs a particular function and requires a specific set of skills.

The classic system development lifecycle is the waterfall lifecycle. In the waterfall lifecycle the activities / stages are performed in sequence – a representation of the waterfall lifecycle is shown in *figure 1.3*. Note that the waterfall lifecycle can be represented with more than the five stages – the additional stages would normally be subdivisions of the stages shown.

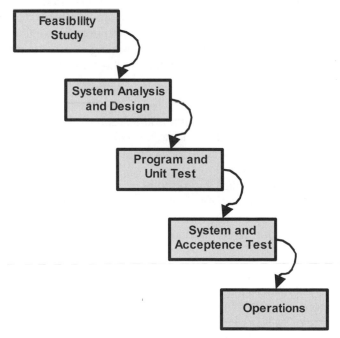

Figure 1.3 Waterfall Lifecycle

The activities of the five stages, in summary, are:

◆ Feasibility study:
A short study to determine if the proposed system is technically feasible, financially worthwhile and ethically justified. The feasibility study produces a report that is used to determine if the project should get the go-ahead. If the project is to proceed the feasibility study will include the terms of

reference, a project plan and budget estimates for the future stages of the development.

◆ System analysis and design:
A full study to determine the requirements for the computer system and to map those requirements onto the computer hardware.

The stage includes a detailed study of the business needs of the organisation. This study is then mapped onto a logical system and that in turn is translated into a design for the technical implementation. The system analysis and design stage may well consider options for changing the business process and will also need to determine the appropriate hardware and system software to be used for the project.

◆ Programming and unit test:
Converts the design to computer code and tests each component of that computer code.

Computer programs need to be written for each part of the system. Using a conventional programming language programs will be written as a series of modules (possibly by a number of programmers). Each of these modules should be the subject of separate and detailed testing.

The alternatives to conventional programming are a 'fourth generation language' (4GL), application generator, or the use of bought in software packages.

◆ System test and acceptance test:
System testing, by the project team, and acceptance testing, by the users.

In the system and acceptance tests the separate modules of the system are brought together and tested as a complete system. The system needs to be tested to ensure that:

  ◆ The interfaces between the modules work (Integration Test).
  ◆ The system works on the intended platform and with the expected volumes of data (Volume Test).
  ◆ The system does what the users require of it (Acceptance Test / Beta Test).

◆ Operation:
Using the system including error correction and enhancement.

The system is made live and is used for its intended business purpose. The IS function will be involved in training the users on the new system and associated procedures. There will be a support function that deals with queries and errors as they arise. There may (will) also be enhancements to improve the system and to deal with changes in business requirements.

Eventually the business requirement will change radically and / or the system (hardware and / or software) will become outmoded and a new system will be required. The lifecycle starts again.

The lifecycle is included in this introductory chapter to illustrate the role of the IS function within a organisation. There are alternative approaches to system development and the lifecycle, and the system development process is dealt with in more detail in **Part V**.

Exercises

The following exercises are designed to aid your understanding of the material presented in this chapter. The exercises can be used for self study or selected exercises can be used for tutorial discussion.

1. An information system is a business application of the computer. List some of the business applications that you come across in everyday life.

2. Information systems are often specialist applications and, in some cases, they are very large systems. Desktop packages such as word processors and spreadsheets are also used for business applications (in effect individual information systems). List some business applications of desktop applications.

3. From the information provided in the chapter, write a job description for the system analysis role in an organisation.

4. List the stages of the waterfall lifecycle and add to that list the tasks performed by the system analyst at each stage.

5. Write a job description for the project manager of a system development team.

Assignments

As well as the above exercises, based on the material in the chapter, it is also advantageous to do your own research. Below are essay questions on two IS related topics that are not covered in any detail in this book. Choose one of the topics and write an academic essay of about two thousand words. Reference all the material taken directly from the sources and include a full bibliography.

1. The use of computers and telecommunications can enable work to be done at a location remote from an organisation's office; a development known as teleworking (or telecommuting in North America). Discuss the nature of teleworking, its impact on the individual, the organisations for which the teleworkers work and its likely future development.

2. Computers are extensively used in schools and colleges but normally only for the study of IT topics or as an adjunct to more traditional teaching practices. Some educationalists suggest the much wider use of computers in education, with information and communications technologies (ICTs) largely replacing face-to-face contact in the classroom. Research and explain possible future uses of ICTs in education and assess their likely impact on the various institutions and different client groups that may be affected.

Chapter 2
Case Study

Summary

The chapter is devoted to the case study of Universal Home Stores (UHS). UHS has invested heavily in its IS / IT systems. All its stores are equipped with EPOS systems that interact with the merchandising and stock replenishment systems in the head office and the distribution centre. The organisation works on the basis of 'quick response supply' with stock sold one day been replenished overnight and then stock is reordered from suppliers using electronic data interchange (EDI). The sales and stock systems feed the management information systems, the accounting systems and interface electronically with the credit card companies used by UHS.

The overall IS / IT infrastructure is large and complex – the intention is to convey to the reader the extent of the IT infrastructure required by a large organisation. Don't be worried if you don't take in all the detail on a first read, we will be returning to the case study in subsequent chapters.

2.1   Using Case Studies

Case studies are widely used in the study of information systems, particularly at an intermediate and advanced level. Case studies can be used:

◆ To illustrate how organisations develop and make use of information systems.
◆ As an exercise for practising system analysis and design techniques.

Teaching cases tend to tell half the story and then leave the student to make the business decisions or choose the IT solution in tutorial discussion. Doubtless it is a good teaching technique but a book full of such (incomplete) cases can be a frustrating read. This chapter contains one large (and complete) case study:

◆ Universal Home Stores (UHS).

This is a fictitious organisation (but based on real systems and organisations). The case study is used in a number of chapters to illustrate topics that include business activity, IS infrastructure, order processing and EDI systems. Further (shorter) case studies are given throughout the book where they help to illustrate the topics being discussed.

2.2 Universal Home Stores

Universal Home Stores (UHS) is a large UK multiple retailer selling fashion goods and some giftware. The head office is in Nottingham as are the data centre and the distribution centre. It operates 120 stores in the UK and is represented in all major urban areas and shopping malls.

As with most large retail groups, UHS makes extensive use of information and communications technologies (ICTs) in running its business. This case study is based on interviews with a number of key UHS personnel involved in the provision and use of the ICT infrastructure at UHS.

❖ **Barry – IT Operations Manager**

The role of operations is to run the central computers at the head office data centre. Most of the business systems are focused on the central computer systems. Currently UHS has two large IBM mainframes, a number of UNIX servers and a data warehouse system. Mainframe software includes the operating system (MVS), the transaction processing monitor (CICS) and a relational database (DB2). The data centre is operated twenty-four hours a day and seven days a week.

The principal use of the mainframe computers is the critical sales, stock and replenishment system. One mainframe runs this system while the other is used for development, subsidiary tasks and as a backup machine in case of any failure in the other system.

UNIX servers are used for a variety of functions that do not need to be on the mainframe or where the best available software was designed for the UNIX environment. Significant UNIX systems include: personnel / payroll, purchasing decision support, e-Shop, intranet, inter-organisational messaging and the general ledger.

The data warehouse is a specialist machine with massive amounts of online storage that is structured for rapid data searches, pattern recognition and online queries. All sales data is held on the data warehouse for at least five years.

All central computers are interconnected and they are in turn networked to all head office departments (using a local area network (LAN) system), to the distribution centre, the newly developed e-Shop and to every store (using UHS's private network leased from Mercury Communications – a wide area network (WAN)). There are also network links to UHS's supply and credit card partners using the facilities of the IBM Global Network.

While the main computer systems are in the data centre there are also numerous PC and specialist systems located throughout the head office, distribution centre and stores. In the head office nearly all staff have a PC on their desk which is used both for desk-top applications (principally word processing, spreadsheets, intranet and e-Mail) and as client / terminal systems to access the facilities of the central computer systems. The distribution centre and the shops have PC systems but they also have their own specialist systems – electronic point of sales (EPOS) at the stores and a semi automated warehouse system at the distribution centre.

Barry's Operations Group is responsible for the running of the central computers and supporting the system software that is used on those computers. Barry reports to Keith, the Information Systems Director. The other groups in the data centre reporting to Keith are:

◆ Strategic Information Systems – managed by Karen.
◆ System Development – managed by Yousif.
◆ End User Support – managed by Geoff.

Strategic Information Systems is the smallest group within the data centre. Its role is to look into the future, study the latest IT and IS developments and to see how these can be usefully and profitably applied in UHS. The role is a business analysis function (and the group was called the Business Analysis Group until it adopted a new title at the beginning of the year).

Systems Development is responsible for the systems analysis, programming and implementation of any new project devised by the business analysts. Much of the work of the group is in the maintenance and enhancement of existing systems. The central sales, stock replenishment systems were developed by the group and have been enhanced and updated over the years, a process that still continues. Many other systems have been bought-in and then adapted to UHS' requirements – generally this is a cheaper approach than developing new applications in-house.

End User Support provides first instance assistance for all IT users outside the data centre. The support function is centred on a help desk but there is also an IT officer in each of the stores and at the distribution centre. Most day to day problems are resolved in first line support but any corrections to software have to be passed on to Systems Development for action.

Two further functions in Information Systems are e-Commerce and Information. Both of these functions have a manager supported by a researcher and a secretary. The managers report to the IS Director but, given their size and nature, they are designated as functions as opposed to the other four groups within the division. The e-Commerce and Information managers are interviewed later in this case study.

The current staff complement of the IS Division is approximately 275 people (excluding the further 120 IT Officers in the branches who count as store staff).

❖ **Susan – Store Manager (Sheffield Branch)**

There are two large branches in Sheffield, one in the city centre and a second at the Meadowhall shopping mall in the lower Don Valley – Susan is responsible for the city centre branch.

All UHS shops are similar. The corporate image, employment policies, merchandise and IT policies are all determined by head office. There is some variation of stock policy between stores to take account of the size of the premises, turnover and the preferences of the local population – again these variations are largely determined by head office. The role of the Store Manager is to make sure that UHS policies are effectively implemented and that the resources of the store are deployed to best advantage.

The main IT system in the store is the electronic point of sale (EPOS) system. There are 32 EPOS terminals in the store linked to the EPOS controller in the back office and hence to the central system at the head office.

The EPOS terminal is based on a standard PC that is adapted for the specific purpose. Besides the processor (running the current MS Windows operating system) the terminal has:

◆ The barcode reader.
◆ A special reduced keyboard consisting of numbers and control keys in keypad format.
◆ A small screen that lists the product lines and total of the current transaction – the screen is limited to 10 products but can be scrolled.
◆ A repeater screen for the customer showing the current transaction line or the total, once all items have been entered.
◆ Two hard disks. The first hard disk holds all product codes, descriptions and prices plus all the product transactions and credit / debit / store card transactions recorded at that terminal during the day. The second hard disk is slightly smaller and is a duplexed copy of the transactions.
◆ A magnetic stripe card reader. This is used to read credit cards, debit cards, the UHS store card and staff cards when staff log on to use the system. There is the possibility of having a smart card reader to read cards with chips on them but this is an expensive option and the cost is a subject of dispute between the Retail Consortium and the credit card companies.
◆ A cash tray for coins, notes and cheques.

The EPOS terminals are linked to the back office EPOS controller by a LAN. A full keyboard and mouse can be connected to the system for maintenance purposes.

The EPOS controller is again a PC-based system – in this case a server. It is linked to head office via the WAN and the EPOS terminals via the LAN. The EPOS controller holds the product codes, descriptions and prices for all items stocked in the branch. These are updated daily by an overnight transmission from head office. These product details are, in turn, transmitted to each EPOS terminal first thing in the morning before the store opens. The EPOS controller also holds details of all the product and card transactions. These are downloaded from the EPOS terminals at the end of the day and then automatically transmitted to head office overnight.

Resilience is a vital aspect of the EPOS system – if the EPOS system is not operating the store can not open – if sales data is lost the replenishment system can not send fresh supplies – if the credit / debit / store card data is lost then people are not charged and their accounts are not updated. Resilience is built into the EPOS system – the main features are as follows:

◆ There are 32 EPOS terminals – if a few are not working then there are still enough available for the store to operate.
◆ If the product / price update from head office or the EPOS controller fails then the EPOS terminal can still operate with data it has stored in it (if necessary a limited amount of data, such as a new special offer, can be input through the keyboard).

◆ If the sales / card data can not be downloaded from the EPOS terminal to the controller then the EPOS terminal can continue to operate – there is space available for at least two days' sales.

◆ If the EPOS terminal suffers a serious failure then the sales and card data should still be secure – it is duplexed on two hard disks and if necessary a disk can be removed and the data retrieved on another machine.

◆ The sales and card data is not deleted from the EPOS terminal until it has been uploaded to the EPOS controller and then copied onto a tape streamer.

◆ Each store has a second EPOS controller that can be used if the first controller fails. The second controller does not have duplexed data but the tape streamer output from the first controller is used to replicate the state of the failed controller.

◆ If the card / sales data can not be transmitted to head office it remains secure on the controller. If necessary the tape streamer output can be sent to head office.

In addition to the EPOS system there are a number of PCs in the administrative offices of each shop. These are used for word processing, spreadsheets, e-Mail and the company intranet but also they give access to the head office systems. This gives the store manager and her staff access to merchandise, stock, accounts and personnel information. One small system that is specific to the store level is cash management where money banked is recorded, reconciled with till totals and with the cash floats retained for the next day's trading.

❖ **Jade – Merchandising Manager**

Merchandising, the buying function, plays a critical part in the success of UHS. To be a success, in a very competitive environment, the store has to stock the right product, at the right price and in the right quantity. Fashion is very fickle: get the styles or colours wrong and you have the twin problems of lost sales and remaindered stock that nobody wants.

For UHS the buying function means placing 6,000 contracts per season. The buyer's job is based on fashion knowledge, negotiating skills and planning ability. At UHS the buying function is assisted by a decision support system (DSS). This system uses a bought-in DSS engine and has access to all current and previous contracts plus an interface with the data warehouse and hence the full details of all previous sales for the last several years. Using the DSS the buyers can see what garments (including size and colour) sold when and where and whether they had to be discounted to achieve the sale. What sold last year is not necessarily an accurate guide to what will sell in the coming season but it is, nevertheless, a useful input to the buying decision.

Buying decisions lead to contracts and these are recorded on the Contracts System and will be used at a later stage when the product is called-off from the supplies and moved into the store.

The agreement of the contract leads onto the Product Mix Planning System. As the buying decisions are made for each season the Mix system is used to plan which lines, colours, sizes, and quantities will be allocated to each of the shops. Some lines are allocated to all stores but there are variations depending on the store size and regional preferences. The Bournemouth store will, for instance, get a larger allocation of the more conservative lines to appeal to the large community of retired people in that area.

The Mix system is also where the retail price is recorded. This is also another difficult decision as UHS obviously wants to make a reasonable profit but must also price in line with the competition and market expectations. The information from the Buyer's DSS is an important input to the pricing process.

❖   **Jon – Distribution Manager**

Jon's primary responsibility is the distribution centre but he also has an intimate knowledge of the Replenishment System and that is where this section starts.

The Replenishment System is at the heart of UHS's operations. The inputs to the Replenishment System are the Contract System, the Mix System and the daily sales data from the EPOS systems at the stores. There are two levels of replenishment working in the system:

◆   The replenishment of the shops from the Distribution Centre.
◆   The replenishment of the Distribution Centre from UHS's suppliers.

The first of these is operated using the parameters established by the Mix system and the second uses the Contracts system. Both levels operate on a quick response basis. Stores only have the stock that is on display and expect overnight replenishment. The Distribution Centre is essentially about breaking up lorry load deliveries from the suppliers into deliveries to the individual stores and any stock holding is (largely) incidental to that process.

Starting at the shop, let's assume that Susan's Sheffield shop stocks four medium, blue, fleece body warmers and sells two of them. The sales data is transmitted to head office and the system notes those two sales. The system then:

◆   Checks the Mix system and notes that Sheffield should store four of this product.
◆   Checks the sales history and the season. If this product has been selling well in Sheffield it might seek to increase the stock holding. If it is getting towards the end of the season it might seek to gradually reduce the stock holding at the shop.

Let us assume that the preliminary replenishment decision is to send two of this item to Sheffield. The next stage is then to see if the product can be sourced:

◆   First step in sourcing the product is the Distribution Centre – if the product is in stock, it is assigned to Sheffield and that is the end of the replenishment computation for this item.

If the product can not be sourced from the Distribution Centre then the 'calculation' becomes more complex:

◆   The product might be on order from the supplier with an agreed delivery date – part of this delivery can be pre-allocated to Sheffield.
◆   If the product is not on order then it can be ordered but this will depend on the contract, the overall planned demand, the likely lead time and the

remaining duration of the season. Supplier ordering is electronic and is discussed by Faisal later on.

◆ In addition to sourcing the required product it is important to ensure that the branch has a good overall stock. If the store is going to be short of medium blues then the system can increase the allocation of other colours and (possibly) of the product range.

The replenishment process is complex and highly tuned and this is just an example. Over the 120 stores and 6,000 contracts the system can be making 4.5 million replenishment decisions each working week.

Stock allocations from the Distribution Centre are transmitted to the dedicated Distribution Control System. The Distribution System will then prioritise allocations and route picking instructions to a printer in the section of the centre where the goods are held. Picking of goods is a manual process but the goods are then put into specially designed containers that are guided along an automated conveyor system to the loading bay for the store that is to receive the goods.

The system calculates the load for each store and the optimum use of the delivery fleet. Where a lorry is to be sent to two or three stores then the goods are loaded in reverse order of delivery. The system also works out the route and schedule for the lorry and can include calling at a supplier's premises on the return journey to pick up some incoming supplies.

Stock coming into the distribution centre is also processed using the Distribution Control System. All suppliers are required to deliver product in standardised containers and with UHS barcode descriptions. These barcodes are read when the goods are unloaded and checked off against the corresponding replenishment order. The barcodes also serve to guide the packages along the conveyor system to their destination in the Distribution Centre.

❖ **Faisal – e-Commerce Manager**

The e-Commerce function is the newest within the IS Division. Faisal initially joined the Strategic Systems Group but after only one year was given the separate responsibility of e-Commerce strategy. Faisal reckons his e-Commerce degree from Manchester Metropolitan University was the main factor that identified him for the job.

UHS was already making extensive use of e-Commerce when Faisal's post was created. The type of electronic commerce that was in use was electronic data interchange (EDI). The use of EDI means that the replenishment orders generated by the UHS system are transmitted electronically to the supplier's system using the IBM Global Network. Using EDI there is no need to print out orders, post them and then key them into the supplier's computer – they are delivered electronically to the system that needs them, ready for processing. The orders are coded using the international EDI coding system, EDIFACT.

The replenishment orders are just one of several EDI transmissions. Further uses of EDI include:

◆ Predictions – UHS transmits details of sales of each item to the supplier. This allows the supplier to assess how the well or badly the product is doing and anticipate future demand. If, for example, the blue body warmers are outselling the black they might prioritise production of the favoured colour in anticipation of further orders.

- ◆ Availability – the supplier transmits details of its stock to UHS so that the figures can be taken into account when placing future replenishment orders.
- ◆ Order Conformation – the supplier confirms the receipt of the replenishment order and the expected delivery date for the goods.
- ◆ Delivery Note – the supplier sends an electronic delivery note to the Distribution Centre that can be matched to the original replenishment order and to the barcodes on the packaging of the physical delivery.
- ◆ Invoices – at the end of the month, after the month when the delivery took place, the supplier sends an electronic invoice that can then be matched to the original replenishment order and the corresponding delivery note.

The EDI system does not cover supplier payment. Instead electronic payment instructions are sent to the Bankers Automated Clearing Service (BACS) where the payment is credited to the supplier's account. The supplier also receives a paper payment advice. Note that the replenishment order is technically a call-off order. The contract specifies the goods that will be bought (although this might be varied). The call-off order then instructs the delivery of a part of the contract at a specific time.

Faisal is responsible for the EDI system but the main purpose of creating Faisal's post was to investigate the use of the Internet for business-to-consumer (B2C) transactions, an e-Shop. The start of UHS's e-Commerce study coincided with the e-Commerce crash of 2000 which rather settled the argument about how deeply UHS should go into consumer e-Commerce, at least in the short term.

In the event, UHS has opted for an extensive web site that catalogues most of its products, each with a picture and description. Online sales have however been limited to giftware items such as ties and socks where delivery is easier (the normal post can be used) and after sales is less problematic (there is less likelihood of goods been returned because they don't fit). The cataloguing of items that are not for sale online is seen as a form of advertising, the customer can check out merchandise online and then come to the shop with a fair idea of what they require. To date online sales have been relatively modest and the revenue generated does not cover the cost of the B2C e-Commerce operation. However there are perceived to be many less tangible benefits of running the web site and the company is pleased with progress thus far.

❖ **Nic – Accounts Manager**

The primary tasks of Finance are the financial welfare of the organisation and the production of the company's accounts. To perform these functions, Finance needs its own information and this is the one exception to the central sourcing of data from the data warehouse. The information for Finance is normally held on ledgers. However, before examining the ledgers let's look at the processing of Accounts Payable.

When the delivery arrives in the Distribution Centre the delivery data is matched against the replenishment order and the 'delivered order' is passed to Accounts Payable. Subsequently the invoice from the supplier is matched against Accounts

Payable and the account passed to Supplier Payments. Payment is made and hence the account is settled.

All transactions of a financial nature, the raising of a replenishment demand through to the settlement of the invoice, and all transactions on other systems such as payroll require a posting to the General Ledger. Each posting to the General Ledger comes under a sub-head for the part of the business it belongs to and each posting cancels out the previous posting for that transaction. Thus, for example, when an invoice is received it is recorded as outstanding and when it is paid that sum is subtracted from the outstanding invoices account.

Further ledgers are:

◆ Fixed Assets Ledger – all assets (buildings, furniture, IT equipment, etc.) owned by UHS with a value of over £100.
◆ Sales Ledger – any sales that don't go through the EPOS system.

Examples of the financial management reports used at UHS are:

◆ Actuals vs budget reporting for revenue expenditure.
◆ Trading revenue (sales) vs plan (by store and product group).
◆ Sales per square metre, profit per square metre of shop floor space comparisons.

The financial systems are also used in the production of the corporate accounts.

Other financial systems (shared responsibility with the personnel function) are the Payroll and the Pensions Administration Systems. UHS has approximately 14,000 staff on its monthly payroll.

❖ **Everton – Information Officer**

The Information Group's role is to ensure that business information and company information is readily available to everyone in UHS who needs it and that the information supplied is accurate, timely, relevant and consistent.

For a retail organisation the basic requirement is the appropriate analysis of sales – who is buying, what they are buying, when they are buying, the cost of sales, the stock lead times and so on. The policy on business information is to have a single source and that is the data warehouse. All sales data from the EPOS system is loaded onto the data warehouse. Centralising sales and related data on the data warehouse goes at least half way to ensuring accuracy and consistency. The other half of the story is to ensure that the enquiry / report generator software is used correctly, and the Information Group includes staff who are available to advise, help and audit the use of company information.

The second area of information is company information: boardroom developments, company statistics, personnel information, policy and procedures and so on. As with most companies, UHS had large amounts of paper and manuals. Often they were not available to those who needed the information and, where information was available, it was very possibly not the latest version. All this company information is now on an intranet supplemented by e-Mail notifications of significant changes. The use of an intranet does not ensure that the information is up-to-date but it does make sure that everyone can access the latest version.

❖ **Acknowledgement**

Universal Home Stores is a fictitious creation. The author acknowledges the use of an educational document issued by British Home Stores:

> BHS Information Technology Department (1994) *The Role of Computers within BHS*, BHS.

This document has been used as a teaching source for a number of years – it is now somewhat dated and hence its replacement by the UHS case study.

Exercises

At this stage, the main requirement is to read the case study – it will be used in subsequent chapters and, in particular, it will be extensively analysed in *Chapter 6*. For the present the following exercises are suggested as an aid to concentration and understanding:

1. Draw a structure chart of the departments in Universal Home Stores.

2. Draw a simple diagram of the UHS IT infrastructure.

3. Explain (briefly) the meaning of the following acronyms and terms:
   - EDI.
   - Quick response supply.
   - Call-off orders.
   - EPOS.
   - General Ledger.

Note that suggested assignments for *Part I* are given at the end of *Chapter 1*.

Part II
Business

Information systems are used by businesses, public sector organisations and non-governmental organisations (NGOs). To create and to understand information systems we should have some idea of their organisational context, and these next four chapters are intended to provide that understanding.

For our study of business / organisations we use a layered model that relates management functions to the operation of the organisation and the organisation to the external environment in which it operates.

The use of IS / IT is an essential component of the operations of most organisations. The use of IS at the operations level of the organisation is the basis of providing information to the management level. The imaginative use of IS / IT can be an important contributor to the competitive advantage of the business (and the lack of appropriate IS / IT can be a source of competitive disadvantage).

The use of networks, in particular the Internet, extends the scope of the organisation's IS / IT outside its boundaries to trading partners and administrative bodies in the business environment.

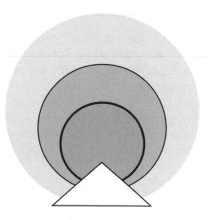

Chapter 3
The Business Environment

Summary

To produce a relevant information system the IS practitioner, and hence the IS student, needs to have some understanding of business and organisations.

To introduce business we use a three layer IS business environment model. The model makes the point that the everyday functions of the business (operations layer) do not exist in isolation but in the context of the ownership, structure and culture of the organisation (management layer) and the society in which the business operates (environment layer). These three layers are relevant to the study of business but also to information systems which need to meet requirements at all levels of the organisation and often of business partners.

Following on from the IS business environment model the outer, environment level is discussed. There is a wide range of topics that could be covered but for the purposes of this book we concentrate on globalisation and the technological environment.

3.1   The Information System Environment

An information system is a business application of the computer. To design an application system that will be productive for the organisation, we need to understand the aims of that organisation and how the organisation operates.

Information systems vary greatly in size and scope. At one end of the scale there are small departmental information systems doing relatively minor tasks – recording leave or processing travel claims could be examples. At the other end of the scale are the large, corporate information systems that are central to the efficient execution of the organisation's core activities; examples of such information systems are:

- A bank with a central record of all customers and their accounts. The data is accessible at the branches and, with limitations, at ATM machines and over the Internet. Information derived from the account data is available to departments such as marketing, the actuaries and to management.

- An airline that must have a database of its flights together with the crew rosters and the passenger bookings. The flight data is then used as the basis for making bookings, by the airline's staff and by travel agents (high-street and Internet), often via one of the large airline booking systems. The bookings are then used by the check-in staff to allocate seats and to organise the loading of the aircraft. As with the bank, the data is also used by other internal departments such as marketing and the management of the company.

♦ A manufacturer of consumer products with a stock control, production planning and order-processing system. In this case the database records all the customers that the company does business with and the products that it makes and supplies. As orders come in from the customers stock is picked, packed, despatched and the customer is invoiced. As stock is sold the production plans are updated so that appropriate quantities of each product can be manufactured to meet anticipated future demand.

The corporate information systems, as indicated above, affect staff at all levels within the organisation and the external entities with which the organisation does business:

♦ At the operational level the system processes business transactions – the input of customer orders and the subsequent delivery notes and invoices, that are sent out to the customers, are examples. The system can affect employment and impacts on the way staff do their everyday work. An appropriately designed system, that is sensitively introduced, can increase efficiency without adverse effects on staff – a poorly executed system will have the opposite effects.

♦ For the management of the company, operational information systems accumulate vast amounts of data that can be analysed in various ways to inform management in their tactical and strategic decisions. The obvious type of information is a summary of the level of sales. More obscure information could be, for example, the level of sales to passengers transferring from partner airlines and the revenue that generates. The scope for management information and decision support information (from internal information) is virtually unlimited. The problem is likely to be one of too much information rather than the reverse (and possibly the information system could be used to help sort that out).

♦ External to the company are the organisations that the company does business with or with which it exchanges information. These external entities are customers, suppliers, government departments and the like. The organisation exists within the business and societal environment and it only thrives if it is successful in its relations with that environment. The information systems of the organisation can also extend outside the organisation using business network and Internet links.

The relationship of the information system with the various levels of the organisation and its external interactions is shown in *figure 3.1*.

3.2   The IS Business Environment

The information system's business context, shown in *figure 3.1,* is a starting point to examine the nature of business, its environment and how IS and IT can and should interact with that environment.

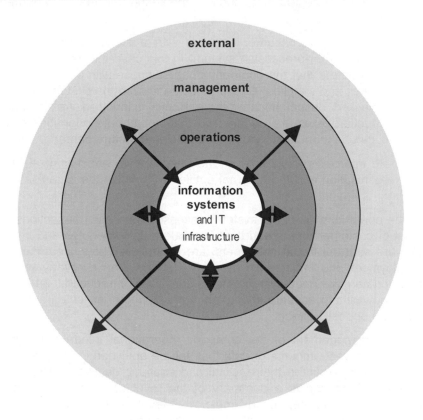

Figure 3.1 IS and Business

The diagram of IS and Business puts forward a three layer business model to guide our study of the business context of IS. The model is derived from Needle's business in context model (Needle, 2004) and includes input from Porter's generic value chain (Porter, 1985). The three layers and the main activities at each layer are:

❖   **Operations**

The inner layer of the model is the day to day operation of the business – production for manufacture and service delivery in other economic sectors. As well as production, Porter would include inbound and outbound logistics, and they can also be applicable to service sectors such as retailing.

   In addition to the basic operation of the business there are further operational level activities that service the internal functioning of the business. Both Porter and

Needle list a number of activities, and those that seem most representative and relevant to this text are:

◆   Marketing.
◆   Purchasing.
◆   Finance.
◆   Personnel / Human Resources.
◆   Innovation.
◆   IS / IT (not included by Porter or Needle).

The operations level of the model will be further discussed in *Chapter 6*.

❖   **Management**

Operational processes take place within the framework of the organisation and under the direction of the management. The organisation, in turn, has to exist within the society (external environment) in which it does business.

   The role of management is to determine the strategy and structure of the organisation and then to facilitate the efficient delivery of product or service within that context. The organisational factors we will concentrate on are:

◆   Ownership.
◆   Structure.
◆   Culture.
◆   Strategy (and business models)

These aspects are developed in *Chapter 4* and *Chapter 5*.

❖   **External Environment**

The organisation exists to serve its customers / clients and it does so in the social and economic context of the societies in which it operates. The organisation has to reflect, or at least fit in with, the community it serves, and in turn it will have some influence and modifying effect on that society. The business and social environment is the outer layer of the model.

   Needle lists the state and politics, social and cultural factors, labour market and trade unions, the economy and technology as factors in the external environment. These factors are all very relevant to the study of business and Needle makes some excellent points linking the political, history and economic factors that affect the business environment. For this book on information systems I will (regretfully) restrict coverage to a brief look at the state, labour, consumers and the economy and then concentrate on two elements:

◆   Globalisation.
◆   Technology.

The external environment is further considered in the remainder of this chapter.

The IS business environment model, with IS affecting all three layers, is shown in *figure 3.2*.

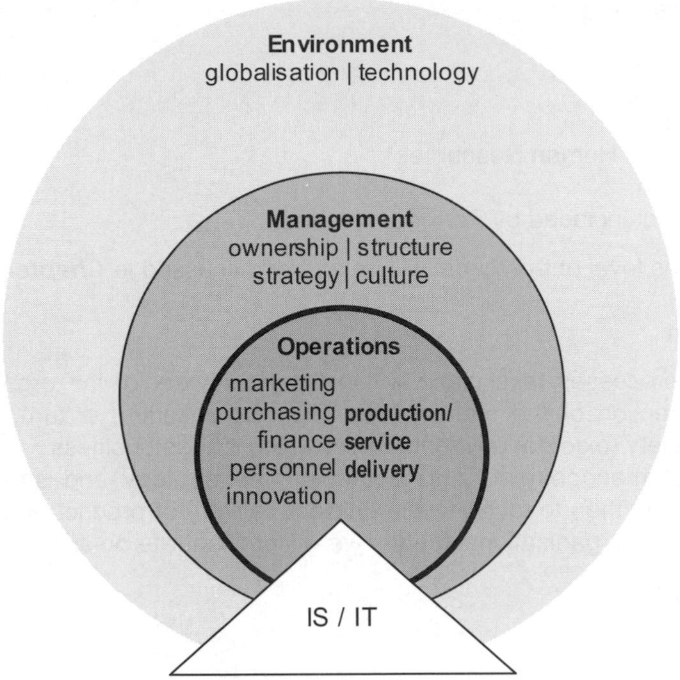

Figure 3.2 The IS Business Environment

3.3 Businesses and Organisations

Before we start on the external environment let us first quickly examine the terms 'business' and 'organisation'. Starting with the term business, we can define that as:

> A business is an organisation that manufactures products or sells a service with the aim of making a profit.

And there are many such organisations at work in our society. They range from the very large global companies such as the Ford Motor Company and Esso Petroleum to small businesses such as the local builder and the corner shop.

However businesses are only part of the picture. The university or college at which you are studying is probably not, within the definition given above, a business. For the college, university and bodies such as government departments, local authorities and (non commercial) hospitals we can use the wider concept of the organisation. Organisations are in most respects similar to businesses. They:

- ◆ Employ and pay their staff.
- ◆ Manage their service delivery.
- ◆ Account for their income and expenditure.

They also use IS and IT in much the same way as commercial organisations and hence non-commercial organisations are as important to our study as commercial organisations.

Organisations may be large or small and commercial or non-commercial but that is only part of the diversity. Wild (1985) identified four basic types of production (activity):

◆ A transformation of raw materials (or components) into manufactured articles.
◆ A transformation in the nature of ownership.
◆ A change of location.
◆ A transformation in the state of the customer.

Transformation of raw materials into finished articles is manufacture. It covers making things such as cars and computers and would also include other processes such as making bread and bottling milk. Manufacturers normally work with a complex network of suppliers. The car maker uses other manufacturers to supply some basic materials, such as the steel for car bodies, but also components such as lights, seats, etc. Food processors might be responsible for a greater part of the end product but they too will buy in the basic ingredients and items such as the packaging for the products. There is a tendency to think of businesses in terms of manufacture but it is only one sector in the overall economy.

Transforming the nature of ownership is about selling things – and intermediaries that wholesale and retail goods are a substantial sector of the economy. Many items are manufactured in bulk quantities and then distributed through the supply chain to the eventual customer. The manufacturer produces bulk supplies of a limited range of items and, in the case of products such as groceries, the individual customer requires limited quantities of a wide range of products. This transformation is the business of the supermarkets, shops and the suppliers with whom they work.

The change of location category is about transport. This includes the transport of people by road, rail, sea and air and also the transport of goods by similarly diverse means. In both cases there is substantial provision by a wide diversity of organisations.

	Commercial			Non-commercial
	large	medium	small	
manufacture	Ford Motors	Dyson vac. cleaners	Morgan cars	-
selling	Safeway supermarkets	independent cash & carry	corner shop	-
transport	British Airways	Stobart Transport	local taxi company	-
service	Barclays Bank	Endsleigh Insurance	solicitor	hospital, school, social services

Figure 3.3 Classifying Organisations

The final category, transforming the state of the customer, covers most services (and is possibly a bit of a catchall). Education and hospitals obviously have a role in transforming the state of the customer (hopefully for the better) but banks, insurance companies and many government departments are also placed in this category.

These categories further emphasise the diverse nature of the organisations that together constitute and create the business environment. *Figure 3.3* gives a table of these categories and examples for each case.

3.4　The External Business Environment

Businesses have to work in the economic, political, legal and social context of the countries in which they operate. Businesses also affect their environment by, for example, the jobs they create and by lobbying government bodies on industrial and financial policy. The process is two-way.

Factors in the external environment include the following.

❖　**The State**

The state is defined by Scott J. (1979), taking a lead from Max Weber, as:

> The body which has a monopoly over taxation, the money supply and the legitimate use of violence.

A nice definition, think about it! For most Europeans these functions are shared between the national governments and the institutions of the European Union.

Needle (2004) lists the functions of the (liberal) state as:

*   to protect the workings of the free market against forces that might otherwise disrupt it, such as excessive monopoly power of either business or trade unions;
*   to provide and / or control goods and services to individuals such as defence and education, where provision by other means would be impossible or inappropriate;
*   to take a longer-term view of economic, social and environmental change than individual businesses are capable of doing.

In fulfilling these functions the state spends a great deal of money, employs a large number of people and creates many laws and regulations. Businesses make extensive use of the infrastructure and services provided by the state but are liable to object to fiscal and regulatory provisions that they see as against their corporate interest. Legal / regulatory provisions that affect organisations include:

*   The law of contract.
*   Company law.
*   Patent law.
*   Consumer protection.
*   Data protection.
*   Health and safety.
*   Labour and trade union laws.

There is a trend for organisations to locate their operations in countries where they see the conditions as most favourable. This can include direct relocation assistance from the host government.

❖ **Culture**

In addition to the state and formal rules and regulations, organisations are affected by the culture of the society in which they operate. Examples of this difference of culture could be:

◆ North America (USA) where the emphasis is on enterprise and self-reliance (often coupled with a good measure of self-belief). Wealth and power are prime measures of respect and there can be a corresponding lack of respect for citizens who find themselves at the bottom of the heap. Work can be informal but there is great emphasis on enthusiasm and company loyalty – holiday leave is minimal by European standards. Besides work (and money), traditional concepts of family and religion are central to the lives of many in heartland America. Social provisions are limited – school education is universal but further education, healthcare and housing are largely dependent on what the individual can afford. The social safety net in terms of unemployment and other welfare provisions is minimal. The United States is (largely) an immigrant country but it was also a slave owning country. There is great social mobility but that sits side by side with a continuing undercurrent of racial discrimination.

◆ For Europe, commerce and making money do not have the same central place in society that they have in North America – in some European countries being 'in trade' has been seen as a second-class occupation. The Europeans have the concept of the 'social market economy' that attempts to marry enterprise with comprehensive social provision for the old, sick and unemployed. Work, and the companies which provide employment, are generally treated with a greater cynicism than one would expect in North America. Social attitudes are generally liberal; there is generally less dogmatism on concepts of religion and traditional family structures. Europe is a continent of nation-states, each with their own language (or languages) and long-standing culture. For most European countries, immigration is seen as a recent phenomenon. There is extensive racial prejudice against the non-white immigrant populations.

◆ Japan has moved from being a very closed country to a leading world economic power since the Second World War – the leading Japanese manufacturing companies are as large as or larger than their American counterparts. Japanese industry differs from its American and European counterparts. The large Japanese manufacturing companies are conglomerates with a range of interests spanning, for example, heavy engineering to consumer goods. These large Japanese companies have worked hand in glove with their government and without the sort of aggressive capital market provision that typifies the American corporate sector. After many years of dramatic economic growth the economy has been in recession for the last few years – how this current problem will be resolved is unclear. The Japanese workers are seen as having a very strong tie in their companies with, until recently, a job with one of the large corporations being a job for life. Japanese welfare provision is largely company based (which can be problematic for people without the appropriate company connection). Japan is not, in general, an immigrant country.

These pen pictures are necessarily brief and, of course, are open to dispute. Hopefully they capture something of the cultural and employment differences between the three economic areas that have been depicted. The differences in culture and approach to business has been exposed when multinational companies have tried to set up shop in another country and / or continent. Examples include:

◆ Nissan which when it set up its car plant on Wearside in the North East of England in 1986, had some difficulty in incorporating and adapting local cultural and employment practices. These were difficulties that were overcome and the Wearside plant is now one of Europe's most productive (and Nissan is now tied in with the French car maker Renault).

◆ McDonald's which has had a hard time gaining acceptance in some European countries such as France and Italy. Again globalisation seems to be winning through and 'le hamburger' is now part of the local language (tout le monde est américain).

Just as different societies have different ways of working and different ways of doing business a company will also evolve its own corporate culture. This is one of the topics in *Chapter 4*.

❖ **Labour**

Employers take on labour to perform a function, when and where there is a task to be done. They want people:

◆ With the appropriate education, training and skills.
◆ At a price they deem appropriate and which they can afford (which may not be the same thing).

High unemployment enables employers to be less generous with pay and to take less care about working conditions.

Workers will take on a job if they need work and the job seems attractive to them. Low unemployment allows workers to be more choosy about the jobs they take on and the pay and conditions they will accept, particularly if their skills are in demand.

Employment trends in the UK, and other advanced countries, have been away from the primary sector (mining, agriculture, fishing, etc.) and manufacturing to the tertiary sectors (financial, leisure, professions, etc). These effects have been in part a result of automation and in part a result of globalisation, with manufacturing functions transferring to cheap labour countries. The process of deindustrialisation has been more marked in the UK than in countries such as Germany, France and the USA.

A standard topic in any discussion of the labour market is the role of trade unions. However with deindustrialisation, government action to curb trade union power and a less collective attitude amongst working people, the influence of trade unions has been much reduced. That said, there are still many workers who do belong to trade unions; much of the role of trade unions is low profile and concentrates on representing individual members on issues such as victimisation and discrimination.

Governments attempt to ensure that their country offers an attractive labour force by providing, for example, education and training. Legalisation is used to protect the labour force through provisions such as health and safety and the minimum wage. Governments have to attempt to strike a balance between the demands of employers and the needs of the working population.

❖ **Consumers**

All organisations have their customer / client groups. For some companies, such as component suppliers, this will be another organisation further down the supply chain but the product or service is eventually sold to, or delivered to, the ultimate consumer.

Consumer requirements are affected by need, the ability to pay but also by cultural factors, social trends and fashion. Basic requirements such as food have a fairly stable market but for other items the market can be more volatile.

Consumer purchases are affected by the consumer's ability to pay (or willingness to borrow). Where consumers (individual or business) are not doing very well or are not feeling very confident they will not spend or they will delay purchases (e.g. of a new car) to a later date.

Consumer purchases are also affected by fashion – the need to have the latest mobile phone to be 'cool'. Fashion is not rational and is even more difficult to predict and direct than economic and confidence factors. Fashion can require the purchase or replacement of an item even when the current product is fully functional. Fashion can dictate the brand that is chosen even where there are other equivalent, and possibly cheaper, brands available.

Consumer attitudes are not easily directed by business or governments and will not necessarily fit in with the way those organisations see the needs of society or the economy.

❖ **The Economy**

The term economy is normally used to refer to the national economy. It can be measured in terms such as gross national product (GNP) and that in turn can be divided by population figures to derive a GNP figure per head. GNP figures range from close to US$ 40,000 per head in the richest countries (Switzerland and Norway), over US$ 20,000 per head for most western countries to well below $1,000 a head in China, India and most African countries (Economist Intelligence Unit, 1999).

Countries aim to achieve steady growth in their economies whilst maintaining low inflation and an acceptable balance of trade with other countries. High growth tends to exacerbate inflationary trends and leads to trouble further down the line. Negative growth (recession) affects the prosperity of businesses, employment rates and the well-being of the citizens.

The national economy can hide many regional and sectorial variations. In the UK, over many years, London and the south east have prospered in contrast to, say, the north east of England and central Scotland where the economy was built on industries where there has been a long term decline, i.e. coal mining, steel and heavy engineering.

The national economy is in turn part of the wider continental and world economy. Economic progress or recession in one part of the world affects exchanges with trading partners and hence has a knock-on effect on those other economies. Supranational effects are emphasised where a country is a member of a trade block such as the European Union (EU) or the North American Free Trade Area (NAFTA).

The economy and businesses interact with one another. Businesses are very much affected by the economy, witness the business failures and increase in unemployment during a recession. That said, it can be argued that the economy is the sum total of all business activity and that is in turn influenced by the factors already outlined; see *figure 3.4*.

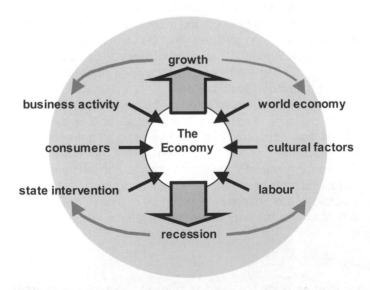

Figure 3.4 Interactions in the Business Environment

Having outlined a number of factors in the external business environment, we will now look at two further aspects of the business environment, globalisation and technology, in more detail; these two factors have a greater direct relevance to IS and IT.

3.5 Globalisation

Globalisation is the trend to source goods from anywhere in the world and to make investment on a similar global basis. People have defined globalisation in many different ways, often with a slant aimed at identifying the supposed harmful economic, political, and social effects of the phenomenon. The definition suggested by Globalisation Guide.org (2002) is:

> Globalisation is the rapid increase in cross-border economic, social and technical exchange under conditions of capitalism.

Globalisation includes the free flow of capital and investment. Many companies have created subsidiaries or bought up competitors in other countries. This has given rise to the phenomenon of the multinational or transnational corporation. Trade sectors where multinational companies operate include:

- Banking: Banking companies such as HSBC and Barclays have grown over recent years to achieve an international presence. Interestingly, US banking laws have prevented the development of large national (retail) banking chains of the sort we are used to in the UK and (for instance) in Canada and this seems to have excluded US banks from the global retail banking sector – there are large US banks with an international presence in the corporate finance sector.
- Oil and petroleum products: This is a sector dominated by a small number of large multinational companies that have the capital to invest in oil exploration and refinery capacity. Global companies in this sector include Exxon (Esso), Shell and BP.
- Automobiles: Two of the best known multinational companies are Ford and General Motors (the latter operating under the Vauxhall badge in the UK and the Opel badge in Europe). Other large automobile manufacturers such as Volkswagen, Nissan and Toyota also have an international presence. The third largest US automobile manufacturer, Chrysler, has also made attempts to establish an international presence but with limited success – it is now grouped with Daimler (Mercedes). There is a case study of Ford at the end of this chapter.
- Computing: This is a sector dominated by US companies with multinationals such as IBM, Intel and Microsoft being market leaders in their own sub-sectors. The conditions that have led to single companies dominating the mainframe, chip and desk top software sector do not apply to, for instance, the manufacture of PCs where there is a greater diversity of supply that includes US and far-eastern companies.

Not all countries and societies welcome the development of multinational corporations. They tend to dominate the market and often squeeze out local manufacturers and suppliers. The setting up of a subsidiary of a multinational provides investment and local jobs but the profits are not necessarily reinvested in the local economy. In many instances the subsidiary is set up to exploit the local labour market, or to gain entry to that national market, but the quality jobs (such as research and development) are retained at corporate headquarters. Large multinational corporations have, in many instances, a turnover greater than the gross domestic product of countries in which they operate – they can have great influence, and sometimes they operate against other local priorities.

Globalisation also includes the free flow of goods ranging from out of season fruits and vegetables to computer equipment and cars that are sourced from all over the world.

In theory it seems to make sense. If products can be grown more easily, or be produced more cheaply, in one part of the world then why should consumers in other countries not have the advantage of the cheaper merchandise? The flip side of such free trade is that imports can have a devastating effect on the local economy particularly where that economy is heavily dependent on one, or a limited number, of products or industries. A further objection is the environmental one against large-scale production processes and the environmental costs of carting components and products great distances when they could be sourced locally.

The ideals of globalisation (if it has ideals!) should tie in with free trade. Many countries whilst preaching free trade set up protectionist barriers to defend indigenous producers and, in some cases, use subsidies (hidden or otherwise) to promote the export of nationally produced goods. The promotion of free trade has been the subject of prolonged international negotiation and dispute – each of the countries involved has tried to gain advantage for its exporters whilst attempting to protect its domestic market from too much foreign competition. Examples of disputes that have arisen in the free trade arena include:

*   The EU's attempt to protect the market for Caribbean bananas against the US insistence on free trade which would favour the produce of its multinationals using large South America estates with cheaper production costs.
*   The US attempt to protect domestic steel producers against more efficient European producers and low cost producers in the Far East.
*   The subsidies given to EU and US food producers which can make imported foods cheaper than locally produced products in third world countries. There is a widespread problem of local farmers being driven out of production and hence adding to the problems of rural depopulation and unemployment in those third world countries.

Free trade is the subject of international consultation and the World Trade Organization (WTO) exists to promote those consultations and to settle disputes. In practice the process is often more about power politics than fairness and it seems to have done little to help the poorer countries (which with the availability of cheap labour perhaps should have been a significant beneficiaries of any move to free trade).

The third element of a global economy, along with the movement of capital and of goods, is the free movement of labour. The EU includes the free flow of labour in its internal market arrangements. On a global scale, many countries have tight immigration rules that (attempt to) preclude a global economy in labour.

In a sense there in nothing new in globalisation. Companies based in rich countries have been investing overseas for centuries. The difference now is one of scale. Much of the move to globalisation is dominated by large corporations, many of them multinational corporations, that no longer have any real ties to, or accountability in, any particular country. In many economic sectors, companies can locate production or source product in the country where the cost of labour is cheapest, the tax regimes are most lax and / or health, safety and environment protection is virtually non-existent.

Globalisation affects some trade sectors more than others. For many years, from before the term globalisation was coined, the manufacture of electronic goods has been transferred from the developed countries, which were the main consumers, to developing countries such as Taiwan, Malaysia and China. Many companies have separated branding, design and marketing from manufacture, with production subcontracted to manufacturing businesses located in cheap labour countries.

Globalisation, as we have already seen, has had its effects in the IT industry. As well as multinational IT companies and the global trade in IT products there is also a trend to outsourcing IT tasks on a global scale. Programming and data entry tasks are being outsourced to cheap labour countries. India is now a centre for outsourced software with a highly organised software industry, centred on Bangalore, doing programming work for many large organisations. Similarly, large data entry jobs, possibly the conversion of large paper archives, can be outsourced to the Philippines; an interesting variation to that is US organisations that send data to Ireland for keying, taking advantage of the time difference to get the work processed ready for the next day local time.

Globalisation is also facilitated by computer and telecommunication systems. Organisations and supply chains are coordinated and controlled by information systems and the location of manufacture or of markets can be largely irrelevant to the administration of the process.

3.6 Technology

Technology has been around since man first cut a flint. Technology, appropriately applied in the production process, has the capability to increase production and reduce costs. As well as being used in production, technology is also a product in its own right – the consumers of technology are both organisations who use it in their production processes and consumers who use technological products in their everyday lives.

The pace of technological change has increased massively over the last couple of centuries and, if the trends are projected forward, that change is set to continue. The first quantum leap in technology (leaving aside the stone age, iron age and the invention of the printing press) was the industrial revolution. In the industrial revolutions automation moved production from the home to the factory and new forms of transport facilitated the distribution of factory output to national and international markets. The industrial revolution, in turn, created massive social (and political) upheaval with the move of people from the countryside and the creation of the urban proletariat.

Recent decades have seen the undoing (or reshaping) of many of the effects of the industrial revolution. The great industries of the industrial era: coal, steel, textiles, railways, etc. have all been reshaped and new consumer product industries and services have grown up to become important elements in the economy. The basic industries of the industrial revolution are now a shadow of their former selves, not necessarily in terms of output but certainly in terms of the labour that they employ. The change has been driven by technology. New production technologies, often incorporating IT, require a fraction of the labour that they once did. The new manufacturing and services industries that have grown up also incorporate IT.

The application of IT to production and the creation of new service industries dependent on IT is seen, by some, as creating a new era: the information revolution or the information society.

Information technology started some 60 years ago with Baby (at Manchester University) closely followed by the US Army's ENIAC system in 1945. The US Department of Defense did a study and estimated the maximum worldwide requirement for computers at six.

The first commercially produced computer was UNIVAC, produced in 1951. By the early 1960s computers were being adopted by most large organisations for data processing tasks. One of the early adopters was Joe Lyons (the UK teas, bakery and corner house chain) that built its own computer to process office applications – its first application was bakery valuations, the world's first routine office application to be run on a computer. These early machines were physically large, using valves for their logic functions. They were used alongside punch card machines (e.g. Hollerith cards) such as sorters, collators and tabulators – these machines had previously been used, by some organisations, for large data processing tasks.

Valve computers were replaced by mainframe computers using transistor and printed circuit technologies. The new computers were easier to program using languages such as Cobol and Fortran and were easier to control as they also incorporated an operating system.

Alongside the development of the new mainframes, companies such as DEC were developing smaller computers for use in laboratories and process control. These small computers also found application as mini computers used by smaller companies and divisional companies for the types of data processing hitherto the preserve of large organisations with mainframe computers.

Following on from the development of the mini was the micro or personal computer (PC). The technology that enabled the development of the PC (and I include the Apple in the category of personal computer) was the replacement of the printed circuit and the transistor with the micro chip. The PC was revolutionary, not because it did anything that the mainframe and mini could not do but because it was (or became) both cheap and small – there could be a PC on every desk and in most households (in developed countries).

The microchip not only enabled the PC but was applied to all other aspects of IT. Microchips are built into mainframe and mini computers (and the distinction between these categories is not as real as it was). Microchips were also introduced into production machinery, domestic appliances and even cars. In manufacture the application of IT to production processes can result in largely automated processes (although extreme automation is still not a cheap option).

Alongside developments in processor technologies there have been dramatic changes in storage technologies and communications:

◆ Online data storage is now plentiful, fast and cheap. A computer system can normally store as much data as the user requires and it can be readily accessed, for a variety of purposes, using the appropriate database technology.

◆ Communications have been revolutionised (a process that has itself been enabled by the application of IT technologies). The organisation's IT is networked to link central computers to the desk top and the factory floor. Networks extend outside the organisation to link the business systems of partners in the supply chain. The general public also has access to IT which can be used, via the Internet, for many purposes including linking into a company's IT systems to transact online.

IT is linked with communications technology to be the key of the information revolution: information and communications technologies (ICT). A timeline of the development of ICT is shown at *figure 3.5*.

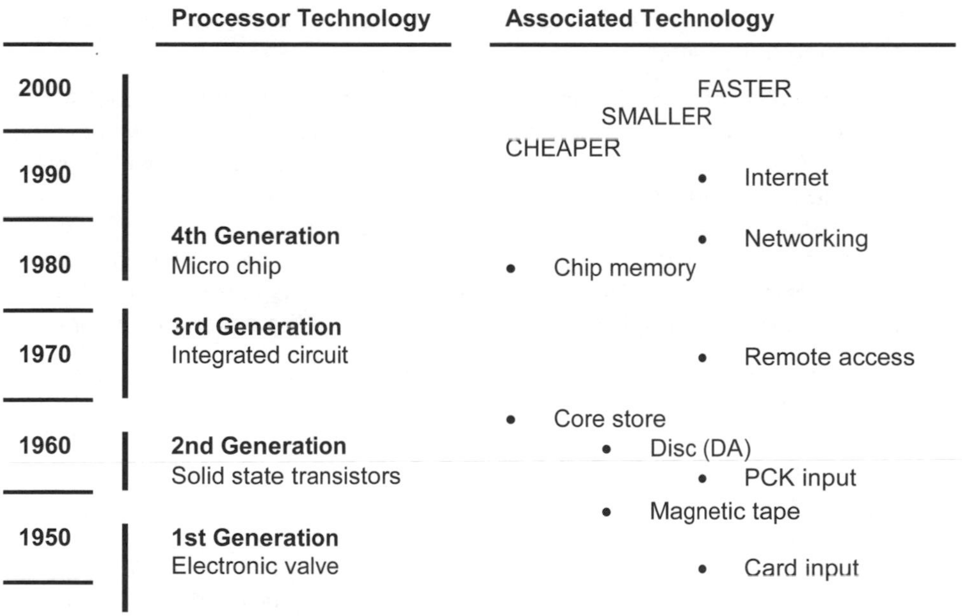

	Processor Technology	Associated Technology
2000		FASTER
		SMALLER
		CHEAPER
1990		• Internet
1980	**4th Generation** Micro chip	• Networking • Chip memory
1970	**3rd Generation** Integrated circuit	• Remote access
1960	**2nd Generation** Solid state transistors	• Core store • Disc (DA) • PCK input • Magnetic tape
1950	**1st Generation** Electronic valve	• Card input

Figure 3.5 The Development of Computer Technology

ICTs have a formidable capacity to automate and integrate but they are not without their problems. Large ICT projects are formidably expensive and the outcome is not always what was intended (or at the cost that was budgeted). ICT systems can store and analyse vast quantities of data and that includes personal data. It can serve commercial purposes and it has beneficial effects for public administration but it also has implications for civil liberties; these are further examined in *Part VI*.

3.7   Case Study: The Ford Motor Company

Ford is well known throughout the world and is an effective example of a multinational company.

The Ford Motor Company was formed in Michigan in the US on 16 June 1903. The founder was Henry Ford. There were 11 investors and the initial capital was US$28,000. The first car was sold to a doctor in Detroit less than two months after the company was set up.

The Ford Motor Company had an international presence from the very early days:

- Ford started exporting cars to the UK in its first year of operation.
- In August 1904 the Ford Motor Company of Canada was set up in Ontario; production began in 1905.
- In 1908 the company opened its first overseas sales branch in Paris.
- The first production facility outside North America was opened in October 1911 at Manchester in the UK.
- Within ten years of its foundation the Ford Motor Company was selling cars throughout Europe, South America and Asia.

Two events were however to distinguish Ford from the many other car makers that were operating at the time:

- The first was the Model T. In 1903 Ford started with the (first) Model A and progressed through the alphabet before reaching its first big winner, the Model T in 1908. The Model T stayed in production for almost 19 years and the total production was about 15 million.
- The second was the production line. The story goes that Henry Ford had seen the lines in the slaughterhouses of Chicago where the carcasses were 'disassembled' stage by stage to remove the various cuts of meat and determined to apply the process in reverse to the assembly of cars.

The Ford Motor Company was the first car manufacturer to create and use a moving assembly line. It was initially implemented in 1913 at the Highland Park plant. The system allowed the workers to stay in one place and perform the same job as the vehicles moved down the production line. With the production line Ford was able to be much more efficient and productive than its competitors and hence it was able to sell its cars at more affordable prices.

The Model T was initially priced at US$850 each. The new assembly line method for producing cars was so efficient that in 1915 Ford was able to drop the price of a Model T to US$250 and eventually to just under US$100. In 1915 Ford sold one million Model Ts.

The Model T, aimed at the mass market, was a revolutionary product for its time. However after some 19 years it was becoming dated. Chevrolet, part of the emerging General Motors (GM) conglomerate, had set its sights on the mass market dominated by the Model T. The new Chevrolets were more modern than the Model T specifically, in place of Ford's antiquated transmission they had a new three speed gear box. Henry Ford was violently opposed to any suggestion that the Model T needed to be updated or replaced. However by 1926 sales of the Model T had plummeted and Henry Ford was forced to accept that it was the end of the line for the Model T. On 25 May 1927 production of the Model T was stopped and the factory closed for six months while a new model was developed – not a great piece of planning (and not a mistake that a company would easily recover from in today's market). The replacement car, when it came out in 1928, was the second Model A.

Ford, unlike many other large corporations, grew to its present size largely through natural growth. There was one early acquisition:

◆ In 1922 Ford paid US$8 million for the Lincoln Motor Company. Lincoln then became Ford's main luxury car brand.

and a new division:

◆ In 1938 Ford produced its first Mercury model. Ford was producing economical cars for the mass market and luxury Lincoln models but it had no mid-priced models; the Mercury models were designed to fill that gap in the product range.

Overseas expansion was achieved mainly by establishing subsidiary companies rather than buying up local manufacturers. Ford started production of the Model T at Trafford Park Manchester in 1913. Ford relocated its UK production facilities to Dagenham in 1931 and opened a second UK assembly plant at Halewood on Merseyside in 1963.

The 1940s saw the Second World War (when civilian car production was replaced by wartime production of jeeps, tanks and aircraft) and in 1947 the death of Henry Ford. After the war, Ford developed in a number of new directions:

◆ In 1956 Ford became a public company (Henry Ford had bought out his original private investors back in 1919). The day of the sale was 17 January 1956 – 10.2 million shares were sold representing 22% of the company.
◆ In 1959 the company set up Ford Credit – an operation that has developed into the automobile industry's largest leasing company.
◆ In 1987 Ford made a major investment in the car rental company Hertz and in 1994 the company took over full ownership.

The Ford Motor Company has been a global player from its early days and from the early days of the motor industry. The late 1960s saw that pattern consolidated with the formation of Ford Europe in 1967 and the Asia-Pacific operation in 1970.

In the late 1990s Ford reorganised again (announcing reorganisations is part of what management do!). The Ford 2000 program created a global management team – the program started with the merger of the North American and European operations. The aim of the program was to:

> ... combine the power, resources, and reach of a world company with the immediacy, agility, and the spirit of a small one.

Ford also embarked on a series or acquisitions of overseas car companies (the first large scale acquisitions since 1922). By the end of the 1920s the big three – Ford, GM and Chrysler – had been established in the US but in other continents and countries the industry remained fragmented. Towards the end of the 20th century there was a sense that small was no longer beautiful (at least not in automobile assembly) and there was a rush to buy up the remaining independent car companies:

◆ In 1979 Ford acquired a 25% stake in the Japanese car company Mazda and in 1986 a 10% stake in the South Korean car company Kia.

◆ In 1987 Ford purchased 75% of the shares of the small, UK luxury car maker Aston Martin. Ford then bought the remaining 25% in 1994.

◆ In 1990 it was the turn of the UK luxury car maker Jaguar, bought for US$ 2.5 billion.

◆ Next to be snapped up was the Swedish car maker Volvo, bought for US$ 6.45 billion in 1999.

◆ Finally (in that round of acquisitions) it was the turn of the UK all-terrain specialist Land Rover, purchased in the year 2000.

And as well as acquisitions in Europe and the Far East, Ford was also expanding in China and India.

Over recent years Ford has taken a lead in trying to standardise development and production across its entire global range. In today's car industry, a lot of emphasis is put on the standardisation of 'the platform'. One platform can be used for a number of models with significant cost savings. The Volkswagen group use just four platforms for all Volkswagen, Audi, Skoda and Seat models. In the case of Ford, the new 'small Jaguar', while a distinctive car, is being built on the Mondeo platform.

Ford of Europe was, at the end of the last millennium, running with six assembly plants: Dagenham and Halewood in the UK; Köln (Cologne) and Saarlouis for Germany; Genk in Belgium and Valencia in Spain. In addition to these assembly plants there were other production facilities such as engines in Bridgend Wales and the newly acquired facilities of Jaguar (Coventry UK), Volvo (Göteborg, Sweden) and Land Rover (Solihull, UK). Dagenham and Cologne were the older plants. Halewood had been developed in the 1960 in conjunction with the British government's regional development programme and had a history of poor quality and difficult labour relations. The Spanish plant was also a response to regional development initiatives and gave Ford the advantage of cheaper labour than was available for its other European operations.

As each major investment decision came up, typically associated with a new model, Ford management set up a sort of competition for that investment between its plants and the countries in which it operates. Examples of this and the restructuring that Ford has undertake to cope with overcapacity are:

◆ The Halewood works, frequently threatened with closure, have been extensively refitted and the labour force retrained to produce the new small Jaguar. Ford decided that it could not justify investing in a new car plant in Jaguar's home in the West Midlands and was prepared to locate production anywhere across its global empire. In the event the job went to Halewood assisted by an aid package worth between GB£40 to 50 million from the UK government. The announcement was made in 1998 and production started in 2001. At the time this conversion was thought to solve Ford's problem of overcapacity in the European market – this soon proved not to be the case.

◆ On the 12 May 2000, Ford announced that car assembly would cease at Dagenham – the last car to leave the plant came off the production line in February 2002. Ford announced that Dagenham is to become a centre for the production of diesel engines, a sort of consolation prize.

The announcement of the Ford Dagenham closure roughly coincided with GM's announcement of the closure of its Vauxhall plant at Luton – in both cases, overcapacity in the European market was given as the reason for closure. Why close in the UK (essentially preference was given to German plants by both Ford and GM)? Why close the main UK production facilities as opposed to the smaller, 1960s, Merseyside facilities of Halewood and Ellesmere Port (GM) which had always been seen as more vulnerable? Numerous reasons have been advanced for the Ford (and GM) decisions. Among these reasons are:

◆ Britain's decision to remain outside the Euro zone – a decision that has been criticised by Japanese car makers which have set up in the UK.
◆ The strength of the pound against the euro – making British production costs higher, but possibly a temporary situation.
◆ British labour laws that make it easier to sack workers than is the case in much of the rest of Europe – a 'flexible labour market' is seen as an advantage in attracting investment but it also makes it easy for that investment to be terminated.
◆ The need to consolidate in the German market – Europe's biggest, and possibly the German consumers are more loyal to their domestic industry than are the British.

Also, possibly, Ford is trying to 'spread it around'. Multinational companies can threaten to remove production from a country but once they have done that they lose the influence that they once had.

Further rationalisation, it is thought, might threaten the plant at Genk in Belgium. Ford also indicated, when making its Jaguar investment decision, that it is not committed to retaining manufacture of specialist marques in their country of origin. The location of investment is a mix of politics and hard-headed economics – loyalty to a country or a long serving labour force don't count for much with a multi-national company. One day it may be a Spanish Volvo or a Land Rover made in Brazil (the engine for the new Land Rover Freelander is now Japanese).

Ford's problems do not end in Europe. In 2002 the Ford Motor Company announced a US\$5.45 billion loss – US\$4.1 million of that down to restructuring costs. The problems were not helped by some difficult product launches, a very public row with Firestone on tyre safety and market uncertainties after the September 11th New York attack. The difficulties at Ford prompted William Clay Ford, great grandson of the company's founder, to take over as chief executive. Restructuring in North America is to see five plants close – three of them car assembly plants. Overall the restructuring will cut Ford's North American production capacity from 5.7 million to 4.8 million cars a year.

Sources include: ford.com and *The Guardian*.

Exercises

1. Make a list of 10 organisations you have come into contact with today (or over the last couple of days) and classify them using Wild's four categories. Note whether your interaction with those organisations involved or was facilitated by ICTs.

2. Look up 'globalisation' on the web and examine the different definitions you can find there. Globalisation is a controversial process and there is a substantial anti-globalisation movement involving development charities and various left wing organisations. Debate the case for and against globalisation.

3. Look up the Ford web site (ford.com seems more useful than ford.co.uk) and see if they are reporting any new developments. Also use other sources to look up news items on Ford (guardianunlimited.co.uk is a useful source). See whether Ford are progressing in solving its organisational and over-capacity problems or if it is still in turmoil. Possibly turmoil is the natural state of business in a rapidly changing, globalised world?

Further Reading

The best textbook I have ever used is Needle's introductory business text. The latest edition (although in many ways I preferred earlier editions) at the time of writing is:

Needle D. (2004) *Business in Context: An introduction to business and its environment*, 4th ed., Thomson, London.

Chapter 4
Business Ownership, Structure and Culture

Summary

Using the IS business environment model introduced in *Chapter 3*, this chapter looks at the management level.

This chapter concentrates on some selected aspects of the structure and strategy of an organisation. These are:

◆ Ownership: there are a variety of forms of ownership – the form of ownership is not necessarily a deciding factor in the way that the organisation is structured or managed.

◆ Structure: organisations have both formal and informal structures – there are a variety of approaches to structure and an appropriate structure is important to the efficient operation of the organisation.

◆ Culture: like people, different companies have different personas – ruthless and efficient or concerned and approachable are two extremes. We look at company culture and the mission statements that may (or may not) embody that culture.

The aim is to give an overall introduction / understanding of how business is organised and managed and to relate these factors to IS and IT. The issue of strategy is also part of the management level but this is dealt with separately in chapter 5. There are many more aspects of organisation / management that could have been covered but those details are beyond the scope of this text.

4.1   The Management Level

The management level can be seen as the interface between the operation of the organisation and the environment in which it operates and which it serves. The management of an organisation must identify the market that is to be served and develop a strategy to ensure the continued success of the organisation. The management must then organise the company to deliver a quality service in an economic manner and enable the organisation to move forward in line with the corporate strategy. The factors identified for study at the management level are:

◆ Ownership.
◆ Structure.

◆ Culture.
◆ Strategy.

See the IS business environment model (management level) in *figure 4.1*.

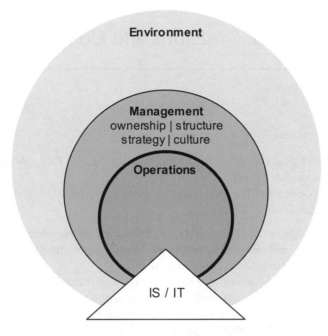

Figure 4.1 The IS Business Environment

4.2 Ownership

Ownership has long been at the centre of the ideological divide but is not now, generally, seen as such a divisive issue. The capitalist model can be caricatured as the ruthless mill owner controlling his factory and its operation with the emphasis being on maximising profit and with the terms and conditions of the employees taking very much a second place. It was in that context that the socialist movement looked to public ownership as the means of ensuring decent conditions for working people. In the words of the (now abandoned) clause four of the British Labour Party constitution:

> To secure for the workers by hand or by brain, the full fruits of their labour and the
> most equitable distribution thereof that can be obtained by the common ownership
> of the means of production, distribution and exchange.

Whatever the truth of the caricature (and there were, and are, examples of the gross exploitation of working people) things, in general and in the developed world, have moved on. Organisations are more complex and:

◆ They are very often run by teams of professional managers rather than the owner.

- The labour force has diverse skills and a much greater ability to switch to other employers.

In these circumstances, the management approach, working conditions and ethos of an organisation do not necessarily directly correlate with the nature of its ownership. The ownership model may be determined by the societal function of the organisation (with public service type functions more likely to be state provided), but also by politics, history and size. Ownership can be divided between the state and private ownership but there are also sub-divisions (and anomalies).

❖ Privately Owned Organisations

There are a number of forms of private ownership. The form of ownership has a rough correlation to size but is also dependent on the history of the company, the legal framework and the type of service being offered. The main forms of private ownership are:

- The public company: quoted on the stock market and owned by shareholders.
- The private company: owned by an individual or a family.
- Professional partnerships: doctors, lawyers and accountants.
- Cooperatives / mutual organisations: owned by the participants.

The category of public company includes most large businesses; names such as Ford, Barclays and Tesco come to mind. These companies have raised capital by issuing shares on the stock market and are owned by their shareholders.

Not all public companies are large – many medium-sized companies are listed on the Stock Exchange. Not all large companies are public companies. Virgin and Clarks Shoes are large companies owned by families or individuals. Other large companies are public but large stock holdings, by the founding family, give an effective veto: Sainsbury and BMW are in this position. In theory the shareholders control the company, in practice owning a few shares gives you no real say (although some pressure groups are now using their right to attend the annual general meeting make their views known). For most companies the majority of shares are held by financial institutions, such as pension funds, and a few wealthy individuals. Normally effective control is vested in the board of directors and shareholders only get involved, if at all, when things go wrong.

Private companies would tend to be at the small end of the scale (although as already noted there are exceptions). A private company may be a small engineering works, an independent retail company or just a freelance IT worker. The author of this book worked for a number of years as a freelance computer consultant; his services were provided through his company, Computa Ltd with a share capital of GB£100.

The private company still has shareholders but that can be for a nominal sum and the shares would be held by the owner-manager, a business partner or a close relative (for example the owner's spouse). The shares in the private company are not traded on the Stock Exchange. For the private company the connection between ownership and control is very real. The failure of the private company may well bring financial hardship to the owners. It is not uncommon for the owners of a private company to have mortgaged their homes to the bank to secure finance for their company – if the company fails they can lose the lot.

A specialist form of ownership is the partnership. This structure is widely used by professionals such as doctors, lawyers and accountants. In these areas it is the individual partner who is responsible for obtaining clients, providing the service and for professional standards. The partnership is a means of providing common services such as office premises and support staff.

The fourth category of private ownership is the co-operative – a form of ownership that might be used by a group of environmentalists setting up a wholefood shop. The co-operative has a long history. It tended to be a socialist alternative to the capitalist model and the co-op stores, in this and other countries, are a prime example. Further examples are farmer's co-operatives where farmers get together to process and / or market their produce, and there is also the John Lewis Partnership, a national chain of department stores.

The co-operative is owned by its workers. It has similarities to the mutual organisation that was owned by its participants. The mutual societies had similar roots to the co-operative movement with working people grouping together to provide themselves with savings or insurance – the mainstream financial institutions were not very interested in providing a service for poor people. Many of these mutual societies grew into large financial institutions and household names – the Halifax, Abbey National, Norwich Union and Friends Provident were all mutuals / friendly societies. These large organisations had long ceased to be rooted in their communities and arguably offered a service that was very little different from their commercial counterparts. In the 1990s many of the large mutuals were 'de-mutualised' and now operate as public companies. There are still mutual societies: the Nationwide is probably the largest. Many poor communities are now finding that none of the established financial institutions offer them an appropriate service and a new generation of savings and loans clubs are being formed – whether they grow in the way that the building societies of the last century grew remains to be seen.

For individuals running their own business an alternative to a private company is self employment. The choice between a (one person) private company and self employment depends on taxation and contractual issues – freelance IT consultants tend to work through their own private companies whereas a builder is more likely to be self employed.

The traditional focus in private ownership has been the maximisation of profit and the shareholder value (sometimes at the expense of the people who work for the company, the communities in which it operates and the long-term prospects of the company, or so it would seem). An alternative view is that of the stakeholder organisation. This view recognises that the shareholders are not the only people who have a stake in the organisation: other contributors are:

◆ Customers / clients – people who use the services of the company. They may be long-term clients and could be in difficulty if the service was not available. The closure of a rural bank branch is an example of where a group of client stakeholders can be left without a service.

◆ Managers and workers – many employers will have worked a good number of years for a company, often giving greater service than is called for by their contract of employment. For many people their lives are built around their jobs and insensitive treatment, discrimination or redundancy is no real reward for years of loyal service.

◆ Local community – towns and villages throughout the country rely on the job opportunities offered by large employers. The closure of a factory or administrative centre creates unemployment but also affects suppliers, local trades people and the future job prospects of the young people of the community. Closures of coal mines in Britain are an example of where the whole *raison d'être* of many towns and villages communities was destroyed.

◆ Society – the effect of decisions of large organisations can be much wider than just the local community in which they operate. Investments decisions by multinationals such as car companies can be on a such a scale as to assume national importance – two American multinationals, Ford and Vauxhall (GM) have recently closed major car plants in the UK, possibly counterbalanced by inward investment from the Japanese multinationals, Nissan and Toyota.

The stakeholder concept is summarised by *figure 4.2*. One way that the workers are encouraged to see themselves as stakeholders is employee share ownership schemes – whether directors will treat them as stakeholders if things become difficult is another question.

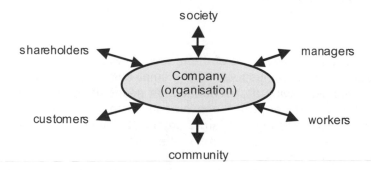

Figure 4.2 The Stakeholder Organisation

❖ **Publicly Owned Organisations**

In addition to the private sector there are a great number of organisations that are publicly owned. These can be roughly divided into:

◆ Public administration: government departments and local authorities.
◆ Public services: schools, universities, hospitals, prisons, courts, police and armed services.
◆ Public enterprises: e.g. the Post Office.

Public administration consists of the offices of central government and the corresponding local government structure. Central to their function, but a small part in terms of employment, is the role of planning and policy advice. The large administrative departments are those which raise revenue (the Inland Revenue, Customs and Excise and local tax departments) and those which dispense welfare benefits (Employment, Social Security and local housing benefit offices). The large administration functions make extensive use of IS and IT.

Education, welfare, law enforcement and defence are all services that employ a lot of people – the National Health Service is, it is said, the world's biggest employer after the Chinese army. IS / IT is significant to these organisations but it is the staff who are central to the delivery of services.

The role of public enterprise has been much diminished over recent years. In the UK, coal, steel, gas, water, electricity, railways and some airlines have all been public enterprises in the recent past. Many of these enterprises have been sold off in a process called privatisation – a process copied in many other countries in Europe and across the world. The Post Office is, in the UK, the last of the large nationalised enterprises. For most of these industries there is a significant public interest in fair treatment of all customers – many of them are natural monopolies. Public policy ensuring, for example, that electricity is available at a fair price even in rural areas, was easy when the state owned the company – under privatisation, state control has been replaced by regulation designed to ensure good service, at a fair price but with a fair return for the private company.

A final category that is neither state or private is the non-governmental organisation, the NGO. These are often charitable organisations and they mix welfare services and political lobbying: Greenpeace, Oxfam and the RSPCA are examples of such organisations.

4.3 Structure

Within an organisation, irrespective of the model of ownership, there needs to be an organisation / management structure. In a small company this can be informal, for example, the boss having a chat about what needs doing next over a cup of tea with her two employees. (In a one person company the boss can talk to himself – and probably does.) For a larger organisation there needs to be a more formal structure – after all there is a limit to the number of people that a manager can talk to over a cup of coffee.

Various models of organisation have been tried over the years. The main models are:

❖ **Divisional Organisation**

For this type of structure the organisation is divided into divisions. Divisions may be product based, e.g. a small car division and a specialist car division, or they can be geographically based, e.g a North American division and a European division. The divisions have devolved responsibility for the conduct of their business and for their financial performance. Divisional structures can be tight or loose, i.e. with varying degrees of central control and common services (finance, personnel, computing, etc.). At one extreme is the holding company, with each division operating as a separate, quasi-independent, company.

The classic example of a divisional company is that of General Motors (GM). The structure was devised in 1921 by Alfred Sloan and termed 'federal decentralisation'. In the US, GM operated its car business under the five marques of Chevrolet, Oldsmobile, Oakland, Buick and Cadillac (in 1926 the Oakland was dropped and Pontiac introduced). Each division developed, manufactured and marketed its own models. The various divisions had their own ethos – Chevys, for example, tended to be fairly basic models with a price that reflected that. Each marque also had its loyal customers: my Canadian father-in-law was a Buick man and was never really happy the one time he ended up with an Oldsmobile. As well as the division there was a head office function, called the General Office, providing support services between divisions but focusing on results. A simple divisional structure chart of GM is shown in *figure 4.3* – the overall picture was more complex with further divisions covering trucks, overseas manufacture and other products such as railway locomotives.

In a divisional structure, each division acts as a profit centre (or as a cost centre). The division is responsible for its income and expenditure. If the division is doing well, selling lots of cars, attracting many clients, etc. it is in a position to expand, update its equipment and / or pay its staff a little better. If the division is not doing very well that soon becomes clear and the division must cut costs, reduce its staff numbers or just try harder to get some more business. The divisional structure encourages entrepreneurship.

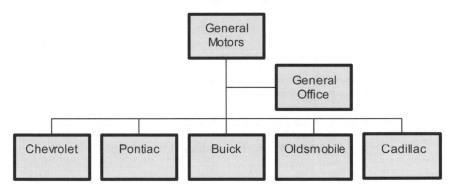

Figure 4.3 The Divisional Structure (GM)

The problem with a divisional structure is that it can make central control more difficult. Divisions can become very powerful and they value their autonomy. Areas of difficulty are:

◆ Central services: how they are controlled and paid for.
◆ Transfer pricing: how one division prioritises and charges for work done for another division.
◆ Diversity: divisions can move into new areas of business and the group can lose focus.
◆ Customer interface: the customer may be faced with different procedures when it is using the services of a number of the company's divisions.

Divisions can also create duplication of effort and a waste of resources. Each division may have its own accountants and its own IT staff, duplicating effort and tackling the tasks in a slightly different way – a functional structure could be used to address this problem.

❖ **Functional Organisation**

The logical alternative to organisation by division is one based on professionalism or skills. In this type of organisation the structure divides, for example, purchasing, production, marketing, accountants, etc. into separate departments – each functional area is managed by specialists from that area.

An example of a type of organisation that uses a functional structure would be a large accountancy firm. Such a firm would have separate departments for accountancy, auditing, insolvency, management consultancy, etc., each staffed by specialists in that particular area. Such a structure is illustrated in *figure 4.4*. Computing may well be organised as a functional grouping within an organisation – the information services department is staffed by the systems analysts, programmers, etc. and makes its services available to the rest of the organisation.

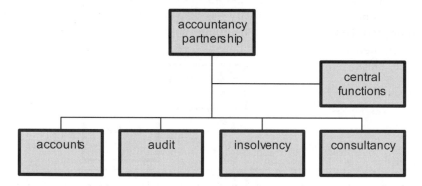

Figure 4.4 The Functional Organisation

A functional structure reinforces and makes good use of skills. Staff in the functional grouping can readily turn to colleagues for help and advice, and tasks can be scheduled and shared within the group of specialists.

The problems with a functional organisation are conflicting departmental objectives and lack of customer focus. Generally the functional grouping is only concerned with one aspect of a task – responsibility for real cost and absolute deadlines is distributed across a number of departments and the job is perhaps less likely to be delivered on time and to budget. A project team can tackle some of these issues and that is what we look at next.

❖ **Project Teams**

A way of creating focus on the task in hand, particularly a transitory requirement such as a building project or creating an information system, is to set up a project team. The project team is designed for the requirements of the task. A building project needs the right combination of architects, engineers and the appropriate building trades. An IS project needs system analysts, system designers, database designers, programmers and so on. Members of the project team may be added or removed during the various stages of the project but the role of the project leader is crucial. It is the project leader's job is to ensure that the project is delivered on time, within budget and that it meets the customer's requirements. The project leader must focus on those objectives – loyalties to a division or a functional department are secondary.

Many organisations use project teams for special, one-off, tasks – a type of organisation that is largely structured around project teams is a large civil engineering or construction company. These construction companies have a small central staff and then set up a team for each project as it comes along. The project team structure is summarised in *figure 4.5*.

Large projects are difficult to manage and are notorious for running late and over budget – the project team is specifically designed for such situations and it provides for focus on the objectives of the project.

The project structure is however essentially transitory. It may get the job done but that can be at the expense of staff job security. Once one job is finished there is no guarantee that there is continuity of employment for the staff involved – the next project may not directly follow on or it may require a different mix of skills. In addition to the continuity issue, the individual experts in a project team can become isolated from fellow professionals with no chance to cross-check ideas and update skills.

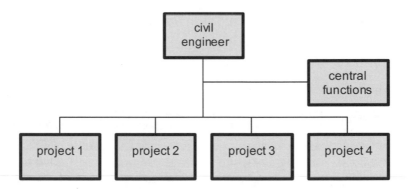

Figure 4.5 Project Teams

❖ **Matrix Organisation**

All three organisational structures discussed thus far have both advantages and disadvantages. The matrix organisation seeks to combine two or more of these structures and hence combine the advantages. Possible matrix organisations are:

◆ Divisions combined with functional specialisms:
This structure could, in theory at least, retain the entrepreneurship of the divisional organisation but cut out some of the duplication and provide a professional home for the various specialists. An example of such a structure is shown in *figure 4.6*.

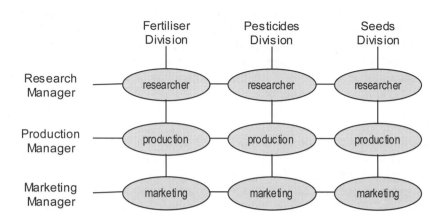

Figure 4.6 Matrix Management in a Divisional Organisation

◆ Functional specialisms combined with project teams:
This is a structure that might be adopted in an IT consultancy or a large IS department. The department could have functional divisions for the systems analysts, programmers and data designers. Staff would report to the divisional head (managing analyst, chief programmer and data analysis manager) on professional and personnel issues but would be allocated to project teams, and report to the project manager, on their day to day work. This structure is shown in *figure 4.7*.

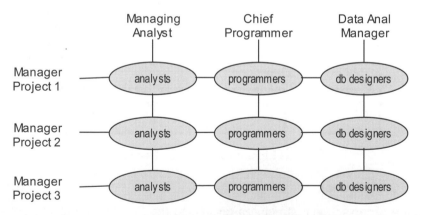

Figure 4.7 Matrix Management in an IS Project

Matrix organisations look good in theory but, in practice, either one axis of the matrix becomes dominant (e.g. the divisions or the project managers take charge and ignore the functional managers) or everyone becomes bogged down in endless meetings discussing the conflicting objectives of the alternative perspectives. As well as taking up management time in meetings the matrix can be confusing for employees who have to report to two bosses and may be receiving conflicting instructions.

Matrixes were popular in the 1970s but that popularity was fairly short lived. There is still, however, an element of matrix management in many organisations. Very possibly your college / university department has a matrix management with subject leaders and course leaders having an input to how courses are structured and delivered. See the exercises at the end of the chapter.

❖ **Other Organisational Structures**

Over the last century while management structures have been studied the nature of work has changed considerably. The Ford Motor Company, when it first started, produced virtually all the components and much of the raw material for its cars on one site – the River Rouge plant had its own power plant and iron forge. In a similar manner the London and North Western (LNW) rail workshops at Crewe even produced its own steel for use in making its engines and other railway equipment (although this vertical integration did not apply in, for example, the Lancashire cotton industry where stages in the process such as spinning and weaving were generally carried out in different mills and often in different towns).

Today, organisations rely heavily on other companies for the supply of goods and services. Ford makes its own car bodywork and assembles its cars but most other components are bought in, including in some cases the engine. Many companies will also outsource services such as catering, payroll and in some cases the complete IS / IT function. This pattern of outsourcing lets management concentrate on the processes it knows well and uses the expertise of suppliers for component parts – it also reduces the capital a company requires to produce its product. The suppliers in turn have their own specialist areas and can sometimes achieve economies of scale by winning contracts from a range of customers. The process of outsourcing is driven by a number of factors, including IT, that make trade exchanges with external suppliers easier and cheaper.

These changes in technology and in company functions are giving rise to new approaches to organisations. These include:

◆ Virtual Organisations:
   The virtual organisation takes outsourcing to an extreme – all the service delivery is outsourced and the organisation then coordinates its suppliers. Examples of industries where such organisations operate are:

   ◆ Package holidays: The transport and the hotels are provided by other companies and the holiday is sold by a travel agent. The holiday company just has to coordinate its contracts, print its brochures and hope that the public will buy its holidays.
   ◆ e-Shops: Many organisations running e-Shops are of minimal size. The product they sell may be supplied direct from a wholesaler and the delivery is by post or a courier service. The e-Shop just has to do its marketing, coordinate the contracts and manage the web site.
   ◆ Electronic goods: There is an increasing trend to outsource the entire production of some electronic goods to factories in the far east. The company whose name appears on the equipment may have designed it and will be marketing it but it has not made it. Hewlett Packard are

market leaders for computer printers but they do not own any of the plants where they are produced.

- ◆ Local authorities, under the previous Conservative government, also looked to be heading in the direction of being virtual organisations. Services such as refuse collection and road repair were outsourced to private contractors and, more recently, administrative functions such as collecting council tax and paying housing benefit have, in some cases, been outsourced.

There are degrees of outsourcing and at what stage a company becomes virtual could be argued. Virtual companies can do well – they can have large sales with minimum capital investment and, in many cases, a capability to cope with fluctuations in demand without sustaining significant damage. When things are going well, the profits can be impressive. Potential problems are:

- ◆ The company does not directly control its production processes or its service delivery – quality can be an issue.
- ◆ There is no asset value in the company.
- ◆ New firms can enter the same market, using the same or similar sub-contractors, with a minimal outlay of capital.

◆ Franchise organisation:
An organisation with a good idea, a marketable format, can sell licences to other organisations for them to use that format. The benefit to the franchiser is that it can grow the business rapidly and generate an income without the need to commit capital. The benefit to the franchisees is that they have a ready-made business concept, hopefully with brand recognition, and the benefit of some central functions such as marketing support.
   The main areas of franchising are in the retail and service sectors – it is the norm in the fast food business and also applies in other areas such as the high street print shop.

◆ Network organisations:
A development or amalgam of the project team, outsourcing and the virtual organisation. This is where the Internet is used to bring together a number of independent and geographically dispersed professionals as a project team for some particular task. Networked project teams are sometimes used for consultancy, IT projects and for academic research.
   Teleworking can also be conducted through virtual networked organisations where programming, translation or other office tasks are sent out from an agency to individual teleworkers on a piecework basis.

Some of these informality / impermanent arrangements are also appearing within large organisations. In the last chapter we saw how Ford expected different plants to compete for new models, and the same sort of competition between internal suppliers is occurring, formally or informally, in many other organisations. It is not uncommon for service departments within an organisation to have to have to prove they provide quality of service and value for money. Examples are the IT department that has to compete for the work of other divisions against outside contractors, and the UK prison sector where the government's prison service has to compete against private contractors for the contract to run a new jail. One could argue that management is abdicating its responsibility for running the organisation and 'delegating' that responsibility downwards – this delegation does not seem to get reflected in the level of directors' pay!

❖ **Structure Charts**

Most medium and large-scale organisations will use a variety or combinations of these structures. A large organisation may adopt a divisional structure but with:

◆ Functional / matrix structures for group services such as marketing, accounting and IT.
◆ Functional structures within each division.
◆ Project teams for product development and major IT projects.

Traditional structure charts have standard, symmetrical hierarchies with a manager having a number of supervisors each with a quota of workers. Classic examples of this structure are an army infantry brigade, an old-fashioned factory or a civil service clerical department. Such a structure is illustrated in *figure 4.8*.

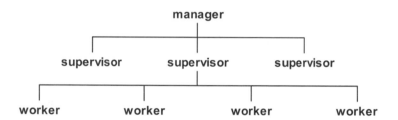

Figure 4.8 Hierarchical Structure

Hierarchical structures are now much less common and, where they exist, they have been delayered. The traditional hierarchy involved many non-productive posts, delayed work (as tasks and decisions were passed up and down the chain) and led to a lack of opportunity for individual initiative. Modern organisational structures are liable to be skewed and flattened.

The skewed structure places management emphasis on important areas of policy rather than head count or resources. *Figure 4.9* shows the structure of Volvo Cars UK (Volvo Concessionaires when it was part of the Lex Group). The major operational functions of car preparation, parts supply and warrantee had about 120 staff but these were represented by just one director – the other directors, dealing with dynamic policy areas, had much smaller departments of between four and twelve staff (accounts also included the IS / IT function with an additional head count of about 25).

The flattened structure reduces the length of the chain of command and gives each member of staff much more responsibility, and space to exercise that responsibility – delegation and empowerment are buzzwords in the new business structure. Managers will find that they have much wider span of responsibility with (say) ten or twelve supervisors reporting to them when previously it might have been four or six. The role of the manager is to agree policy and set targets rather than any detailed supervision.

One organisational theorist has recommended a 'blueberry pancake structure' – flat with lumps in it – I'm not sure about this, but if you are in the US and can get a good blueberry pancake with whipped cream and syrup it is well worth a try.

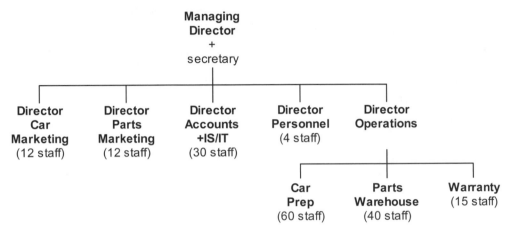

Figure 4.9 Volvo Concessionaires

4.4 Culture

As well as the formal aspects of ownership and structure, organisations have a culture, a way of behaving and doing business. The ethos of an organisation is in part a deliberate creation of the organisation and in part organic. This culture is part derives from society (we looked at some North American, European and Japanese attributes and attitudes in *Chapter 3*) and is in part created in the workplace. The culture of an organisation will affect how it interacts with its customers, employees and all other stakeholders. The culture can be either:

◆ Centralised control and regimentation, or it may be much more informal with delegated authority and the encouragement of initiative.
◆ Innovative with a drive to design new products and develop new markets or conservative with the emphasis on traditional values and established product lines.
◆ Friendly, supportive and informal in the work place or rather impersonal and lacking collegiality.
◆ Open and accountable with remuneration and advancement linked to merit, or secretive with various forms of unfair preferment, discrimination and bullying (all of which is regrettably commonplace in organisations).
◆ Customer centred or focused on internal objectives and rivalries.

◆ Rooted in the community with concern for any environmental impact and for social issues in the societies it serves, or focused on production and profit with little regard for the impact of the company's activities.

Sometimes the culture of an organisation can be summed up in a mission statement and it is this aspect we will concentrate on. An article in *The Grantsmanship Centre Magazine* (Fall 1998) summed up the requirements of a good mission statement thus:

> … accurately explain why your organization exists and what it hopes to achieve in the future. It articulates the organization's essential nature, its values, and its works.

It went on to say that:

> An effective mission statement must resonate with the people working in and for the organization, as well as with different constituencies that the organization hopes to affect. It must express the organization's purpose in a way that inspires commitment, innovation, and courage – not an easy task.

As this extract says 'not an easy task', and many mission statements are just public relations exercises that have little impact on the way management behaves and no noticeable inspirational effect on the staff. In using the mission statement to illustrate the culture of the company we will select only mission statements that seem to reflect the real culture and aspirations of the organisation.

One of the places where we, as members of the public, are most likely to regularly interface with an organisation is when out shopping. As customers we notice the difference between the shop that is clean where the staff are keen to serve you, and the shop that is a bit of a dump where customers are made to feel like an intrusion. As students you may work part-time in a supermarket or a fast food restaurant and you will know how you feel about the way you are treated and how forced is that smile with which you greet the customers.

Sainsbury's is one example of a large supermarket that puts good customer service and reasonable treatment of staff high on its priority list. Its attitude as an organisation is, I suggest, fairly summed up in its mission statement:

> To discharge the responsibility as leaders in our trade by acting with complete integrity, by carrying out work to the highest standards, and by contributing to the public good and the quality of life in the community.
>
> To provide unrivalled value to our customers in the quality of goods we sell, in the competitiveness of our prices and the range of choice we offer.
>
> In our stores to achieve the highest standards of cleanliness and hygiene, efficiency of operation, convenience and customer service, and thereby create as attractive and friendly shopping environment as possible.
>
> To offer our staff outstanding opportunities in terms of personal career development and in remuneration relative to other companies in the same market, practising always a concern for the welfare of every individual.
>
> To generate sufficient profit to finance continual improvement and growth in the business whilst providing our shareholders with an excellent return on their investment.

The attitude and ambience of Sainsbury's is similar to other leading supermarkets but it does contrast with some of the 'stack it high and sell it cheap' merchants where quality, cleanliness and customer service are less in evidence. The ambience of Sainsbury's also contrasts with other shops, for example:

◆ Record or fashion clothes shops where there is an attempt to create a funky atmosphere. Service can still be good but it is provided by young people in loud t-shirts.

◆ Shops where staff are on commission and there is pressure to make a sale (and for the staff to ensure that sale is recorded to their account).

The point in Sainsbury's mission statement about looking after staff is very important here. It is difficult to provide good customer service if the working conditions are bad and the pay is lousy. It is not very easy to take time to help a customer if you know you will then get hassle because the shelf-stacking job is not finished.

The mission statement of Manchester Metropolitan University (MMU), my university, is:

> To be an accessible and responsive institution of higher education of the highest quality.
> To be a centre of excellence in its teaching and research.
> To serve the aspirations of all with the ability and motivation to benefit.
> To meet the needs of industry, business, the professions and the wider community.

How well it meets those aspirations could be debated – but we do our best. In contrast to that of Sainbury's, this mission statement does not include any commitment on staff.

An aspect of the MMU mission statement that could be important is the commitment 'To serve the aspirations of all with the ability and motivation to benefit'. A disabled student who applies to MMU and is not admitted, or comes to MMU and does not get the facilities that he or she needs to be able to study effectively, could point to that line in the mission statement when seeking redress. Similarly, should any member of staff at Sainsbury's feel he or she has been discriminated against on the grounds of race or gender, he / she could cite the mission statement and the line that says 'To offer our staff outstanding opportunities … practising always a concern for the welfare of every individual'. Having committed to a mission statement, neither MMU or Sainsbury's are going to feel comfortable if there is a suggestion that they have acted in a way that seems contrary to that statement and their reputation as responsible organisations.

And finally, on the topic of culture, let's look at the mission statement of Fuji Film. The mission statement on its US web site is:

◆ To deliver the highest quality products and services in the global imaging and information market place to all of our customers.

◆ To be the most excellent manufacturing organization in the world.

◆ To dedicate ourselves to the continuous protection and improvement of our precious environment and safety and health of our associates.

- To commit ourselves to continuously improve the prosperity and quality of life for our associates, their families and our local community.
- To create and sustain in our associates, their families and our community a source of pride in our manufacturing and research and development complex.
- To continue our growth towards profitability, in order to provide the opportunity for reinvestment in our local operators and quality of life.
- To ensure that Fuji Film will be a growing concern well into the 21st century.

OK, but the story goes that the real mission statement of Fuji Film is:

Kill Kodak!

and that is a mission statement that could 'accurately explain why your organisation exists and what it hopes to achieve in the future'.

Exercises

1. Take the list of organisations you identified in *Chapter 1*, Exercise 1 and note down who or what you think owns the organisation. Consider whether the mode of ownership is appropriate and how it affects your experience of its services.

2. For the UHS Case Study, *Chapter 2*, draw a staff / structure chart for the Information Systems Department.

3. Consider your college or university department. Find out which members of staff have responsibility for what (course leader, etc.) and construct an organisational structure chart. You may well end up with a matrix chart. Compare your chart with that produced by fellow students and any official organisational chart – there may well be (legitimate) different interpretations of the same data.

4. Look up the mission statement or your college or university. Assess how well you feel it meets the aims set out in that statement and consider whether its aims adequately meet your needs as a student. If you have a part-time job with a large organisation, see if you can find the mission statement of that organisation and check out how those objectives fit the organisation as you experience it.

Further Reading

The topics of this chapter are again covered in Needle's introductory text:

Needle D. (2004) *Business in Context: An introduction to business and its environment*, 4th ed., Thomson, London.

There are numerous other texts on management covering the area in more detail (and greater complexity). One example of such a text is:

Handy C. (1993) *Understanding Organisations*, 4th ed., Penguin.

Chapter 5
Business Strategy

Summary

A business's strategy is a pattern of major objectives and plans that define the nature, purpose and future direction of an organisation. The strategy of an organisation needs to take into account:

◆ The business environment in which the company operates. The strategy development process tries to anticipate future developments in this environment. The business environment was the subject of *Chapter 3*.

◆ The capabilities and attributes of the company. The strategy development process must make a realistic assessment of the ability of the organisation to successfully cope with any proposed developments. The organisational level of the company is the subject of *Chapter 6*.

The strategy, once determined, guides the future development of the organisation. It may well affect the structure and culture of the organisation, topics that were among the subjects of *Chapter 4*. From time to time the strategy of an organisation will need updating to take account of further developments in the business environment. Sometimes the strategy will not seem to be working out and needs rethinking – the danger is that strategic development is replaced by short-term thinking to the detriment of the organisation and its stakeholders.

The formulation of strategy can be helped by the use of appropriate business models – in this chapter we will look at: SWOT, Porter's model of competitive forces and the Boston Consulting Group matrix.

As well as a corporate strategy, an organisation may do well to have an IS / IT strategy. The factors affecting IS / IT strategy, within corporate strategy, are examined.

5.1 Strategy

Many organisations have a strategy. For some organisations there is a formal strategy derived after an extensive study of the business environment and the capabilities of the organisation. In other organisations it is a much less formal affair that is implicit in the way the organisation is operated and developed.

Strategy is the process of long-term planning as opposed to the management of the immediate. Strategic thinking is the opposite of crisis management. Andrews (1971) in his book, *The Concept of Corporate Strategy*, defines it as:

> Corporate strategy is a pattern of major objectives, purpose or goals and essential policies or plans for achieving those goals, stated in such a way as to define what business the company is in or is to be in and the kind of company it is or is to be.

❖ **Strategy Development**

The concept of a business strategy can be illustrated by a formulation of the strategy development process. Needle (2004) suggests a four stage strategy development process: see *figure 5.1*.

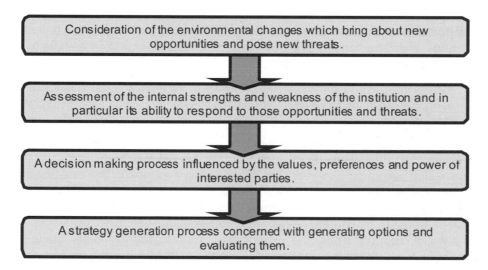

Figure 5.1 Strategy Development Model

The first stage is to:

> Consider the environmental changes which bring about new opportunities and pose new threats.

This relates to the environmental level of the business model. The organisation needs to consider its current market or client base and how that might change over the coming years. It also needs to look for relevant changes that will produce new opportunities. Examples of environmental changes that could provide good opportunities for some organisations (and problems for others) include:

- Concern about global warming and the environment in general, coupled with the emphasis on reduced emissions and renewable energy sources.
- Increasing interest in organic food and growing distrust of industrialised farming and processed food products.
- Government policy and other pressures that suggest an increase in the participation rates in further and higher education.

Negative changes could include an uncertainty about future growth in the economy or increased competition from imports sourced from cheap labour economies.

IT developments are part of the environment. This can include the opportunity to incorporate electronics in products and the use of ICTs to increase company efficiency or to differentiate its services. The continuing development of Internet technologies and the ever increasing number of people with online access is one area of opportunity that might be exploited.

Three models that could be helpful in assessing the business environment, and that are examined later on in this chapter, are:

◆ SWOT (strengths, weaknesses, opportunities and threats).
◆ Porter's model of competitive forces.
◆ The Boston Consulting Group matrix

An opportunity is only advantageous if the organisation has the capability to take advantage of it. The second stage of the strategy development process is to take a searching look at the organisation:

> Assess the internal strengths and weaknesses of the institution and in particular its ability to respond to those opportunities and threats (identified in the first stage of the process).

Traditionally organisations have considerable investment in their plant and the people who work for them. Such organisations cannot just be turned round from (say) making luxury cars to churning out cheap volume cars. The organisation is not necessarily equipped for such a new role and it might not fit the working ethos. Large organisations tend to be ponderous and slow to change direction – a decision from management does not necessarily get the immediate and enthusiastic support from the workforce. Smaller organisations have less investment in what they are currently doing and are generally seen as being better at adopting and adapting to change. Some organisations outsource most of their production / operations keeping only a small management and marketing team – this can give the flexibility to make rapid changes as the investment in production and operating facilities is minimal.

Aspects of the organisation that could be relevant to the assessment (based on Lynch, 1997) include:

◆ Cost structures of the organisation: are we a low cost producer or are our traditions and working practices more suited to the premium end of the market? For example, are we a Ford or a Mercedes?
◆ Economies of scale: do economies of scale exist in the industry? How important are they and is our organisation of the optimum size? For example, can Rover match Ford on production costs for economy cars?
◆ Labour costs: is the cost of labour a significant part of the production cost and are workers with the appropriate skills available in other locations? For example, electronics assembly might be moved to Malaysia or China.
◆ Production output levels: how significant is full utilisation of plant and equipment to cost structures and profitability? For example the steel industry requires a high level of plant utilisation to be profitable.

- Quality: how significant is consistency and can we achieve the required quality standards? For example, the reliability of an aircraft is more crucial than that of a photocopier.
- Innovation: does the market require constant updating of products and can we achieve that level of creativity and speed to market? An example is the mobile phone industry.
- Management capability: have we the management skill and experience to successfully cope with proposed change (a difficult one for management to objectively assess)?
- Labour / management relations: do we have the trust and understanding of the employees and will they wholeheartedly cooperate in any proposed development? If there are disputes with employees, how crucial are these to the operations? For example, changes to working practice on the railways have led to strikes. Will the customers return or will they permanently switch to other modes of transport?
- Technologies and copyright: does the industry rely on patented technology or copyrighted material and do we have access to the requisite intellectual property rights? An example is the proprietary and generic drug industries.
- Brand: do we have a brand that is trusted and respected by customers? For example Heinz is a strong brand for tinned food products.
- Skills: do we have exceptional staff – skills that give us competitive advantage over other organisations? An example is a top research university.
- Other factors: are there other factors that apply to our industry? This list is oriented to manufacture and the emphasis would change for an assessment in the service sector.

This type of analysis is sometimes referred to as 'gap analysis'. Is there a gap between what the management and the organisation can do and what they would like to do? An organisation that wishes to move ahead should be ambitious and optimistic but not unrealistic.

The final stage of the strategy plan is to bring together the external and internal studies and to decide on the way forward. This process is covered by the third and fourth steps in the strategy generation process:

> A decision making process influenced by the values, preferences and power of interested parties and a strategy generation process concerned with generating options and evaluating them.

In some organisations the overall strategy will be determined in an essentially political process and that is then followed by a planning process that puts flesh on the overall strategic decision. Other organisations will identify a number of options and evaluate them before deciding on the strategic direction.

There is no set formula for making such decisions and there are bound to be conflicting advice and different interest groups. Predictions of changes in the business environment over the next five or ten years are, by their nature, speculative. Other organisations are also involved in similar strategy formulation processes and might come to the same conclusions – the predicted new market might be a very crowded place, if it even materialises. The flavour of the decisions to be made is perhaps illustrated by a few examples:

◆   The Lockheed Tristar:
    Lockheed used to be a significant provider of propeller passenger planes but dropped out when the market switched to passenger jets – it concentrated on the military aeroplane and avionics market. When the market started moving to wide-bodied jets it re-entered with the Tristar (powered by a new generation of jet engines from Rolls-Royce). Both Lockheed and Rolls-Royce had a lot of problems financing the development and had to be bailed out by their respective governments (in Britain, Rolls-Royce was nationalised). The Tristar eventually entered service in 1972 and sold reasonably well. Over subsequent years there was a shift by airlines to single source their fleets; if all their planes were from one manufacturer it simplified training, maintenance and spares supply. Lockheed's two main competitors, Boeing and McDonnell Douglas (this was before the European Airbus became a major player) could supply the range of aircraft the airlines needed but Lockheed, with just two variants of the Tristar, could not. The option were: to invest in new variants to consolidate the company's place in the passenger aircraft market, to muddle along, or to quit. This was no small decision given the investment that Lockheed had made in designing a new generation of jets, creating the production capacity and developing the market. The decision when it was made was stark: the company quit.
       Did Lockheed make the right decision? There can be no definitive answer to that. Its analysis was that there was space in the market for two makers of large passenger jets and there was no point in investing heavily to stay in third place. Since those days the European airbus has developed to be joint market leader with Boeing – McDonnell Douglas effectively dropped out of the running and eventually merged with Boeing.

◆   Microsoft's X-box:
    Microsoft has a virtual monopoly of desk-top operating systems and general purpose office software. Interestingly it was not much interested in the Internet when it first started coming to the attention of businesses and the public, but when it 'cottoned on' it made it a centre piece of its strategy and quickly set about supplanting the then leading software supplier, Netscape. With (arguably) not much room for further expansion in the desktop market it has been eyeing the education / leisure / games market – *Encarta* and *Age of Empires* being its best known titles. Microsoft used to argue that the PC was the most appropriate games machine and that dedicated games boxes from Sony and Nintendo would eventually lose out. Now it seems to have changed its tune and has launched its own games machine, the X-box. Production of the X-box is outsourced. The X-box faces a stiff uphill battle against the existing providers (with their established games portfolios) but with Microsoft's resources and determination it would be a mistake to bet against their success.

Where does strategy come into Microsoft's way of working? On both the Internet and on games boxes it seemed to miss the boat and then used its massive resources and market position to make a late entry into the market. There is a whole separate literature on first mover advantage (first to the market with a new idea but with all the problems of developing new technologies and a new market) and second mover advantage (avoid the problems of new technology and developing the market but there is then the need to catch up the market leader). On browsers and now on game boxes, Microsoft was a late comer to the market (and its entry seems in many ways to be opportunist rather than strategic). In the case of the browser it used its dominance of the PC operating system market to become the dominant browser provider. These tactics can not be reused for the games box but, presumably, Microsoft will not be content with anything less than the number one slot (and being number two in this market is not a good position).

◆ GEC / Marconi:
British GEC (not the American company of the same name) was a leading British manufacturing company with extensive interests in areas such as power generation, precision instruments, telecommunications switchgear and defence equipment. The company was run for many years by Arnold Weinstock as a fairly loosely configured holding company, each component company concentrating on its own specialist area. Over the years the company ran profitably and built up a cash pile in excess of GB£3 billion. Eventually Weinstock retired and the new management decided to concentrate on the telecom equipment sector. Subsidiaries that were not in the chosen area of business were disposed of and new telecom companies were acquired (including two American companies, bought at the height of the stock market telecom boom, that eventually proved to be virtually worthless). For a while the stock market loved the new GEC (now called Marconi) but that did not last. There was oversupply in the telecoms equipment market, the telcos (who had themselves run up considerable debts) reduced their orders for new equipment and Marconi started looking pretty sick. From a diverse, cash rich company, Marconi had changed into a heavily indebted company with a declining share of an overprovided specialist market segment – all in the space of a few years. At the time of writing, Marconi is having to shed labour, sell its remaining peripheral assets and its survival is in doubt. The stock market valuation of the new Marconi dived from GB£23 billion in 1999 to a little over GB£100 million at the time of Weinstock's death in July 2002.

GEC / Marconi did the strategy thing and got it wrong. Under Weinstock it was seen as a slumbering giant. The new management decided to change all that and followed the stock market fashion for hi-tech investment. Developing a strategy does not ensure success – following stock market fashions that ignore the fundamentals of business value is, over the long term, a sure recipe for disaster.

Strategy is typically cast in terms of competitive advantage. Porter (1998a) identifies three generic competitive advantages:

◆ Cost leadership: to be the lowest cost operator in the market sector.
◆ Differentiation: to produce goods or services with qualities that distinguish them from competitors.
◆ Focus: to concentrate on one segment of a market sector, a niche market.

Having agreed a strategy there then has to be a process of translating the theoretical strategy into a practical plan than can be implemented by management and carried out at the activity level. Not every aspect of the strategy will work out as intended but hopefully the organisation with a strategy is better placed than the one that does no more than muddle through. *Figure 5.2* represents the ongoing implementation of strategy and the pressures that will continue to affect the outcome.

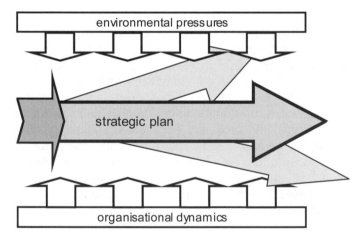

Figure 5.2 Strategy Implementation and Pressures for Change

5.2 Business Models

There are a number of business models that can be used to inform the process of strategy formulation. In this chapter we will look at three of them:

◆ SWOT.
◆ Porter's model of competitive forces.
◆ The Boston Consulting Group matrix.

❖ SWOT

SWOT stands for strengths, weaknesses, opportunities and threats. It is a simple, two by two matrix that corresponds with the first two stages of the strategy formulation process. The model asks four questions:

◆ What are the strengths of my organisation?
◆ What are the weaknesses of my organisation?

♦ What opportunities are present in the environment?
♦ What are the threats in the environment?

The requirement is that we put on our thinking caps and brainstorm these four questions. We should come up with a short list of the main points for each heading – a honest evaluation, not one that simply justifies what we intended to do. Under strengths we need to assess not just what the organisation does well but what it does better than the competition. Factors that might apply include:

♦ Strengths in research and development.
♦ The ownership of intellectual property rights.
♦ Favourable locations in important markets.
♦ Brand reputation and recognition.
♦ Leading position in chosen market(s).
♦ Strong finances.
♦ Modern facilities.
♦ Skilled labour force.
♦ Economies of scale / low operating costs.
♦ Strength in supply chain organisation.
♦ Well developed IS / IT infrastructure.

Weakness would list similar factors but for areas where the organisation is at a disadvantage.

For opportunities we need to look at factors in the external environment such as:

♦ Likely increases in demand for our existing products.
♦ Opportunities for new products for which we have the required expertise.
♦ Opportunities to expand into new geographical areas.
♦ Government support for development in areas relevant to the organisation.
♦ Anticipated economic growth and customer spending power.

And threats can include the opposites of the above (e.g. anticipated decreases in demand) plus:

♦ New competitors entering the market.
♦ Substitute products.
♦ Ethical or environmental concerns.

Strengths ☺	Weaknesses ☹
• Large number of students onsite • Loyal friendly staff • Caters for ethnic diet requirements	• Students only present for 24 to 30 weeks • Most of the trade is at lunchtime

Opportunities 👆	Threats ☜
• Commercial partnerships	• Commercial eateries off campus • Pressure from the university for a commercial return

Figure 5.3 SWOT Analysis – Student Refectory

Figure 5.3 attempts to illustrate the process by presenting a SWOT analysis of the refectory for my faculty at MMU – check out how well the analysis fits the eating places at your university or college. *Figure 5.4* is a similar analysis but for a national airline such as British Airways (the analysis is that of the author, not of British Airways).

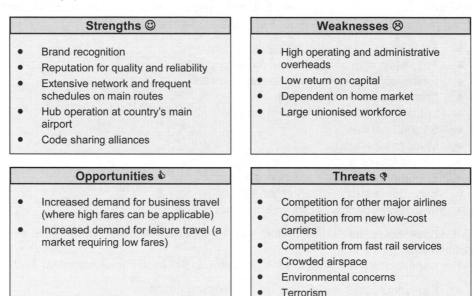

Figure 5.4 SWOT Analysis – National Airline

The strategic choices for major airlines are not easy. Competition with other major airlines is fierce and that has a downward pressure on fares (although British Airways can charge a premium on its transatlantic routes where many customers prefer it to US based competitors). In addition to competition from similar airlines there is increased competition from low cost carriers on short haul routes. The major airlines can try to match the low cost carriers on price but their cost structures make that very difficult. To compete they would probably have to go the no-frills route but that would alienate the premium business market which is their most profitable sector.

❖ **Porter's Model of Competitive Forces**

Porter's model was originally published in his book: *Competitive Strategy: Techniques for Analysing Industries and Competitors* (Porter, 1998a). The model is extensively used in academic writing and is one of the basic business analysis models.

Porter's model helps a company, or an organisation, to look at the competitive environment in which it operates. The point it makes is quite simple but is none the less worth making. The first competitive force is that of the existing competition: competitor airlines, the other PC makers or whatever the case is – fairly obvious and not likely to be ignored. The model however points to four further forces:

◆ Threat of potential entrants.
◆ Threat of substitution.
◆ Bargaining power of buyers.
◆ Bargaining power of suppliers.

The model is represented in *figure 5.5*.

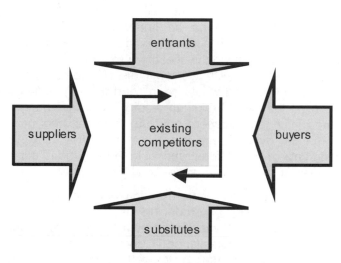

Figure 5.5 Porter's Model of Competitive Forces

Reprinted with the permission of The Free Press, a Division of Simon & Schuster Audit Publishing Group, from COMPETITIVE ADVANTAGE: Creating and Sustaining Superior Performance by Michael E. Porter. Copyright © 1985, 1998 by Michael E. Porter. All rights reserved.

The four external forces are examined, with examples taken from various economic sectors, below:

◆ Threat of potential entrants:

This force is about the ease with which a new competitor can set up in the market in competition with the existing players. If the market is buoyant, with considerable business being done, the natural capitalist process is for new or existing businesses to move in to get a share of the action. New entrants to the market will seek to achieve competitive advantage by offering a superior product or a similar service at a lower price. Factors that inhibit new entrants include:

   ◆ The cost of entry – how much must be spent on research, development, production equipment and marketing before the new entrant can compete in the market.
   ◆ Branding – if existing market player(s) are well known and trusted, will customers / consumers switch to a new brand?
   ◆ Intellectual property rights (IPR) – do existing player(s) have patents and / or copyrights that make new entry difficult or impossible?

This threat of potential entrants can be illustrated using a couple of examples from the IT industry:

* Microsoft, with its Windows operating system, is the dominant supplier in the PC operating system market. IBM with OS2, arguably, had a better product but did not market its system as effectively as Microsoft. Apple has its own operating system but that is a different (and smaller) market. Creating a new operating system and competing with Microsoft can look to be an impossible task. To create a new operating system from scratch would require a massive investment and then, to make it worthwhile, there would need to be a good range of applications to go with it. Even if this were to be achieved there is a fair bet that Microsoft would be in court to allege infringements of its IPRs (and that would take up a lot of time and money even if the claimed infringements were not true). The only real new entrant into the market over recent years is Linux from the free software movement – a very different model from the large IT companies. It will be interesting to see if it makes a real dent in Microsoft's stranglehold.

* Whilst Microsoft has been the dominant player in PC operating systems the position on producing the machines themselves is very different. The market was started by IBM (and Apple) and was joined somewhat later by established IT companies such as DEC and HP. However, as the market developed, a PC became very much a commodity item and it was easy for new companies to enter the market. Over the years there have been many new entrants to the market – those which made a significant impact include Compaq and Dell. Unlike the operating system market (or the chip market) it is very easy for a new player to start building PCs – with the number of operators already competing in the market it could be that a few more would not be really noticed but the leading PC maker must be watching out for the competitor who will come up with that new idea which will give it competitive advantage – as Dell did with its direct sales and just-in-time supply chain management.

◆ Threat of substitution:

As well as potential entrants to the market there is the danger that the product will become obsolete and the customers will switch to something different (or not require the product at all). Classic cases of substitution include the use of synthetic fibres in place of natural fibres and the use of plastic containers in place of glass (although in both cases wool, cotton and glass live on with a proportion of the overall market).

Continuing with the case of the PC, it has long been suggested that many users do not require a full spec personal computer and something much cheaper and linked to processing and software resources over the Internet could be more appropriate and economically viable – the 'net machine'. In the event, the concept never got off the ground – the PC got cheaper and the net machines that were produced never represented enough of a saving to be worthwhile. An alternative threat is that consumers who only require a computer for entertainment and some Internet access will be content with an interactive TV or a game box – possibly, but many consumers are buying these facilities and a PC as well. The threat of substitution in the PC industry looks low – for the present at least.

- ◆ Bargaining power of suppliers:

The ability of the organisation to compete depends not just on the organisation's cost structure and methods of working but also the cost of the goods and services it buys in to be used in its operation. If an organisation is buying in commodity products that are readily available then it should be able to get a good price – steel is one such example where there is overcapacity in the industry and users of the raw material are able to extract very good prices from the producers. If, on the other hand, the required inputs are in short supply or very specialised in nature the supplier will be in a much better position to name its own price – suppliers of medicines to the health services are in such a position as long as their product is in demand and they have a patent that stops generic substitution.

Organisations can reduce the bargaining power of their suppliers by ensuring, where possible, that there is an alternative, competing source of supply. Suppliers can seek to lock in their customers by differentiating their product and providing value added services.

For the makers of PCs, Intel has been the established supplier of processor chips. It ran a successful promotion with the line 'Intel inside' and for many customers a PC was only acceptable if it came with an Intel chip. Recently AMD has gained increased recognition for its rival processor chip; some PC users claim it to be superior to the Intel equivalent. Over a number of years Intel, as a supplier, has had a strong bargaining position – a position that is now much weaker given that the AMD chip is now an acceptable alternative.

In bargaining, the business and its suppliers both need to exercise some caution. If the business pushes too hard the supplier may go out of business and if the supplier takes too greater advantage of a strong market position it will encourage new entrants and substitution.

- ◆ Bargaining power of buyers:

The bargaining power of the buyers is, in most respects, the mirror image of the position with the suppliers.

For a company buying from trade suppliers and selling to trade customers the ideal is to negotiate a keen price with the suppliers but to achieve a decent mark-up when selling on to the customer. The ability to achieve that mark-up relates to factors such as:

- ◆ The cost base of the organisation.
- ◆ Special factors that differentiate the product from the competition.
- ◆ The degree of competition in the marketplace.

The factors that affect the bargaining power of a supplier to the organisation are the same factors as come into play when the organisation deals with its customers. Does the product have that special edge that can be used to get a better deal or is it just the same 'bog-standard' commodity item that many of the competition also offer. To get a competitive edge in dealing with its buyers (customers) the organisation needs to achieve differentiation, focus or cost leadership in its chosen field of business.

A business customer looking for a number of PCs will be able to shop around for the best deal. If the requirement is for 100 mid-range PCs with the usual desk top facilities there are a large number of manufacturers and office supply companies that would be happy to provide them. With no real difference between the products (whatever the manufacturers may claim) the buyer is able to drive a hard bargain – the main limiting factor being the number of sources that the buyer has time to contact and negotiate with.

A special case in applying Porter's model is where the buyer is a retail customer. In most retail situations customers can not haggle on price but they can look for an alternative make or go to another retail outlet.

As is indicated by the examples, not all forces will be equally applicable in each case; check each of them out but don't feel the need to invent threats where none exist.

❖ Portfolio Evaluation

Our third and final model is portfolio analysis using the Boston Consulting Group matrix. The suggestion is that:

◆ A product can be In a high growth rate or a low growth rate market (some dynamic markets such as for cars, PCs and mobile phones are now relatively static but their size would probably justify classifying then as high growth rate – certainly the nature of the competition would seem to suggest that band).

◆ A product or a model can have a relatively high market share or a relatively low share of the overall market.

This gives the four-cell matrix shown in *figure 5.6*.

		Market Share:	
		High	Low
Market Growth Rate:	High	**Star**	**Question Marks**
	Low	**Cash Cow**	**Dog**

Figure 5.6 The Boston Consulting Group Matrix

The four classifications are:

◆ Star: a market leader with a high market share in a high growth rate / desirable market. In the PC market the current market leader is Dell. The star position is a good position to be in but one that has to be defended. It will cost the company money in marketing and product development to maintain the star position. Hopefully the economies of scale, coupled with the sales volume, will make the investment worthwhile. In the case of Dell, other PC makers are trying to copy its production and sales techniques; the market is fiercely competitive and Dell could be a fallen star by the time you come to read this book.

◆ Question mark / problem child: an also-ran position in a desirable and hence competitive market. If Dell and the other leading PC makers are achieving 8% to 20% share of the PC market then it is a bit of a dubious position to be a small PC maker with (say) 2% or less of the market. You still have to update your product when a new chip comes out and you need to advertise and / or get your product taken on by distributors. Your costs can be similar to the market leader, your bargaining power with suppliers is less and your sales are a tenth of Dell's. Unless you can differentiate the product, achieve focus or have realistic hopes of breaking into the big time it is not a healthy position. The question mark is whether to continue or whether to cut one's losses and quit.

◆ Cash cow: in a less glamorous market area the competition tends to be less fierce. There are no great prizes for being the top seller of, for example, self-raising flour. If you are the market leader, as is Homepride in the UK, you don't need to do a lot of advertising – all the supermarkets will stock your product and presumably you will make at least a fair return on your capital and production costs. The product is a cash cow.

Arguably another cash cow situation is where the company has a near market monopoly and not too much threat of new entrants or substitution. Microsoft can treat its Windows operating system and office suite as cash cows to fund its other ambitions, safe in the knowledge that there is no other product about to dent its dominant market position.

◆ Dog: is the description given to the also-ran position in a low growth, static or declining market. Having a low percentage of such a market probably means relatively high unit costs and it is probably not worth the investment that would be necessary to catch up or overtake the market leader. What should a small, traditional flour producer do – the supermarkets are not too likely to stock his brand alongside the market leader and the public would not recognise the product if it was on the shelves. If the product is a dog it is probably best to abandon it.

Note, there seem to be a number of versions of the Boston Consulting Group matrix in circulation. Another version deals with the product lifecycle from inception, through growth, to maturity and eventually decline – this version is not analysed in this text.

5.3   IT / IS Strategy

As well as the overall business strategy the organisation may well wish to develop its IS / IT strategy.

Traditionally the strategy for individual departments or functions has been subservient to the overall business strategy of the organisation and that would normally be true of IS / IT. That said, the use of IT can be a significant competitive weapon and IT can be a vital element in the development of overall business strategy. Cases where companies have achieved significant competitive advantage through the use of IS / IT include:

◆ Apollo and Sabre airline booking systems. These two systems were early examples of airline booking systems developed by American Airlines and United Airways respectively. When these systems were made available for online booking from travel agents the owning airlines listed their flights first and placed those of competitors lower down the list. One of the victims of this was Frontier Air whose route network overlapped with United's. It won an antitrust case to force United to list its and competitor flights in an unbiased order but by that time the damage was done and Frontier was out of business. See, for example Earl (1989) or Whiteley (2000).

◆ Brun Passot is a French office supplies firm. In 1982 it started linking up its customers electronically – initially using the Minitel system and later an EDI system. In the fragmented French office supply market the competitors of Brun Passot were unable to match its IT investment and the company was able to rapidly increase its market share; see Jelassi (1994).

◆ Federal Express is one of the three large express parcel carriers in the US and world wide – its major competitors are UPS and DHL. The major express parcel carriers barcode their packets and have IT systems that record their movements each time the packet passes through a depot. Federal Express introduced an Internet service that allowed its customers to check where their parcel was in the system – this was convenient for the customers and saved Federal Express dealing with many telephone enquiries. This competitive service was matched six months later by UPS but it took DHL a further couple of years before it was able to introduce a matching service. See Whiteley (2000).

e-Commerce is an application area that can be very important to the future development and competitive position of a company (despite the well published dot.com hysteria and subsequent crash). In my book *e-Commerce: Strategy, Technologies and Applications* (2000) I argue that, for many organisations, ICT developments can be an essential part of future competitive advantage and an evaluation of e-Commerce environment needs to be specifically included in the overall business strategy development process.

Exercises

1.   List the major car brands and suggest which of Porter's three generic competitive advantages they seem to be attempting to achieve. For some

manufacturers you may identify different models with different aims – discuss any problems this may give raise to.

2. Check out the SWOT analysis of the author's university refectory (see *figure 5.3*) and see how that compares with the refectory that is available at your place of study. Prepare a SWOT analysis for another organisation you are familiar with – the bookshop where you bought this book or the college / university department in which you are studying.

3. Assume that you are running a rail passenger service – London to Manchester is the example I normally use. Use Porter's model to assess its competitive position (note that some of the four forces are less significant than others for this case).

4. Apply the Boston Consulting Group portfolio analysis to the case of the principal rail services on the West Coast Mainline:
   - London to Birmingham – journey time of under 1 hr 45 min.
   - London to Manchester – journey time of about 2 hr 45 min.
   - London to Liverpool – journey time of about 2 hr 55 min.
   - London to Glasgow – journey time of about 5 hr 30 min.

5. Consider the environmental changes that are likely to affect your university or college department. Also consider the strengths and weaknesses of the department and suggest two or three pathways the department could choose as its strategy for growth and / or development over the coming years. Your answer to question 2 could feed into the first part of this question.

Further Reading

There are numerous specialist books and business books that cover the strategy development process and popular business models. One book, specifically on strategy, that the author uses is:

Lynch R. (2002) *Corporate Strategy*, 3rd ed., Prentice Hall, Hemel Hempstead.

The best book on IT and strategy came out some years ago – it is:

Earl M. J. (1989) *Management Strategies for Information Technology*, Prentice Hall, Hemel Hempstead.

Many more general books cover the strategic process and Needle is, of course, an excellent example:

Needle D. (2004) *Business in Context: An introduction to business and its environment*, 4th ed., Thomson, London.

Finally, it is always worth going back to the original sources, the relevant text for Porter's model is:

Porter M. E. (1998) *Competitive Strategy: Techniques for Analyzing Industries and Competitors*, Simon & Schuster, London.

Chapter 6
Business Activity

Summary

The final layer of the IS business environment model is the operations level. The operations level is where the production process is carried out or where the service is delivered. The production process is most easily envisaged in a manufacturing company making cars, computers, paper clips or whatever. The operations / production level also includes organisations in primary industries, such as farming and mining, and in the service sector such as banking, health and education.

In addition to the central production / service delivery process there are a number of support functions at the operations level. These include:

◆ Marketing: letting potential customers know you are there and persuading them to do business with you.
◆ Purchasing: buying in the raw materials or components for the production process plus the equipment and supplies needed for the functioning of the organisation.
◆ Finance: the organisation has to count its pennies – it should know how much it is earning and how much it is spending and it must then report to its stakeholders.
◆ Personnel: the organisation needs to recruit the right people for the job and then make sure they are trained, paid and disciplined (should that prove to be necessary).
◆ Innovation: the world moves on and yesterday's mobile phone is now (for some) an embarrassment – the company must update, improve or re-invent its products and / or its service delivery.

Also at the operations level is the IS / IT functions – that is what the remainder of the book is about.

6.1   The Operations Level

The third and final layer of the model is the operations level – the place where the cars are built, the merchandise is sold or the students are taught. The operations layer is essentially about that production / service delivery function but also includes a number of other operation level functions:

- Marketing.
- Purchasing.
- Finance.
- Personnel.
- Innovation.

See the IS business environment model (operations level) in *figure 6.1*.

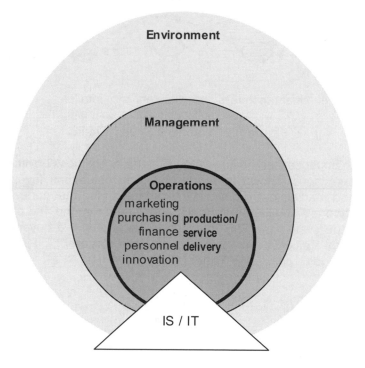

Figure 6.1 The IS Business Environment

The production process takes place in the context of the management level and the business environment but it is also dependent on the suppliers to the organisation, and it requires that there are customers or clients prepared to pay for the product.

The process of buying in raw materials, components or merchandise from a supplier, processing it in some way to 'add value' and selling it on to a customer for further processing or for use is referred to as a supply chain. A generic supply chain is illustrated in *figure 6.2*.

The supply chain is central to the operations of most businesses in the manufacturing and selling (wholesale and retail) categories and these are illustrated in *figure 6.2*. Transport industries and services are also dependent on suppliers and customers but the supply side is generally less central to their operations (the transport of goods provides the physical linkages in the supply chain). The use of ICTs is central to the coordination of a modern, complex, just-in-time supply chain and this is discussed in the chapter on EDI in *Part III*.

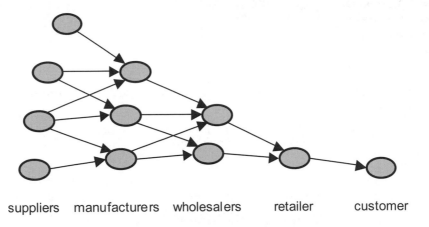

suppliers   manufacturers   wholesalers   retailer   customer

Figure 6.2 A Generic Supply Chain

The supply chain model can be integrated with the IS business environment model to produce the model shown in *figure 6.3*. The operations level functions of purchasing and marketing are obviously vital in ensuring that good quality inputs at the right price are obtained from the suppliers and that the end product is sold at a profit to the customers. This matches the suppliers and buyers (customers) aspects of Porter's model of competitive rivalry (see *Chapter 5*); it is also similar to Porter's generic value chain, see Porter (1998b).

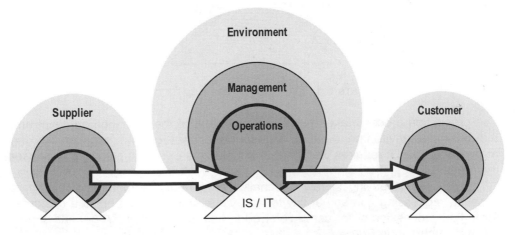

Figure 6.3 The Business Operations Model

6.2   Marketing

In the early days of the Soviet Union the government banned advertising as a wasteful, capitalist activity and in many ways they were right – many companies spend a fortune on advertising and none of that expenditure adds any value to the products (although some adverts are better entertainment than the shows that they come with). The problem the Soviets then had was that the potential consumers did not know that a product was available and were hence unlikely to make a purchase.

A marketing operation can be fairly modest and passive. The corner shop that sells newspapers and convenience goods just needs a half-decent shop window and possibly a leafleting campaign round the local community. The local builder may not do much more than paint company details on his van and pay for an advert in the Yellow Pages.

Marketing on a national scale can also, in some instances, be reasonably low key. UK students find out about university courses from their school teachers, university web sites and the documentation provided by the admissions clearing houses. There is however increasing competition for students and the likelihood that marketing efforts will be ratcheted up – it is already happening. The problem, of course, is that the more time and money that is expended on marketing, the less resource there is available for educational facilities and teaching students.

The most aggressive marketing is carried out in a few market sectors – soap powder is the classic case. In these sectors, marketing costs are a significant part of the product price and, by themselves, do nothing to get your clothes cleaner or to enhance the utility of the product. Where competition is strong then it is easy for marketing battles to break out. The only gainers are the advertising agencies and the advert-carrying media – the losers may be the small organisation that can not afford to compete in the marketing game and the consumer who ultimately foots the bill for the marketing costs, without necessarily getting the best available product.

There is an established mantra for marketing – the 'four Ps'. These are:

- Product: The product or service has to be one that is required by and / or attractive to the consumer.

- Price: The price needs to be right. It needs to be one that the consumer is prepared to pay and, preferably, one that covers the company's operating costs. Interestingly, reducing the price does not necessarily help sales. Some markets are price sensitive but in other cases a low price can be seen as an indicator of poor quality and consumers may well go for a higher priced, designer label, product on the assumption it is of better quality.

- Promotion: The product or service has to marketed. There is no advantage is having a great product, at a good price, if the consumer does not know it is there – the role of advertising has already been discussed.

- Place: The final 'P' is place. The product or service has to be available to the consumer – on the shelves in the shop, in an office that can be easily accessed by clients or delivered in the required quantity and on time to the commercial customer. Many manufacturers have the twin task of persuading the shops to stock the product and the public to buy – to achieve sales the supplier needs to be successful in both arenas.

Marketing has to be supported by an efficient production and distribution function. Having found customers, or created a demand, the organisation must then deliver.

6.3 Purchasing

All organisations need to purchase inputs for their production / operations. For many organisations, particularly in the service sector, this may not be a crucial factor (the office supplies need to be there but they hardly make or break the operation) but for operations such as manufacture, wholesale and retail it is a crucial aspect of the business. For these operations we have the concept of the supply chain or value chain. A simple, generic supply chain has been illustrated in *figure 6.2*.

Real supply chains are more complex and stretch across much more than five levels. Car assemblers and supermarkets number their suppliers in the hundreds or possibly thousands. Smaller organisations will work through wholesalers who can more easily deal with a large number of suppliers and then pass on the goods, in the quantities required, to their customers.

Many organisations have a purchasing department and the staff may well have been trained in the 'buying business'. Getting the right deal on primary inputs to the production process is vital to the quality and costing of the end product. Traditionally organisations would bulk purchase the materials they needed for their production process and then keep a stock in their warehouse / stock room. These processes of purchase and stock control are being replaced by:

◆ Supply chain management.
◆ Just in time manufacture.
◆ Quick response supply.

This newer terminology reflects an effort to decrease stock (which ties up capital and incurs handling charges) and to improve quality by total quality management (TQM) systems in cooperation with selected suppliers.

The supply chain, as illustrated, is about primary supplies – components for manufacturing and merchandise for selling. A further aspect of purchasing is secondary supplies – typically the stationery for the office and the consumables for the shop floor but also including items such as computers and services such as cleaning. For many service sector organisations secondary supplies are the main purchasing requirement.

Whilst considerable effort has gone into creating efficiency and taking cost out of the primary supply chain (and e-Commerce is a important element of this) the area of purchasing secondary supplies has been relatively neglected. Kalakota and Robinson (1999) assert:

> Large companies spend more than 5 to 10 percent of revenue on office equipment, supplies, software, computers, peripherals, and other so-called non-production goods.

Purchasing these secondary supplies is another task for the purchasing function. Unlike primary supplies, where there is a streamlined process and extensive use of IS and IT, the purchase process for secondary supplies is often bureaucratic and time consuming. The cost of processing the order often exceeds the cost of the goods – 95% of purchases involve paper based processing. ICTs, in the form of e-Procurement systems, are being gradually introduced into this area, hopefully with the effect of making the process quicker and cheaper for all concerned.

6.4 Finance

The basics of accounting were summed up by Charles Dickens, speaking through Mr Micawber, in his book *David Copperfield*:

> Annual income twenty pounds, annual expenditure nineteen nineteen six, result happiness. Annual income twenty pounds, annual expenditure twenty pounds ought and six, result misery.

It seems to be an old-fashioned view not always applied in company (or personal) finance. The currency is also outdated: for those too young to remember, £19.19s.6p is £19.98 and £20.0s.5p is £20.02 (using symmetrical rounding) and that may yet need to be reinterpreted as annual income €32.23 ...!

Wilkins Micawber is well known for waiting for something to turn up – possibly the Enrons and Worldcoms of this world had similar hopes to get them out of the black holes that they had created in their accounts. However, a well regulated company will have a clear picture of the state of its finances and it is the job of the finance and accountancy department to maintain those accounts.

The responsibilities of the finance department can be divided into financial management, management accounting and financial reporting (Needle, 2004):

◆ Financial management: This is concerned with raising capital to finance the organisation's operations and with ensuring that the company can generate sufficient funds to cover the cost of raising that finance. Sources of funds include issuing shares, borrowing from the bank, state funding and internally generated funds.

◆ Management accounting: This is the application of accounting techniques to provide management with information to assist it in the process of planning and control. Management accounting includes:
  • Budgeting and budgetary control.
  • Cost accounting.
  • Investment appraisal.
  • Cash flow management.

◆ Financial reporting: This is the collection and presentation of data used in financial management and management accounting. It includes the balance sheet and a profit and loss account. These accounts have to conform to the relevant statutory and professional accountancy requirements. They form the basis of the annual report to shareholders and the tax authorities. In the UK the accounts have to be lodged with Companies House and are available for public inspection.

An extract from the accounts of my company, Computa Ltd., is shown in *figures 6.4 and 6.5*. The company was selling my services as an IT consultant and the accounts are therefore different from a manufacturing or retailing organisation which would have greater sums invested in assets or stocks. The figures are the balance sheet and profit and loss account for 1990 (before I took a vow of poverty and became an academic!). Hopefully these examples give some idea of the nature of financial reporting – the process is much the same for a large company, just add zeroes on the right side of all the figures.

Computa Limited
Profit and Loss Account

	1990	1989
Turnover	45,436	**47,018**
Cost of Sales	12	**21**
Gross Profit	45,424	46,997
Administrative Expenses	18,546	17,620
Operating Profit	26,878	29,377
Interest Receivable	618	784
Profit on Ordinary Activities before Taxation	27,496	30,161
Tax on Profit on Ordinary Activities	6,907	7,643
Profit for the year	20,589	22,518
Dividends	20,589	22,437
	-	81
Accumulated Loss brought forward	-	(81)
Net Profit	£0.0	£0.0

Figure 6.4 Computa Ltd – Profit and Loss Account

Computa Limited
Balance Sheet

		1990		1989
Fixed Assets		2,873		3,317
Current Assets:				
Stock	159		2,581	
Debtors	606		2,118	
Cash at Bank and In Hand	4,931		3,911	
	5,696		8,610	
Creditors: Amounts falling due				
within one year	8,469		11,827	
Net Current Liabilities		(2,773)		(3,217)
Total Assets less Current				
Liabilities		£100		£100
Capital and Reserves:				
Share Capital		100		100
Profit and Loss Account		-		-
		£100		£100

Figure 6.5 Computa Ltd – Balance Sheet

Keeping accounts accurate and up-to-date requires care and a lot of arithmetic. In many ways accounts are an ideal computer application and accounts were one of the earliest applications to be automated. Most modern companies use an IS for accounts. In a small company this will be a series of spreadsheets or a PC accounts package. A larger organisation will have a much more complex facility where all transactions in (say) the Order Processing system are automatically updated to the General Ledger for each processing step that has a financial implication. The General Ledger system should be able to provide detailed figures of the value of orders received, orders despatched, write-offs, accounts payable, accounts received, etc., at any time and for any given period.

Accountants fill many of the senior positions in UK organisations. Sometimes it seems that UK companies are more concerned with 'bean counting' than with the production of goods, delivery of service or the research and development process that is necessary to develop the next generation of products.

6.5 Personnel

Many organisations claim that their staff are their most valuable asset (although some of us could, perhaps, be forgiven for asking why the organisation does not therefore take better care of its assets).

The policy of the organisation on recruitment, training, remuneration and 'disposal' of its staff is the responsibility of the personnel function – called 'human resources' in some companies. These functions are carried out in conjunction with the line managers of the various departments within the organisation. Personnel is responsible for the personnel policy of the organisation and for making sure that is operated within the law. The line manager seeks to ensure that he / she has the appropriate staff for carrying out the work of the department. Thus, in most organisations, functions such as recruitment, training, appraisals and redundancy will be joint processes involving both line managers and personnel professionals.

The responsibilities of the personnel function, in a little more detail, include:

◆ Recruitment: The organisation needs to recruit staff with the necessary skills, aptitude and attitude – not an easy task when recruitment decisions have to be made on the basis of not much more than an application form and an interview. Recruiting new staff and giving initial training is not cheap – for many professional jobs the rule of thumb is that recruitment costs add up to a total equivalent to the first year's salary.

An alternative to recruiting 'permanent' staff is to use contract staff or outsource tasks. Contracting gives flexibility but the cost of that can be premium rates and the loss of staff loyalty to the organisation.

◆ Training: Once staff have been recruited it is necessary to keep their skills up-to-date. The personnel department will normally have a training strategy that is implemented in consultation with line managers. Training can be sourced from outside or can be conducted by an in-house training department. Initial job training often consists of working alongside an experienced member of staff for an initial period. Increasingly skill training, particularly IT skills, is provided using computer aided learning (CAL) packages. Sometimes training can be away from work in an hotel or training centre – however companies are becoming increasingly cost conscious and such treatment is increasingly reserved for senior managers.

◆　Pay: Staff must be paid. Arguably the organisation wants to pay as little as it can get away with but it needs to balance that with the need to retain and motivate staff. In many instances there is 'a going rate for the job' and the company needs to roughly match that rate if it is going to get the staff it needs.

Having recruited staff and agreed a rate of pay it is then normal for those wage or salary rates to be reviewed on an annual basis. This may be a straight 'offer' from the employer or it may be negotiated with staff representatives, typically a trade union. Some staff, for example many shop floor workers and university lecturers, are paid a set rate for their grade (e.g. the senior lecturer pay scale) whereas in other organisations staff will be paid on a performance related basis. Paying people on the basis of their performance sounds attractive but in many cases performance is difficult to assess. A study in a civil service department found that white male managers tended to assess the performance of their white male staff more highly than other staff members – not an appropriate, or unusual, outcome. Some football clubs are now proposing performance related pay for their players. On current form, that doesn't sound too good for the players at my team – Sheffield Wednesday.

Sometimes, pay for high earners is referred to as remuneration or a compensation package – it is not clear what they are been compensated for.

◆　Appraisals: In addition to any individual salary review, many organisations operate a staff appraisal system. The staff appraisal is typically an annual process where staff evaluate their own performance and discuss that performance and their aspirations with line managers. Some organisations operate a reverse appraisal system where staff also appraise their managers – most organisations are not that brave.

◆　Redundancies: Sometimes organisations need to 'let people go'. This may be a group of workers that are surplus to requirements or an individual whose performance has been judged unsatisfactory. Whatever the reasons, redundancies have to be handled with care (and hopefully sensitivity and generosity). There are legal and procedural requirements that need to be met before staff can be dismissed.

◆　Health and safety: Workplaces are not always the safest of places. The dangers of a mine or a building site are readily appreciated but there are dangers, albeit less dramatic, in all workplaces. It is the duty of all employers to pay proper attention to the health and safety of their work people. In the UK, health and safety procedures have to be worked in consultation with representatives of the employees – usually this is the personnel department and the trade unions (if the staff are union members).

◆ Payroll and pensions: The personnel department is responsible for staff and therefore, typically, has responsibility for administering the payroll and the pensions procedures. In almost all cases the payroll is computerised and in many cases the running of the payroll is outsourced to a specialist computer bureau. The personnel / payroll section of the organisation needs to ensure that the staff data is kept up-to-date.

◆ Trade union relations: Where the staff are represented by trade unions the personnel section will take the lead in consultations / negotiations with those trade unions. The obvious issue is the negotiations about wage and salary increases but there are also likely to be many other consultations / disputes about issues affecting the working lives of union members within the organisation.

The personnel area is the subject of extensive regulations. This includes health and safety, race and sex discrimination, equal pay and trade union law. It is the job of the personnel department to provide expertise in these areas. Hopefully the organisation treats its staff fairly – certainly it needs to act with due regard to the law – and there are employment tribunals and other remedies open to employees / ex-employees who feel they have been treated improperly.

The task of personnel is a mixture of hard-headed business and of caring for real people who lead complex and sometimes difficult lives. It is a difficult balance to strike and one that is not always achieved.

6.6 Innovation

Innovation is concerned with both products and process. It is included in the activity level but will have strong links with the strategic level where future plans will, very likely, depend on new products and updated services. Needle (2004) sums up innovation thus:

> Innovation is the process through which new ideas and inventions become a business reality in the form of new products, processes and marketing strategies, and new methods of organisation and management. Its importance to business survival and growth is acknowledged by many firms through the creation of special units such as research and development departments in manufacturing industry.

The obvious form of innovation is the introduction of a new or updated product. Examples of this include:

◆ A new, or updated, model of a car.
◆ Mobile telephones incorporating a digital camera and able to send a picture.

The description is wider than the introduction of new products in manufacturing industry – it would also cover changes in the service sector:

◆ The introduction of Internet banking.

◆ The replacement of large, relatively infrequent, double-deck buses with small buses and a more frequent service.

It can also include a change in the way the product is constructed, the substitution of plastic for glass packaging or the use of composite materials in place of metal in aircraft construction.

Aside from updated products or services, innovation can also be in the structure of the organisation or the way that things are produced. These changes may not directly impact the consumer but can be of indirect relevance in making the product cheaper or the organisation more responsive to customer demand. Examples of such 'behind the scenes' innovation include:

◆ Process innovation: new ways of making a product or delivering it to the customer. Robots in production could be an example of such a change.

◆ Organisational innovation: a new way of structuring or running the organisation. Creating a customer service function for market segments or outsourcing IT are examples in this area.

◆ Marketing innovation: a new way of promoting or selling the product – the use of e-Commerce would be a topical example.

And there is a final classification of innovation, the pseudo innovation. This is a marketing ploy to suggest innovation where no real change has taken place. An example is the 'new improved formula' in the marketing of soap powders.

Most organisations are involved in some sort of innovation – in manufacturing there is (or should be) the research and development function – in services there may well be a department looking at new or restructured services. Even your degree is re-packaged every few years – possibly you have new degree titles such as e-Commerce and multimedia – in some cases another example of pseudo innovation!

6.7   Production / Operations

Finally, and central to the operations level and the whole organisation, is the production process. The nature and organisation of the production process varies greatly and is, in part at least, determined by the type of industry that the organisation operates in. The diversity can be illustrated by revisiting Wild's four categories:

◆ Manufacture: this can be highly organised and automated as in the production of cars but it could be a much simpler process such as making paperclips. Further production-type processes are mining, farming and craft industries.

◆ Selling: would tend to suggest the large supermarkets and the high street retail chains but it also includes the corner shop and the wholesale business for both trade and retail goods.

◆ Transport: covers moving of goods and / or people by land, sea and air. Also, arguably, in this sector is the telecomm industry where the object is the transport of speech and data.

◆ Service: this is a diverse category covering banking, insurance, health, education and so on – each of these has its own production process. The operations of financial services, to take one example, are very dependent on the use of IS / IT within the organisation.

The production process can be represented as a system diagram: see *figure 6.6*. The diagram illustrates that:

◆ Any production process requires a variety of inputs.
◆ The production process has a number of outputs (effects) in addition to the intended product or service – some of the effects, such as waste (pollution) and (possible) losses are not desirable.
◆ The process will incorporate feedback mechanisms to attempt to make sure that supply matches demand and that the required level of quality is achieved.

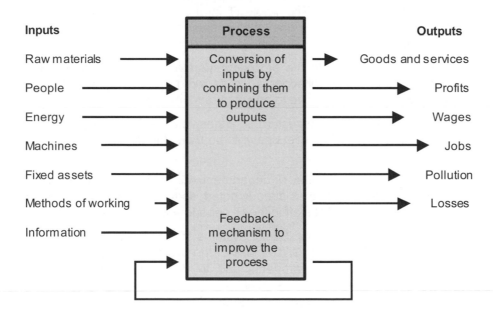

Figure 6.6 Production – System Diagram

6.8   IS / IT

The final activity included at the operations level is IS / IT. Most organisations of any size will have an IT department (although its name will vary). This department is responsible for the provision of IS / IT facilities throughout the organisation. The IS / IT function can be shared with the user departments or it may be devolved to the divisions. There are advantages in having a central IT department which coordinates policy, harmonises provision and makes best use of the available expertise. The flip side of that argument is that central IT can become over-bureaucratic and non-responsive to the needs of departmental users. Another alternative is that all or part of the IS / IT function may be outsourced.

The task of the IT department is to provide IS / IT facilities to the user departments. This can be seen as having four components:

♦ Business information systems: The software that is used for running the payroll, order processing system or whatever other system the business needs. This software may be produced 'in-house' by the organisation's own system analysts and programmers, the development may be outsourced or it may be bought in as a package. The process of developing a system is outlined in *Part V* and bought in ERP (enterprise resource planning) packages are discussed in *Part III*.

♦ IT infrastructure: The business information systems operate on computer systems linked internally and externally by a data network. The organisation may have central servers, possibly mainframe computers, running organisational applications. These are linked to other servers in the departments and / or the branches and hence to machines on the desk top or the factory floor. The whole IT infrastructure needs to be set up, maintained and updated. The components of the IS infrastructure are discussed in *Part IV*.

♦ Desk top: In addition to the business information systems there will be standard desk top applications such as word processing, spreadsheets and e-mail. These also need to be set up and maintained.

♦ Support: the IS / IT infrastructure is extensively used in all aspects of the organisation's work. The users have to be trained in its use and supported when things go wrong.

The structure and staffing of the IT department will depend on the organisation and the nature of its work (and as already noted, some or all of the functions may be outsourced). The specialist staff in the IT department could include:

♦ Business systems analysts: Senior systems staff with an understanding of both the business and of IS. The task of the business systems analysts is to consult with user departments and to devise new or improved IT systems that will assist the business.

♦ Project leaders: Team leaders of a group of IT (and possibly user staff) set up to develop a new system or install a major upgrade to IT facilities.

♦ Systems analysts: These are people who pick up projects from the business systems analysts and, in consultation with the user departments, do the detailed work to translate the business requirement into a detailed system design.

♦ Programmers: The staff who take the system design and convert it into program code to be deliver the IS facilities on the IT infrastructure.

♦ Database analysts / database administrator: As well as designing the system there is a need to map the data requirements onto database structures. This role should include standardising data definitions and structures throughout the organisation – a crucial role if the organisation is to be able to coordinate and audit its activities.

◆ System programmers: As well as the business software there is the system software to look after – the operating systems and the like on the desk top, servers and the mainframes.

◆ Operators: The desk top users operate their own machines but the servers and the mainframes also need to be looked after. For small machines this may be the job of the technicians (combining the role of system programmer and operator), for large central computing facilities there is a separate operators function.

◆ Help desk: A place for the users to ring in about any sort of difficulty. The help desk staff will help users with simple queries and pass more complex problems onto the appropriate technical area within the IT team.

An example organisational structure for an IT department is shown in *figure 6.7*.

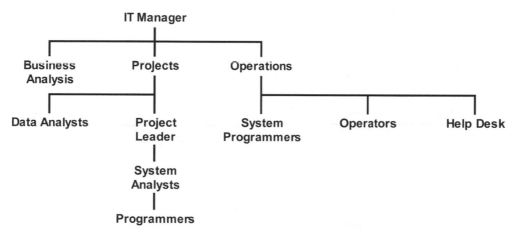

Figure 6.7 IT Department Structure Chart

The sort of systems that are required by the various operational functions include:

◆ Marketing:
  ◆ Customer information management systems (CIM).
◆ Purchasing:
  ◆ Procurement systems.
  ◆ EDI / electronic markets.
◆ Finance:
  ◆ Invoicing, Accounts Payable, General Ledger Systems, etc.
  ◆ Banking systems.
◆ Personnel:
  ◆ Personnel records system.
  ◆ Payroll / pensions systems.
◆ Innovation:
  ◆ Computer aided design systems (CAD).

- ◆ Operations:
  - ◆ Manufacturing: computer aided manufacturing (CAM).
  - ◆ Services: banking systems, insurance systems, etc.
  - ◆ Order processing / stock control.

The use of these systems is integral to the operation of many organisations – here are pen-pictures of the use of IT in the main business operations of two distinct types of business:

- ◆ Car assembly:

  Car assembly is a highly automated business, in terms of both the machinery on the production line and the information systems that are used to help organise that production. Central to the operation of the assembly plant is the production planning and control system which holds the schedule of which models and variants are to be produced. As the plan is developed the component suppliers are sent electronic (EDI) messages from the system informing them what components are expected to be required and when. Small components might be stocked at the assembly plant but larger components are required on a 'just in time' basis. As production of a particular car gets underway the suppliers can be sent 'call-off' orders for the components needed for that particular car. Components are delivered to 'track side' packed in the order they will be required for production – a process that Rover calls 'sequenced delivery'. Notice of the requirement for a sequenced delivery can be short – in the case of Nissan on Wearside it is less than one hour for some components. As well as the systems that control production, the car assembler will use IT / IS in:

  - ◆ Car design – much of the work that used to be done with models and in the wind-tunnel can now be done using powerful computer aided design (CAD) systems.
  - ◆ Production planning is a complex operation that must ensure there are enough cars, in the right place, for likely demand but avoid the possibility of overproduction with new cars stored for months or years awaiting a sale. There is much work, using appropriate IT systems, before the marketing projections become the production plan.
  - ◆ Car supply – the cars that are produced have to be shipped to dealers at home and abroad in response to orders and in anticipation of likely demand – a mixture of push and pull. The car supply requirement is coordinated using IT systems.
  - ◆ In addition to assembling and supplying cars the car maker also has to supply parts and refund dealers for warranty work – both functions require further IT systems.

- ◆ Banking:

  High street banks offer a series of personal and business account services all coordinated by IS and the use of IT. Central to the bank's operation is the data centre – typically containing large mainframes and duplicated in a separate location for security reasons. The systems at the data centre hold details of all the bank's customers and their accounts. The system is networked to the branches, the ATMs and for some customers there is Internet access or even mobile banking. Every transaction is recorded on the system – transfers in, cheques paid and transactions such as standing orders and direct debits which are automatically applied by the system. In addition to managing the individual accounts the system will calculate the overall balance sheet of the bank, and customers' money can then be lent out to other customers requiring loans and mortgages. The systems in the bank are linked electronically to other banks using networks such as SWIFT and CHAPS and money (or the electronic representation of money) can be transferred between banks and other financial institutions both within the country and across the world.

In addition to personal and small business accounts the banks provide an array of other services all backed up by an extensive IT provision. The large high street banks typically spend in excess of UK£100 million on IT a year, which gives an idea of the scale of their ICT provision and usage.

In addition to their industry-specific information systems the car assembler and the bank would need a number of more generic systems including payroll, personnel and accounts.

Exercises

1. Choose a couple of products, say computer games and a new breakfast cereal, and consider how they should be marketed. Does the marketing of the product rely on intermediaries or can the product be sold direct? How does the use of intermediaries affect the marketing process?

2. Take an organisation you know (for example your college or university). List the types of supplies it needs to purchase and from where these might be sourced. Assess how crucial the purchasing function is to the operation of the organisation.

3. Use the Internet to look up some details on the responsibilities of organisations in the personnel area – race and sex discrimination and health and safety could be good starting points.

4. The section on innovation suggests six types of innovation. List these six types and suggest a further example for each.

5. Take the system diagram given in the sub-section on production and apply it to specific industries – making computers and cornflakes or providing insurance and education. Substitute specifics for the input and output categories and assess the relative importance of each category to the selected industry.

6. IT provision in universities is somewhat different from most organisations. There is an administrative requirement, provision for academics and some specialist computers but the vast majority of users are students with their own special requirements and behaviour patterns. Check out how IT is

structured and supported in your university or college – draw a structure chart for the IT staff.

Further Reading

The topics discussed in this chapter are covered in more detail in:

Needle D. (2004) *Business in Context: An introduction to business and its environment*, 4th ed., Thomson, London.

Students are recommended to read the relevant sections.

Assignments

Readers can reinforce their understanding of the material presented in Part II by carrying out their own further research and relating it to the models presented in these chapters. Topics suggested for research and assignments are:

1. IBM used to be the world's largest computer company but it has been supplanted by companies such as Microsoft, Oracle and SAP. Investigate the changes that have taken place in IBM and relate them to the IS business environment model.

2. Microsoft is the predominant supplier of PC operating systems, office software and web browsers. Investigate how it established this position and how it sidelined competition in these areas. Assess its current competitive position and what threats it might have to contend with (freeware is one aspect that will need to be assessed). (This could be a group assignment with four people investigating operating systems, office software, web browsers and competitive threats, respectively.)

3. The Internet and the World Wide Web are being used internally and externally by many organisations across a wide range of their operational functions. For each operation-level function included in the IS business environment, find examples of the use of Internet applications and assess their advantages and disadvantages. (For group work, each member of a team could be assigned to separate operation-level functions.)

The results of these assignments could be an essay or take the form of a student presentation followed by a class discussion.

Part III
Business Use of Information Systems

This section looks at the business use of information systems. The application of IS and IT in organisations is both widespread and diverse and it would not be sensible or realistic to attempt to catalogue all its uses. The aim is therefore to give a number of examples that will help the reader acquire an overall impression of the scope, nature and importance of IS and IT. There is a bias in the examples towards large organisations; the reader is less likely to be familiar with these applications of IS than with the use of PC desk top packages.

We start with by examining the UHS case study from *Part I* and build a system diagram of applications used by UHS. The aim here is to show the diversity, complexity and interconnectivity of the IT and IS used by a large organisation.

Following on from the UHS study we look, in more detail, at two applications that are widely used: payroll and order processing. This shows that business systems consist of a number of sub-systems and brings out how the system designer needs to tailor the system design to meet the circumstances and requirements of each organisation.

Over the years the capability of information systems has been extended by the incorporation of new techniques. Three 'technologies' exampled in this section are:

◆   EDI which is used for business-to-business e-Commerce.
◆   Internet systems used for business-to-consumer e-Commerce.
◆   Artificial intelligence (expert) systems.

The prime purpose of most information systems is the processing of business transactions. This function accumulates vast amounts of data. We look at how this data is then used for the vital function of providing management information.

Finally we look at the application of, and interfaces between, desktop, end user and corporate information systems.

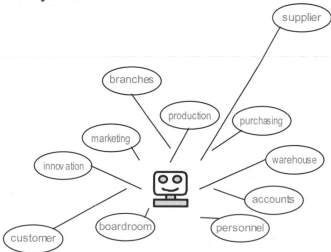

Chapter 7
The IS Infrastructure

Summary

At home most people have a single PC with a dial up Internet connection to an ISP, and that is about it. At work we may also have a PC on our desks or possibly some specialist computer controlled equipment such as an EPOS terminal. If we work for a medium or large organisation our desk top or shop floor equipment will be joined to a local and / or wide area network and have access to a complex web of IT equipment and business information systems.

The organisation will have information systems for its core business activities. For a shop these are EPOS systems and stock replenishment; the bank needs ATM machines and systems that keeps records of its customers' transactions and the university has to have records of all its students and their progress through their studies. The complexity of these systems tends to increase with the size of the organisations, and large organisation will have multi-million investments in their main business systems.

In addition to their main business systems, organisations will have numerous small systems – some of these will be used by individuals and others will be at the department or company level. Examples of these systems are payroll, personnel, purchasing and accounting systems.

The third level of the IS infrastructure is desk top productivity aids such as word processing, spreadsheets and e-Mail. These are functions that we may use at home but at work they may be more structured with form letters, standard filing, archive procedures and security and privacy provisions across the whole infrastructure.

This chapter seeks to emphasise the scope and complexity of this provision by analysing the Universal Home Stores case study that was presented in *Part I*.

7.1   Understanding the UHS Case Study

You should already have read the Universal Home Store (UHS) case study in **Part I** and we will now use that case study as an example of the IS infrastructure in a large organisation.

The case study is complex and possibly you found it hard going. Ideally, to fully appreciate the details of the UHS operations, we would get you to draw a system diagram of UHS. Alternately you could jointly develop such a diagram in a tutorial session with your tutor (which is what I do with my students). However, this is a book and it is the author who must provide the answers. Hence I have developed a number of diagrams that should help to emphasise and explain the information in the case study. Try to follow them through in some detail, on your own or in a tutorial. The aim is to get some appreciation of the nature of the IT / IS infrastructure used by a large organisation. It is very different and much more complex than the sort of computer infrastructure and computer usage you will experience in education (often even the people who work for large organisations don't fully appreciate the IT / IS infrastructure that supports their business – much of it is hidden from most of the people in the organisation).

7.2 The Overall Organisation

The first diagram we might draw is a sort of geographic diagram of the organisation – the information we need is all in the first interview with Barry, the Operations Manager. The diagram is shown in *figure 7.1* – the components of the diagram, including the IT provision, are:

◆ The Data Centre: The central provision of IT and IS. Two IBM mainframes, a number of UNIX boxes and the data warehouse machine. All the equipment is networked together and there are network connections to the head office, distribution centre, all stores, suppliers and the credit card companies.

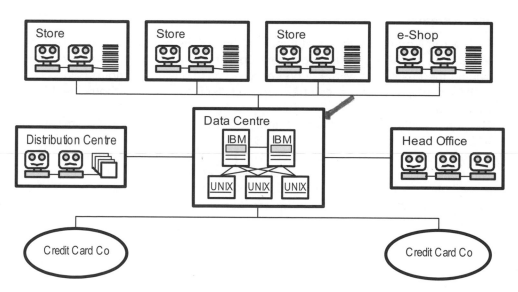

Figure 7.1 UHS Structure / IT Infrastructure Diagram

◆ Stores: The main system used at the stores is the electronic point of sales system (EPOS). This consists of the EPOS terminals, that all shoppers are familiar with, linked to an EPOS controller in the back office. The link to and from the data centre systems is via the EPOS controller. Each store also has a small manager's / administrative office with networked PCs.

◆ e-Shop: The heart of the e-Shop is the Internet server which hosts the e-Shop. This is then linked to systems at the data centre for catalogue data and for back office functions.

◆ Distribution centre: The main processing for the distribution centre takes place on the head office machines. The IT at the distribution centre is focused on the automation of the goods-in and goods-out processes with barcode recording of the movement of packages, computer controlled conveyer systems and the like. The design of distribution centres needs to be optimised for the types of goods been processed – apparel, particularly the clothes delivered on hangers and rails, is one of the more difficult product categories to handle and organise.

◆ Head Office: Unlike the stores and the distribution centre, this is essentially a normal office environment. All staff have a PC on their desk, use desktop applications and are linked by the network to servers and hence to the data centre.

◆ Outside links: In addition to UHS's internal infrastructure the UHS systems have links to the systems of trading partners. The main categories of links are to the credit card companies and to the suppliers.

The IT infrastructure exists to deliver the business functionality and it is that we will look at next.

7.3   Sales System

UHS is a retail outfit and the most important part of the operation is its 120 stores. The success of the stores is dependent upon having the right merchandise and providing the customers with a good service. These basics are not provided by IT but UHS could not run its complex and efficient operation without the IS / IT infrastructure.

The main system at the stores is the EPOS system. We are all familiar with EPOS systems: they consist of the EPOS terminals where the goods are checked out and the controller in the back office. The system is shown in *figure 7.2*.

The basic EPOS terminal is PC based but adapted for the specific application. The keyboard and the screen are both smaller than a standard screen – the input data is just codes and prices and screen output is also quite limited. Additional equipment includes:

◆ A small repeater screen for the customer.
◆ A magnetic stripe reader to read credit cards, debit cards and the UHS store core.
◆ A barcode reader.
◆ The cash drawer.

An important requirement of the EPOS terminal is security and resilience. In the Sheffield store (instanced in the case study) there are 32 terminals and it does not greatly matter if a couple are not operating. What is important is that some EPOS terminals are operating and thus the terminals can work in 'stand alone' mode if the back office controller / server system is down. To work in stand alone mode the terminal needs to store the price list. Also important is that data is not lost – the whole just-in-time replenishment system is dependent on accurate sales data. To guard against the loss of sales data the data is duplexed in the EPOS terminal.

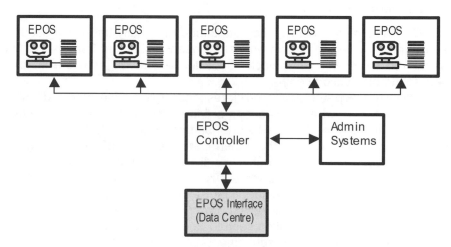

Figure 7.2 Store Based EPOS Systems

Note that all EPOS terminals are not the same – the requirements of the supermarket, with a high volume throughput, are different from the DIY store, the corner shop and a clothing retailer such as UHS. The typical UHS customer buys just a few items of relatively high value – these are mainly clothes, and items such as jackets and dresses need to be handled with greater respect than a tin of beans.

The EPOS terminals are linked to the controller / server in the back office. The server is an interface point between the head office systems and the EPOS terminal – the business functionality of the controller is limited to keeping transaction totals and a few enquiry functions for the store's administrative staff. The system is used when the cash in the tills is reconciled with the sales totals.

The interfaces with head office are:

◆ Product and price data downloaded from head office – this data is stored on the controller and passed on to the EPOS terminals.
◆ Sales data that is 'collected' from the EPOS terminals and subsequently passed on to the head office systems – every single item that has been sold is recorded and included in the transmission.
◆ Credit card and store card data that are 'collected' from the EPOS terminals and passed to head office in the same way as sales data.

The EPOS controller is duplexed. If one EPOS control is non-operational then hopefully the second machine is available – and if that fails then the EPOS terminals can work in stand alone mode.

The final part of the store system is the desk top systems in the manager's and administrative office. These run normal desk top systems, e-Mail and access the

UHS intranet. The manager and administrative staff also have access to the sales and takings summaries in the EPOS controller and to management information systems at head office.

7.4   Replenishment System

The EPOS sales data is sent to the data centre on a daily basis and used by the Replenishment System to decide what stock needs to be sent from the distribution centre to the store and what stock needs to be ordered from the supplier for delivery to the distribution centre.

UHS works on a just-in-time / quick-response basis. The stores do not hold stock 'out the back' – what they have to sell is on the shelves and on the racks. If at the start of the day the Sheffield store has three size 14 blouses of a particular style and colour and it sells all three then there are none left. Not having a stock room saves space and saves double handling goods but it does make efficient quick-response supply vital. The three size 14 blouses need to be replaced by next morning – failure to have the right stock available results in dissatisfied customers and, very probably, a lost customer. The distribution centre also keeps minimum stock – it is a distribution centre rather than a warehouse. The aim is to be able to supply the overnight requirements of the stores from the centre but then to replace these goods from the suppliers on a just-in-time basis.

The Replenishment System is at the heart of UHS's operations. It runs on the mainframe at the data centre and its database includes details of every product that UHS is selling. For each of these product, by size and colour, there also need to be figures for the stock at each store, at the distribution centre, stock that is on order and (where data is available) stock that is held by the suppliers. In addition to its stock database the replenishment process takes inputs from other systems:

◆   Contracts Systems: details of all contracts that are held with suppliers, see *7.5*.
◆   Mix System: details of the intended stock holding for each store by product (including size and colour) and season, see *7.5*.
◆   Sales System: details of every item sold at each store during the trading day, discussed in the previous subsection.

The Replenishment System is easily stated by example but complex to implement (and even more complex when tuned to achieve minimum stock holding combined with maximum availability). Taking the example of the size 14 blouses from above – the branch was Sheffield and we will call the style Carmen blue – the process is as follows:

◆   The EPOS data is read and the stock holding at Sheffield for size 14 Carmen blue blouses is reduced by one for each sale. The resultant stock holding is zero.
◆   The Mix System is checked and that shows that the stock required for this product at Sheffield is three.
◆   The stock at the distribution centre is checked and shows 21 – three are allocated for dispatch to Sheffield.

◆ The sales history calculated by the Replenishment System shows this product is selling well and 21 items, now reduced to 18, will not last long.
◆ The Contract System shows an outstanding contract for supply of this item and returns from the supplier shows that stock is available. The system formulates a call-off order, on the supplier, for a further 200 of the product.

This calculation is repeated thousands of times a night for every product sold at each of UHS's 120 stores. The outputs from the system are the delivery order to be sent to the Distribution Centre System and the call-off order to be sent to the supplier. For the distribution centre the delivery orders must be sorted for efficient picking and into lorry loads for delivery. For the suppliers, orders will be batched and sent off electronically, see **7.6**.

The system, together with its interfaces, is shown in **figure 7.3**.

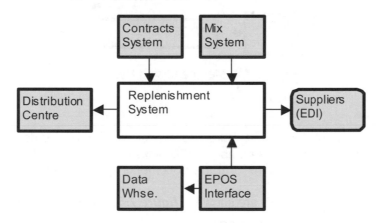

Figure 7.3 Central Replenishment Systems

The EPOS data is stored on the Data Warehouse System. We will look at that system in a bit more detail at **7.12**, and it is also shared with the suppliers using EDI transmissions, see **7.6**.

7.5 Merchandising

The Replenishment System works to the parameters set by the Mix and Contracts systems. Setting up these requirements is the function of the buying department.

The buying function requires judgement and flair and that is something computer systems do not provide. However the judgement of the buyers needs to be supported by information about UHS customers and their buying patterns, and here the system can help.

The buyers can access all sales data on the Data Warehouse. This includes all EPOS data, as described above, but also data collected about methods of payment and through the store card system. The buyers can access this data using queries formulated through the Buyer's Decision Support System (DSS).

Once the buyers have made a purchase decision and the details are agreed with the suppliers it is recorded on the Contracts System. As well as signing a contract with the supplier the merchandising department needs to decide which products will be stocked in which store, in what quantities and for how long (the season). These decisions are recorded on the Product Mix System.

The systems that support the merchandising functions are shown in *figure 7.4*.

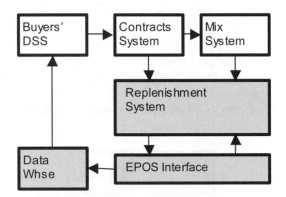

Figure 7.4 Merchandising Systems

7.6 EDI Systems

The Replenishment System is linked to the stock control / order processing systems of the suppliers by a number of EDI links – EDI is a standardised way of exchanging electronic versions of trade documents and is examined in detail in *Chapter 9*.

The EDI links used by UHS are shown in *figure 7.5* and outlined, briefly, below:

- ◆ Predictions – the UHS EPOS data is summarised and sent as EDI messages to the appropriate suppliers so they can work out how well their products are selling and hence anticipate demand.
- ◆ Availability – the supplier sends UHS its stock figures as an EDI message and these are recorded and taken into account in the replenishment calculation.
- ◆ Call-off order – the electronic replenishment order, from the UHS Replenishment System to the supplier, requesting more stock.
- ◆ Order confirmation – an electronic reply from the supplier that confirms that the order has been received and when delivery is to be expected.
- ◆ Delivery note – when the goods are about to be despatched an electronic delivery note is sent to say the goods are on their way.
- ◆ Invoice – a further EDI transmission from the supplier requesting payment from UHS.
- ◆ BACS payment – an electronic payment instruction to the Inter-bank Computer Bureau who in turn make an electronic payment to the supplier.

Accounts Payable and Supplier Payments are looked at in *7.7*.

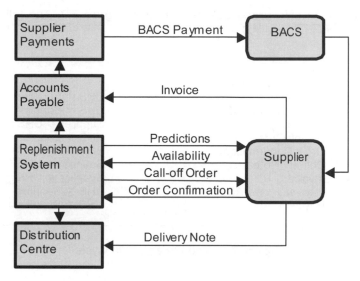

Figure 7.5 EDI Links with Suppliers

7.7 Accounts Payable

The final stage in the ordering process is to pay the supplier for the goods that have been delivered. The process starts with the goods-in function at the distribution centre. The first step is that the EDI delivery note is matched against the call-off order in the Replenishment System. The electronic delivery note is supplemented by barcodes on the cartons and these are scanned in and matched to the call-off order plus delivery note. Where the system works well, and it usually does, call-off orders that have completed the goods-in stage are passed to the Accounts Payable System.

The job of Accounts Payable is to match delivered orders to invoices. Where EDI is not used this can be a time consuming business as paper invoices, with differing formats, are matched against the appropriate order (or orders) from the set of all outstanding orders. The use of EDI eliminates this chore and most of the delays and queries that used to occur. The EDI invoices have a standard format and the order codes will have been accurately transferred from the order and delivery documentation. Once matched, the invoiced orders are passed to Supplier Payments.

The final stage in the ordering cycle is to pay the supplier. As with the other steps in the cycle this has now been automated and payment is made electronically through the Bankers Automated Clearing System (BACS). In each monthly run of Supplier Payments, UHS adds up the amount payable to each supplier and formats it as an electronic cheque. All these electronic cheques are then sent to BACS where the money can then be transferred from UHS's account to the account of the appropriate supplier (it is the same system as is used by most payrolls to pay employees direct into their bank accounts). In addition to the payment the supplier is sent a hard copy advice note detailing the payment and the invoices that it covers.

The Accounts Payable processes are shown in *figure 7.7*. The full order trade cycle is reiterated in *figure 7.6*.

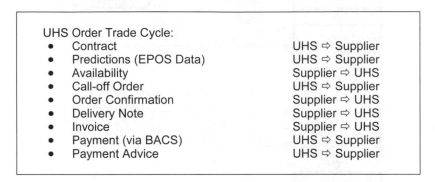

UHS Order Trade Cycle:
- Contract   UHS ⇨ Supplier
- Predictions (EPOS Data)   UHS ⇨ Supplier
- Availability   Supplier ⇨ UHS
- Call-off Order   UHS ⇨ Supplier
- Order Confirmation   Supplier ⇨ UHS
- Delivery Note   Supplier ⇨ UHS
- Invoice   Supplier ⇨ UHS
- Payment (via BACS)   UHS ⇨ Supplier
- Payment Advice   UHS ⇨ Supplier

Figure 7.6 The Order Trade Cycle

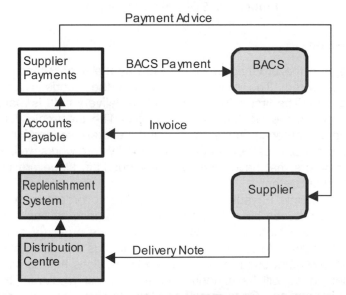

Figure 7.7 Accounts Payable

7.8 Accounting

Accounts of income and expenditure used to be kept in large books known as ledgers and the name has been retained although the books, for most organisations, have long been replaced by computer systems. The three main ledger systems are:

◆ General Ledger:
  The General Ledger (GL) is updated every time there is a transaction with a financial implication – every order, delivery, invoice, payment, transfer of

goods within UHS, sale and payroll transaction. To achieve these updates the GL has interfaces with all the main UHS systems. The system can be used to obtain details of the financial position at company level or for any of the cost centres within UHS.

◆ Fixed Assets Ledger:
The Fixed Assets Ledger records the value of all property and equipment owned by UHS. The ledger is largely free-standing with details of purchases being manually entered. At the end of the financial year the value of assets is recalculated (using standard depreciation rules where appropriate). All changes to fixed assets and their valuation are posted to the General Ledger.

◆ Sales Ledger:
The vast majority of sales take place through the EPOS system. This free-standing system deals with any other sales, for example, equipment or surplus stock. Any sales have also to be posted to the General Ledger and, if appropriate, the Fixed Assets Ledger also has to be updated.

The accounting systems are shown in *figure 7.8*. All three ledger systems are bought-in packages; there is not a lot of business advantage to be gained from writing one's own. Supplier Payments and Accounts Payable were described in the previous subsection.

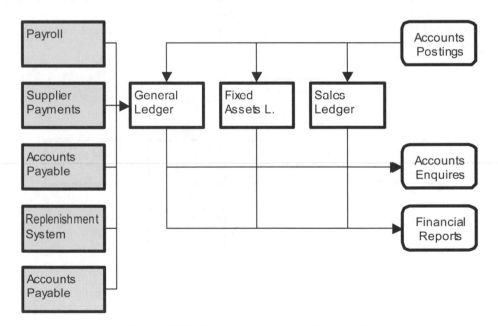

Figure 7.8 Accounts Systems (Ledgers)

7.9   Card Systems

The EPOS system records the sales but it also has to process the customers' plastic cards. These include credit cards, debit cards and the UHS store card (the store card is a loyalty scheme, not a payment card). The EPOS system has a card reader and keypad for cards that are authorised by pin numbers.

Credit cards and debit cards are read and then checked against the database at the appropriate credit card company for authorisation. This check is done automatically: the interchange is routed through the UHS network to the data centre and from there through an open network connection to the credit card company. The credit / debit card payment, once authorised, is stored in the EPOS system and transmitted to the data centre, with all the other sales data, at the end of the day. The credit card data is then routed to the Credit Payments System where the payments are recorded, posted to the General Ledger and transmitted to the credit card companies for payment. The Credit Payment System is also used in resolving any queries and in checking the payment is complete when it is received from the credit card company.

Store card transactions are checked, at the time of the transaction, with the Store Card System at the data centre – this enables the sales assistant to inform customers of the state of their store card account. The store card data is then stored in the EPOS system and included with all other EPOS data in the transmission at the end of the day. The store card data is then used to update the Store Card System and the data is included on the Data Warehouse with the details of the purchases made by the store card holder.

The system infrastructure involved in processing card transactions is shown in *figure 7.9*.

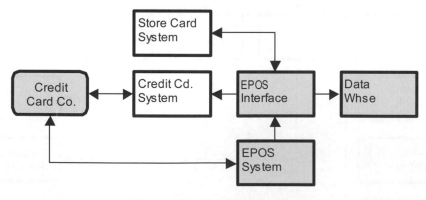

Figure 7.9 Card Processing

7.10   Distribution Centre

The main replenishment decisions and replenishment order processing are the responsibility of the head office and the data centre – the systems at the distribution centre work within these parameters.

The responsibility of the system at the distribution centre is to keep track of where stock is stored. To do this it has, in effect, a duplicate copy of the product database held at the data centre, although some of the details held for each product are not the same. The main processing at the warehouse is:

- The replenishment orders sent to the supplier are copied to the warehouse once the order confirmation has been received.
- When new stock arrives from the suppliers the barcodes are read and the new stock is allocated to a warehouse location. The barcode information is also forwarded to the data centre so that it can update its records.
- Despatch orders for goods to be sent to stores are received and processed into picking instructions for the relevant warehouse section.
- The system calculates lorry loadings and the picking data is also used by the automated conveyor system to route the cartons to the despatch bay and to check that the load is complete.
- The system also works out a lorry fleet utilisation plan, that is continuously updated, to ensure that the lorries are used effectively and efficiently.
- The distribution system includes stocktake and stock adjustment facilities. Adjustments to stock figures on the Distribution Centre System also have to be passed to the Replenishment System for parallel updating and for onward transmission to the financial accounting systems.

The distribution centre system is shown in *figure 7.10*.

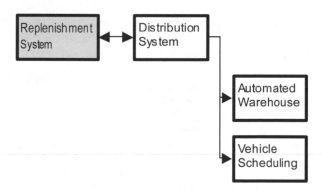

Figure 7.10 Distribution Centre

7.11 Payroll and Pensions

UHS employs some 14,000 people and the Payroll is used to calculate their salaries, tax, national insurance , etc., all the normal functions of a monthly payroll. The Payroll uses a bought-in package and is run on one of the UNIX boxes. The Payroll System is a shared responsibility of Personnel and the Accounts Department. The Payroll is also accessible at the stores, where the manager has a Staff Records System and can update the payroll staff file and record attendance for hourly paid staff.

The Payroll System also links to the Pension System where pension contributions are recorded and payment is made to members of UHS staff who have retired.

Personnel also has a Staff Records System (a recent acquisition that is to take over from the system of paper files where staff details are currently kept). The plan is to establish a link between the Payroll and Staff Record Systems to ensure that the staff details in both systems are kept in step. (Arguably, what is needed is an integrated personnel system that included payroll but UHS did not want to replace the payroll package they were using.)

The Payroll, Pensions and Personnel systems are shown in *figure 7.11*.

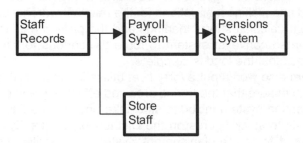

Figure 7.11 Personnel, Payroll and Pensions

7.12 Management Information

EPOS data is used for replenishment processing but is also used for management information (MI). To make sales data available, efficiently and on a consistent basis across the organisation, it is loaded onto the Data Warehouse System.

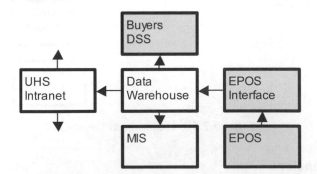

Figure 7.12 MIS and the Data Warehouse

A data warehouse is a large database usually held on a specialised machine, and that is the case at UHS. The system holds all EPOS data for a period of several years, a vast amount of data. The system is not designed for transaction processing but for management information – it can search through large amounts of data quickly and, if needed, use specialised software to identify patterns. The system interfaces with a Management Information System (MIS) package, available to every desk top computer user within the organisation, and with the Buyers DSS, which has already been discussed.

UHS also has an intranet for disseminating information within the organisation. The intranet carries the organisation's key performance indicators and these are regularly updated from the Data Warehouse System.

The data warehouse and its linkages are shown in *figure 7.12*.

7.13 e-Shop

The e-Shop is a new venture that has had to be grafted onto the existing IS infrastructure. There are essentially three parts of the system:

♦ The catalogue. This is derived from the Contracts and Mix Systems which have been modified to indicate which goods are for sale in the e-Shop. The data from the Mix System is supplemented by further descriptive and pictorial information held on a new Catalogue System. The catalogue is then used by the e-Shop to generate the product pages as they are required by the online e-Shop customer.

♦ e-Sales. Online sales are recorded on the e-Sales System and then transmitted to the Replenishment System at the end of the day (to the Replenishment System, e-Sales are very much like the EPOS input from any of the stores.

♦ e-Shop. This runs on a separate server and other systems are insulated from it by a firewall. The web pages are generated from the Catalogue System and the sales are recorded on the e-Sales System as indicated above.

The e-Shop does not store any product. Goods that are ordered are supplied overnight from the distribution centre (the e-Shop has priority if there are shortages in any line of merchandise) and can be packed and despatched next day. The e-Shop is located in the same premises as the distribution centre. The e-Shop Systems are summarised in *figure 7.13*.

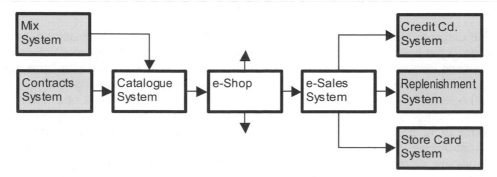

Figure 7.13 e-Shop

7.14 The UHS System Diagram

Having identified all the (major) UHS systems we can now put them all together as a single system diagram. This is shown in *figure 7.14*.

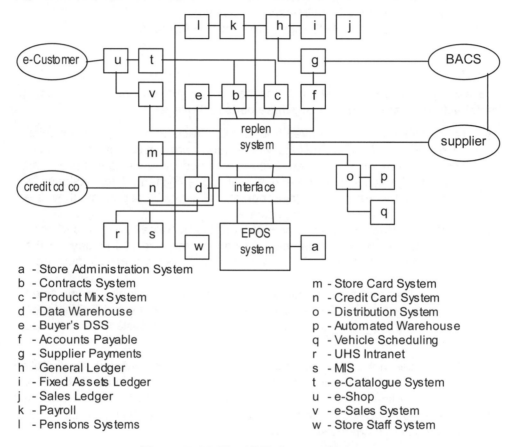

a - Store Administration System
b - Contracts System
c - Product Mix System
d - Data Warehouse
e - Buyer's DSS
f - Accounts Payable
g - Supplier Payments
h - General Ledger
i - Fixed Assets Ledger
j - Sales Ledger
k - Payroll
l - Pensions Systems

m - Store Card System
n - Credit Card System
o - Distribution System
p - Automated Warehouse
q - Vehicle Scheduling
r - UHS Intranet
s - MIS
t - e-Catalogue System
u - e-Shop
v - e-Sales System
w - Store Staff System

Figure 7.14 The UHS System Diagram

The diagram is complex – and that is the major point. The IS / IT infrastructure of large organisations is complex, it consists of many systems and most of them interface with one another and with groups of users. The IS / IT infrastructure has been built up over many years and is constantly developing and changing.

The IS / IT infrastructure of a large organisation, such as UHS, is of a different order of magnitude and complexity to any computer facilities we are likely to use at home or at college (although the IT network of most universities is a complex infrastructure – for students the emphasis is on the provision of IT and there is no significant IS requirement). UHS and other organisations do have large numbers of PCs, with the desk top facilities we are used to. The difference is that those PCs also plug into large, multi-user information systems backed up by equally large database facilities. These IS are complex, they must be resilient and they are also required to be secure.

Exercises

1. Make a list of the systems that use EPOS data and the uses that are made of that data.

2. What is meant by the initials MIS and DSS? Can you suggest what is the essential difference in the intention of the two types of system?

3. Draw a flow diagram of the steps involved in replenishing shop stock from the distribution centre and a second diagram of the steps in replenishing the distribution centre from the suppliers.

Note that the system diagrams in this chapter do not use any formal diagramming conventions and you may also use any appropriate representation in tackling these exercises. We will be looking at IS diagramming conventions in *Part V*.

Chapter 8
Example Systems

Summary

The main information systems used by medium and large organisations are complex. They may be developed 'in-house', bought in as a package system or the processing can be outsourced to a third party. To illustrate the nature of such systems this chapter looks through two widely used systems types:

◆ Payroll: All organisations have to pay their staff but many outsource the function to a specialist bureau. For the payroll system the organisation must update the standing data: details of the staff, rates of pay and any variances that apply that week or month. Once all the data is updated the payroll can be run, producing the pay and pay slip for the staff but also calculating pensions, tax and national insurance. To pay a large number of staff, reliably and on time, requires a well-designed and efficiently run system.

◆ Order processing: Many organisations have significant order processing functions. At the retail end of the supply chain the business has to order in stock to put into its shop. Further down the supply chain the organisations will be both taking in orders from their customers and sending out replenishment orders to their suppliers. The order processing system has to hold data on the products and normally on customers and suppliers. The system processes incoming orders to produce picking lists, delivery notes and invoices. On the replenishment side it issues replenishment orders and then processes goods-in and invoices.

Payroll and order processing are just two of the systems that an organisation might use – they are selected to illustrate the nature of information systems, their complexity and some of the issues that arise when such systems are designed.

8.1   Example Systems

In *Chapter 7* we had a look at the systems used by Universal Home Stores. The intention was to illustrate the complex web of systems that would be used by most medium or large organisations. This chapter follows on from that point to look at a couple of those business systems in more detail. The systems chosen are payroll and order processing.

The systems are illustrated by using a dataflow diagram (DFD) and, for order processing, an entity relationship diagram (ERD) – the two basic diagrams from structured analysis and design. Note that:

◆ The ellipses are externals – usually someone who interacts with the system, e.g. the personnel office staff.

◆ The boxes are processes – where the tasks are performed.

◆ The open-ended boxes are datastores – we can see them as files in the context of the use of DFDs in this chapter.

We will discuss these techniques in more detail in **Part 5**.

There are several intentions in describing these systems – these include:

◆ Demonstrating the complexity of the overall information system and the sub-systems that are used within that system.

◆ Showing the way that IT systems and human systems interact and work together.

◆ Illustrating the way that system analysts have to think about user requirements when designing a system.

Readers are asked to bear these points in mind when reading the case study and to use their imagination to fill out the picture that the author is attempting to create. It is noted that a large IS may well take 20 to 30 development staff two or three years to create.

8.2 Payroll

All organisations have to pay their staff and, except for some very small organisations, the norm is to use a computerised payroll system. The running of the payroll does not 'add value' – it is just a function that has to be done, and many organisations outsource the job to a specialist bureau. Using a bureau means that the bureau concerns itself with the intricacies of payroll calculations and changes in taxation and hence the company can concentrate on its own business processes without needing to employ payroll experts.

The main processes involved in running the payroll are shown in **figure 8.1**. The processes and their implications are described in more detail below.

❖ Payroll Standing Data

The first three processes are concerned with maintaining the data on the people to be paid and the rates they are to be paid. This information has to be supplied by the personnel department. It is updated during the period (week or month) before the payroll is run. It is useful if the personnel department has terminal access to the system and then last minute changes can be made, should this prove to be necessary. For example, if a new member of staff joins part way through the month it is necessary for him or her to be entered onto the system in time for the payroll so that he or she is paid for the work that he / she has done.

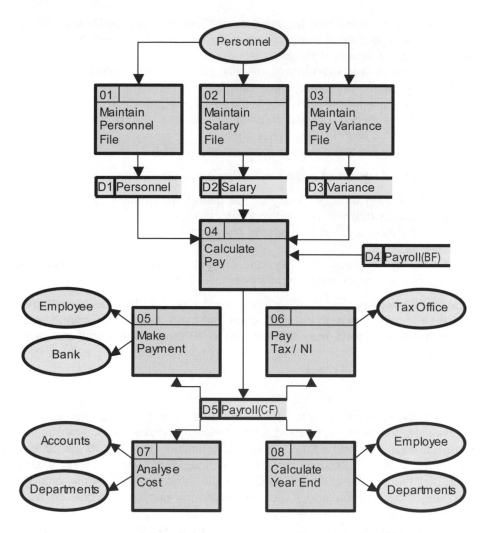

Figure 8.1 Dataflow Diagram of Payroll System

The three main standing data functions are:

◆ Maintain Personnel File (Process 01):
The payroll needs a data file of all the people who are to be paid, we will call it Personnel (D1). For each person the file has to contain:
  ◆ The payroll number, NI (national insurance) number, name, office location and address.
  ◆ The salary grade code (see salary file) and tax code.
  ◆ Details of any other deductions, e.g. pension scheme, charitable donations, and court orders.
The personnel data can be added (for a new employee), updated (where the details of an existing employee changes) or logically deleted (when a person leaves – the personnel record will be marked as deleted but

retained on file to calculate the last period's pay, the P45 and deal with any queries that subsequently arise). The data must be as accurate and up-to-date as possible – the system can help with this by including comprehensive validation to make sure that no invalid data is entered into the system (the system can not stop incorrect data but it can prevent invalid data being accepted).

◆ Maintain Salary File (Process 02):
Some organisations pay each employee a individually agreed salary and some allocate each member of staff to a grade and then pay them in accordance with the salary scale for that grade (see also *Part II*). For the former requirement, the individual's salary is included with the other data on the personnel file and there is no need for a salary file. In the latter case there is a grade code on the personnel file and that corresponds to an entry on the salary file. Where there are large numbers of staff it is much easier to update salary scales than the wage rates for each of hundreds of members of staff. The salary file is shown as datastore D2.

The salary file contains the grade code and the rate of pay for that grade code. For some jobs there is a pay scale for the grade and where that applies the pay scale has to be stored. Accessing the pay scale needs to be thought about – if the personnel file contains the grade and point on the scale then it will have to be updated each year; if it contains the grade plus the date and point at which the person joined the pay scale then the system can calculate which point is applicable when the payroll is run.

The salary scale file needs to be updated to contain the latest salary scale when a new rate of pay is agreed. It needs also to contain previous salary scales so that back pay and queries can be dealt with. The salary scales for a grade need to be set up with a start date and the system calculates which is scale applicable for any particular run.

◆ Maintain Variance Data (Process 03):
The final element of standing data is the variance data – datastore D3. Variances are one-off changes to be applied to the current payroll run (and as such, it could be argued, are not properly classified as standing data).

Variances are used for overtime, sick leave, bonuses, etc. This data is input during the current period and then applied in that end of period payroll run – the variances applicable to the next period will be different. Some organisations where, for instance, there is a lot of overtime or salespersons are paid commission will have a lot of variances. Other organisations, e.g. universities would have not very many transactions on the variance file.

❖ **Payroll Calculation**

At a given time, as near to the end of the period as possible (but leaving some time for recovery if anything goes wrong) the payroll calculation run is started. The payroll staff have been busy updating personnel details, variances and, if necessary, the salary scales. That is in many ways the end of their task. Once the payroll commences there is no more intervention required – the system takes over.

The payroll calculation is Process 04 on the diagram. It can be seen as having two parts:

♦ Calculate gross pay: To calculate an employee's gross pay we need to get that person's details from the personnel file (D1); look up the pay scale that corresponds to their grade code on the salary file (D2) and find any variances that apply to the individual on the pay variance file (D3). The gross pay is then the required proportion of the salary (one week's or one month's) plus or minus any variances. Simple in principle but more complex when all the exceptions and variations are taken into account.

♦ Calculate net pay: Following on from the gross pay calculation, taxes, NI, etc. are deducted to calculate the net pay – the money the employee is actually going to get. Taxes have to be calculated for the financial year to date and then the tax payable this month is the total tax due minus the tax already paid (a bit complex but it works). To achieve this we have to read in last month's payroll details (datastore D4 on the diagram) and find the brought forward (BF) payroll details for the person we are looking at.

After the pay calculation we format a new payroll record and write it to a carry forward (CF) payroll file (datastore D5 on the diagram). The carry forward payroll details are used for payment and reporting in the next stage of the processing and are also the input to the net pay calculation in the payroll run for the next period.

To achieve this matching of one person's details from several different files we must pay attention to the file structures. If, for example, we have the personnel (D1), variance (D3) and payroll (D4/5) files in the same order, presumably employee number order, then the details for the next employee will normally be the next record on each of these files. The pay calculation is 'controlled' by the personnel file – we start with the first person on that file and then just process each person until we reach the end of that file.

❖ **Payment and Reporting**

Having calculated the payroll we now must pay the staff. Payment could be made by cash, cheque or electronically direct into the employee's bank account, with the last of the three now being the normal option. To make the payment we must read the payroll CF file (D5) and format an electronic cheque. The details of each employee's bank are on the personnel file and, in our example, have been replicated on the payroll file. The electronic cheques are made out for each employee and sent to BACS, the inter-bank computer bureau, where the money is transferred to the appropriate bank account for each employee.

As well as being paid each person has to get a pay slip detailing the gross pay, deductions and net pay for the period. This detail can again be taken from the payroll CF file (D5). Some care is needed in designing the system for such a print run – the issues include:

♦ Confidentiality: the pay slip is confidential and needs to be in an envelope. For a large payroll the process for stuffing the envelopes will need to be mechanised. Alternatives are special stationery that will fold up into an envelope or chemically treated, three-part paper where the confidential details only appear on the second of the three sheets.

◆ Distribution: the pay slips have to be dispatched to the various offices within the organisation and distributed to the staff. If they are printed in pay number order they will have to be hand sorted which takes time. It is much easier to sort the payroll file by office location and then print the payslips pre-sorted by location.

◆ Print crashes: printers are not the most reliable pieces of kit and they can be even more problematic when using continuous pre-printed or multipart stationery. For a large payroll it is advisable to have a re-start mechanism programmed in so the print run can be restarted from the last good payslip produced (as opposed to having to restart the print run from the beginning). Where pre-printed stationery is used there will also have to be test prints to ensure that the print is correctly lined up in the right place on the form.

The making of payment and the printing of the pay slips are shown as Process 05. Further tasks that need to be performed using the brought forward payroll file include:

◆ Paying tax and NI (Process 06): the organisation is responsible for the deduction of tax and national insurance from the pay of its permanent employees. These deductions then have to be paid and accounted for to the Inland Revenue (from large organisations the Inland Revenue takes electronic payments and an electronic exchange of information).

◆ Cost analysis (Process 07): the organisation will require management and financial information from the payroll. The information required will depend on the organisation – an obvious requirement is the staff costing per division or department so that this can be fed into the analysis of that department's financial performance. Further reports will be required, perhaps particularly at the end of the year or when there is a wages negotiation taking place. Often it is useful to sort the data file for reports – if the requirement is for departmental totals then we can sort the file into department code order and analyse the pay for each department in turn.

◆ Calculate Year End (Process 08): at the end of the financial year every employee (UK employees) has to get a P60 specifying pay and tax totals for the year. Also the system will perform some sort of archive of this year's final payroll file before the system starts again with zero year-to-date pay figures for the new financial year. There are also likely to be further year end management information reporting requirements (both for the financial year and possibly for the company's own end of year).

The system described here is just an outline of what a payroll system needs to do. Each organisation that runs a payroll will have a system configured for its own needs. The general principles of the system will be similar to that described above.

The payroll is unusual, for a business IS, in the way it has to run. The focus of the system is on a single run at the end of the week or month. Prior to the run the standing data is updated by the personnel / payroll department but the actual payroll run and subsequent prints are just a big batch job requiring no user intervention. The data structures have to facilitate both online access (to update the standing data) and efficient batch running – not an easy trick to pull off. This is further discussed in *Part IV*.

8.3   Order Processing

Wherever goods are traded the organisation involved needs an order processing and stock control system. Once the order arrives at the supplier it has to process that order and then, in turn, replenish its stock by making more product or ordering in fresh supplies.

Order processing systems are used by retailers, wholesalers, manufacturers and by other organisations for secondary supplies. The order processing system may be integrated into the whole IS infrastructure of the organisation (as is the case with our Universal Home Stores case study) or it may be a more modest, freestanding, system. For medium and large organisations it will be computerised – for a small shop it may be entirely manual, almost intuitive, but the principles are the same.

The order processing system be split down into three major subsystems, see *figure 8.2*.

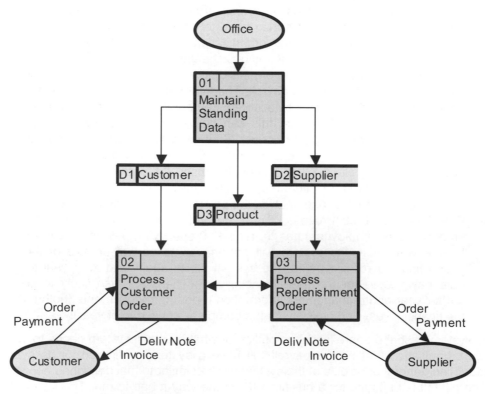

Figure 8.2 Dataflow Diagram of Order Processing System (Level 1)

The three major subsystems are:

◆ Process customer order.
◆ Process replenishment order.
◆ Maintain standing data.

The standing data is applicable to both the customer order and the replenishment order sub-systems and that is where we will start.

❖ **Order Processing Standing Data**

To use an order processing IS we must have a file of product / stock data. In addition to that, to process customer orders, we may well need a customer file and for replenishment orders we will require a computerised list of suppliers. There is a second level data flow diagram for this sub-system, shown in *figure 8.3*.

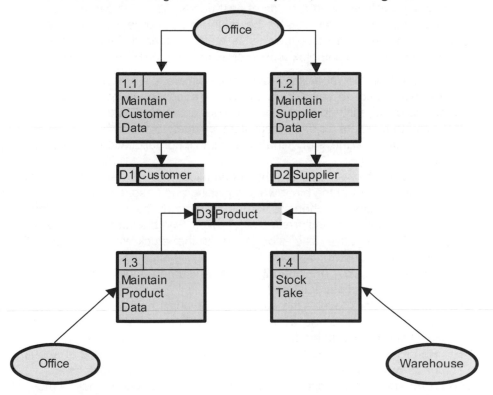

Figure 8.3 Order Processing – Standing Data Sub-systems

For each product that is made, bought or sold we need product / stock data. On a computer system we require a unique code for every record and for the product that will be some sort of product code. For grocery and general merchandise there are the EAN / UPC codes (also used as a barcode) and that would be a good starting point. For other products the firm may have to invent its own product codes.

In addition to the product code there will be:

◆   Product description and possibly other product data.
◆   Price information.
◆   Stock totals.
◆   Warehouse information.

For a small order processing system the information may be fairly minimal but for more complex systems there may be several hundred data items for each product. Examples of some of the complexity include:

◆   The basic price data is the purchase price and the selling price. Prices may however vary for the quantity supplied and for specific customers or classes of customers (the variations may be special prices or percentage discounts). Additionally prices will change over time and the invoicing and accounting systems need records of past prices. All of this can add up to a complex structure which has to be maintained – organisations need to balance the enthusiasm of their sales staff for special deals against the effort of keeping too complex a price structure in good working order.

◆   Stock totals, on the face of it, seem quite simple – we have 200 cans of beans, we expect to sell 400 in the next period so we had better order some more. In reality it is (or can be) more complex. Stock totals that we may wish to maintain for each stock item include:
    •   Free stock – the stock that is available for allocation to any new orders.
    •   Allocated stock – stock that has been allocated to orders but is still on the shelves, or in the bin, awaiting picking and despatch.
    •   Backorder stock – when stock runs out we may 'backorder', i.e. orders that are saved up until fresh stock arrives. The backorder stock total is in effect negative free stock – it is the stock we need to fulfil outstanding orders.
    •   On-order stock – the quantity of replenishment stock that has been ordered but not yet delivered.
    •   Re-order stock level – the stock level at which new stock must be re-ordered (if it takes one week for fresh stock to arrive then the re-order level should / could be the maximum normal weekly demand).
    •   Re-order stock quantity – the minimum quantity of stock that should be re-ordered when the free stock falls to the re-order stock level.
    The art (or science) of stock management is to have enough stock to meet all the orders that come in without having large quantities that just sit in the warehouse, tie up space and capital and possibly, eventually, get written off. Using the above stock quantities we can calculate replenishment needs: see for example *figure 8.4* (not the most sophisticated of stock calculations but it gives the basic idea).

The product file is shown on *figure 8.3* as datastore D3.

Where orders are taken from trade customers and payment is on invoice or statement we need a customer file. Each customer is allocated a customer number and there will also be details such as name, address, credit limit and contact details held for each customer. Having a customer file reduces the amount of data that has to be handled each time an order is placed – typing in the customer number accesses all the other customer detail. Arguably more significant than that, is that it allows a check to be kept on customer credit – customers may only be accepted onto the books after their credit has been checked and they will only be supplied with goods if they are reasonably reliable with their payments.

> If   re-order-stock-level > free-stock – backorder-stock + on-order-stock
> then   re-order-Quantity = re-order-stock-quantity + re-order-stock-level –
>   (free-stock – backorder-stock + on-order-stock)
> else   No action.

Figure 8.4 Order Processing – Replenishment Calculation

For a large system, customer details will get more complex. Amongst the additional data that might be held is:

◆ Delivery information – some customers will have a number of sites and will wish to specify the address where the goods are to be delivered. Each site can be a separate delivery point with its own delivery point code and address.

◆ Billing information – some customers will want goods delivered to one address but the invoice sent to the head office – or possibly one of several different offices where the various accounts are administered. Each office can be a separate invoice point with its own invoice point code and address.

In addition to customer files held for business-to-business systems, customer details may also be held for retail customers, particularly by online or catalogue operators. Where the goods are paid for prior to despatch there is no need to check on the customer's credit status but the details may still be used for despatch and for promotional purposes. The customer file is shown as datastore D1.

The third major category of standing data is supplier data. If the order processing system includes replenishment then the system needs to know which is the supplier for each product, the contact details for that supplier and possibly further details as well. The supplier file is shown as datastore D2.

Each of these three categories of standing data has to be maintained. New products, customers and suppliers have to be put up, existing details have to be updated and redundant records are marked as out of use (we can not normally delete the details as they are required for orders still in the system and then for accountancy and audit purposes).

A final area of maintenance is the stock take. If everyone uses the computer system properly then the stock figures should remain accurate (if you have an order processing / stock control system and then bypass it for some transactions you end up in a real mess). However, over time, discrepancies can develop between theoretical stock (the count on the system) and actual stock (the stock in the bin or on the shelves) and these discrepancies need rectifying. To make sure that the stock totals are accurate it is normal to do a stock take – one a year, once a quarter or some sort of continuous system (because the business can not afford to stop operating while the stock take is done). Stock take requires that the actual stock is manually counted and then the stock take count is reconciled with the theoretical stock totals held on the system. Any discrepancies have to be investigated, accounted for and the theoretical stock totals updated to the actual stock totals.

❖ **Process Customer Order**

Process customer order breaks down into five major steps (some of which may not be used in a direct selling retail system), see *figure 8.5*. The steps are:

◆ Enter and allocate order.
◆ Print picking list.
◆ Confirm pick and despatch.
◆ Invoicing.
◆ Receive payment.

The first step is to enter and allocate orders (process 2.1). If the orders come in on paper then we will need order entry clerks to type the orders into a form on the screen – a simple enough task but it takes time and adds to costs. Also we need procedures to follow if there are any errors on the order form or the goods are not available in stock. Alternative ways of receiving orders are:

◆ Telephone orders – the customer rings in and the order is typed in while the customer is on the phone. With the customer on the phone we can sort out any misunderstandings and any problems with stock availability can be discussed – possibly the customer will accept an alternative product.
◆ e-Orders – orders from an e-Shop or the customer's replenishment system, see e-Order Processing below.

As the order is entered into the system it is allocated a unique, computer generated, order code (it may be that the customer also has an order number but that could duplicate with codes from other customers). Also as the order is entered into the system it is validated – it must be in the correct format and it must cross-check with the standing data on the system. These cross-checks (secondary validation) include:

◆ Customer – the system reads the customer data and checks that the customer code is valid, that it exists on the system and it is a customer that we still wish to do business with.
◆ Product – for each product (order line) on the order we must read the product data and check that it is a valid product code and one we are still selling. If the customer is on the phone we can read back the product name, which gives a further check against any mistakes.

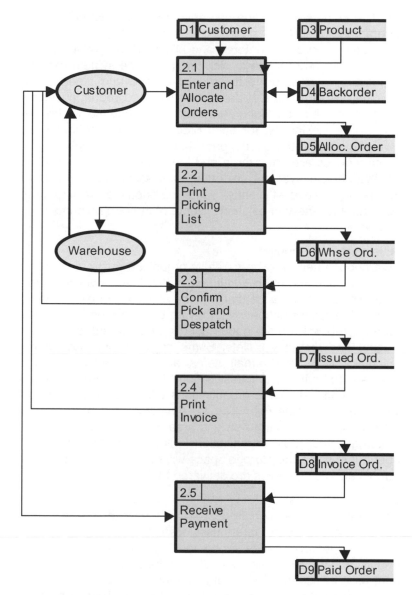

Figure 8.5: Order Processing – Process Customer Order

Having read the product data for each product we can proceed to allocate stock. If there is sufficient stock available we subtract the order quantity from the free stock total and add the quantity to the allocated stock total. If there is not sufficient stock we can backorder the product – this means holding the order until there is stock available (see datastore D4) and adding the order quantity to the backorder total. A complication is if an order has some order lines that can be fulfilled and some which have to be backordered – do we backorder the whole order or split the order with some of it being backordered and some been fulfilled in the normal timeframe? (The same sort of issue can arise if we have some stock but not the full order line amount.)

Some time after the order is entered and allocated the picking process begins (Process 2.2). For the warehouse to pick the goods the system needs to add the warehouse location information to the order line data and produce a picking list (the basic picking list is a piece of paper that lists the product code, quantity and warehouse location – it is the document that the warehouse worker uses). At its simplest, there is a picking list for each order and the warehouse staff wander round the warehouse, find the goods, pack them in a box and label it for despatch. That said, warehouses are often large and the products can be of disparate size and weight. Warehouse systems are often complex in order to cope with these parameters and to achieve efficiency. Some warehouses are largely automated. Warehouses adopt a variety of solutions. Some of the requirements and variations are explored below:

- ◆ Organising the warehouse:
  The warehouse needs to be carefully organised to promote efficiency, to minimise the time and effort that it takes to add new stock into the shelves, racks or bins and to balance that with the efficiency of picking the products from their location for despatch. It may be that the products are heavy and / or bulky – this will require goods handling equipment (some form of fork lift trucks) and probably pallets. Some organisations have a mixture of large, bulky items and small items and may need to segment the warehouse so that each classification of goods can be appropriately racked and handled. Some organisations take in bulk supplies and break packs down into small quantities for despatch: this may require a bulk storage area and a separate picking area which is kept supplied from the bulk storage area. Most organisations will have a fixed location for each product but in some the storage space will be allocated dynamically by the system when fresh supplies are delivered to the warehouse.

- ◆ Printing the picking list:
  The picking list is traditionally just what it says it is – a simple list of products, quantities and warehouse locations – the information that the warehouse operative needs to do the job. For some warehouses the picking list is printed as a series of sticky labels that can be attached to the product as it is picked – the label could include a barcode for automated sorting of the product in goods-out. In some cases the picking requirement will be displayed on a small screen on the fork lift truck, in a picking bay or on a hand held device. The 'full monty' is an automated picking system with no need for a picker or a picking list but obviously the robot picking equipment needs the same sort of picking data.

- ◆ Consolidating the pick:
  Picking each order individually is not necessarily the most efficient way to proceed – particularly if the warehouse is large and it takes several minutes to move from one location to the next. This problem can be eased by sorting the pick lists so that staff can move round the warehouse in the most efficient sequence. It may be more efficient to split the orders by

warehouse area and to consolidate a number of picking lists (e.g. the picker walks round once with a list of 100 products for 20 orders as opposed to 20 times with individual orders). The downside is then sorting the product out into the individual orders (but automation may take care of that).

◆   Despatch:
Once the goods are picked they have to be packed and despatched. At its simplest the warehouse worker takes round a cardboard box and packs the goods as they are picked – possibly the system can calculate the size of box that is needed for the order and print labels for the box at the same time as the picking list is produced. Some warehouses have standard size containers for picking and these are then placed onto an moving belt system that can sort the boxes for the appropriate goods-out bay – some shops use this sort of system in their regional depots. Other warehouses may need to do the packing after the picking – this can range from wrapping up a couple of books to shrink wrapping pallets of bulk groceries or machine parts.

Picking and despatch are ideally one step. On occasions there will be a problem with the pick: the stock that the system thought was available can't be found or is damaged, and the system needs to be updated to show what has actually been despatched rather than what the system thought should be despatched. Thus it is arguably necessary to have an additional step that confirms that the pick is completed and the actual quantities sent. The procedures to be adopted need to be as quick as possible – except where there are delays or errors to record it is a waste of time. The process of confirming the pick (Process 2.3) could just consist of typing in the picking list identity number with additional procedures if exceptions have occurred. Where the picking details are displayed on a device that the picker takes with him or her then confirmation / exceptions can be dealt with as the picking takes place.

As well as picking documentation we will need a despatch note – a form sent out with the goods to tell the customer what is in the consignment. This could be printed with the picking list (the one document could serve both purposes). It would seem to be better to print it out after the pick has been confirmed and any amendments have been made. The problem with printing it out at the end of the process is that the document then has to be retrieved and married up with the consignment which could be a tad messy – more decisions for the system designers.

Once the goods have been sent we can then invoice the customer (process 2.4). Invoicing practice tends to be dependent on the traditions of the business sector. The invoice may be sent with the goods, despatched by post or be sent at the end of the month (for all orders from that customer in the month). Some trade sectors send an invoice for each order and then a statement at the end of each month – the invoice is ignored and payment is made of the statement. Whichever procedure is adopted the system has to have a process for printing the invoices. It is a fairly simple batch process but it also needs to include procedures for reminder invoices that are sent to late payers.

The final step on the customer orders side is to process payments (Process 2.5). As payments arrive we have to identify which invoices the payment is for (not as easy as it sounds if the customer is paying for part of this and disputing that – or simply misquotes the invoice / statement reference) and mark those invoices as paid. Once the invoice is paid, that is the end of the story but we keep the data available for management information and accounting: see below. If payment is not received within reasonable time we have to send a reminder invoice or, when the situation gets serious, stop further orders for that customer.

This outline of processing customer orders covers the basic processing and some of the possible complications. To keep the complexity in bounds I have omitted mention of e-Commerce, self-invoicing, etc. – some of these re-engineering developments are outlined in the e-Order Processing subsection below.

❖ **Process Replenishment Order**

As already said, processing replenishment orders is very much the mirror image of processing customer orders. The customer orders outlined above, very probably, came from the buyer's replenishment system. Equally the organisation that processes customer orders can have its own replenishment system for buying in new stock to replace the goods that have been sent out to the customers: see for example the supply chain models at *figures 6.2* and *6.3* in *Part II*. The data flow diagram for the replenishment subsystem is shown as *figure 8.6*. The steps are:

- ◆ Calculate replenishment requirements.
- ◆ Print replenishment order.
- ◆ Receive goods.
- ◆ Match invoice.
- ◆ Make payment.

The steps in a little more detail (but less detail than for order processing) are as follows.

The first step is to decide what to buy (Process 3.1). This may be done in a periodic run, say once a week, where all stock totals on the product file are reviewed and the replenishment decisions are made. Where stock totals are to be kept low and replenishment is fast the replenishment calculation may be made daily or even as part of the customer order processing as stock is allocated to orders. The frequency of the replenishment decision is a matter of balancing the stock held against the size and frequency of the replenishment order and any discounts that may be available for volume. An example replenishment calculation is shown as *figure 8.4*.

Once we have decided what we need we can send out the replenishment orders (Process 3.2). The product data contains the supplier code so we can access the relevant supplier data – we may well sort the replenishment requirements into supplier code order so we can include all the requirements from each supplier on a single order. Replenishment orders can then be printed and sent out or they may be faxed or sent electronically: see the subsection on e-Order Processing.

Once the replenishment order is sent we have to wait for the goods and their delivery documentation to arrive. When the goods do arrive they have to be put into the rack, bin or on the shelf. The physical process of goods-in is accompanied by the administrative process of matching the delivery note to the replenishment order held on the system (Process 3.3) – we need to know what replenishment orders have been received so that we can update free stock, allocate any outstanding back orders, calculate future stock requirements and authorise payment when invoices come in. The process of matching the delivery note will also indicate where the goods are to be stored – particularly if the system works on dynamic allocation of storage space. If the goods are required for immediate despatch, then the merchandise is sent straight from goods-in to goods-out – a procedure known as 'cross docking'.

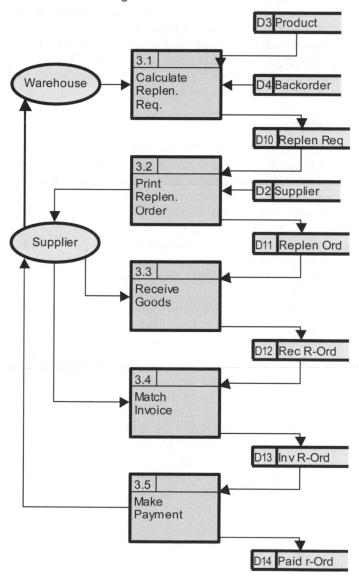

Figure 8.6 Order Processing – Process Replenishment Order

Some time after the goods arrive there will be an invoice. As with goods-in this is a matching process (Process 3.4). This time we are checking the invoice against the replenishment order and the delivery note. If the goods haven't arrived or were not satisfactory we will not pay. If the goods have arrived we need to mark the order to be paid. Where the supplier issues both invoices and statements we probably ignore one of these documents (all a bit of a waste of time but that's business) – arguably we don't need an invoice at all but we will come to self invoicing later on.

The final step is payment. It could be that we pay the invoices as they are processed but more than likely we save them up for a weekly or monthly payment run (and then possibly delay them a bit longer so that the money stays in our bank account rather than being with the supplier) – not friendly, particularly for small businesses, but that is the way much of business operates.

Two of the processes in this side of the system are matching processes (plus the invoice matching on the customer order side). These are not the most computer friendly procedures but they are jobs that have to be done. EDI can help a lot with these: see e-Order Processing below.

❖ **e-Order-Processing**

Most orders printed out from one computer system are typed into another and the same is true of most of the other documents involved in trade exchanges. Typing in the details from these documents takes time, causes delay, introduces errors and all that costs money. Using paper to transmit data from one computer system to another does not make a lot of sense. It should be more accurate and efficient to communicate electronically – an e-Commerce transaction.

As well as orders generated by a customer's order processing system there are orders for secondary supplies, orders from small businesses and orders from retail customers. Many of these orders can now come in from the web and again this is part or e-Commerce.

The basic e-Commerce transactions between the customer's replenishment system, the e-Shop and the supplier's order processing system are shown in *figure 8.7*. Some of the advantages of e-Order processing are:

♦ The e-Shop gives the organisation a retail outlet with much reduced staff and premises cost. Orders from the e-Shop go straight to the order processing system with no need for data entry.
♦ Electronic orders from the customer's replenishment system can be processed as quickly as the trading partners want them to be. There are no postal delays, no data entry costs and no transcription errors.
♦ Electronic delivery notes can be used and they automate the process of matching the delivery to the replenishment order. That said, they don't prove that the physical delivery has taken place – they can be used in conjunction with a barcode labelling system on the delivery cartons.
♦ Electronic invoices neatly automate the process of matching to the order and the delivery note – the only disadvantage is you can no longer argue that the invoice must have been lost in the post.

◆ Electronic payments cut out the chore of writing or printing the cheques. They are the norm for payroll and they are increasingly used for trade transactions.

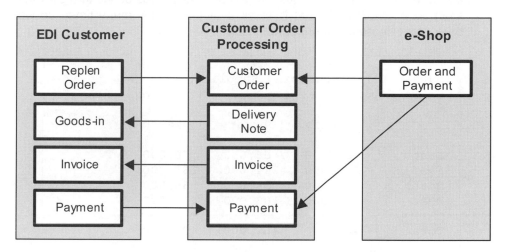

Figure 8.7 e-Order Processing – Electronic Exchanges

A further change that is being introduced in order processing, often in conjunction with electronic data interchange, is self invoicing. The procedure is that the customer pays for what is delivered and the invoice step is abandoned. Ford UK successfully introduced this change for transactions with its component suppliers and reduced the staff involved in supplier payments by over 90%.

The technology for inter-system e-Commerce is EDI – this is further discussed in *Chapter 9*. The second major area of e-Commerce, the business-to-business and business-to-consumer e-Shop, is the topic of *Chapter 10*.

❖ **Order Processing Management Information**

A computerised order processing system means that we have a full detailed history of all the products we have bought and sold back to when the system started (or it last crashed and we had not done the proper backups – not something that happens in a well organised IS department!). Having all this data means that we can have virtually any management information we want (although it may take a little time to programme the request). Some examples of the management information we may ask for are:

◆ Sales reports – what has been sold when and to whom. Numerous combinations can be derived: one report could be monthly sales values by month and region for the year to date. A simplified version of such a report can be seen in *figure 8.8*. The report shows a problem with March sales in the eastern region, something the management would want to follow up.

◆ Invoicing reports – what invoices are outstanding and for how long; is the total customer debt increasing or decreasing; are there any bad debtors that need following up?

◆ Stock reports – what is the stock turn (how many times do we turn over the stock in a year?) and what is stock availability (how many times do we back order because we are out of stock?).

```
Dave's Data Processing Supplies
Sales Report by Region              March 2003

             January    February      March

South        67,000      68,000      70,000
East        246,000     244,000     168,000
North        56,000      54,000      58,000
West         96,000     103,000     104,000


Total       465,000     469,000     400,000
```

Figure 8.8 e-Order Processing – Sales Report by Region

These are just a few examples of the sort of management information we can ask for. The accountants will also be looking for financial information and will use the system to drive the General Ledger and other finance systems. Management information is further discussed in *Chapter 12*.

❖ **Order Processing Data Structure**

The data requirements for a system can be shown on an entity-relationship (ER) diagram – this representation helps the system analyst design the database. The data requirements for a simple order processing system are shown in *figure 8.9*. These data requirements can be summarised as follows:

◆ Each Customer will place zero, one or more Orders.
◆ Each Order will have one or more Order-Line (there is an order line for each product ordered).
◆ Each Supplier will receive zero, one or more Replenishment-Order.
◆ Each Replenishment-Order will have one or more R-Order-Line (one for each product ordered).
◆ Each Supplier will supply one or more Products.
◆ Each Product Category will have zero, one or more Products.
◆ Each Product will have zero, one or more Order-Lines (on different Orders).
◆ Each Product will have one or more Prices (keyed on start date).
◆ Each Product will have zero, one or more R-Order-Lines (on different Replenishment-Orders).

If the data structure is implemented on a database system the connections on the ER diagram can be used in order processing and in producing management information.

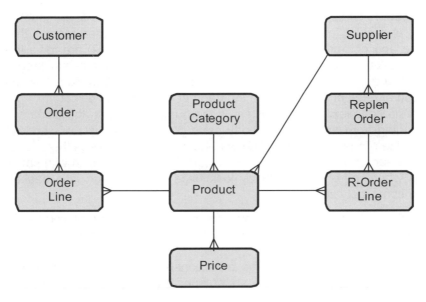

Figure 8.9 Order Processing – Data Structure

8.4   Case Study - Parts Order Processing at Volvo UK

Finally we look at an example order processing system – that used for parts supply by Volvo Cars in the UK.

Volvo Cars supplies parts to its dealers for use in their workshops and for supply to members of the public or other garages. The UK Volvo parts warehouse is located at Crick in Northamptonshire – centrally located in England and convenient for the motorway network. The characteristics of the operation can be summed up as:

◆   There is (essentially) one source of supply, the Volvo European parts warehouse at Gent in Belgium.
◆   There are a limited number of customers, the 200 or so Volvo dealers in the UK.
◆   There is a large range of parts – most parts for the full range of Volvo cars going back a good number of years (Volvos generally last a long time).

The main aim of the parts division is to support car sales and the reputation of the marque. The key targets are about stock availability and speed of order fulfilment. Volvos need repairs like any other cars – hopefully they don't break down too often but what is really bad for the reputation is if the car is then in the garage for several days waiting for a part. The aim is that for at least 95% of rushed orders the part will be at the dealer next day. If the part is not in stock at Crick it will be on the ferry overnight from Gent, cross docked in the warehouse and with the dealer within 48 hours. In the unlikely event that the part is not in stock in Gent it can be flown from the main plant in Gothenburg and still make the overnight delivery from Gent.

The system deals with two sorts of orders. Stock orders are submitted by dealers, at regular intervals, to replenish their own parts storeroom – the orders are large and non-urgent. Vehicle off the road orders (VOR) are for a job in the dealer's workshop where the dealer does not have the part in its stockroom – they are small, urgent and attract less discount than stock orders. Note that car parts are priced at retail and then sold to the trade at a substantial discount.

The main complexity of the system is the number of parts, the disparity in their size (ranging from an engine or body parts down to small screws and washers) and the size of the warehouse. The warehouse is segmented – there is specialist handling gear for volume / large / heavy parts but also a section with small plastic drawers where parts are put in zip-lock bags and collected in a basket. Other areas of complexity are:

◆   Parts supersession – a part on a older model may be replaced by another part introduced on a later model (with dealers still ordering the original part number).

◆   Kits – a part number may be a kit consisting of two or more separately stocked parts. Kits may be superseded by an individual part and visa-versa.

Aspects of the system that make things simpler include:

◆   There is only one supplier and a limited number of customers. The customers are all franchise holders – their operations and requirements are similar and, ultimately, they will do what they are told.

◆   There is no competition – Volvo dealers must use Volvo parts (even if the same part might be cheaper from other sources).

◆   On the customer side there can be standardisation of the way orders are submitted – the dealer's systems are agreed and developed in conjunction with Volvo.

◆   With only 200 customers it is relatively easy to optimise the picking of stock orders. They can be divided by warehouse sector, consolidated with other orders, sorted into aisle / bay / bin order. Deliveries for each dealer can be put together in goods-out.

As noted in the case study in **Chapter 3**, Volvo has recently joined the Ford group. One can expect some standardisation and rationalisation and possibly the parts operation will be part of that process. The general characteristics of the business are similar for parts operations across all car manufacturers – the requirements of this operation are substantially different from, say, an office stationery supplier with hundreds of suppliers and a couple of thousand customers.

Sourced from the author's own experience as IS Parts Project Manager at Volvo UK.

Exercises

1. Why might some organisations outsource their payroll operations? Do the reasons for outsourcing payroll also apply to order processing?

2. Using the formula in *figure 8.4* and the following stock figures:
   - free-stock   60
   - backorder stock   0
   - on-order stock   50
   - re-order-stock-level   200
   - re-order-stock-quantity   50

   calculate the appropriate re-order quantity. If the on-order-stock arrives later today and there are three orders for 80, 30 and 50 before any more stock arrives, what will the backorder figure be?

3. Orders may be sent in on paper and then they have to be keyed into the system – this takes time and can be error prone. What other media / methods can be used to submit orders and what are the advantages / disadvantages of each approach?

Chapter 9
EDI Systems

Summary

Electronic commerce (e-Commerce) is 'the formulation of commercial transactions at a site remote from the trading partner and then using electronic communications to execute that transaction' (Whiteley, 2000).

One of the 'technologies' used in e-Commerce and in information systems is electronic data interchange (EDI). It was the first of the e-Commerce technologies and it enables companies to link their information systems with those of their customers and their suppliers and to automate the supply chain in the form of an inter-organisational information system (IOS).

EDI was developed as a way of codifying structured data, such as orders and invoices. The EDI standard gives an application-independent and machine-independent way of encoding business transactions. EDI, when used in conjunction with a value added data service (VADS), allows senders to choose when and how to send their transactions and receivers to pick them up and decode them at a time convenient to themselves.

EDI decreases the time taken to exchange and process trade documents from several days to a matter of hours – it can be as quick as the trading partners need it to be and it removes the costs and errors associated with data entry from paper documents. EDI facilitates just-in-time manufacture and quick response supply.

9.1 Electronic Commerce

Information systems are used within organisations but they also have interfaces with other organisations and individuals – order processing, discussed in the last chapter, is an example of such a system. Many of these interfaces are, in effect, with the information systems of the communicating organisation and it will often make sense for the interface to be directly between the two systems, a process that is referred to as electronic commerce (e-Commerce).

e-Commerce is nicely summed up by the following definition given by the European Union Esprit program (1997):

> Electronic Commerce is a general concept covering any form of business transaction or information exchange executed using information and

communications technologies, between companies, between companies and their customers or between companies and public administration.

Electronic commerce includes electronic trading of goods, services and electronic material.

e-Commerce, I would suggest, is implemented using three different 'technologies'. These technologies are:

◆ Electronic data interchange (EDI). Used for regular and repeated, business-to-business transactions. The subject of this chapter.

◆ Internet commerce. Used for one-off business-to-business or business-to-consumer transactions, for example buying a book from amazon.com. Discussed in *Chapter 10*.

◆ Electronic markets. Used to allow the customer to choose the best offering from a range of similar, competitive products: the airline booking systems used by travel agents are the best example. Briefly covered in *Chapter 10*.

The three technologies serve different e-Commerce requirements. There is some overlap: the position is shown diagrammatically in *figure 9.1*.

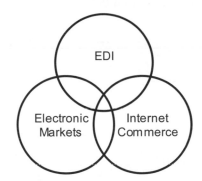

Figure 9.1 e-Commerce Technologies

9.2 What is EDI?

EDI is electronic data interchange. EDI is used for transferring data between computer applications – normally in an automated manner without the need for staff decision making or staff involvement with individual transactions. The normal use of EDI is for trade documentation exchanges such as orders and invoices, and this use of EDI has been introduced in *Chapter 8*.

EDI is sometimes called *paperless trading*, which sums up the nature of EDI quite neatly. A more formal definition, from the International Data Exchange Association (IDEA), is:

The transfer of structured data,
by agreed message standards,
from one computer system to another,
by electronic means.

The definition has four elements and I will use them to explain what EDI does and how it works.

EDI is an important element of the IS infrastructure of many organisations. It is also a good example of the application of information and communication technologies to business requirements.

9.3 Structured Data

EDI is used for *the transfer of structured data*. This means that we are dealing with formal documents as opposed to text (or any of the other elements of multimedia documents). Formal documents are what business information systems process (as was illustrated in *Chapter 8*). Unstructured documents are a different class of computer applications and are largely the preserve of desk top productivity systems such as the word processor and the e-mail system.

An example of a formal document is an order. The order will have a fixed format (although each organisation is likely to have its own format). The order consists of codes, values and (if necessary) short pieces of text – each element of the order is defined and serves a specific purpose. An example of an order is shown in *figure 9.2* – the order is from a bookshop to a publisher ordering a number of copies of a couple of books.

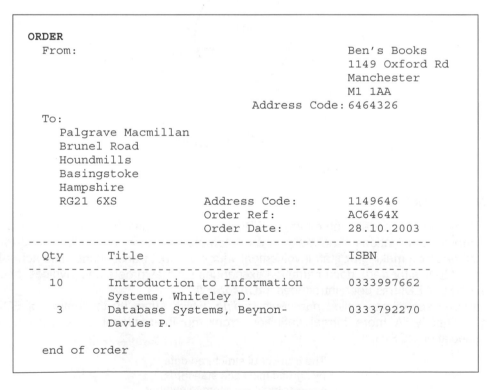

```
ORDER
  From:                                       Ben's Books
                                              1149 Oxford Rd
                                              Manchester
                                              M1 1AA
                            Address Code: 6464326
  To:
     Palgrave Macmillan
     Brunel Road
     Houndmills
     Basingstoke
     Hampshire
     RG21 6XS              Address Code:      1149646
                           Order Ref:         AC6464X
                           Order Date:        28.10.2003
     ---------------------------------------------------------
     Qty       Title                          ISBN
     ---------------------------------------------------------
     10        Introduction to Information    0333997662
               Systems, Whiteley D.
      3        Database Systems, Beynon-      0333792270
               Davies P.

  end of order
```

Figure 9.2 Example Order

Note that while the full postal addresses are given on the order there are also address codes which is all that the IS needs on its order transaction – given that the customer and supplier details are held in standing data. Similarly the order shows the book title but this is not needed in the IS as the ISBN fully identifies the product that is required.

9.4   Agreed Message Standards

The orders are structured data but, in practice, every organisation does its orders a little bit differently. In addition to the differing layouts the organisations have different computer systems and again the record layouts and physical storage characteristics differ from system to system. All of these factors make the exchange of electronic data difficult.

It would be possible for a couple of organisations to agree a common format for the electronic exchange of order data but then, as other organisations joined the scheme, discussions could need to be reopened to accommodate the needs of the new participants. For EDI there is a more general *agreed message standard*, for example at a trade association level, so that all organisations using that sort of data exchange can readily participate. The agreed message standard does not belong to any one business or rely on any specific technology – it is system and machine independent.

EDI standards have, over the years, been developed by a number of trade organisations – examples of such standards include:

◆   Tradercoms: a UK standard for general merchandise – widely used by multiple retailers such as supermarkets. Developed by the Article Numbering Association (ANA) who are also responsible for EAN code allocation (the article numbers used in barcodes).

◆   Odette: a European standard used by the vehicle assemblers for ordering components and, latterly, the exchange of specifications and design information.

These early EDI standards (and there are many more for different trade sectors in different countries) served well but were problematic when trade took place across trade sector boundaries or internationally. These developments resulted in attempts to develop more general standards. The resultant standards were:

◆   ANSI X12: an American standard designed to cover the requirement of all trade sectors.

◆   EDIFACT: a European / United Nations initiative to develop an international standard for all trade sectors.

EDIFACT stands for Electronic Data Interchange for Administration, Commerce and Transport. It is the defacto international standard – even the Americans accepted it and agreed that X12 users should migrate to EDIFACT at some, unspecified, future date.

To illustrate the EDIFACT standard, *figure 9.3* shows the EDIFACT message and data segments that would be used to transmit the order shown in *figure 9.2*.

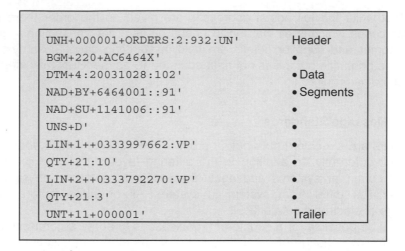

Figure 9.3 Example EDIFACT Order

As can be seen:

◆ The message starts with a UNH header segment and finishes with a UNT trailer segment. The header gives the message number (000001), message type, i.e. order, and some EDIFACT version identification data. The message number is repeated in the trailer along a count of the data segments (including the UNH and UNT segments) – this allows for some message validation by the system that receives the message.

◆ The BGM and DTM segments identify the order. The order number is AC6464X and the order date is 28 Oct 2003. The other data items are qualifiers, for instance, the date and time segment (DTM) can be used for many purposes: in this instance the 4 indicates that in this is an order date and the 102 that it is in century date format.

◆ The two NAD segments specify the buyer (BY) and the supplier (SU). We could send the full text address but, as we have mutually agreed codes for both the buyer and the supplier, the codes are all we need. There could be more NAD segments specifying delivery points, invoice points and the like, if they were required.

◆ The UNS segment separates the order header from the order lines.

◆ Each order line is represented by a LIN and supplemented by a QTY segment. The LIN specifies the product code (ISBN number) and the QTY the order quantity.

◆ Data elements are separated by a <+> and, where composite data elements are used the component data elements are separated by <:>. Composite data elements normally includes an item of user data and one or two qualifiers, as indicated for the DTM segment above. The data segment separator is <'>.

The example looks simple enough, and for a specific application EDIFACT will often be very simple. The overall EDIFACT standard is both huge and complex and can be a considerable problem to interpret for someone not used to the task.

9.5   From One Computer System to Another

EDI messages are (ideally) output from one business information system and automatically input to another computer system. They are for regular, repeat trade transactions that do not require manual intervention. The archetypal examples of EDI usage are the supermarket replenishing its regional warehouse from the large food processors and the vehicle assembler buying in components from its suppliers of wheels, light fittings, etc. Let us use these two requirements to emphasise the point that EDI is intended for communications *from one computer system to another*:

The large supermarket, for instance Tesco, Sainsbury's or Safeway, collects details of its sales from the EPOS system. The EPOS data is used by the stock control system to calculate the delivery requirement of each store and this is then supplied on a daily basis from the regional warehouse. The system also calculates the regional warehouse's stock position and determines the replenishment requirement. For most products, with the possible exception of some fresh food lines, the supermarket will have a contract with the supplier. The supermarket's replenishment system can then automatically generate and send an EDI order to the supplier. The large suppliers such as Heinz, Kellogg, etc. will take the EDI order straight into their own order processing system where it will be processed automatically to produce picking documentation for the warehouse and update the production plan.

The automotive manufacturers such as Ford, Nissan and Rover are also extensive users of EDI systems. Production scheduling of vehicle assembly is a complex task, with each variant of a model requiring differing components. The vehicle assemblers plan their production schedules for some time ahead and send EDI forecasts of what they expect to require to their component suppliers. The car makers are, however, attempting to respond quickly to specific customer requirements and production schedules can change up to the time that the build of a specific vehicle commences. Some smaller components are held in stock but many of the larger assemblies and components are just-in-time, sequenced delivery to the assembly line. EDI orders are sent out for these components as the vehicle is been built. Delivery times can be as short as an hour with the electronic order being sent straight into the supplier's order processing system and the supplier having a warehouse facility co-located with the customer's assembly plant. Suppliers of components, such as seats, may keep part assembled stock and then complete the assembly, e.g. by fitting the required seat cover, at the last minute when the order arrives – this allows the supplier to meet short lead times without holding excessive stock.

EDI was envisaged as a universal trading mechanism but that is not the way it has worked out – the set-up costs are too high except where there are large numbers of standardised transactions to be made. Instead of a generalised network there has developed a pattern of hub and spoke trading. The hubs are the large customer organisations, such as the supermarkets or the vehicle assemblers, and the spokes are their suppliers. See **figure 9.4** for a simplified version of the arrangement (using a supermarket as an example).

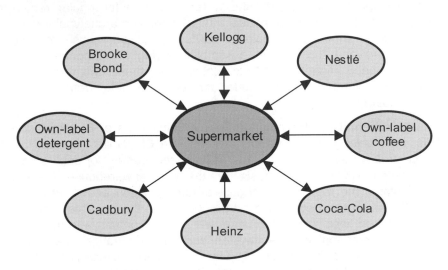

Figure 9.4 Hub and Spoke Trading Pattern

Many of the hub organisations have a hundred or more suppliers and they typically instruct all of them to implement EDI to meet their requirements. Some of the suppliers will also supply other hub organisations and may need to include variations in their systems to meet the differing requirements of each hub organisation. Some small suppliers may not have fully automated order processing systems and could simply print out the EDI order. EDI will also be used for other trade transactions such as delivery note, invoice and payment.

9.6   By Electronic Means

The EDI transactions, once encoded into the required EDI standard, are sent *by electronic means*. The electronic means could be a disk or tape that requires physical delivery but it would be normal to use a network. The network can be a direct dial up link, it may be the Internet but, very often, it is a commercial value added data service (VADS).

The VADS, also known as a value added network (VAN), provides two significant advantages for the EDI user:

◆   Time independence: the messages can be sent when it is convenient to the sending organisation and picked up at a time convenient to the recipient. Where, for example, orders are time critical the supplier will have to retrieve the customer's messages at regular intervals. However, if the order turnaround time is longer, say, 48 hours then the supplier might retrieve the EDI orders from all its customers once a day and and use a batch run of its order processing system to allocate stock and schedule the day's deliveries.

◆ Protocol independence: the sender and receiver have to agree on the EDI standard and how they will use it but they do not need to use compatible network protocols and communications equipment. The large hub may, for instance, have a high speed permanent connection to the VADS whereas a small supplier may dial up once a day to download its orders.

Time and protocol independence are provided by the VADS's computer system using its post and forward facilities. Continuing with the example of an order, the process is as follows:

◆ The customer sends its orders into the VADS, at a time that is appropriate to its schedule, using a communications port that meets its network requirements.

◆ The VADS strips off the transmission protocol data and stores the EDI orders in the customer's postbox.

◆ The VADS checks its postboxes for incoming messages and sorts them into the mailboxes of the intending recipients.

◆ When the supplier wishes to process its orders it sends a message to the VADS, using a communication port that meets its network requirements, and requests a download of its orders from its mailbox.

◆ The VADS sends the orders to the supplier using the appropriate transmission standard and protocol. The orders in the downloaded interchange may have come from a number of customers.

The process is illustrated in *figure 9.5*.

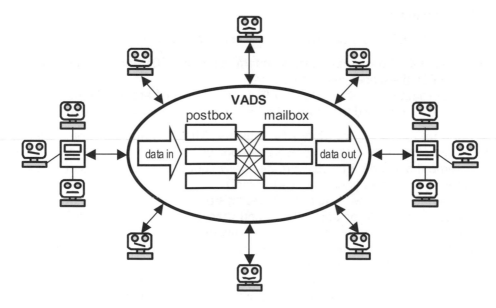

Figure 9.5 The VADS System

In addition to the basic post and forward service, the VADS offer its customers:

- A secure and reliable service. It charges premium rates and attempts to make sure that the service is more secure and reliable than alternatives such as the Internet.
- Data security. EDI messages can be stored in the VADS, after the initial download, and retrieved if the recipient suffers any data loss.
- Consultancy. The staff at the VADS have considerable experience in EDI and usually offer a consultancy service. They may well also offer EDI software and validation services for EDI messages. All these services are charged.
- Trusted third party services. The VADS can record transactions and arbitrate in any disputes between trading partners. If a customer and a supplier are arguing whether an order or an invoice has been sent the VADS can use its records to settle the dispute.

The main problem with using a VADS is that the data services, and any additional services, have to be paid for. Arguably the charges are not that great but with companies seeking to cut costs, wherever they can, some have focused on VADS charges. The Internet is an alternative to a VADS service and is considerably cheaper. Some organisations have moved to using the Internet for EDI but there are still concerns on security and reliability. To move to using the Internet for EDI services requires the agreement of the hub organisation which may be less keen than some of the supplier organisations.

9.7 EDI Implementation

To implement EDI the organisation needs software that will:

- Translate the internal transaction format into the EDI standard and transmit the EDI messages into the network.
- Interrogate the network for any EDI messages that are awaiting download, retrieve them and then translate them into the internal message format.

The normal approach is to buy EDI software. The software may come from the VADS supplier, a third party software vendor or be part of an order processing / procurement package. EDI software generally supports several EDI standards and a number of networks (including the Internet).

To interface the user's application software with the EDI software the user produces a serial file of transactions and then the translation into EDI format is parameter driven. The vendors of EDI software make the process as simple as they can but interfacing an order processing system to EDI can still be a sizeable (and hence expensive) undertaking.

In addition to the EDI software we also need to agree with our trading partners precisely what we are trying to achieve and how we are going to do it. Possibly the trading partners have been doing business for many years using paper documents but EDI requires much more precision. With paper documents the data entry staff can interpret the data and make allowance for different formats but with EDI everything has to be precisely defined and accurately encoded. Reaching agreement on EDI can be a time consuming business involving management, procurement and technical staff. Most organisations that set up EDI trading arrangements draw up an EDI agreement that specifies:

- The EDI standards to be used (normally a subset of the complete EDI standard will be agreed).
- The codes to be used for products, customers, suppliers, etc. Quantities can be an issue – does the quantity refer to a pack or an individual item and how are bulk goods to be measured in terms of quantity and quality?
- The network to be used.
- The frequency of the interchange, with some definition of acceptable deviation from targets.
- How any disputes are to be resolved.

Disputes that may arise from electronic trading are an interesting issue. There are established laws of contract and legal precedence for trade conducted using paper documents. How these laws should be interpreted when the trade is conducted electronically is not entirely clear.

The full EDI system is represented in *figure 9.6*.

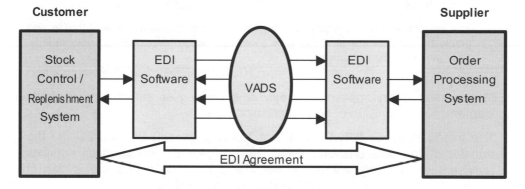

Figure 9.6 The EDI Trading System

9.8 EDI Examples

As has already been mentioned, EDI is extensively used by large retailers and by car makers. These usages of EDI are illustrated by the following example:

Tesco is the leading UK supermarket and it has taken a lead is setting up EDI links with its suppliers (and subsequently Internet e-Commerce with its customers using its chain of superstores as its local depots). The initial roll out of EDI at Tesco was in 1989. Electronic trading with the suppliers is driven from the EPOS systems and the EPOS data. This system records every item that is sold and hence: updates stock records, drives the replenishment of the stores from the regional warehouse and, in turn, the replenishment of those warehouses from the supplier:

For each of the company's 578 stores in the United Kingdom, electronic point-of-sales (EPOS) data is adjusted to take account of known weather, seasonal and promotional factors to generate a replenishment order that appears in the suppliers' computer system via EDI links.

(Wheatley, 1997)

As of the end of 2000 Tesco was doing the bulk of its replenishment using EDI. Of Tesco's 2,000 suppliers, 1,500 were EDI enabled (and most had been trading using EDI systems for a number of years). The remaining 500 smaller, seasonal, suppliers receive EDI orders but do not respond with electronic advanced shipping notices and invoices. Tesco is using a third party supplier (Kewill) to provide a cost effective facility for these small trading partners. The aim, in the words of a Tesco Product Manager, is:

... to achieve a single business-to-business process within our company, where EDI messages can be sent and received with all 2,000 of our suppliers.

(Kewill, 2000).

In addition to its use of EDI, Tesco is also making its EPOS data available to suppliers using Intranet technology in a system called Tesco Information Exchange (TIE). This lets suppliers inspect their customer's sales and stock data and helps them anticipate the requirement for product in advance of receiving the EDI order. In the words of another Tesco's Project Manager:

The electronic POS data provided by TIE provides and early view of trends and gives the supplier the ability to take corrective action, especially on volatile lines like new products and promotions.

(GE Global eXchange Services, 2002)

EDI has also been applied in areas other than just straightforward trading documentation. Examples of such applications are:

The Inland Revenue (UK Government Tax Department) is using EDI for the transfer of tax data between itself, large employers and financial services providers. A case highlighted on the Inland Revenue's web site is that of Standard Life, a leading mutual financial service company.

Standard Life's initial EDI system was for the PAYE returns on 100,000 annuity policies. The forms used for this purpose are the P45 (3,000 per annum), P46 (15,000 per annum) which are sent to the tax office and the P6s that are returned once the P46 has been processed. Using paper (and hand written P46s) the process would take at least 22 days and the error rate was 28%. Using EDI the turnaround time is six days, the error rate is drastically reduced and there has been a very significant saving in administration costs.

The case study of UHS in Chapter 2 also included the use of EDI. UHS uses a system of quick response supply to make sure that it has the right merchandise in its shops whilst keeping minimum stock levels at its distribution centre. UHS works with its suppliers so that they know what is selling and it knows what they have in stock. This information is maintained using two EDI exchanges:

◆ Predictions – details of sales – sent by UHS to the suppliers.
◆ Availability – details of stock holding – sent by the suppliers to UHS.

UHS's replenishment calculation is based on EPOS sales data from the stores but also takes into account the contract position, the stock at the distribution centre, and the availability data sent by the supplier. The replenishment calculation results in the:

◆   Call-off Order – replenishment order – sent by UHS to the supplier.

UHS has then used EDI to ensure it is kept informed of the progress of the order – this allows it to make alternative replenishment decisions if there are any supply problems and to speed the processes in the distribution centre. The EDI exchanges involved are:

◆   Order Confirmation – sent by suppliers to UHS.
◆   Delivery Note – sent by suppliers to UHS.

The trade cycle is then completed with the invoice and payment exchanges. These exchanges are:

◆   Invoice – sent by suppliers to UHS.
◆   Payment – electronically through the banking system using the BACS system.

9.9   EDI Advantages

For the medium or large organisation, with a sophisticated IT infrastructure and conducting numerous trade exchanges with its customers and suppliers, EDI has many advantages. Organisations which use EDI include multiple retailers (supermarkets, DIY chains, etc.) and manufacturers who use a large number of components (e.g. automobile assemblers). The most obvious advantages are:

◆   Speed of transaction. The transaction is being processed in the recipient's computer system within a day (and very possibly within an hour if that is the agreed service level). The contrast is with a paper transaction that has to go out through the sender's mail room, through the post, in through the receiver's mail room and then be keyed into the order processing system. A four day turn-round would be a very good figure for a paper transaction.

◆   Error reduction. There should be no room for misunderstandings and there are no transcription errors. The order in the supplier's computer system is precisely the order the customer sent (and if the customer made a boob, then that is clearly the customer's problem).

◆   Cost cutting. The order entry clerk and many of the staff dealing with invoice queries and supplier payments becomes redundant or can be transferred to other work. Note also that seasonal peaks, staff holidays, etc. no longer create a backlog in the order entry area. These cost savings will need to be offset against the system development and network costs.

Less obvious advantages are:

- Reduced stock holding. As orders can be processed much more quickly and reliably there is less need for stock. Using EDI, manufacturers have moved to just-in-time manufacture, where components are delivered to the production line as and when they and needed, and retailers have moved to quick response supply, where the shelves in the shop are restocked by overnight deliveries. These changes allow stock holdings to be reduced and, in some instances, stock rooms and warehouses to be closed. Reduced stock holding reduces the capital tied up in stock. Reduced stock holding also reduces goods handling costs and wastage through damage and theft. Reduced stock holding at the retailer or manufacturer can lead to some increase in stock holding by the supplier who has to meet ever more stringent delivery and availability targets.

- Business opportunities. Having the capability to trade electronically makes it easier to take on new contracts with customers who demand that business is transacted in that manner. Equally, having an established EDI relation with a customer can help lock-in that customer – having to establish electronic trading relationships with a new supplier is an additional incentive to continue with the existing arrangements.

- Cash flow. Electronic invoicing will reduce the turnaround time of invoices and, more importantly the number of queries. This should speed payments and hence improve cash flow.

Exercises

1. List the four main elements of an EDI system.

2. List the transactions that take place between trading partners that seem suitable for EDI implementation. Suggest some business communications that would not be suitable for this technology.

3. The advantages given for EDI compare EDI with paper orders; if the orders were sent by fax, which of the advantages would still apply?

Further Reading

The recommended text for further details of EDI is:

Whiteley D (2000) *e-Commerce: Strategy, Technology and Applications*, McGraw Hill, Maidenhead.

The full official documentation of the EDIFACT standard is on the UN web site at:

http://www.unece.org/trade/untdid/welcome.htm

The reader may look at this if he or she wishes but, be warned, it is large, complex and not readily understandable, unless you are used to interpreting EDI standard documentation.

Chapter 10
e-Commerce Systems

Summary

The second e-Commerce technology is Internet e-Commerce (i-Commerce). Internet e-Commerce uses the World Wide Web to set up an online shop where users can buy products or order services. Internet e-Commerce is used for both business-to-consumer and business-to-business transactions. The use of the World Wide Web provides a point and click environment where the user can search for and select products – it differs from EDI where the purchasing decisions are in the context of a contract and the transactions are application to application.

For Internet e-Commerce the 'shop front' is the World Wide Web but this has to connect to a back office system where orders are received and processed.

The use of the World Wide Web for shopping has advantages but there are also difficulties. Areas where an e-Shop differs from a conventional shop are:

◆ The user can not touch, smell or try on the product.
◆ Payment is normally electronic and there are user concerns with the security of online payments.
◆ The purchase process may be quick but tangible goods have to be delivered and that takes time and costs money.
◆ The e-Shop is remote and that can be difficult if there are problems with the service or the customer wishes to return the goods.

These areas are more problematic for some classes of products and for some customers than to others. Organisations that run e-Shops and people who design them need to be aware of the problems and to ensure that their e-Shop does as much as it can to reassure and provide good service.

The third e-Commerce technology is electronic markets. The chapter suggests that EDI, i-Commerce and e-Markets provide a 'complete set' that meets the need of all types of trading relationships, where the participants wish to trade electronically.

10.1 Internet e-Commerce

EDI, discussed in the previous chapter, is a technology for the regular exchange of structured data between the information systems of trading partners. EDI, however, is not appropriate for less formal business-to-business or for business-to-consumer exchanges and this is where Internet e-Commerce can come in.

The use of the Internet for commercial services started in the 1990s with the advent of the World Wide Web and the start of home use through Internet service providers (ISPs). The archetypal business-to-consumer e-Shop is amazon.com. Amazon was established as an online bookshop in 1995 but there are now e-Shops that sell almost anything that an individual or a business may wish to buy.

Note that business-to-consumer e-Commerce was not invented in the mid 1990s when e-Commerce sites started appearing on the World Wide Web. Similar transactions were available on videotex systems back in the late 1970s – the French Minitel was the most successful of these with over six million subscribers.

10.2 The e-Shop

The most obvious part of the Internet e-Commerce operation is the web site – the e-Shop. The web site must attract the customer, display the product and transact the business. A mock-up of a web site containing the basic (very basic!) requirements is shown as *figure 10.1*.

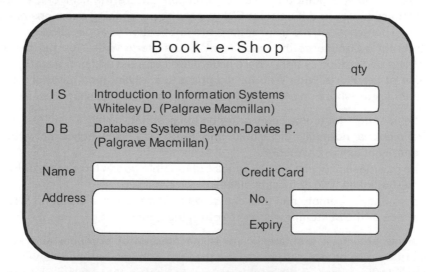

Figure 10.1 A Simple e-Shop

Most e-Shops will be much more sophisticated than the example that has just been shown. A full service e-Shop selling tangible goods will normally include:

◆ The front page. This needs to tell the customer, clearly and concisely, what the e-Shop does and provide access, by index and / or search engine, to the rest of the site. Often the e-Shop will try to include something eye catching on the front page. The front page is also a good place to include any special offers. That said, the user's screen size is limited and if the front page is too cluttered, or too slow to download, customers can be frightened away before they even start using the e-Shop. The front page may include a log-in procedure for customers who are already registered with the site and, in some cases, a registration procedure for new users.

◆ Information. It can be helpful and reassuring to give the customer more information on who the company is, what it does and how it trades (privacy policy, delivery, etc) – this data can be provided on additional information pages.

◆ The catalogue. A series of pages detailing the goods for sale. Typically there will be a name, picture, description and price. For many categories of goods the e-Shopper is at a disadvantage because the goods can not be seen, touched, smelt or tried on and the details given must try to make up for these deficiencies. In some cases the web has advantage over a conventional shop, for example an online music shop can conveniently provide short samples of the tracks on a CD. The e-Shop should exploit any advantages that the web has to offer.

◆ The shopping basket, trolley or cart. Many e-Shops use a supermarket analogy with an electronic shopping basket to hold the goods that have been selected. Customers need to be given the opportunity to check the basket and 'return goods to the shelves', should they change their minds.

◆ Checkout. Continuing with the supermarket analogy, once shoppers have finished their shopping they 'proceed to checkout'. For electronic shopping there is no need to add up the bill – this has already been done. The checkout does include payment (which must be done electronically) and then customers must give their name and address details (if they are not already registered with the site) so the goods can be delivered.

This is shown diagrammatically in *figure 10.2*. Note that the asterisk on the product box indicates an iteration. The sequence of use is variable and the diagram does not purport to document this detail.

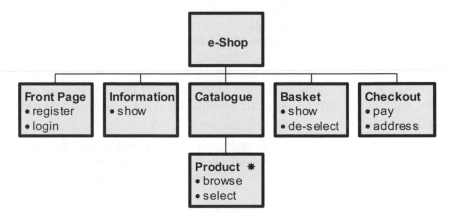

Figure 10.2: The e-Shop – Structure Chart

e-Shops for tangible goods follow much the same basic pattern, be they selling books or bathtubs. e-Shops for services often require a different approach – for services such as airline tickets, insurance, etc. the customer specifies the details of the service he or she wants and the system generates a quote.

10.3 The Back Office

The web site of the e-Shop is only half the story. The web site is what customers see and where they select their goods. The web site then has to be connected to the back office system where the payments are processed and fulfilment actioned.

The back office is primarily an organisational matter. The e-Shop having taken an order needs to ensure that the goods (that have already been paid for) are despatched rapidly and reliably.

The basic requirement for the back office is a warehouse with appropriate arrangements for the despatch of goods, replenishment of stock and processing of returns. It may be that fulfilment is outsourced or transferred to suppliers but it still has to be the responsibility of the e-Shop to make sure that delivery occurs in accordance with legitimate customer expectations. Many e-Commerce companies, particularly in the early days, did not pay enough attention to the requirements and complexity of the back office operations and poor (or appalling) service was, all too frequently, the result.

An e-Shop of any size is going to need an order processing system to manage its fulfilment. Order processing for an e-Shop is not fundamentally different from the generic system outlined in *Chapter 8*. The order entry comes direct from the web site which should obviate the need for manual data entry for that part of the process. Also the payment is made at the time of ordering – the payment has to be processed as part of the order entry but there is no need for the invoicing and receive payment processes.

To get the orders into the order processing system the web site that has been displayed on the user's (client) machine has to 'talk' to the back office system on the server. This is done through:

◆ The <form> provision of HTML where text boxes, radio buttons, etc. can be specified on the web page. Any user input is then transmitted to the server when the submit button is clicked.

◆ A CGI or ASP program on the server that collects the web input and processes it – in many cases the processing will be relatively simple with the data being passed onto a conventional order processing system for further action.

Note that many e-Shops are not written in straight HTML but the pages are generated, at run time, using CGI or ASP procedures. This enables the web page to be displayed using up-to-date data from a database and taking into account any relevant customer parameters.

The relationship of the client system and the back office processing on the server is shown in *figure 10.3*. The server is shown as a single system but it may well be spread across several servers, partly for security reasons, and it may have links to legacy systems used by the organisation in its other (non e-Commerce) operations.

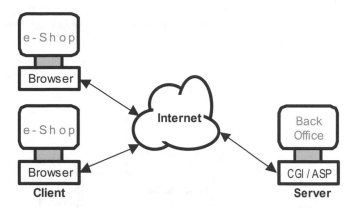

Figure 10.3 The e-Shop as a Client–Server System

10.4 The Complete e-Shop

The basic requirements of a e-Shop are fairly simple but to do any quantity of business on the web the basic will not be enough. *Figure 10.4* is a model developed by Whiteley, *et al*. (1999) for the evaluation of e-Commerce sites and used in the book *The Complete e-Shop* (Whiteley, 2002). It serves as a checklist of items to be considered or included when designing an e-Shop. In summary an e-Shop needs:

- Search: The e-Shop will only make sales if people know it is there. This has to be tackled in a number of ways including:
  - Choosing a good name – a url that people have a chance of remembering.
  - Making sure that search engines can find the site by registering with the search engines and using well chosen keywords on the site.
  - Advertising both online, e.g. on a search engine, and in the conventional media. Advertising can be expensive and you need to check that the return will justify the expenditure.
  - Being funky. If the site really appeals and provides a great service to one customer then she might recommend it to her mates.

- Company: It can be a good idea to give the customer some information on the company – if the customer feels wary about doing business it may provide reassurance. Some companies have a message from the chairperson and others may have copies of annual reports or pictures of the company's premises – think about what approach would reassure the sort of customer you are after.

- Customer: At some stage in the transaction you have to get customer details. You can ask customers to register before they use the site but that could frighten customers off (why should customers give away their address and risk being spammed when they don't even know if they want to use the site?). The alternative approach is to allow unfettered access to the site and only take customer details when there is a sale and those details are needed. Customer details can either be retained for marketing and for use when the customer uses the site again or they may be discarded. Whichever approach is taken, don't upset the customer (too much!) and make sure you meet the requirements of any applicable data protection legalisation (which may not amount to much if the operation is registered in a jurisdiction with lax data protection laws).

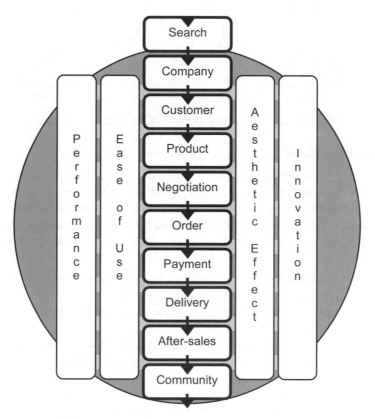

Figure 10.4 Web Site Design Checklist

◆ Product: The products have to be displayed in such a way that customers can find them and understand what they are buying. e-Shops come in all shapes and sizes and sell a diverse range of products. If there are a large number of choices on the site then it needs a good index and a site search engine. The product itself needs to be displayed attractively and customers needs complete, but succinct, information on what they are getting and what they are paying. For some products, such as clothes, the Internet is generally at a disadvantage compared with a conventional shop. For other products such as books, CDs and possibly holidays and wine there is the possibility of giving more information than is readily available in most shops (although setting up an extensive online catalogue is obviously an overhead for the e-Shop).

◆ Negotiation: Bargaining takes place when large business-to-business contracts are negotiated and for large ticket items such as houses or cars. It is not the norm for typical e-Shop transactions such as buying a book or a plane ticket and it is not readily replicated online. There are auction sites and with online shopping one can, with reasonable ease, shop around for the best price. However negotiation is not a part of most e-Shops – their goods and services are fixed price offerings.

◆ Order: The order process needs to be simple and understandable. For tangible goods it normally involves selecting the product and this is then added to a virtual basket, trolley or cart. For services there is typically a form to fill in and the best sites take the users through carefully designed and clearly marked stages.

◆ Payment: In the e-Shop the goods or services are normally paid for online and prior to delivery. Payment and the security of payment are big issues for e-Commerce and the users of e-Shops. It can be argued that online payments are no less secure than many other forms of electronic payments but that is not how many punters see the situation. Payment and the security of electronic payments is further examined at **10.5**.

◆ Delivery: The smart way to do business is to let other people do the work. In a supermarket customers pick, pack and deliver the goods for themselves. In an e-Commerce operation the fulfilment process is down to the e-Shop – picking, packing and despatch has to be paid for and the customer has to wait for the goods to arrive. The fulfilment process is further discussed in **10.6**.

◆ After sales: The requirement for an after sales service varies from product to product and service to service – there is not, for instance, a lot of need for after-sales on a book but products such as electronics might not work and clothes that were bought online may not fit properly. For some products the Internet has real advantages. Many products, such as electronic goods, are supported by extensive web sites. The use of the web cuts out the need for paper documentation, allows the information to be updated and can provide facilities such as interactive decision trees for fault finding. The disadvantage of online shopping occurs when goods have to be parcelled up and returned – it is much easier and cheaper to take a product back to a conventional shop where the problem can be discussed, face-to-face, with a 'real' person.

◆ Community: Some web sites have a buzz. If a site can build up a sense of community then people will come back and possibly make repeat purchases. In a conventional store we might try to achieve this effect with a coffee shop. Online we can provide a chat room or some form of personalised service or participation. eBay has a community following and supports this with specialist pages for specific groups of enthusiasts.

◆ Usability: Four aspects of this are shown on the model:
  ◆ Performance – the web site needs to load quickly, work with a range of browsers and has to be reliable – no 'dead links'.
  ◆ Ease-of-use – the site needs to be intuitive for the novice user without being fussy for the returning customer – not an easy trick to pull off.
  ◆ Aesthetic effect – to attract the customer the site needs to look interesting and exciting. The overall effect needs to fit in with the type of business that is being done – a web site for a bank will have a different aura from one designed for a pop group.
  ◆ Innovation – there was a stage when web sites prided themselves on doing something new and different. Not so important now but a flight simulator for the kids on the airline site won't do too much harm – provided Gran knows that the real pilot has already passed all the tests.

10.5 Online Payment and Security

Payment: In the e-Shop the goods or services are normally paid for online and prior to the delivery of the goods. Payment is typically by credit card but can also be made using a number of other mechanisms:

◆ Credit cards are simple enough to use online. The customer types in the card number and expiry date and the e-Shop can automatically check its validity. The credit card is vulnerable as, if the details fall into the wrong hands, it can be used (with or without possession of the card) for a number of further transactions before the problem is detected. The customer has a measure of protection as the credit card company normally has to pick up the tab for fraudulent use. A drawback for the suppliers is the fees they have to pay to the credit card company – these can be high for a small online trader.

◆ Debit cards are similar to credit cards but not as widely accepted or used. They do not offer the customer the same protection against fraudulent use as a credit card.

◆ e-Cash is an attempt to recreate real money in a virtual environment. To make it work both the user and the e-Shop have to join the same e-Cash scheme. The user then deposits an amount of money in his or her e-Cash account – an electronic purse. To make a payment the user authorises the transfer of some of that money from his or her account to the e-Shop he / she is using. The advantages are that the amount of loss the user can suffer is limited to the amount in the electronic purse and also that the scheme is suitable for small payments (where the use of a credit card would not be appropriate). The disadvantages are that the user is shelling out money up-front and that there are no universally accepted e-Cash schemes. It is noted that while the scope for fraud when using e-Cash is limited there have been problems with the security of payments into the e-Cash schemes. Another aspect of the use of e-Cash is that the transaction is effectively anonymous – if you are doing something online that you are not very proud of then the evidence will not be printed out on your next credit card statement.

◆ Accounts are offered by some sites – share trading and gambling sites are among the sites that offer such schemes. It is similar to e-Cash but the use is limited to the one site. For operations such as share trading and gambling it allows payment but also facilitates the return of money when the customer makes a sale or has a win.

◆ Offline payments are a way of reassuring customers who are particularly concerned about e-Shop security. Payment may involve giving part of the credit card number online and the remainder by phone or fax or simply sending a cheque in the post. The processing involved complicates the sale for the e-Shop and the despatch of goods will normally be held back until the payment has been received and processed.

The big concern about online payments is security. The normal method of payment is a credit card and problems can arise in four areas:

◆ Impersonation – the person making the transaction may not be the owner of the credit card that is being used. The transaction uses the 'customer not present' protocol and the normal check of a signature and being able to look the person in the eye do not apply.

◆ Interception – it is possible that the transmission could be intercepted, the card details stolen and, subsequently, used fraudulently. Possibly not very likely and, as most e-Shops provide for encrypted transmission, this part of the process should be fairly secure.

◆ In the e-Shop – the credit card details may be stolen from the e-Shop, by a member of staff or by a hacker. The e-Shop needs to design security into its technical and personnel procedures. Technical protection includes the use of firewalls and the encryption of stored data – the evidence is that many sites have not paid enough attention to this aspect of their business.

◆ Fraudulent e-Shops – the final possibility is the bogus e-Shop, a web site that looks like an e-Shop but has no intention of despatching any goods or selling any service. The bogus e-Shop cashes your payment and very likely passes the card details on for further fraudulent use. They can be difficult to detect and to deal with as an e-Shop can be set up by almost anyone and on a server that is in another legal jurisdiction. Normal advice is to stick to e-Shops that look professional and with brands you recognise – which is a bit unfortunate for the legitimate, new small business trying to set-up online.

These problems, or some of them, can also be applicable to other forms of online payment. For example, they apply to debit cards and e-Cash but with e-Cash the damage is limited to the amount held in the electronic purse which is presumably much less than a credit card limit.

The security of online payments is of great concern to many consumers. There is a steady growth in online trade but security concerns still stop a significant number of people shopping online. There is always the suggestion that some technical development will stop or reduce online frauds – probably not true – however good the encryption it will not stop impersonation or fraud in the e-Shop (could try a retina scan device connected to the PC, I suppose!). A fundamental issue with e-Commerce (and mail order / telesales) is that there is no exchange of value when payment is made. In a shop the customer exchanges payment for the goods – online the customer pays now and hopes to get the goods or service delivered a few days later.

10.6   Delivery

Having ordered online, an apparently hi-tech process, it seems a bit ironic that the customer has to wait days (or even weeks) for the product to arrive. In part, this is an inevitable part of direct selling but the supplier needs to do all it can to ensure that goods are delivered quickly, reliably and economically. The way goods are delivered depends, in part, on their size and value. The alternatives include:

- Post – the postal service is relatively cheap and reasonably fast. It is good for small items that are moderately priced. If the package will fit through the letterbox that saves the worry about what to do with the packet if the customer is out. Amazon.co.uk uses the post for most of its deliveries.
- Express parcel services – these are used for larger or more expensive items. The service costs more and there is the problem of what to do with the packet if the customer is not in to receive it (which is a frequent occurrence for domestic deliveries).
- Local delivery – perishable items and bulky items normally need to be delivered from a local depot. Setting up a network of depots and the supply chain to service it is obviously an expensive undertaking. Examples of goods needing local delivery include:
  - Groceries – the large supermarkets are using their supermarkets as the local depots. There is a suggestion that a specialist e-fulfilment depot would be more efficient but that would require investment and volumes to justify that investment. Customers of online supermarkets normally have to agree a delivery slot that is possibly a couple of days from the time of ordering – this requires a degree of organisation and foresight that not all of us can achieve.
  - Domestic appliances (cookers, refrigerators, etc) – the large multiple retailers already have depots for home deliveries from their bricks and mortar stores and can use the same network to deliver to their online customers.
- Electronic delivery – some products, such as music, software, greeting cards and even books can be delivered electronically. This eliminates the wait for delivery and much of the costs of fulfilment. Large downloads can be problematic for people with slow connections and, for example, a CD burnt on a blank disc is not quite the same as the 'proper' CD in its own box with all the documentation (possibly I am old fashioned – I like my CD collection).
- Service delivery – many services transactions can also be delivered electronically. Bank, insurance and ticket transactions can all be confirmed

online. In some case this is followed up by a confirmation through the post but this is often dispensed with – airline e-Tickets are an example.

♦ Other delivery schemes – the delivery of online purchases is only really satisfactory if the item can be posted through the letterbox or delivered (reliably) electronically. Schemes that have been tried, to overcome the problems of delivering packets to domestic addresses, include:

  ♦ Larders – a safe box, possibly including refrigerated space, installed at the house and with a combination key known to the owner and the delivery company.

  ♦ Local collection point – e-Deliveries to a local garage or convenience store where customers can easily pick up the packet when they return from work.

In addition to the problems of physical delivery there is also a security concern – unless goods are signed for there is no proof that delivery has taken place. Presumably there are goods that don't get despatched or are lost in transit but there is also a problem of some customers complaining that goods have not arrived when delivery did in fact take place.

10.7 Electronic Markets

The third of the e-Commerce technologies is the e-Market. This is where a computer system is used to 'display' the products or services of a number of vendors and buyers can visit (electronically) and pick the best buy on the basis of price, quality and / or service.

Markets are applicable for commodity products (products with standardised characteristics) and an e-Market has similar restrictions (there is not a lot of point in comparing the price and quality of potatoes and carrots unless one is prepared to substitute one for the other). The best current examples of e-Markets are the airline booking systems. These systems list all the flights of most airlines and are used by travel agents to look up suitable flights for their clients – the customer can then choose on the basis of convenience and price. These airline-booking systems can also be accessed by the public through the sites of online travel agents. A number of financial and commodity markets can also be classified as e-Markets.

e-Markets were predicted to achieve a much wider usage than has been the case – they fit in with liberal economic theories on free markets. The action of a free market, where there is adequate (or excess) supply, is to drive prices down. This action of a market can benefit the customer but is not necessarily advantageous to the supplier. The e-Market relies on the suppliers providing information and there are instances where proposals to set up e-Markets have had to be abandoned as suppliers were reluctant to participate (note that the creation of the unbiased airline booking system was not the intended outcome of those who created the original airline booking systems).

Stock markets and airline-booking systems have relied on proprietary systems but recently there have been moves to create Internet enabled e-Markets. A number of these markets have been set up and some of them have already failed.

e-Markets will continue but their potential to expand into fresh trade areas remains doubtful.

10.8 The Complete Set

The three e-Commerce technologies now provide us with an appropriate IS solution for all major categories of trade exchange. EDI, as we saw in the last chapter, is appropriate to frequent trade transactions between businesses and i-Commerce is used for one-off transactions between businesses or between businesses and consumers. e-Markets play a much smaller role but they have a place where a commodity market exists and the players, in that market, are prepared to cooperate in such a system.

Business-to-business transactions are typically through established trading relationships and on credit terms (the goods are supplied first and paid for on the receipt of an invoice). This is a standard part of the EDI trade cycle but trade through an e-Shop or an e-Market can also be on credit terms – sales to each business customer are totted up and invoiced at the end of the accounting period. Business-to-consumer transactions are not usually on credit terms and payment can be made electronically through the e-Shop.

The three e-Commerce technologies, together, make a complete set – there is an e-Commerce technology that can be appropriately used for any trade transaction.

Much has been made of the growth of e-Commerce for business-to-consumer transactions although, whatever the impressive values quoted, the truth is that i-Commerce accounts for only a very small proportion of retail sales (some of the growth has been at the expense of other forms of direct selling such as mail-order and telesales). More growth has taken place in business-to-business e-Commerce where electronic trading is the norm for many transactions in many trade sectors. Another application of e-Commerce is business-to-administration and consumer-to-administration where interactions with public authorities (government, local authorities, etc.) are increasingly available (or required) using electronic means. The growth of e-Commerce has required the re-engineering of many business processes and the associated information systems. This type of trade is now referred to as e-Business. The potential e-Business links of an organisation are summarised in *figure 10.5*.

10.9 Case Study – amazon.com

The best known of all the e-Shops is amazon.com – it claims to be the world's biggest bookstore (a claim that does not really stand up to examination – we will come to that later).

Amazon.com was founded by Jeff Bezos and started in a converted garage in Seattle by Jeff, his wife and a couple of employees. Amazon was registered as a domain name on 01 November 1994 and started trading in July 1995. The story goes that Bezos drew up a list of 20 types of products that might be sold on the web and, after evaluation, books seemed the best bet. Bezos had no background in the book trade.

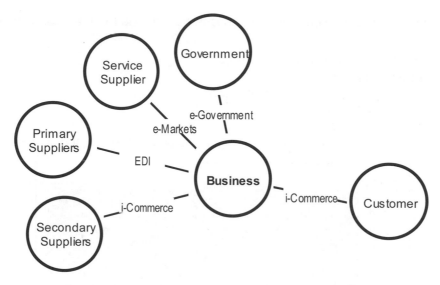

Figure 10.5 e-Business Links from an Organisation

Amazon was not the first online / Internet bookshop but was launched at an ideal time just as the web was coming into use (the first Internet bookshops used e-Mail for ordering). Bezos was (and is) a very clever and determined man and he attracted people of similar calibre to get his business started. Sales grew rapidly, and were matched by equally impressive losses, see **figure 10.6**. At the time there was a notion that losses did not matter in the 'new economy' and a high rate of 'cash burn' was almost a virility symbol – a nonsense that was part of the dot.boom bubble and was eventually to lead to the dot.bomb crash in 2000. As Spector (2002) reports, in December 1998:

> [Amazon] Shares were trading at a stratospheric 97.4 times sales (while Wal-Mart traded at 1.6 times sales).

The dot.bomb crash was a salutary lesson for the business-to-consumer sector and many online companies went out of business. For amazon it was a wake up call and it had to start looking at its costs, organisational structure and profit (or rate of losses). Some impressive progress has been made on these fronts. Amazon claims to be in profit on US book sales but, at the time of writing, losses continue.

The amazon.com site is, on one level, just a conventional e-Shop. That said, most of the things it does are done rather better than the competition. From the start amazon had a clear front page and it took pains to make sure that it worked effectively and efficiently with any browser or Internet connection that the customer was likely to be using. There are some things that a conventional bookshop does well and some that are more effective online. If you want a Starbucks coffee whilst browsing for a book (and that you can get in large American bookshops) then an e-Shop is not for you. If you know which book you want and need to find it quickly a computer search engine should be better than searching through the shelves (although you can't take the book away with you if and when you find it). Features that amazon has included in the book catalogue are:

◆ Full bibliographic details of the book.
◆ Expected delivery times.
◆ The publisher's description of the book.
◆ A picture of the front cover.
◆ Readers' reviews.
◆ Suggestions of other books that might also be of interest to the customer.

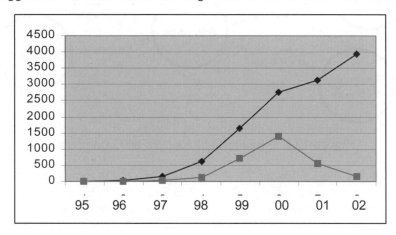

Figure 10.6 Amazon Annual Sales and Losses
(◆ Sales and □ Losses in million US$)

In some ways, the amazon user has more information than the customer in a conventional book store – certainly there is more information than would be the case if the book was not in stock and had to be ordered.

Bezos was not content to just have the most famous online brand name and the world's biggest (online) bookstore – he wanted to expend the amazon brand to other areas of online retailing. A couple of years after starting the online bookstore amazon started adding a number of further categories of merchandise: these included groceries, pet supplies, toys, electronics, music CDs and videos. Some of these categories were started by acquiring, or investing in, existing e-Shops. Most of these enterprises have not been a startling success – music CD and videos seem to be the main exception (perhaps Mr Bezos should have been mindful of his original ranked list of 20 possible business areas).

Amazon (and other online retailers) can run with low inventory (some try to run with zero inventory). According to Spector (2002), at amazon a book stays in stock for on average 18 days but the supplier does not get payment for 53 days – allowing for credit card clearance at 2 days this gives a negative operating cycle of 33 days. In contrast, in a physical book store the book is held for an average of 161 days but the supplier is paid after 84 days – assuming a credit card purchase that gives a positive operating cycle of 79 days. Whereas a conventional bookshop is paying to stock its shelves, the online bookstore is, in effect, getting a loans from the wholesalers and publishers to help it run its business. This difference is in addition to the disparity in operating costs. The costs of a book-shop (including premises and employees) are about double those of an online operation such as amazon. On the negative side, amazon spends about a quarter of its revenue on marketing compared with about 4% for traditional retailers.

Amazon.com is the best known of all the dot.coms. In a short time period it has built up a impressive brand name and very substantial sales. Whatever its sales total is when you come to read this book it should be put in context of the overall total of book sales, $26 billion for the US domestic market (Spector, 2002). Amazon.com lists well over one million books but only stocks a fraction of them – the titles that are not stocked are bought in from the publisher or a wholesaler when an order arrives. A large American bookstore (Barnes and Noble or Borders) will carry in excess of 100,000 titles on its shelves and can, of course, take orders for all of the titles that amazon lists.

10.10 Other e-Shops

Besides amazon there are e-Shops serving just about every imaginable area of retailing. Further well known dot.coms include:

◆ eBay – an online auction site – a bit like the small ads in a local paper or a trading magazine but with a bidding process thrown in. This site has a sense of community about it with many regular users. It has been argued that it is a consumer-to-consumer model – there is a case for that classification but the business eBay is in there taking a commission.

◆ Expedia.com – an online travel site that interfaces to the airline booking system (Worldspan). The main offering is airline seats but most travel needs, e.g. hotels, and ferries can also be booked.

The best known examples of Internet e-Commerce are 'pure play' e-Shops but many established, 'bricks and mortar', companies also have their own web sites. Areas where 'bricks and clicks' operations have become established include:

◆ Airlines – all major airlines now have web sites that inform customers, sell tickets and give details of their customer loyalty schemes. Using their web pages the airlines can make substantial savings over the costs (including commission) of selling tickets through other channels. Low cost airlines, such as easyJet reduce costs by only using direct sales (web and telesales). See Doganis (2001) and Whiteley (2000) for further discussion of e-Commerce in the airline industry.

◆ Supermarkets – customers can order their weekly groceries online and save the hassles associated with the weekly trip to the supermarket. Groceries are bulky, include perishable items and the customer has to book a delivery slot for a day or two after the order is submitted. Tesco is the best known provider in the UK and seems to have done better than some of the US equivalents (including HomeGrocer.com, at one stage part owned by amazon and which ceased trading in 2000).

The dot.com site tends to be the US version and many of the large e-Shops also have a .co.uk version. Amazon.com, in addition to the US site runs sites for Britain

(.co.uk), France (.fr), Germany (.de) and Japan (.co.jp). Normally it is best to use the national site as opposed to an overseas version – if nothing else the shipping charges will be less. An exception is where goods are available in the US that are not (currently) marketed elsewhere.

Exercises

Use the Internet for an online shopping trip and see how easy it is to find what you want, how well the sites work and whether you get good value for money. Set yourself an objective before you start. Suitable subjects are:

♦ A flight to New York. Choose a set of dates, e.g. the first Friday in February and returning the following Monday. Set out from your home town choosing the most convenient airport but balancing that with getting a good deal (and if you live in North America set the destination as Paris).

♦ You have come to university / college with your expensive new PC and you are now rather worried about the level of thefts from student accommodation. A large dog is one possibility but seems a bit impracticable. Get online and find some insurance for your PC that would suit your circumstances and your budget.

If this is done as a class exercise compare results. Which search engines with what search keys worked best (or did some students find their e-Shop in other ways)? Did the sites found / sites used belong to the service providers or were they the sites of agents / brokers? Was the site attractive and easy to use or was it a bit rubbish? Who got the best deal and how did they find it?

Further Reading

The recommended text for further details of Internet e-Commerce and e-Markets is:

Whiteley D (2000) *e-Commerce: Strategy, Technology and Applications*, McGraw Hill, Maidenhead.

Further details on the user design requirements for an e-Shop are given in:

Whiteley D (2002) *The Complete e-Shop*, Chandos, Oxford.

And the chapter *e-Commerce@airline.co* is very good in:

Doganis.R (2001) *The Airline Business in the 21st Century*, Routledge, London.

Following the stock market euphoria for e-Commerce companies and the subsequent crash there have been a number of studies that make interesting (and relatively light) reading. These include:

Cassidy J (2002) *dot.con: the greatest story ever sold*, Penguin, London.
Kuo J. D. (2001) *dot.bomb: Inside an Internet Goliath – from Lunatic Optimism to Panic and Crash*, Little Brown, London.
Spector R. (2001) *amazon.com: Get big fast*, Random House, London.

Chapter 11
Expert Systems

Summary

Most IS / IT applications use the computer's abilities for high speed calculation, data manipulation, communication and large scale data storage – this applies to all the applications discussed, thus far, in this section of the book.

There are, however, many tasks that require more than just calculation and data manipulation – they require judgement which is a part of intelligence. Computers are not intelligent but we can use their capabilities to simulate intelligence – this area of research and application is known as artificial intelligence (AI).

Research into AI has been extensive and wide ranging. The two main approaches to AI can be categorised as knowledge based systems (KBS) and artificial neural networks.

KBS are also referred to as expert systems. A KBS is set up with a database of 'knowledge' – 'facts' from the problem domain coded in some knowledge representation formalism, typically 'if – then' rules. The system can then be fed with details of a problem and will use its 'knowledge' to give expert advice. How a KBS is set up and how it operates is further explained in the chapter.

The alternative approach to AI is the neural network. This is a attempt to use the computer to simulate human thought processes. It is a newer process than KBS and still the subject of extensive research.

AI systems are used for a number of applications where conventional computing is not appropriate. Early KBS packages tended to concentrate on the field of medical diagnostics. More recent application areas have included in the fields of fault detection, financial advice and fraud detection.

11.1 Artificial Intelligence

Computers have the ability to calculate, manipulate text and store vast quantities of data – but they don't think. The processes performed by the computer are governed, step by step, by the instructions in the program they are running. Their utility is the ability to execute complex sets of instructions accurately, reliably and at great speed. This ability can be applied to tasks such as:

◆ Processing large numbers of business transactions – examples of this are the payroll and order processing systems we have already looked at.

◆ Controlling complex machinery such as process control in a chemical plant, power station or an aircraft cockpit.
◆ Evaluating large scale models such as those used in weather forecasting or modelling wave action on coastal defences.
◆ Desk top applications such as word processing or spreadsheets.

These applications can be complex and the list includes tasks that could not be done (with the same degree of complexity) without a computer. However these tasks do not require the computer to exercise judgement – the computer does not have the attribute of intelligence.

Tasks that require judgement can be seen as the domain of the expert (although people exercise judgement, in and out of work, at all levels and are not necessarily considered to be 'experts'). Expert tasks that can not sensibly be tackled by conventional computing include:

◆ The doctor who sees a patient and has to judge, on the available evidence, what the problem is and what treatment would be appropriate.
◆ The bank manager who is asked for a loan to set up a small business and has to judge if the bank would be wise to advance the money.
◆ The exam board that needs to determine a student's degree award in the context of any special circumstances applicable to that student.

Conventional use of computing may help with these decisions. An IS can be used to provide information on the case in question and to analyse similar, relevant cases, but conventional computing can not make a reasoned, intelligent judgement. To apply IT to the decision process we require a different type of computation. We refer to this class of application as artificial intelligence (AI):

> The discipline devoted to producing computer systems that would require intelligence if done by a human being.

The field of AI research and practice can be divided into two principal approaches:

◆ Knowledge based systems (KBS).
◆ Artificial neural networks.

In this text we will concentrate on the former approach. The intention is to give an introduction to how KBS functions and an overview of the application of AI. Most computing degree courses will include modules on AI, at intermediate or advanced level, for those students who wish to further pursue their study of this topic.

11.2 Knowledge Based Systems

The definition of a KBS, also referred to as an expert system, is a little more specific than our general definition of AI:

> A system containing knowledge that can perform tasks which require intelligence if done by a human being.

The key to the KBS is 'knowledge'. To set up a KBS it is necessary to 'extract' knowledge from an expert in the field and codify it in a way that can be used by a computer. The process is not easy. Much of the 'knowledge' we use to make judgements is subconscious – we would be hard pressed, for example, to express and codify all the judgements we make in deciding to cross the road or ask a fellow student out for a drink – see *figure 11.1* for an example of the complexity of codifying knowledge and deciding what knowledge is relevant to the problem.

If we are out for a walk in the countryside we might say, 'Look at that bird, I think it is a wren.' How do we know, how do we form that 'expert' judgement?

First we may say:

> 'It is a bird because it can fly.'

OK but say the person you are with is an argumentative type (probably doing a university computing course). She asks: 'What about ostriches or penguins?' OK, not too many ostriches or penguins in the New Forest but let us modify the knowledge base:

> 'It is a bird because it can fly – unless it is an ostrich or a penguin.'

Sounds OK but then your friend is not going to let it go there. 'What if its wings have been clipped or it is dead – are you going to tell me that a dead bird is no longer a bird?' We could have a metaphysical argument about dead birds (what do you call a dead parrot? a polygon!) but better to update our knowledge base:

> 'It is a bird because it can fly – unless it is an ostrich or a penguin or has had its wings clipped or it is dead.'

Now your friend says: 'It could be in a cage or it might have got its feet stuck in concrete'.

Figure 11.1 Identifying a Bird

Once we have the knowledge (in a appropriate form) it can then be used with the circumstances of a particular case to reach an 'expert' conclusion. An alternative definition that more fully describes the way a KBS operates is:

> An expert system is a computer system that operates by applying a inference mechanism to a body of specialist expertise represented in some knowledge representation formalism.

(Beynon-Davies, 1991)

The mechanism for reaching that conclusion is the inference engine. It takes the user's input and applies if–then rules. Normally the rules will lead to a partial conclusion and the rule set will be applied again until the inference engine is ready to give its 'expert opinion'. The components of the KBS are further explained in the following subsections.

11.3 If–Then Rules

The normal way that knowledge is codified is in the form of 'if–then' rules. MYCIN, for example, contains approximately 4,000 such rules. A brief outline of MYCIN together with an example of two of its rules is give in *figure 11.2*. You can imagine that developing 4,000 such rules was a formidable undertaking.

MYCIN was developed by Stamford University to assist in the diagnosis and treatment of meningitis and bacterial infections of the blood. A problem with this class of infection is that early diagnosis and treatment is vital but the lab tests take some time. A patient seen, at an early stage, by an expert has a better chance of appropriate treatment and survival than a patient seen by a doctor with less expertise in the field. The idea was that a KBS could make the appropriate expertise much more widely available. The MYCIN system was trialed and assessed to be as good as the experts in the field.

MYCIN contains about 4,000 if–then rules. Two of the rules are:

if the stain of the organism is gramneg **and**
the morphology of the organism is rod **and**
the patient is a compromised host
then there is suggestive evidence (0.6) that the identity of the organism is pseudomonas

if the stain of the organism is grampos **and**
the morphology of the organism is coccos **and**
the growth conformation of the organism is chains
then there is suggestive evidence (0.7) that the identity of the organism is streptococcus

Figure 11.2 MYCIN If–Then Rules

The process of formulating the rules is known as knowledge engineering. Normally the rules are written by a KBS specialist working with the person or people who know about the field being examined – the domain experts. Formulating the rules is a complex and laborious task. A very real problem is to find domain experts who can spare the time to fully participate in the process.

To illustrate the workings of a KBS, we will use a much simpler example with only 14 rules. The example is to identify creatures spotted in the countryside and the rules are shown in *figure 11.3* – they are simplistic (and incomplete) but, hopefully, they serve to illustrate the process.

Rule:
R1   **if** flies **then** bird.
R2   **if** not flies **then** animal.
R3   **if** bird and small **then** small-bird.
R4   **if** bird and large **then** large-bird.
R5   **if** animal and four-legs **then** quadruped.
R6   **if** animal and two-legs **then** human.
R7   **if** bird and perched **then** passerine.
R8   **if** bird and foul-like **then** gallinaceous.
R9   **if** quadruped and hops **then** rabbit.
R10   **if** quadruped and runs **then** fox.
R11   **if** quadruped and not hops **then** hedgehog.
R12   **if** small-bird and passerine and red-breasted **then** robin.
R13   **if** small-bird and passerine and brown **then** wren.
R14   **if** large-bird and gallinaceous **then** pheasant.

Figure 11.3 Example If–Then Rules

11.4 Inference Engine

The if–then rules are applied to a particular case using the inference engine. For early KBS systems the developers used to write their own programs but now it is possible to buy ready written programs – known as KBS shells.

The workings of the inference engine are summarised in *figure 11.4*.

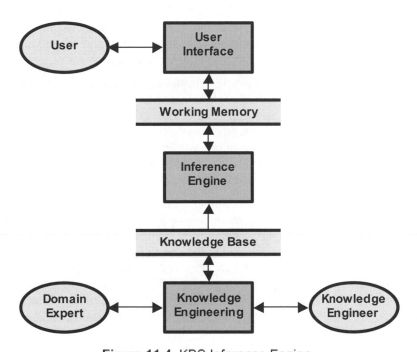

Figure 11.4 KBS Inference Engine

The basic mechanism of the inference engine is as follows:

◆ The user is asked to input the details of the case to be examined, through the *user interface*. The user may not be able to supply all the information that is asked for but the *inference engine* will 'do its best' with the information that is available. The user input is stored in *working memory*.

◆ The *inference engine* then loops using the rules in the *knowledge base* and the data in the *working memory* as follows:
   • It searches the *knowledge base* for applicable rules, i.e. rules where the antecedents (factors required to evaluate the if condition) are available in working memory. For example if there is a rule <if A and B then C> and A and B are both available in *working memory*, then the rule is applicable.
   • It selects the most appropriate of the applicable rules and 'fires' it – the consequence of the rule (the then) is added to *working memory*.

For example, if the rule <if A and B then C> is the most applicable, then C is added to *working memory*.

◆ The inference engine ceases looping when an end condition is met. This could be a consequence that gives an end result or it could be that there are no more applicable rules that have not already been applied. The user is then given the result through the *user interface*.

Different KBSs will apply more sophisticated ways of applying the inference mechanisms. The MYCIN example included a probability and the inference engine would take this into account in deciding what rules to fire and what weight to give to the answer. Other techniques that might be employed are:

◆ Forward and backwards chaining: The examples given in this chapter are forward chaining – the inference engine checks whether the if conditions (antecedents) are met and applies the then condition (consequence). The alternative, backward chaining, approach assesses the desired then clause (consequence) and then works in reverse to establish the conditions that are required for that goal to be achieved. KBS systems can use forward chaining, backward chaining or a combination of the two.

◆ Fuzzy logic: The examples given in this chapter use binary logic – the condition is true (value 1) or false (value 0). In many areas where experts work, things are not necessarily that simple. Fuzzy logic recognises uncertainty and ascribes a value in the range from 0 to 1 to the outcome of a test. On this basis, in our example, rather than categorising a bird as large or small we might set a degree of largeness, thus while a swan may be large (value 1) and a wren small (value 0) other birds such as thrushes and ducks would get a intermediate degree of largeness, possibly 0.2 and 0.4 respectively.

The inference engine we will use for our example is very simple and is shown in pseudo code in *figure 11.5*. The pseudo code makes it look more difficult than it is. To explain it in words:

◆ We collect the input data from the user.
◆ We search the knowledge base until we find an applicable rule (where the antecedents are in working memory but the consequence is not in working memory) – then we fire it.
◆ Once a rule is fired we return to the beginning of the knowledge base to start the search again.
◆ We continue searching the knowledge base and firing applicable rules until there are no more rules that meet the applicability test – then we output the expert opinion.

```
data:
          working-memory: array parameters (1:n).
          rule-base: array rule (1:m).
          rule-count: integer.
          rule-found-ind: integer.
process:
          input       user parameters to working memory.
          rule-count := 0.
          rule-found-ind := 1.
          while     rule-found-ind = 1:
                    rule-count := 0.
                    rule-found-ind := 0
                    while     rule found-ind = 0 and rule-count < number-of-rules:
                              rule-count := rule-count + 1,
                              If        rule-base(rule-count) antecedents
                                        in working memory and
                                        rule-base(rule-count) consequence
                                        not in working memory
                              then      place rule-base(rule-count) consequence
                                        in working memory,
                                        rule-found-ind := 1.
                    end-while.
          end-while.
          display results from working memory.
end.
```

Figure 11.5: Inference Engine – Pseudo Code

11.5 Running the Example Expert System

Using the rule base given in *figure 11.3* and the inference engine shown in *figure 11.5* we can now run our example knowledge base. The creature we saw In the woods could fly, was small, brown and was sitting on a twig. This data is input into working memory and the KBS uses the inference engine and its knowledge base to work out what sort of creature it is. The working of the KBS is shown in *figure 11.6*. We loop round searching the knowledge base for a rule that matches the data but has not already been used. We then fire that rule and add the new data it generates to the knowledge base (the addition is shown underlined). Once all applicable rules have been applied the answer we get is that the creature was a wren (OK, it could have been several other birds but that is the best I can do with 14 rules).

You could be underwhelmed by such a simple example. A realistic example would have a large knowledge base and a more complex inference engine; it would overwhelm us. I therefore have to ask you to scale up the example in your imagination. Examples of real KBS applications are given in the next subsection.

Initial state:
>   Knowledge base: can fly, small, brown, perches
Pass 1
>   Select: Rule 1
>   Knowledge base: can fly, small, brown, perches, <u>bird</u>
Pass 2
>   Select: Rule 3
>   Knowledge base: can fly, small, brown, perches, bird, <u>small bird</u>
Pass 3
>   Select: Rule 7
>   Knowledge base: can fly, small, brown, perches, bird, small bird, <u>passerine</u>
Pass 4
>   Select: Rule 13
>   Knowledge base: can fly, small, brown, perches, bird, small bird, passerine, <u>wren</u>
Pass 5
>   Select: No applicable rules
Final state:
>   Knowledge base: can fly, small, brown, perches, bird, small bird, passerine, <u>wren</u>

Figure 11.6 Example If–Then Rules

11.6 KBS Applications

There have been a number of KBS systems developed across a number of areas. We have already exampled one of the early medical information systems, MYCIN. Further examples of KBS applications are:

◆ Investment management: Selecting investments and knowing when to sell them is a complex business. The difference in the returns achieved from a well managed portfolio and one where the managers did not make the optimum decisions can be considerable. Fund managers have a great deal of information, some of it market statistics (delivered by IT systems) and some of it little more than gossip. The Pareto Partnership is an investment company that has spent over £1 million on an expert system that assists it with its portfolio management. The system has about 2000 rules and also employs other techniques such as forward and backward chaining and fuzzy logic. In 1998 the system was reported to have achieved a return of 3.4% – a return that matched the top quarter of human investors (Bocij *et al.*, 1999).

◆ Crop management: A US Government agency has an expert system that analyses weather patterns and crop data and, after reviewing all the relevant information, advises farmers about irrigation, fertilization and the optimum time to harvest to maximise crop yields (http://www.goldhill-inc.com).

11.7 Artificial Neural Networks

As has already been stated, an alternative approach to AI is the use of artificial neural networks. The approach in this type of system is to try and simulate / approximate to the working of the human mind. This is done by having a number of simple processing units (the neurons) that are connected by communications channels (the network). The operation of the network is governed by processing rules normally derived from an algorithm. Most neural networks have some sort of training whereby the weights of connections are adjusted on the basis of preset patterns, i.e. the neural network learns from examples.

> These systems use a similar process to biological intelligence to learn problem solving skills by 'training' or exposure to a wide range of problems. The learning occurs through interactions between nodes which are similar to the neurons of the brain.
>
> (Bocij *et al.*, 1999)

A recent application of neural networks has been to improve checking of Visa credit card transactions for fraud at Barclays Bank. The neural network has been trained using past transactions, both valid and fraudulent, and is able to predict the likelihood of fraud on an account. Since its installation by Barclays Bank in 1997 it has been recognising over £100,000 of fraudulent transactions a month (Bocij *et al.*, 1999).

11.8 AI at MMU

The Intelligent Systems Group in my department at Manchester Metropolitan University has developed a lie detector using artificial neural networks.

The system uses video input of the subject's face and the images are then analysed for minuscule gestures that indicate whether the subject is telling the truth or is lying. The image processing is done by a series of neural networks.

The system is claimed to be more accurate than the traditional polygraph, or lie detector machine. It is also possible to train people to fool the polygraph but such techniques are not applicable to this video analysis system.

The author's involvement in the system was as a guinea pig. The test was a box with a £10 note and a pair of glasses in it. Test subjects, on a random basis, either took the money or left it in the box – in both cases they were asked to deny taking the money. The subjects were then interrogated using a standard script and the machine was used to identify those telling the truth and those who were lying. I took the money and, as part of the publicity for the system, was exposed on TV as a thief and a liar! The system is still being developed but is seen as having applications in a number of security and law enforcement areas.

11.9 Continuing Developments

Finally let us note that the study of AI has been around for a while and there is still a long way to go. AI was defined in the 1940s by the British computer scientist Alan Turing who said:

> A machine has artificial intelligence when there is no discernible difference between a conversation generated by the machine and that of a intelligent person.
>
> (quoted in Freedman, 1999)

AI has made significant advances and is now applied in a wide variety of applications. AI is still a specialist area and setting up any sort of AI system is a time consuming process. AI systems are in use but the number of applications remains limited. AI has not yet passed the 'Turing test', and possibly that is a good thing.

Exercises

1. Attempt to codify the knowledge you apply in deciding to cross a road. Note, if you think it is simple then you have not thought about it enough!

2. Use the example KBS with an alternative inputs and determine the type of creature that has been spotted. Suggested parameters are: doesn't fly, four legs and it hops.

3. Conceivably, AI systems could replace humans in many decision making processes. What are the social and ethical implications consequent on handing over the decision making process to machines? Applications could possibly include university admission, student assessment, judgements in criminal cases – consider these and / or similar examples. Suitable for a tutorial discussion.

Further Reading

There are many books available on KBS and on AI but most are aimed at intermediate and advanced level students doing AI specific modules. A more detailed treatment of KBS, at an introductory level, can be found in:

> Curtis G. (2001) *Business Information Systems: Analysis. Design and Practice*, 4th ed., Prentice Hall, Harlow.

There are a number of demonstration KBS systems available on the web – the best known is probably the whale identification system. Links are on the web site.

Chapter 12
Management Information

Summary

The basic function of most business information systems is the processing of business transactions: processing orders, selling insurance, maintaining a bank account or whatever. The processing of those business transactions produces data, large volumes of data, and this in turn can be used for the production of management information.

Management information is essential for the functioning of the modern organisation with the emphasis on quick response to customer demands while making efficient use of resources in a fast changing market place. A great deal of effort has gone into the production of management information, either as a subsystem of the business information system or as a specialist system such as:

◆ Executive information systems (EIS),
◆ Decision support systems (DSS),
◆ Data warehouse systems.

Management information can be produced on paper or presented on screen in a tabular or graphical format. To be useful, management information needs to be accurate, timely and relevant.

12.1 Transaction Processing and Management Information

Up to now, in this part of the book, we have looked at information systems mainly as business transaction processing or data processing systems. I have explained the payroll as having the principal purpose of calculating wages and paying the staff. I have explained order processing in terms of translating orders into deliveries of goods that are then invoiced and hopefully paid for. These systems, of course, also produce management information. The payroll can, for example, produce an analysis of staff costs across the various divisions and departments. The order processing system is used to provide management information on stock, sales and so on. The use of the information system to inform the management decision making process is a vital element of IS provision and is discussed in this chapter. It is however emphasised that management information is not the prime purpose of most computer applications systems – many authors seem to set out to give the contrary impression.

The relationship of transaction processing to management information is shown in *figure 12.1*. The example is of an order processing system that processes orders and produces delivery notes and invoices. All the order data is stored on the database along with the customer and product data. The database can then be used by the management information system to correlate and summarise the data and produce information for management at all levels.

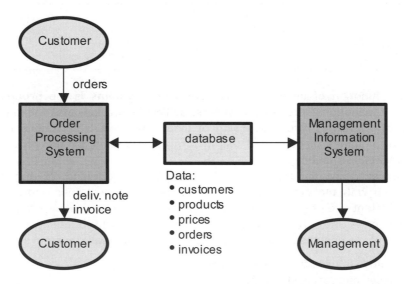

Figure 12.1 Transaction Processing and Management Information

Note that the transaction processing system will also interface with accountancy systems that then produce accounting information.

12.2 Levels of Decision Making

Management information produced from the organisation's information systems needs to be appropriate for the intended purpose. The levels of decision making in an organisation can be represented using Anthony's triangle: see *figure 12.2*.

Anthony's triangle represents the management structure of the organisation. At the top of the organisation there is a relatively small population of senior managers. Their role is, or should be, to determine the strategic direction of the company. Their decisions are passed down through the management hierarchy, a process represented by the control line on the diagram. Below the strategic layer is middle management – their role is the tactical planning and control of the organisation's activities. The third tier is the operational level, the base of our triangle. The operational level is concerned with day-to-day decision making at the production level. Feedback is passed back up the structure to the tactical and strategic level (who take not a blind bit of notice – whoops, I am not supposed to say that!).

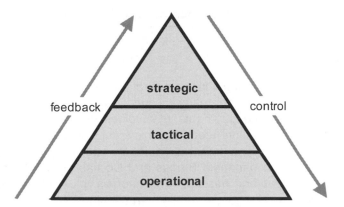

Figure 12.2 Decision Making Levels in the Management Hierarchy

Reporting / information requirements differ at each of the levels of the triangle. In general terms the requirements can be summarised as follows:

◆ **Strategic**

Strategic level decision making is, in general, the province of the top tier of managers / the board of directors. The decisions appropriate to this level are major marketing, organisational and investment decisions. Examples are to build a new factory, open new branches or invest in a new product range. To assist in making this level of decision, top managers will need reports on trends from both inside and outside the organisation. From the organisation's information systems they need summary reports on trends in sales and / or the overall financial performance of each division. From outside the company they will need to be informed on the performance of their competitors and on trends in the national and international economy. If we take the example of a sales report, a top manager may want a monthly report showing sales per region and the trends that are developing in the sales figures. This level of management ties up with the management level in the business environment model in *Part I*.

◆ **Tactical**

Tactical planning is the function of middle managers. The middle manager is aware of the strategic direction set by the board and must endeavour to ensure that the organisation meets strategic targets. The middle manager needs to be aware of what is happening within the department or at the branches and take action to deal with events or take advantage of trends, as they occur. Examples would be a marketing manager who may want to adjust prices, make a marketing push to deal with a problem or take an opportunity shown by an analysis of sales. Most of the information for tactical management comes from within the organisation, much of it from the company's information systems. Continuing with the example of a sales report, the middle manager would need sales reports for every

…anch in the area and, at a more detailed level, for each product range …ithin the branches.

Operational

The final level in the triangle is the operations level. This is where the day to day activity of the company occurs: stacking the shelves in the supermarket, matching payments to invoices or teaching students in a university. The information needed at this level is is short term and almost exclusively internal. The information is on specific cases that require action: there are no bananas, Bloggs and Co has not paid the last three invoices or Jatinger has missed three tutorials, plus an assignment and needs chasing up.

These reporting requirements can be represented in terms of time horizon, level of detail, source and frequency on a chart: see *figure 12.3*, derived from Curtis (1998).

	Strategic	**Tactical**	**Operational**
Time horizon	Long term	Medium term	Immediate
Level of detail	Summary	Categories	Specific cases
Source	Mainly external	Internal	Departmental
Frequency	Annual / monthly	Monthly / weekly	Weekly / daily

Figure 12.3 Characteristics of Information at Management Levels

12.3 Structured and Unstructured Decisions

As well as requiring different levels and sources of information the nature of decision making is different at different levels of management:

◆ Structured Decisions

At the operational level decisions will tend to be structured. A structured decision is one where:

- There are clear rules on how the decision is to be taken.
- The information on which the decision is to be taken is clear and readily available.
- The information requires no interpretation.

If these conditions are met the decision will be repeatable. If the same information is presented several times, or if different people were given the same rules and information, the decision outcome would be the same in each instance. Examples of such decisions are:

- Deciding the amount of income tax to be deducted from a worker's pay.

- Sending an invoice reminder where a bill has not been paid.

The information available at an operational level will normally meet the requirements for structured decisions. Many of the decisions that would have been made by clerical or shop floor workers will be programmed into the relevant IS. In the case of the income tax example, this would be part of the payroll system. Invoice reminders can also be automated, as is the case with the red bills from utility companies – other organisations may take a less structured decision where they chase up some customers but act more leniently where they judge that a stiff reminder could jeopardise the business relationship.

◆ **Unstructured Decisions**

Decisions tend to become less structured as one progresses up the management hierarchy. An unstructured decision is one where:

- There are no clear or complete rules on how the decision is to be taken.
- The information on which the decision is to be taken is unknown or not readily available.
- Any information that is available requires interpretation.

In these circumstances the decision will not be repeatable. The same person on different occasions, or two different people, may make very different decisions in what might appear to be similar circumstances. Unstructured decisions are greatly affected by 'gut feelings' or intuition. Examples of such decisions are:

- Deciding whether and where to build a new supermarket.
- Deciding which university to go to and which course to choose.

The risk involved in making an unstructured decision can be reduced by collecting as much information as possible and by consulting appropriate experts, i.e. trying to make the decision more structured. Information that could be available will come from both inside and outside the organisation and will be uncertain and / or need interpretation. Some internal information will come from the information systems but other information will be more informal / anecdotal. External information can include statistics from government and trade associations but it will also come from reading newspapers and from chatting to managers in other organisations – a good excuse for a round of golf at the company's expense? The strategy formulation process, discussed in *Part II*, involves research on environmental factors and internal strengths and weaknesses but the eventual strategic decision requires a value judgement, an unstructured decision.

Not many decisions are totally unstructured (and purely structured decisions may well be automated). Most decisions lie on a spectrum between structured and unstructured and the position on that spectrum has some approximation to levels of management (as illustrated by Anthony's triangle). A third factor is the scope of decisions. Higher managers make broad decisions that affect the future direction of the company whereas, lower down the hierarchy, decisions have a narrower scope. That said, focused decisions can still be very important for the individual concerned. Examples are the decisions a doctor or a bank manager may make on an individual case. These three dimensions of decision making, hierarchy, structure and scope are put together in the diagram shown as *figure 12.4*.

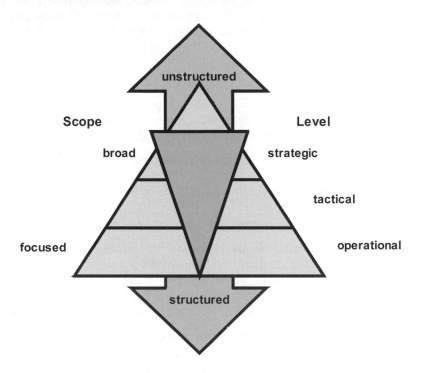

Figure 12.4 Dimensions of Decision Making

Next we will look at the way that information systems can contribute to the management and decision making process.

12.4 The Analysis Report

To inform decisions with information from internal systems we must produce reports that are printed on paper or shown on a computer screen. The basic type of report is an analysis report where we tabulate the information on a two-dimensional grid. An example of an analysis report could be a monthly report of top management showing sales, by month and by region. A simple illustration of such a report is shown in *figure 12.5*.

The manager, looking at the report in *figure 12.5*, might start with the 'bottom line'. From that bottom line we see a steep rise of sales for February and then a fall back in March – seems a bit odd but March sales are still above January so, arguably, that is not so bad. Possibly we would just put the report to one side but make a mental note to check which way things are going in April.

```
Sales Analysis by Region                        03 Apr 03
                                                   (IR01)
                    January       February       March
SE England           97,000       103,000        94,000
SW England          157,000       169,000       172,000
Central England     232,000       263,000       187,000
N England            67,000        87,000        91,000
Scotland             63,000        72,000        84,000
Wales                23,000        24,000        23,000
        Total       639,000       718,000       651,000
```

Figure 12.5 Analysis Report – Sales by Region

If our manager felt a little less hassled (no pressing engagement at the golf club) then she might look a bit more closely. If she did look at the figures by region she might see that the SW, North and Scotland had maintained a rising trend, the figures for Wales had remained fairly steady, and the dip in sales in March was accounted for by poor figures in the SE and Central regions. Having identified these anomalies, the next step would be to find out why – possibly there would be an abrupt call to the SE and Central regional managers to get to head office early the next day and explain the problem (their problem!).

The SE regional manager, having received a summons to head office, is going to have a look at his analysis reports (if he has not already done so). One of the reports he has is for sales for each product category for each month in his region: see *figure 12.6*.

Looking this report it soon becomes clear where the problem is – meat sales have collapsed. The manager needs to work out why, possibly by looking at some more detailed reports. What was the problem: a problem with getting product from the supplier, special offers from competitors or has everyone in the SE region turned vegetarian? From the tone of the call from head office it seems that his story had better be a good one!

Hopefully this illustration shows the use that can be made of analysis reports and the hierarchy of detail that might be used to inform different levels of management. You might also notice that the use of an analysis report requires detailed inspection. There are advantages to that but we could make the manager's job easier by presenting a report with a more immediate impact. We will come on to some alternative ways of presenting information in the next two subsections.

To produce this report the system has to read through all the sales that have been made in the current year, look up the prices and add up the required totals. Not a difficult task to program but it will take some time to run – presumably there will be a lot of sales on the database that have to be read through (the design of the database can help shorten the run time – this is looked at in **Part IV**). Note that if you have to produce such a report then make sure that the totals cross-correlate

– observe that the total line in *figure 12.6* matches the regional total line in *figure 12.5*.

```
Sales Analysis by Product Category              03 Apr 03
SE England                                        (IR02)

                    January        February        March

Fresh Meat          24,000         23,000          9,000

Fruit & Veg         15,000         17,000         16,000

Frozen Goods         8,000         10,000         12,000

Dry Goods           31,000         33,000         35,000

Other Goods         19,000         20,000         22,000

      Total         97,000        103,000         94,000
```

Figure 12.6 Analysis Report – Sales by Product Category

The reports shown are just two of the analysis reports that might be produced from an order processing system. *Figure 12.7* lists other analysis reports that might be produced, which is not to say that all of them should be produced – there is a problem of having more information than can be usefully used. A similar long list of possible reports could be given for most other categories of IS.

Order Processing Analysis Reports – Examples

- Sales by month for current year.
- Sales this month by sales area.
- Sales this month by product category.
- Number of orders by month for current year.
- Value of orders by month for current year.
- Age of credit (unpaid invoices) analysis.
- Credit outstanding per month for current year.
- Value of stock by product category.
- Stock turn.
- Stock availability.
- Number of orders on backorder, by month, for current year.
- etc.

Figure 12.7 Example Analysis Report Titles for Order Processing

12.5 Other Report Types

As well as, or in place of, analysis reports we may use other types of report to highlight aspects of the available information. Additional report types include:

◆ **Exception Reports**

Often in examining management information we are looking for problem areas that require attention. As we have seen above, with an analysis report, we can search through and find exceptions, but it could be more helpful if the system identified the exceptions for us, which is what the exception report is designed to do.

We could have an exception version of the sales analysis report. Such a report would give details of any area where sales fell by a given percentage or failed to meet target. This might not be the best approach – better to get the whole picture. If however we had 500 shops or 2,000 sales people an exception report might be more helpful (it could give the top 10, an average figure and those who failed to meet the target (thus putting the exceptions in a general context).

A more common and useful example of an exception report would be that of invoices not paid after a given period. Note that for this (and for many other reports) the order is important. If the report is given in customer number order then the consistent bad payers are highlighted. An example is given at *figure 12.8* – note that Mike's Meat seems to be a problem whereas, possibly, Fred's Fish just needs a gentle reminder.

```
Unpaid Invoice Report                    03 Apr 03
(Invoices unpaid after 60 days)            (IR03)

Customer       164923        Mike's Meat Ltd
                                          Rem.    Part
   Inv No.    Date         Total          No      Paid
   6023465    15.10.02       7,026.00     4        Y
   6133492    16.11.02      13,974.00     3        N
   6246555    14.12.02      18,127.00     2        N
   6319845    15.01.03      11,849.00     1        N

Customer       170029        Fred's Fish
                                          Rem.    Part
   Inv No.    Date         Total          No      Paid
   6137426    19.12.02       7,623.00     2        N
```

Figure 12.8 Exception Report – Unpaid Invoices

To produce an exception report we must first set parameters to define what an exception is. This can be a problem area. There is no point in setting an exception level that reports virtually every case, e.g. 60 days would be inappropriate if the average time to pay an invoice is 90 days. It is also necessary to update exceptions periodically: for instance, expecting a increase of sales of 5% when inflation is 2% is very different from the same target with inflation at 7%.

Exception reports are more likely to be applicable at the tactical and operational levels of the hierarchy.

◆ **Key Target Reports**

Another approach is to set 'key targets' and to then have a brief report that monitors performance against those key targets.

For this approach the key targets should be limited in number, carefully selected and achievable. *Figure 12.9* shows a key target report for a warehouse. The five targets chosen are:

- Stock turn – the number of times that the (average) stock item is sold in the year – the target is 12.
- Stock availability – the proportion of orders that can be met using stock that is in the warehouse – the target is 98%.
- Orders processed day 1 – the proportion of orders that are processed on the day they arrive – the target is 98%.
- Backorder time – the time it takes to get stock and process the order where the stock was not initially available – the target is 2 days.
- Write-offs – the proportion of stock that gets lost, damaged or too old to sell – the target is 2%.

```
Key Target Report - March 2003                   03 Apr 03
SW Warehouse                                        (IR04)

                          Target         Actual

   Stock Turn:            12.00          10.31

   Stock Availability:    98.00%         99.25%

   Orders proc day 1:     98.00%         83.96%

   Backorder Time:        2 days         3 days

   Write-offs:            2.00%          3.46%
```

Figure 12.9 Key Target Report

The report shows a reasonable performance. The stock turn is down but availability is above target, which suggests that stock levels could be reduced a bit – and that might also help on write-offs. The throughput of orders on day one is well below target (but not disastrous). This needs looking at. Is it just a temporary problem caused by high demand or staff absences or is there a need to strengthen the order processing area?

Target setting has, over recent years, become popular in the public sector – targets are set for trains on time, students passing exams, etc. All of these require a key target report to show performance against the target. In many cases the target is political and unlikely to be met. In some cases the data to make the measure is not readily available and resources are diverted from achieving the target to collecting data to monitor the target. (In the case of our order processing example, all the data to monitor the target should be available from the order processing system – the only additional item of data required is recording the date the order was received.)

Key target reports would usually be aimed at the strategic and tactical management levels.

◆ **Ad-hoc Reports**

As well as formal reports that might be produced on a regular basis there will also be occasions when other information is required. These could be for almost any reason, possibly there is a proposal for a new sales campaign and information is required that is not available from regular analysis.

The problem with ad-hoc reports is that they can take a time to prepare to test and possibly to run (if there is a large database that is not optimised for the intended enquiry). The preparation time can be considerably reduced by the use of a fourth generation language / report generator where the report is specified by parameters rather than being programmed in the traditional way. Some report generators are used by users, thus relieving the IT department of the task. A further problem is testing the ad-hoc report to ensure that the results obtained are correct (and there are examples of important management decisions taken on the basis of incorrect information from ad-hoc reports). One useful 'trick' is to make the ad-hoc report produce control totals that cross-check with a tried and tested, regular report.

An example of an ad-hoc report I remember being involved in was at Volvo. There had been a hit and run accident and the police had got a speck of paint, analysed it and determined it was from a Volvo of a certain model and date range. Our problem was to find the registration numbers and owner details of cars that met that specification. Three of us came in overnight, took over the mainframe when scheduled processing finished, wrote a program and had a list of cars ready for the police before the office opened next morning.

◆ **Data Enquiries**

The final type of report is the data enquiry. All systems need to give the facility to look up each element of standing data and any transaction. For an order processing system, just for the customer order side of the system, we will need enquiries for: customer, product, order and invoice. The enquiries will be by key: order reference, etc., but may also include alternative search keys for cases where the key is not known, e.g. all orders for a specified customer.

This is very much an operational level enquiry / report. It is simple enough but vital for the everyday operation of the system.

12.6 Graphical Presentation

The example reports given thus far have a simple layout using a Courier typeface – the sort of layout that has usually been available from larger machines using bulk printing facilities.

This type of report layout can be improved using ink jet or laser printers – the sort of printers that are typically used with PCs but can also be available for bulk printing. The utility and credit card companies use such facilities to produce the bills that they send out to their customers.

Modern printing facilities can also be used to present reports in a graphical form. The sales analysis report presented in *figure 12.5* would show the trends more clearly if each region's sales were shown as lines on a graph: see *figure 12.10* (although there is a limit to the number of regions that can reasonably be presented on one page).

One problem with graphs is the temptation to analyse everything, even when it does not provide any useful information. Pie charts seem to be a favourite for presenting useless information. We could have a pie chart showing the proportion of the sales total achieved by each region – it could look pretty but it seems unlikely to inform any management decisions.

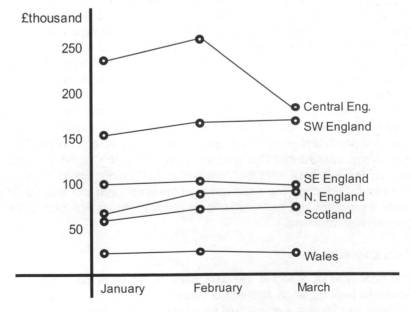

Figure 12.10 Analysis Report – Sales by Region

12.7 MIS, EIS, DSS and Data Mining

As already outlined, most of the data for management information is going to come from the organisation's transaction processing systems. This data can be analysed as a sub-system of the main transaction processing system or it can be fed across, possibly in a summarised form, into a specialist management reporting system. These specialist systems are variously classified as:

- ◆ Management information system (MIS):
  Originally a specialist system for analysing business data and producing reports for the management of the organisation. The plane makers Lockheed were one of the pioneers in this field. Nowadays usage of the term can be much broader / less well defined. In the US the term MIS is generally taken to refer to any business computer application and it will very probably include transaction processing as well as management information facilities.

- ◆ Executive information system (EIS):
  A system designed to provide analysis and reports used by top managers. The system normally has its own database that holds data extracted from the company's business information systems and possibly outside sources (such as stock market data). The system will have ad-hoc reporting facilities which allow executives to specify their own analysis using point and click technology. The system will also include facilities to produce analysis in graphical format for inclusion in management presentations.

- ◆ Decision support system (DSS):
  Similar to an EIS but designed to support decision making. The system will have its own database and be able to analyse past and current performance but will also have tools to test out the effect of policy decisions. The sort of question that may be asked is a 'what if': What if we invest in a new factory with predicted effects on sales? What will be the effects on cash flow? This is a more complex tool than the EIS and possibly used by the executive's research / support staff rather than the executive in person.

An opposite approach to abstracting data to a specialist MIS is to store all available data on a specialist data warehouse system. These systems are used by organisations with large volumes of transactions – multiple retailers are a typical user and the UHS case study in *Part I* included the use of a data warehouse. Using the data warehouse the retailers are able to record every sales transaction and associate those transactions with specific customers where a store card has been used. The data warehouse can then be used to analyse customer shopping habits and inform the design of the shop layout or a promotional campaign.

The special quality of the data warehouse is the ability to traverse / analyse large volumes of data at high speed – a process known as data mining. The analysis performed using the data warehouse could take place on the database of the main IS but as neither the equipment, nor the data, is optimised for analysis and retrieval, it would take too long (and disrupt the processing of standard business transactions).

12.8 Information and Operations

Business information systems can spawn vast quantities of information and this information is readily supplemented from sources outside the organisation, using both old and new media sources. Frequently there is more information than people can cope with and often it is removed from the context that would make it meaningful. Information is seen as 'power' and as a 'precious resource' but, as with anything, we can have too much of a good thing – we use the term 'information overload' (but that is only one aspect of the problem).

The emphasis on information and its power to shape and take forward an organisation can be overdone. The basic function of any organisation is the delivery of the product or service – that is what the customer or sponsor pays for. Appropriate information is vital to the efficiency and appropriateness of the operation of the organisation but it is not an end in itself.

Organisations put a lot of effort into streamlining their operations but there is an equal need for economy in the use of 'information workers' in the management levels and support functions. An often quoted example is the level of measurement, recording and reporting that is expected of school teachers which does nothing to enhance, and can detract from, the education delivered to the pupils. Similar examples exist in many organisations but they are usually not reported (it is the management jobs that are created by the task of assessing and discussing management information – managers are not about to deliberately put themselves out of a job). A recent report on the relative decline of British Airways (BA) (Clark, 2002) reports that:

> BA's reaction to every crisis is to drop a few more planes and routes. But it is a top heavy company with a rather overblown HQ.

It is for these reasons that this book looks at business systems as primarily operational systems and secondly as management information systems.

Exercises

The following exercises are proposed to reinforce the material in this chapter. Each of them can lead to a tutorial discussion.

1. Many readers of this book will have recently joined a college or university. To gain a place you will have filled in an application form that was then assessed by the admissions tutor. Let us assume that we are looking at a course in a prestigious university. It has an equal opportunities admissions policy, we have three candidates and one place to fill. All three candidates have two As and a B in their GCSE A-level exams and good references from their school. Dipesh went to a well known local public school and has been an active participant in the sports, social and community activities offered at that school. Andrew comes from Liverpool and has been at a comprehensive school in a run down part of town – he does not include many out of school activities in his application. Louise comes from Stratford upon Avon, attended the town's grammar school and is just finishing a 'year out' on a community project in Mexico. Is the decision of

the admissions tutor structured or unstructured? How can he / she fairly decide between these three candidates? Should there be some form of rating system and what factors should be included?

2. The government is greatly exercised by setting targets, monitoring performance against those targets and then finding excuses when the target is not achieved. Further and higher education is not exempt from this process. Areas where targets have been set include recruitment from less privileged backgrounds (by various ethnic and socio-economic categories) and the dropout rates of students after they start their courses (at each stage of the course). Your college or university wants to monitor the achievement of these targets across all its departments. Choose one of these target areas and sketch an analysis, key target and exception report for the requirement (make up some target figures if you need to). Assess the appropriateness of each report to the management information requirement.

3. Look up data warehouses on the web. See what more you can find out about how they work, what they are used for and how AI can be used for information retrieval.

The issue of management information also comes up in one of the assignment topics given at the end of the final chapter of this section.

Further Reading

Management information is also a topic in other introductory IS texts but, I suggest, they do not add a lot to what has already been covered in this chapter. There are more advanced books on management information but they are probably not suitable to the expected readership of this text. Hence there is no recommended further reading – read this chapter carefully, do the exercises and have the rest of the week off!

Chapter 13
From DP to Desk Top

Summary

Systems range in size from single user desk top applications to corporate information systems with hundreds or thousands of users. The software may be bought in or could have been developed specifically for the application. Bought-in applications range in size (and price) from the ubiquitous Microsoft package to large enterprise resource planning (ERP) systems. This range of systems requires a range of IT provision, starting with the desk top PC and ranging up to the central mainframe or corporate server.

In this chapter we identify four categories of information system provision:

◆   Corporate (strategic) systems.
◆   Functional support systems.
◆   End user systems.
◆   Office support systems.

Each of these categories will tend to have a different software and IT provision. All of them will be networked to form the IT infrastructure of the organisation.

13.1   System Types

In this part of the book we have concentrated on business information systems – the corporate systems or, possibly, department systems that are specifically designed for the job that they do and the type of business that the organisation operates. We have looked at the stock control / order processing system but there are many others, for example: banking systems, insurance systems, ticket booking and, closer to home, a student registration / record system. These systems are an essential part of the operation of the enterprise – they can be referred to as corporate and, in some cases, strategic information systems. Features and facilities in this class of system can differentiate the organisation from its competitors and contribute to competitive advantage.

Besides these corporate systems there are further sets of computer applications. These might be classified as:

◆   Functional support systems (for want of a better term): A set of more generic systems that are used by many / all organisations but are not necessarily specific to the type of business the organisation is in. The obvious example of such a system is the payroll but further examples include human resources (HR) systems and accountancy systems. These can be seen as departmental systems as opposed to corporate systems. Many of them will have interfaces with corporate information systems – this is particularly true of the accountancy systems. They are vital to the efficient running of the organisation but, of themselves, do not usually contribute to the competitive advantage / distinctiveness of the organisation – they are not strategic information systems.

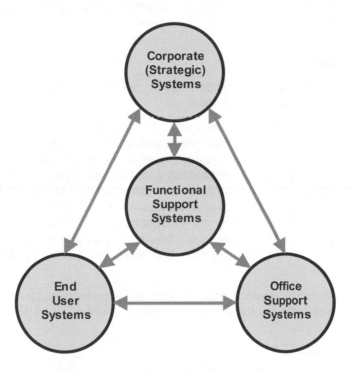

Figure 13.1 Information System Types

◆ End user systems: Small systems developed by the user or bought in for departmental use. EIS and DSS systems, with their user report writing interfaces, may fit into this slot. Also in this category are the small, user written, database applications that are used for a number of minor tasks. Some of these systems, particularly the EIS and DSS, will interface with corporate and functional information systems.

◆ Office support systems: This is the PC on the desk top used for word processing, spreadsheets and through the network for e-Mail and intranet / Internet access. The software used is not specific to the organisation and its use fits, broadly, into general office procedures such as writing letters, producing reports, calculating budgets and communicating with colleagues (sometimes for work related purposes!). This use of computers is very different from the application specific, shared use of computing represented by strategic information systems and functional support systems. That said, sometimes the use of desk top applications becomes quite sophisticated and their use starts to overlap with other categories of IS usage.

These four categories of information systems, and the interfaces between them, are shown in *figure 13.1*. This generalised diagram ties back to the variety of systems and plethora of interfaces that we identified in the UHS case study: see *Chapter 7*. This diagram could also have been drawn as a Venn diagram – this would have indicated that these are overlapping categories but it would not have shown the interfaces.

13.2 Sourcing Software

Software can be bought in or written specifically for the organisation. Bought-in software can be categorised as follows:

◆ Desk top productivity packages: This category includes the word processor, spreadsheet, mail client and Internet browser. The market is dominated by Microsoft. Arguably this is an inappropriate monopoly but it does have the advantage of creating a de facto standard that facilitates the interchange of data files. There are alternative suppliers and these are generally cheaper – they have a very small market share as organisations are reluctant to break from the Microsoft norm. Some of the alternative suppliers come in the shareware / free software category – an interesting development in an industry that has been dominated by the large IT corporations.

◆ Shrink wrapped applications: These are application specific but not company specific packages. Two of the most widely used such packages are:

  ◆ Sage Accounting systems.
  ◆ Peterborough Payroll systems.

These types of package are available from other suppliers, for other applications and for both PC and server systems. Also in this category are:

  ◆ EIS and DSS systems. These packages include database software, information retrieval and report formatting facilities. They are set up with data from the organisation's functional support and corporate systems.
  ◆ Application packages: There are a large range of industry specific packages available covering requirements ranging from hotel management to the doctor's surgery.

These packages provide a fair degree of customisation but, ultimately, users have to fit their business into the provision of the package.

◆ Enterprise resource planning (ERP) systems: These are a much more ambitious approach to bought-in software and the intention is to provide an integrated set of applications that run all the major functions of the organisation. The concept, as expressed by Bocij *et al.* (1999 – with minor modifications by this author), is:

> A software system with integrated functions for all major business functions across an organisation such as production, distribution, sales, finance and human resources management. It is normally purchased as an off-the-shelf package that is tailored by a consultant. A single ERP package typically replaces many different previous systems.

For a manufacturing organisation the ERP can include:

- ◆ Order Processing.
- ◆ Materials Management.
- ◆ Production Planning.
- ◆ Sales and Marketing.
- ◆ Logistics.

and accounting and human resources software can also be included in the overall system.

ERP systems have some of the disadvantages of all bought-in software – the organisation has to fit the package (although ERP systems can be modified and added to by the customer organisation). The claim is that ERP packages incorporate 'best practice' and hence fitting in with their way of working has the benefit of updating the organisation's procedures. ERP systems are not shrink-wrapped software. They are expensive and installing ERP is a major project – not all ERP projects go smoothly.

The major supplier of ERP systems is the German company SAP (which now vies with Oracle for distinction of being the world's second largest software company (after Microsoft)). Other suppliers of ERP systems are J. D. Edwards, Peoplesoft and Oracle (who have built applications on top of their database product).

Other, more industry specific packages can match ERP for size, complexity and cost but would not generally be called ERP. Examples are integrated banking and supermarket systems – the Worldwide Chain Store package is an example of a package implemented by a number of supermarkets.

These categories of bought-in software map fairly well onto the IS type diagram of *figure 13.1*. The desk top productivity packages are the main resource of the office support systems and the ERP matches the requirement for corporate systems. The third category of shrink-wrapped applications can meet the requirements of many functional support and end user systems.

The main alternative to package software is to write your own (or get a software house to write it for you). Traditionally, medium / large organisations had their own IT departments and when a business system was required they would design and develop it. Such an approach was time consuming, costly and often the system that was produced did not live up to expectations. Also, in many cases, the software being developed served the same function as packages developed by tens or hundreds of other organisations – hence the opportunity for generic software products.

All that said, people still do develop software. Two areas where in-house developed software is still applicable are:

◆ Small systems: In many cases a requirement can be met by a PC based IS 'knocked up' using an application generator / database package such as MS Access. For someone familiar with Access this can be done relatively quickly and easily and the process is under the control of the user / developer. It could be that there is packaged software that would do the job but often it is more trouble to check the market than to write your own. One area where such packages are used is university departments where (in many cases) each department has its own package to keep track of student progress (possibly if universities has better central IS provision that would not be necessary).

◆ Strategic systems: Large organisations may well have special require-ments or wish to do something rather different from their competitors (in the hope of gaining some sort of competitive advantage). In these circumstances the organisation may need to write its own software.

We should also recognise that large systems are typically a network of sub-systems developed, modified and added to over many years. Maintaining and enhancing these legacy systems is still a job for the in-house software development team. (Why do we call these facilities 'legacy systems'? Very often they are the main business systems of organisations. They may be old but they do the job – very possibly better than any of the alternatives that might be deployed to replace them.)

The final alternative to packages or writing your own application is to 'borrow' one (and I am not suggesting software piracy). One area where such an arrangement is commonplace is payroll. Many organisations have their payroll run by specialist bureau services. The organisation provides staff and salary data and the bureau runs the software. With this arrangement, most of the hassle associated with running a payroll is outsourced to the bureau – there is no competitive advantage to the organisation in running its own payroll. A new concept in 'borrowing' software is the business application Internet service provider (ISP). The idea here is that the ISP has specialist business software and its customers access its facilities on a pay-as-you-go basis via the Internet. Sounds OK but the success of the model is in doubt. Experience seems to suggest that there is not much point in using the model for cheap packages (you can buy your own) and for expensive packages the support costs are likely to be too high. A number of business application ISPs have started up but some of them have not lasted very long.

13.3 IT Infrastructure

In addition to the requirement and the software we need the IT infrastructure. We start with the desk top (or factory floor) PC. The PC, linked to a network, serves several purposes:

◆ Desk top productivity – running word processing, spreadsheets and the like.

◆ IS platform – running free standing IS applications – for an individual or a small office where several users share the one dedicated PC (they may well have their own PCs for other functions).

◆ Communications – linked to the network the PC is used for e-Mail and Internet access.

◆ Client – the PC can be the client part of a client–server system (part of the IS runs on the desk top and other functionality and data storage are on a shared server system).

◆ Terminal – the PC can be a terminal to a remote IS running on a central server / mainframe system.

◆ Development system – the PC can be used for the development of software, to run on the PC or on another platform.

The network links the desk top to server systems. The server system can be just another PC or it may be a much bigger box. There can be servers in the branches or departments that are in turn linked to central server and / or mainframe systems. The server system can have one or more functions:

◆ IT facilities – a print or file server.

◆ Communications – as an e-Mail and / or Internet server.

◆ Client–server systems – as the server component.

◆ TP system – a central system accessible from the desk top.

For client server and TP systems the central (server) platform is likely to have batch functions that are not directly accessible from the desk top. The components of the IT infrastructure are dealt with in more detail in *Part IV*.

13.4 Outsourcing

The traditional way of providing IS and IT for an organisation is to have an IT department. The organisation buys the IT equipment, writes rents or buys the software and the IT department manages and maintains that IT infrastructure. Ways of working change and organisations are sub-contracting / buying in many of the provisions and services that used to be provided in-house. Reasons for outsourcing can include:

◆ Management can concentrate on the core business.

◆ Contractual clarity with the outsourcing company.

◆ Expertise from a specialist provider.

◆ Reduced cost and reduced capital investment.

But there are also problems in contracting out such a vital part of the firm's infrastructure (it is a bit more complex than office cleaning or food preparation in the staff canteen).

Outsourcing can cover the whole IS / IT provision or separate aspects of it such as desk top support. Some organisations that have outsourced IS / IT provision have, at the end of the contract, taken the function back in-house. It can be difficult to re-establish an IT capability after it has been disbanded (or sold off).

13.5 The Complete Picture

We can now put these aspects of the IS / IT provision together to give a generalised picture of the IT infrastructure. We now have:

◆ Office support systems – running on the desk top and using general purpose desk top software.
◆ End user and functional support systems – on departmental servers using shrink-wrapped packages or in-house database applications.
◆ Corporate (strategic) systems – legacy or ERP systems running on main-frame or central server systems.
◆ A mixture of in-house and outsourced provision.

The full structure is most applicable to larger organisations. Smaller organisations may have more of a two-tier structure (desk top and functional support).

The whole structure will be networked. The desk top uses the network to access corporate, functional support and end-user systems. Data from the corporate systems is used to feed functional support and end user systems (and there can be other interfaces as shown in *figure 13.1*). The organisation is also networked outside to customers, suppliers and to other sources of information and authority. The overall infrastructure is shown in *figure 13.2*; note this is a generalised picture and the specifics will vary in individual organisations.

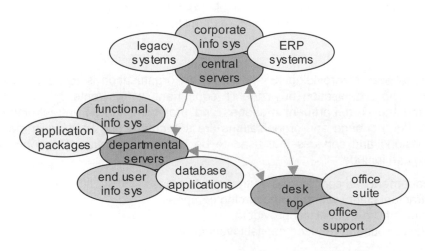

Figure 13.2 The Corporate IS / IT Architecture

Exercises

The purpose of this chapter is to put the topics covered in *Part III* in context and to provide a starting point for *Part IV*. The requirement is that you read the chapter. There is only a single exercise (see below) and no recommended further reading.

1. List advantages and disadvantages of purchasing packaged software as opposed to house development. Suggest circumstances where packaged software would be advised and where a bespoke, in-house development might be more appropriate.

Assignments

The exercises presented at the end of each chapter are designed to reinforce the students' knowledge and understanding of the topics presented. Assignments require further research; assignment topics for *Part III* are:

1. At my university (and many others) we take registers for each class and tutorial. The attendance information is then collated and the course leader / year tutor chases up students who seem to be lacking in application. The year tutor / course leader will also keep the head of department informed on the overall progress of the cohort. Let us assume all the attendance figures and assignment marks, for each student and all modules, are on a database:

   - Suggest information / reporting requirements for the course leader. Outline the type of report that would be most appropriate to each of these functions and suggest how frequently that information should be produced.
   - Sketch a report layout of the report you are recommending for the year tutor / course leader.

2. Many organisations have outsourced all or part of their IS / IT function. Investigate IT outsourcing and write an academic essay on the topic. The essay should include discussion of the functions (or combination of functions) that might be outsourced, contractual issues, the advantages and the disadvantages of outsourcing to the organisation and examples of organisations that have outsourced IS / IT. The recommended length is 2,000 words – full referencing is required.

Part IV
Information Technology

Having looked at the information systems that organisations use, we will now take a look at the information technology that those systems run on.

In the study of IS, or if we are going to be a systems analyst, we need to be aware of what IT is available and what it will do to support and facilitate our IS. We do not necessarily need to know how it works and it is not part of the study of IS to know how to build or repair IT equipment.

The first aspect of IT we will look at is computer equipment – the 'box'. These range from the standard PC, costing a few hundred pounds, up to supercomputers, costing several million pounds. Each information system needs an appropriate processor, or processors, to run on.

As well as the processor the information system will need to store its data, normally on a fixed disk drive. We need to be aware of the types of equipment that are available and how the data can be organised. Appropriate structuring of the data is vital for large systems. Normally a database management system will be used to manage storage and retrieval of data in a business IS. Disk drives are slow in comparison with processor speeds and it is vital we get the data structures right if the system is to produce the necessary performance.

Finally, we will very probably make use of a network. The system may be linked to other information systems and will also be networked to its users: in their workplace, at home, or possibly while they are on the move. Networked systems use techniques such as transaction processing, client server and distributed systems; these architectures have to be understood when the IS is designed. Networked computing is used by organisations but is also available to the general public using the Internet.

Chapter 14
Computer Systems

Summary

We start our study of information technology with the computer system. The sort of computer we normally see is a personal computer (PC). The personal computer runs desk top productivity packages like word processing and spreadsheets. For the business user it can also run small applications and for the home user it may also be used for games.

The PC is only one category from the range of computers that can be utilised. In this chapter we will examine the spectrum of available computer systems and give some pointers as to what sort of systems might be required for which type of business information system. The computer systems we look at are:

- ◆ Personal computers – desk top machines used for personal productivity applications, small business systems and to access networked systems and services.
- ◆ Network servers – back office machines used for file storage, e-Mail and Internet services.
- ◆ Enterprise servers – used for larger, multi-user (corporate) information systems.
- ◆ Supercomputers – very powerful computers used for large mathematical and modelling problems.

We also briefly review the peripheral / ancillary equipment that might be incorporated into, or linked to, the computer system.

The chapter starts with a look at the way that the computer works. It is a very brief look, just enough to dispel some of the mystery and possibly give some idea why some processes work well on computers and others can be more problematic or time consuming.

14.1 The Processor

A computer system consists of the processor and a number of peripherals such as disk drives, printers and the control console. On a PC, many of these elements are integrated into the same box / package as the processor whereas on bigger systems they are likely to be separate units. We start with the processor.

Processors come in all shapes and sizes and over the years the technologies used to construct the system have changed dramatically. That said, the basic principles by which a modern computer operates are much the same as the first computers that were built about 60 years ago. The four essential elements of a processor are:

◆ Memory: the computer system has a memory where the program is stored together with any data that is used while the program is operating.
◆ Decode unit: logic circuits that take an instruction from the program, decode it and switch in the function of the arithmetic unit required for the execution of that program instruction.
◆ Arithmetic unit: the logic circuits that perform the program instructions: add, subtract, etc. The arithmetic unit will have one or more registers that store the data items that are currently being worked upon.
◆ Interfaces: slots where the control console, storage devices, printers and the network are connected.

The configuration of these elements is shown in *figure 14.1*.

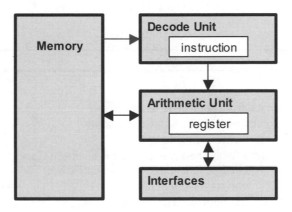

Figure 14.1 The Processor

The computer system is a digital computer; program instructions and the data are represented in binary format (some early scientific computers were analogue but this technology is no longer used). Binary numbers work to the base of two (as opposed to decimal numbers that work with the base of 10). *Figure 14.2* shows some example binary numbers and their decimal equivalents. Take the number 102 as an example. In decimal it is 1x100 + 0x10 + 2x1, and in binary it is 1x64 + 1x32 + 0x16 + 0x8 + 1x4 + 1x2 + 0x1 giving 1100110 as its binary representation.

If we want to add two numbers together, e.g. C = A + B, this could (depending on the machine code of the computer system) require three simple machine instructions:

1. load A into the register,
2. add B to the register,
3. store the register contents in C.

decimal	binary	decimal	binary
0	0	8	1000
1	1	12	1100
2	10	16	10000
3	11	32	100000
4	100	64	1000000
5	101	102	1100110

Figure 14.2 Binary Numbers

These instructions, together with the data, are held in binary format in memory – each instruction or data item is held in a separate word in memory (some machines use bytes and an instruction or data item is held in one or more bytes). The position is represented in *figure 14.3*.

address	instruction	use
1	00001 0001010	load from A
2	00010 0001011	add from B
3	10010 0001100	store in C
	data	
10	0000 0000 0100	A
11	0000 0001 0101	B
12	0000 0001 1001	C

Assume:
- Words in memory contain 12 binary bits.
- The program instructions are in data stores 1 to 3.
- The data is in data stores 10 to 12.
- The program instruction has a five bit instruction and a seven bit address. The instructions used in this example are:
  - 00001 load data store to register.
  - 00010 add data store to register.
  - 10010 move register to data store.

Figure 14.3 Example Machine Code Instructions

The decode unit and the arithmetic unit use a complex array of electronic logic gates to perform their function. The logic capability of each gate is very simple: for example an OR gate with two inputs will output:

◆ zero   if both inputs are zero.
◆ one   if one, or both, input is a one.

The truth table for an OR gate and an AND gate are shown in *figure 14.4*. *Figure 14.5* shows the truth table for adding two binary digits together (the half adder); note that the truth table for the carry matches that of the AND gate.

OR Gate Table		
A	**B**	**C**
0	0	0
0	1	1
1	0	1
1	1	1

AND Gate Table		
A	**B**	**C**
0	0	0
0	1	0
1	0	0
1	1	1

Figure 14.4 OR and AND Gate Truth Tables

A	B	Sum	Carry
0	0	0	0
0	1	1	0
1	0	1	0
1	1	0	1

Figure 14.5 Half Adder Truth Table

The half adder can be designed using six logic gates: see *figure 14.5* for the truth table and *figure 14.6* for the circuit.

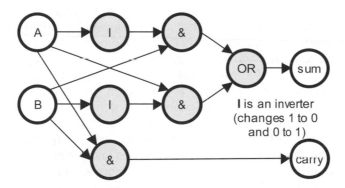

Figure 14.6 Half Adder Logic Circuit Diagram

The half adder adds two binary digits together and is the basic building block of a simple arithmetic unit. To add two binary numbers we must process each pair of binary digits and add in any carry from the previous stage of the addition process (as we do when adding two decimal numbers together). These requirements are met by:

◆ Feeding the two binary numbers from the registers into the adder (these are shift registers and the next bit is sent when the register is triggered by a clock pulse). The sum is also sent to a register.

◆ Using a second half adder to add in any carry (from the previous 'column' of the addition) to the sum of this addition. The carries from the two half adders are then put through an OR gate and output as the carry for the next 'column'.

The two half adders, thus linked together, are called a full adder. Building a functioning computer is obviously more complex than this but this illustrates the basic building blocks.

This subsection is no more than a very brief introduction to what a computer system is. Arguably it is more information than you need for the study of IS (but I think it is important to have some idea how the machines that we use function). Possibly your course of study will include other units where the design of computer systems, and the associated technologies, are studied in detail.

14.2 The Development of the Computer

The first electronic computers were produced in the 1940s. These were valve machines: each valve served the function of a logic gate (the valve looked rather like a domestic light bulb but was about half the size). These first machines were large and slow by modern day standards. That said, once the technology had settled down, they performed well on the tasks required of them. These machines did not have operating systems and middle-ware programs and so all their computing power was available for the task in hand.

Following on from the valve machine came the transistor, the integrated circuit and now the microchip. Each of these developments made computer systems cheaper, smaller, more reliable and that in turn allowed the development of more powerful computers. The transistor was the replacement for an electronic valve. It served the same logic function but it was the size of a small, capsule-shaped pill as opposed to a small domestic light bulb. Subsequently the transistor was replaced by integrated circuits. Initially an integrated circuit had several 'transistor equivalents' placed on a chip of semi-conductor material and later this evolved into the microchip where a whole processor, or a section of memory, could be fabricated on a wafer of silicon. These changes of technology can be represented on a time-line with the valve machines forming the first generation; transistors the second and integrated circuits the third. Some authors would also show the use of the micro-chip as a fourth generation. Further details of this evolution and its implications have been given in *Chapter 3*.

Despite the changes in technology, the basic principles of the operation of the electronic computer have not changed since their genesis in the 1940s. The technology is being refined all the time but the last generational change in technology was well over 20 years ago. The types of machines and their availability have, however, changed radically.

14.3 Classification of Computer Systems

The early computers were large, expensive, required a controlled environment and were only used by government departments and large companies. From these early machines evolved a number of categories that can be summarised as:

◆ The mainframe:
These machines are the direct descendent of the first and second generation machines. They were large, expensive and formed the central computing facility of a company. The term mainframe is no longer in vogue

but some systems still require large, central computing facilities and, whatever we call it, something similar to the mainframe still lives on.

◆ The mini:
The advent of the transistor and the integrated circuit meant that a computer did not have to be so large or expensive. These developments led to specialist machines for scientific tasks and for process control. From these machines evolved the mini computer. It was like a small mainframe but it could be afforded by smaller organisations or it might be installed in a department of a large organisation. It could also operate in a normal office environment.

◆ The micro computer (or PC):
The next step on was the processor on a chip, which gave rise to the micro computer, or the PC as we generally know it. The PC is what its initials suggest: a personal computer (as opposed to a shared computer). The PC (and I include the Apple in this category) is now on the desk top, on the factory floor, in schools and colleges and at home. Normally the PC is linked through some sort of network to a server, and that machine may well be something bigger than just a PC.

◆ The supercomputer:
As computers got smaller they also got bigger in terms of processor power. The biggest computers became known as supercomputers and were designed to solve large modelling and simulation problems, the sort of problem that could not have been tackled before the advent of the supercomputer. The Cray range of machines perhaps typifies the supercomputer but there are a number of other companies out there competing for this type of business.

◆ Servers:
As networks grew the central computing facilities became less of the property of the IS / IT department and more of a corporate resource – accessible from the desk top and the factory floor, using a networked PC. In this context, and with the incorporation of PC technology into larger machines, the distinction between mini computers and mainframe computers has started to evaporate (and mainframes became associated with high costs so the mainframe vendors have wished to move away from the term). Arguably all central computers are now just servers, but there is a distinction between the server that is just a PC box providing e-Mail and additional file space and a large machine, costing hundreds of thousands of pounds, and running complex information systems for tens or hundreds of users. We will call the former a network server and the latter an enterprise server.

The evolution of these categories of computer systems is summarised in *figure 14.7*.

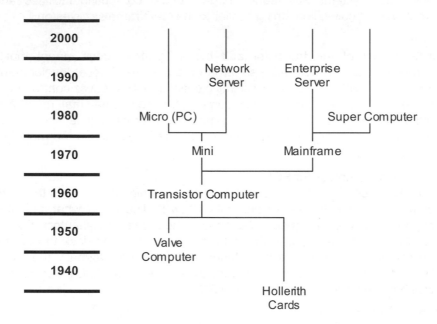

Figure 14.7 Computer Generations – Computer Systems

14.4 Supercomputers

Supercomputers are very powerful computers that can perform a vast number of mathematical calculations at very high speed. A leading manufacturer of supercomputers, and a firm that once dominated the supercomputer market is Cray. The definition given on their web site is:

> A supercomputer is defined simply as the most powerful class of computers at any point in time. Supercomputers are used to solve large and complex problems that would be insurmountable by smaller, less powerful computers. Since the pioneering Cray-1® system arrived in 1976, supercomputers have contributed enormously to the advancement of knowledge and the quality of human life. Problems of major economic, scientific and strategic importance are typically addressed by supercomputers years before they become tractable on less capable systems.

Supercomputers are used for a special class of problem that requires a great deal of processing power. Their speed is typically measured in megaflops, that is millions of floating point operations per second. These systems are not appropriate to the type of commercial payroll or order processing system that was discussed in the previous section. Most of the processing time in commercial systems is spent reading and writing records onto a database; that is not what supercomputers are about.

The supercomputers can be broadly classified as vector processors or array processors. The vector processor gains its processing speed by performing multiple calculations on vectors (one-dimensional arrays) simultaneously. The array processor, on the other hand, passes elements of the array to separate arithmetic units, each of which then executes the same set of instructions. The effect of each approach is much the same. Both systems are only of advantage where the problem involves large arrays of data, such as is the case in large modelling or simulation exercises.

One of the many applications of supercomputers is weather forecasting. All the meteorological offices round the world are linked together in an electronic network and they exchange their weather readings (using an EDI-like system). These weather readings can then be loaded into a three-dimensional model of readings across the world and up through the atmosphere – the world and the atmosphere are divided into a grid. The climatic conditions in areas for which there is no weather reading can be interpolated from the readings in the surrounding squares and the readings can be rolled forward a step at a time, say in 10 minute intervals, to predict what the weather will be a day, a week or a month ahead. The accuracy of the forecast depends on the availability of readings and the veracity of the model. It is also dependent on having a fine grid and a short interval. Both these factors increase the processing requirements and hence the need for the supercomputer.

Other applications that supercomputers have been used for are:

♦ Oil and gas prospecting where known geological data is used to create a model and hence predict the location of new deposits.
♦ Numeric wind tunnels where aircraft or car designs can be 'tested' with more precision and less expense than a 'real' wind tunnel.
♦ Sequencing the genome.
♦ Military applications including battlefield simulation (possibly not all applications are as beneficial to humankind as the Cray web site suggests, but that depends on your point of view).

The world's largest supercomputer, as this book is being written, is the Earth Simulator. The motivation for this project came from the 1995 Kobe earthquake. The plan is ambitious – to simulate the earth. The model includes the atmosphere, the ocean and the ground – each divided into a vast number of cells. The computer is then used to calculate how changes in one cell (could) affect other cells and hence predict future environmental events such as earthquakes (Mathews 2003). This computer uses kit from the Japanese NEC company and is located in Japan. The system has 640 nodes each with 8 vector processors – a total of 5120 processors. Each processor has a peak performance of 8 gigaflops (thousand million floating point instructions per second) and the overall system has a maximum performance of 40 teraflops (trillion (10^{12}) floating point instructions per second). Figures of that order are rather incomprehensible to most of us but let us just say, it's fast.

Cray and NEC are the largest specialist suppliers of supercomputers. Other large supercomputers are made up of large arrays of standard boxes. ASCI White in the US uses 8,192 IBM RS6000 processors to deliver 12.3 teraflops and the Tera Supercomputer in Europe uses 2,560 Compaq Alpha processors to deliver a 5 teraflop performance.

My own department at Manchester Metropolitan University has recently installed its own supercomputing facility. The instillation consists of a four-processor NEC SX/5 and a single processor SX/6. Both are based on vector processors capable of performing up to 256 numerical calculations simultaneously. The SX/5 can deliver 19,220 megaflops and the SX6 7,575 megaflops.

The primary user of the instillation is the Centre for Mathematical Modelling and Flow Analysis (CMMFA). CMMFA specialise in hydroinformatics and computational simulation software for industrial blastwave hazard analysis. One of its projects, in the area or hydroinformatics, is concerned with analysis of violent overtopping of waves at seawalls, events that can lead to extreme hazards to users of road and rail links that run along seawalls. CMMFA is developing mathematical models to simulate these events. These models, using Navier-Stokes equations, cannot be solved analytically and computational techniques must be used. Using the NEC machines for their simulation work, a job that took 48 hours on a Intel P4 can be run in 9 hours on the SX/6 and 3 hours 40 minutes on the SX5.

14.5 Mainframe / Enterprise Server

The mainframe / enterprise server is a large computer running business applications that are accessed by large numbers of staff spread throughout (and possibly outside) the organisation. An example of such an application is the order processing system discussed in *Part III*.

Traditionally large computer systems came from proprietary manufacturers such as IBM (or ICL in the UK). These machines were expensive and had their own architectures and operating systems – hence it was difficult to switch suppliers as the software would need to be converted or re-written. IBM was the predominant supplier of mainframes but its architecture (or at least the machine code interface) was copied by clone manufacturers such as Amdahl and Hitachi. In order to escape reliance on one manufacturer and to obtain cheaper kit, a number of organisations downsized some or all of their applications onto UNIX boxes (open systems). These were non-proprietary systems that were more cheaply available but did not necessary have the sophisticated / integrated operating system / middleware infrastructure of the mainframe system. Over the years the size of the machines available as open systems has increased and some of these systems, e.g. the large SUN servers, are now as large as the traditional mainframe. A distinction that possibly remains is that the UNIX system is often used for one application whereas the mainframe will be running a variety of information systems.

Large organisations that still use mainframes include banks, insurance and utility companies (although a few of these have moved to distributed, open architecture, systems). Large organisations that are totally reliant on their IT infrastructure may well have two mainframe centres at opposite ends of the country (or opposite sides of the world). At any time, one of the centres is used to run the system and the second is on 'hot standby'. The standby system matches the first, runs the same system and has its data updated in parallel – should the first system fail (or be knocked out by some more severe event), the second system can take over with, hopefully, no interruption to the service.

As we saw in the UHS case study in *Part I*, organisations may well spread their applications across a variety of platforms. Some may be on a mainframe because of their size but others may be on smaller, networked boxes because they are mainly used by just one department or because the software was available for that particular type of machine.

14.6 Network Server

The network server is typically a smaller machine than the enterprise server and, in many cases, is just a PC that is not a lot different from the desktop clients that are networked to it.

The functions of the network server are largely technical, IT related (as opposed to the IS function of the enterprise server). These functions can include:

- ◆ File space – the network server can have a large amount of disk storage space that is then available to be used by the client machines.
- ◆ Software – applications can be loaded onto the server and then accessed from the client machines. This saves space, maintenance and can reduce software licence costs.
- ◆ Communications – data can be passed through the server from one client system to another. The most obvious such application is e-Mail.
- ◆ Internet access – the end users can access the Internet via the network server. With all users using the same access point it may be possible to afford a higher quality connection and to install a higher standard of data security and firewall protection.
- ◆ Internet server – the network server can also be an Internet server.

There does not have to be a strict distinction between the network server and the enterprise server – some server systems will serve both purposes or, in a large organisation, the desk top will be linked to a local network server which is in turn linked to other departmental and enterprise server systems.

14.7 Personal Computer / Workstation

The personal computer sits on the desk top and is used by one person – hence the term 'personal computer'. The personal computer is typically the PC with a common, IBM / Intel clone architecture but Apple Mac and UNIX workstations are also used in much the same way and for many of the same purposes as the standard PC.

The typical PC comes as a package incorporating not only a processor but also disk storage and the control console (video and monitor). The PC is used at home, in the office, on the factory floor, and can be incorporated in special purpose equipment, e.g. the EPOS terminal.

Arguably the most remarkable thing about the PC is the number of them that are in use. The PC is now standard office equipment and is also in widespread use in the home. The PC is a business computer but also serves as a:

- ◆ Terminal to access business systems running on server systems.
- ◆ Word processor / calculator (using spreadsheets).
- ◆ Communications device for e-Mail systems.
- ◆ Internet access device.
- ◆ Educational tool.
- ◆ Games machine.

I think we can safely assume that all readers of this book have used a PC and many will own their own kit. The readers will be familiar with most usages of a PC but not necessarily its use for business information systems.

14.8 Peripheral Equipment

The computer (processor) system is of little use without additional equipment to input commands, input data, store data and output the results of the processing that takes place. In the PC a number of these functions may be incorporated in the package but on larger systems they may be separate devices. The principal categories of peripheral equipment used with the basic computer system are:

- ◆ Control console – there needs to be a device that facilitates communication with the operating system. On the PC it is the keyboard, video and mouse which are also used for the user interface to application programs. On larger systems there may well be a separate workstation dedicated to the control console function.
- ◆ Data terminal – normally a keyboard, video and mouse. On the PC this is the same kit as is used for control. For larger systems the data input will be from networked terminals or from other systems. Data can also be captured from specialist equipment – the barcode reader is an example of this.
- ◆ Storage – there needs to be a device that stores the system software, application software and data. Typically this will be a fixed disk unit. Many systems will have additional storage devices. These can include:
  - ◆ Additional hard disk units to accommodate large volumes of data.
  - ◆ Exchangeable storage devices that allow the media to be removed and archived or transported. Examples are magnetic tape, CDs and diskettes.
- ◆ Output devices – such as printers and plotters.
- ◆ Network connections – linking to user terminal systems, other business systems and the Internet.

14.9 Choosing the Right Box for the Job

For PC applications and, at the other extreme, supercomputer applications the requirement is normally fairly obvious. The problem is choosing the appropriate infrastructure for medium to large business applications which could use:

- ◆ A central computer system with access from desk top terminals using some sort of transaction processing system.

◆   A distributed system using desk top clients and one or more server systems.

The choice of approach is dependent on both the requirements of the system and the policy of the organisation. It may be that the organisation has an existing IT infrastructure using central enterprise servers and the new requirement can be added without any significant additional IT investment. An alternative scenario is that new investment is required and a client / server system is seen as a cheaper and more flexible approach.

It can be that both the central system and the distributed system / client server approach are viable alternatives. Arguably the principal determinant is the nature of the data. If there is a lot of data that needs to be accessible by all users then there is a strong argument for a central server system – airline booking systems and banks are both examples of this case. If on the other hand much of the function is operated at a division or branch then the client server system may well be a viable alternative,

Exercises

The following exercises are recommended to accompany *Chapter 14*:

1.   For *figure 14.4*, work out the decimal values of A, B and C – check that C is the correct answer.

2.   The college / university PC labs are normally networked to a server system. What facilities do the servers in your PC labs supply?

3.   Most banks are based on a branch network but they hold their account details on mainframe systems. What are the advantages of having account details and processing centralised in this way?

Further Reading

Hopefully this chapter gives sufficient coverage of the range of computer systems that are available to the system designer. Students who wish to follow up on how computer systems are designed and how they function can reference Clements or Stallings (see below).

Clements A. (2000) *The Principles of Computer Hardware*, 3rd. ed., Oxford University Press, Oxford.

Stallings W. (2003) *Computer Organization and Architecture: Designing for performance*, 6th ed., Prentice Hall, Upper Saddle River, NJ.

Chapter 15
Files and Data Structures

Summary

Modern computers, used by individuals and organisations, hold large amounts of data. The data may be in textual form, such as word processed documents and stored e-Mails, or it may be business system data recording business and financial transactions. The data may be owned or used by one individual, accessed by a number of people in the organisation, or be shared with other organisations or the public.

For the data to be usable it has to be organised and structured, and the basic element of that structure is the file. The file is the unit that is recognised by the operating system and is accessed by the program.

The file is composed of a set of records. The file must have a data structure to give efficient access to the record, and the record must have a structure that that is known to any application that is required to use it. For many applications the data structures are crucial to the viability of the system. For a large, multi-user system, get the file data structure wrong and the system will grind to a halt. The three basic ways of organising and accessing data are serially, using an index (index sequential) or calculating the position of the record (hash random). These three file data structures, together with the way they relate to the hardware and system requirements, are the subject of this chapter.

Many applications require access to a number of data sets, and this can be organised using a database management system. Databases still use the basic file data structures but provide for sophisticated ways of accessing data while hiding the complexity from the application. Databases are the subject of the next chapter.

15.1 What is a File?

All computers, from the largest mainframe to the ubiquitous PC, use 'secondary storage' devices, and the file is the unit of storage on those secondary storage devices.

Secondary storage is any medium to which the computer can write data in machine readable format. The essential secondary storage device is the hard disk but other secondary storage devices include the diskette, the optical disk and various sizes and shapes of magnetic tapes. Secondary storage is distinct from the main memory of the computer. The main memory holds data and program code when the program is running but that data has to be written to a file, on a secondary storage device, if it is to be retained after the process is completed and the computer is switched off.

This book is being written using Microsoft Word and the text is saved to a file on the hard disk when I finish working on it. The file holding this chapter is on a PC and is relatively small. Files used by business information systems can be much larger and may be on mainframe or central server systems with vastly more disk space than a PC system. All data retained on a computer system is held on files. That data may be:

◆ Software:
All the software used on a computer will be held in files on secondary storage. This includes the operating system, system software and application programs. The basic format for a PC software file is the executable (.exe) file and there are equivalent forms for other operating system environments. Further files may be used for software including the program source files (on the machine where the software is developed and maintained).

◆ Data:
Data is perhaps typified by the business data used by information systems. Examples of data are:
  ◆ Standing data such as the customer and product files in an order processing system or the personnel file in a payroll system.
  ◆ Transaction data such as the order file in an order processing system or the monthly payroll file in the payroll system.
The concept of data files also extends to the data used with desktop software, such as the document files used by word processors or the HTML files of the World Wide Web.

◆ System:
A third category of files are those used by the system. Complex software, such as the operating system, has its own data files. These files are used for various system parameters and for storing run-time information where it might be required to facilitate system recovery.

◆ Archive / security:
Program or data may be copied off the computer system onto a portable medium (diskette, optical disk or magnetic tape) for:
  ◆ Security in case the working copy on the hard disk is lost or corrupted.
  ◆ Archive where the data is no longer needed for every day use but is to be retained, in machine readable format, in case there is a need to access it at a later date.
  ◆ Interchange where the software or data is to be sent to another user. The most obvious example of this is the software issued on CD-Rom by the various software companies.

For many business information systems the data will be held on a database. The database is a sophisticated way of organising and accessing data but the data on the database is still held on one or more files. The way data is organised and accessed on a database is the subject of the next chapter.

15.2   The Disk

A PC will typically have a single hard disk drive inside the processor box while larger machines may well have several drives that are external to the processor. Whatever the configuration of computer, the essentials of the disk are much the same.

For the study of IS we don't need to examine the electronics of the disk but we do need a general idea of how it operates. In general terms the disk consists of:

◆   One or more platens coated with the magnetic sensitive material, ferric oxide. These platens are much like the disks you can see through the shutter of a diskette but they are probably bigger, there may be several of them and they are mounted on a fixed spindle.
◆   Read / write heads (one for each disk surface that is to be used) mounted on an arm and with the heads suspended above the surface of the disk.

In operation, the disk platens are spinning and the read / write heads can be moved in and out over the surface of the disk. The disk drive is shown diagrammatically in *figure 15.1*.

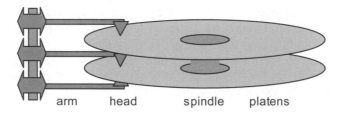

arm   head   spindle   platens

Figure 15.1 The Disk Drive

The data on the disk is recorded on tracks. These tracks are a series of concentric circles on the disk. The heads can be positioned to write data to or read data from the rotating platen. The tracks are not part of the physical makeup of the disk but are defined by the positioning of the head as it is stepped in or out over the surface of the disk. The disk drive has to be very precisely engineered so that the positioning of the head over a given track is exactly the same each time the disk is used.

The disk is also divided into sectors. Each sector of each track is a block. The tracks, sectors and blocks are shown diagrammatically in *figure 15.2* (although there will be many more tracks and blocks on each platen than the diagram shows).

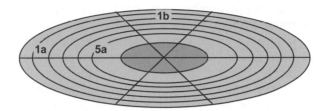

Figure 15.2 Tracks, Sectors and Blocks

The diskette is much the same as the hard disk; it is a single platen, slower and holds much less data than a hard disk but it operates using the same principles. Other secondary storage devices are:

◆ Magnetic tapes / tape cassettes which record the data in the same way as disks but the read / write heads are stationary and the tape is moved serially over the heads.

◆ Optical disk where data is read using light (as opposed to the magnetic recording used on other secondary storage devices). Optical devices generally use the CD or DVD format. Many are read only but increasingly CD / DVD writers are being installed. The CD / DVD has a much greater capacity than the diskette and may well supersede that technology.

15.3 Files, Blocks and Records

As indicated earlier, a set of data will be held in a file. All the words and diagrams for this chapter are held in a single file on my hard drive. They are separated from the other Word files that have been set up for the other chapters of this book. In a similar way, an information system can have a number of files each holding a different set of data. A payroll system (as outlined in *Part III*) would have separate files for personnel data, salary tables, variances and the monthly payroll.

On a disk drive we can have a number of files. The location and separation of these files is logical (not physical). There will be a directory recorded on the disk listing the names of all files on that disk and indexing the location of those files (the directory will be in a standard place, known to the system, such as track zero). The location of the files will be recorded in terms of the tracks and blocks that the file occupies. Thus, on the disk shown in *figure 15.2*, one file might be on track 1 occupying blocks 1a, 1b and so on to 1f with another file occupying tracks 2, 3 and 4, and so on.

The computer operating system reads the directory of each disk that is loaded and hence knows what files are available and where they are located (on Windows we can interrogate this by clicking on the device icon and getting a list of the available folders and files). A program is able to connect to the files it is to use through the operating system, using this directory information.

The physical file consists of a number of blocks (above I suggested that there was a file on track 1 consisting of blocks 1a to 1f). The block is the physical unit of data that is read or written at any time (that is the basic principle although it can be more complex).

The logical file consists of a number of records. If our file has details of products for an order processing system then we will have one record per product. Each record will have the product code, the product name and the other details of the product that the system needs (we normally make sure each record on our system has a unique identifier and, in this case, a product code meets that need).

The records are then packed into blocks – possibly we can fit six products per block and thus, for the file on track 1, we can fit 36 products. The position is illustrated in *figure 15.3* – we can see that products 140101 to 140106 are in block 1a, 140107 to 140112 are in block 1b and so on (a file of up to 36 products is unlikely to require a computer system to administer it but it serves to illustrate the overall principles).

block	records:					
1a	140101 blue pen	140102 pencil	140103 rubber	140104 chalk	140105 clips	140106 staples
1b	140107 red pen	140108 marker	140109 ruler	140110 crayon	140111 label	140112 ink
1c	140113 ribbon	140114 cartridge	140115 paper	140116 card	210101 board	210114 bag
1d	210115 folder	210116 pouch	210117 compass	210118 tag	210119 stamp	210120 wallet
1e	210121 band	210126 fastener	230231 scissors	230233 knife	231001 glue	231002 paste
1f	231003 tape	231032 string	231033 pin			

Figure 15.3 File, Records and Blocks

The vital point that we must remember, when we consider file and database designs, is that while the program processes an individual record the system reads and writes a block at a time. Thus to process product number 210116 we will have read block 1d which gives us the six product records from 210115 to 210120. If subsequently we wish to process product 210119 the system will not have to access the disk again as it already has the record in memory (the program will issue a read instruction but, as the data is already in memory, the system will simply transfer the record from its block buffer to the program's record buffer).

15.4 Accessing Data

Accessing data on the hard disk (or the diskette) involves the following four steps:

♦ The read / write head has to be positioned over the required track.
♦ The system has to wait, while the disk rotates, until the required block is under the read / write head.
♦ The block of data has to be read from the disk and transferred to a block buffer in the memory of the program requiring the data.
♦ The required record has to be unpacked from the block and made available to the program that required it.

The first two steps are mechanical and take a considerable time when compared with the electronic transfers of the later two steps. With a disk drive we can access the data in one of two ways:

♦ Serial access – we start at the beginning of the file and read through all the blocks and hence all the records, in the order they are held on the file.
♦ Random access – we select a particular record, work out which block it is in, and go straight to that block.

Serial access is a fast way of reading a lot of records. It virtually eliminates the need to move the read / write head (one of the slowest parts of the operation) and each block read delivers a number of records. Random access, on the other hand, is much slower. For each access we can expect to have to move the heads to the required track and then, once the block is read, there is only one record of interest. We have to choose the type of access that the application needs whilst we try to optimise the way the data is structured so that run times do not become excessive.

15.5 Serial Files

The simplest way of organising data is the serial file. For this type of file the records are just stored one after another in whatever sequence the system designer chooses. Continuing with our example of the product file, using a serial type of organisation the file would appear as shown in **figure 15.4** (I have shown the file as having three records per block and some of the keys are not used – this is to keep the diagram compact and so that the same data-set can be used to illustrate other types of file organisation).

To read the file we simply start at the beginning, read each block in turn and hence unpack and process each record. Serial access is the best approach if we need to process every record (e.g. to check stock levels and calculate replenishment). It might be less appropriate if we need to find all records with a product category of 22. It would not be the preferred option if we required the product with a code of 210121.

To write, or update, a serial file we start with a blank file and write the records, packed into blocks, in the sequence they are made available by the program. If we are selecting records from a larger file, for instance if we want a new file of all products with a product category of 22, this could be an appropriate approach. If, however, we were updating an existing file with just one new product record, it might seem to be a long-winded way of doing the job.

To summarise, serial files:

♦ Provide serial access efficiently.
♦ Do not provide random access.
♦ There is no problem with overflow (an issue that comes up when we look at direct access files).
♦ Do not require significant vacant space to be left in the file (although a new copy is created when the file is updated).

For a magnetic tape device, sequential access is the only way of processing the data. On the other hand, with a disk drive we can program the device to go straight to the block, and hence the record, that we want. Next we will look at a couple of file structures that facilitate this approach.

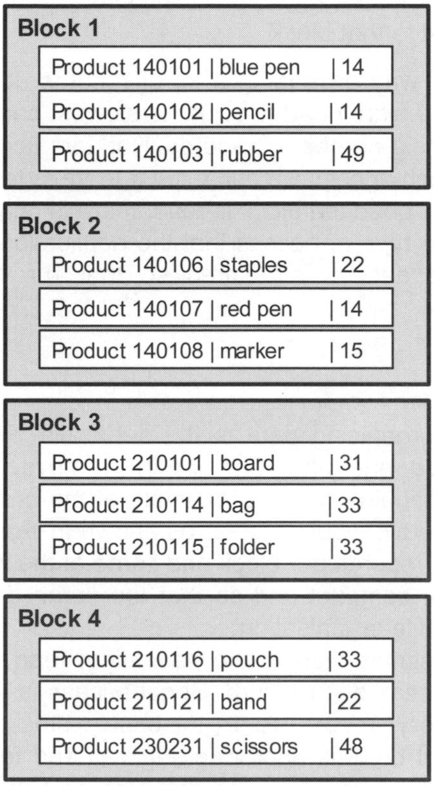

```
Block 1
    Product 140101 | blue pen    | 14
    Product 140102 | pencil      | 14
    Product 140103 | rubber      | 49

Block 2
    Product 140106 | staples     | 22
    Product 140107 | red pen     | 14
    Product 140108 | marker      | 15

Block 3
    Product 210101 | board       | 31
    Product 210114 | bag         | 33
    Product 210115 | folder      | 33

Block 4
    Product 210116 | pouch       | 33
    Product 210121 | band        | 22
    Product 230231 | scissors    | 48
```

Figure 15.4 Serial File
(Showing Product Code, Product Name and Product Category)

15.6 Index Sequential Files

The index sequential file structure allows for both serial and direct access. To facilitate direct access we have, as the name of this file structure implies, an index. The position is as represented in *figure 15.5*.

The file is set up using a load utility program. This program loads records from another (serial) file leaving spare space in each block. In our example we show room for three products in each block with one of those spaces left unused (a more realistic example might have room for 20 records in a block with only 13 records present on initial loading.

As well as loading the data the utility program would also set up the index. The index has to be in a standard place and I have shown it in block zero. The index contains an entry of the highest record key in the block. Note that once the index is set up, using the load utility, it cannot be changed unless the file is set-up again.

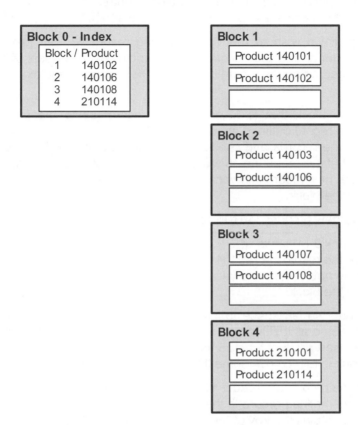

Figure 15.5 Index Sequential File

Reading the file can be sequential or direct. To read the file sequentially the program just starts at the beginning and reads the blocks and records in turn, as it would for a serial file, but ignoring the index entries. Reading the file in direct access mode involves the following steps:

◆ Read the index block – block 0.
◆ Search the index for the first entry giving a key that is greater than or equal to the required key.
◆ Read the block indicated by that index entry.
◆ Unpack the records and process the required record (or the appropriate exception condition if the record is not found).

To illustrate this further, assume we wished to read product 140107. The steps that would be taken are:

◆ Read the index block – block 0.
◆ Examine first entry in index   – is 140102 >= 140107 – No.

- ◆ Examine second entry in index – is 140106 >= 140107 – No.
- ◆ Examine third entry in index – is 140108 >= 140107 – Yes.
- ◆ Read the block 3 as indicated by that index entry.
- ◆ Unpack the records and process the product 140107.

For updating, if we wish to modify an existing record we can just change the relevant data items and the record can be written back as part of the block it belongs to. Inserting a new record is, however, a bit more complex. The steps are as follows:

- ◆ Read the block that is to contain the record (using the procedure for reading a record outlined above).
- ◆ Unpack the records and check that the record that is to be inserted does not exist (if it is found that is presumably an exception condition).
- ◆ Insert the new record into vacant space in the block.
- ◆ Rewrite the block.

So, to insert a new product 140104, the steps that would be taken are:

- ◆ Read block 2 (which is where product 140104 would be if it was on file).
- ◆ Unpack the records – 140104 is not there so we can proceed.
- ◆ Insert the new record into vacant space in the block.
- ◆ Rewrite the block.

That works out: we left space to insert a record and now we have used it. The index is unaffected as it still points to the highest key in the block. If, however, we now wish to insert product 140105 there will be a problem. It should go into block 2 and the block is full. To overcome this problem the system will:

- ◆ Insert the record for product 140105 in an overflow block.
- ◆ Insert a small tag record in the home block – block 2 in this case. The tag record contains the key of the additional record and the block where it can be found.

The file after these two updates is shown in *figure 15.6*.

The final requirement is to delete a record. This follows much the same procedures as for amend but the record is removed from the block before it is written back. Note that the record to be deleted can be the one that has its key in the index. If this happens the index still remains unchanged and all the access procedures outlined above will still work out. *Figure 15.6* includes the deletion of product 140108 from block 3.

  Eventually the index sequential file can become a bit of a mess. There will be an uneven distribution of spaces available for updating and ever more records ending up in overflow. As the use of overflow increases, access times will increase and there is the possibility of the file failing, e.g. if overflow becomes full. Normal practice is, every once in a while, to read off the index sequential file to a serial file and reload it using the load utility. Once the file is reloaded the records are again evenly distributed and the overflow is emptied out.

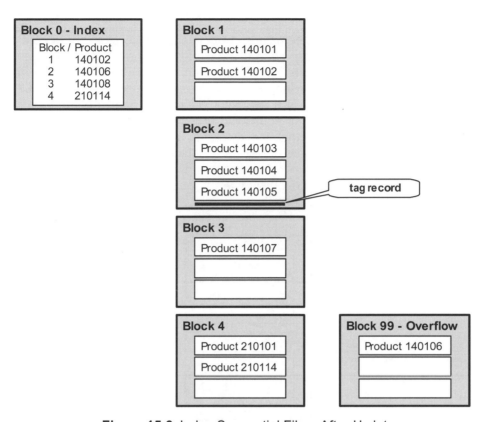

Figure 15.6 Index Sequential File – After Update

Note also, a large index sequential file can have a two, or possibly three, level index and some implementations have the index in a separate file – we will not go into the details of these complexities in this book.

To summarise, index sequential files:

- Provide serial access with reasonable efficiently.
- Provide random access, again with reasonable efficiency.
- There can be a problem with overflow – the position needs to be watched.
- It requires vacant space to be left in the file for new records to be added.

15.7 Hash Random Files

An alternative to using an index for direct access is hash random. This approach uses an algorithm on the key to calculate the block where the record is to be stored. The basic requirement of the algorithm is that the answer is within the range of the blocks in the file. It is advantageous if the algorithm produces a random distribution, as it should cut down on any problems caused by clustering in the set of keys.

Using the data we had in the index sequential example and assuming that there are five blocks available, the algorithm could be:

block = remainder of (key / 5) + 1

Thus for key 140101 we get a remainder of one and hence store the record in block 2. When the record needs to be read the same algorithm produces the same block address. Once read the record can be amended or deleted if that is the requirement. The file produced by applying this algorithm is shown in *figure 15.7*.

The file shown in *figure 15.7* is a very simple example and a real application would need more than five blocks and would hopefully accommodate more than three records per block. Note that the algorithm shown is not a randomising algorithm but it should split clusters of keys over adjacent blocks.

With an appropriate algorithm, overflow should not be a great problem but it can occur and normal practice is to overflow into the next block with available space and to insert a tag record in the home block.

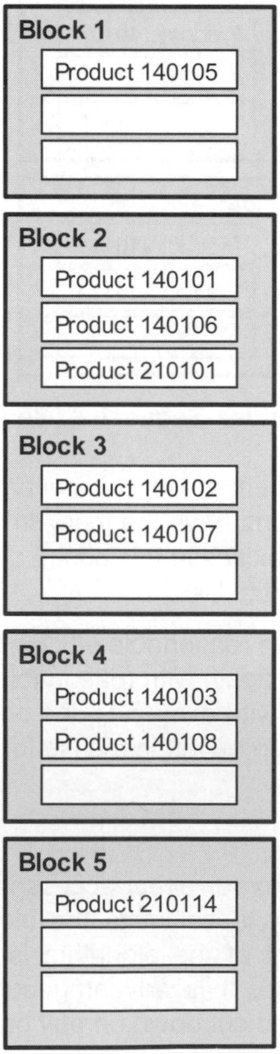

Block 1
Product 140105

Block 2
Product 140101
Product 140106
Product 210101

Block 3
Product 140102
Product 140107

Block 4
Product 140103
Product 140108

Block 5
Product 210114

Figure 15.7 Hash Random File

In summary, the random access file:

- Provides random access efficiently.
- Does not provide serial access (there seems no real reason why a hash random file should not be read serially but the file handling software, normally, does not allow it).
- There can be overflow but it is not normally a real problem.
- Requires space to be left to facilitate updates.

15.8 File Handling Software

The processing of the three file types, serial, index sequential and random, has been described as if the programmer needs to be aware of the methods used. At one level this is true, the designer and the programmer need to be aware of how the file access systems work as it will affect the run time of their programs and hence the level of service given to the user. That said, the access methods are actually hidden in the file handling package – the software provided to the program by the compiler. The programmer will only need to include read and / or write statements and supply a key where appropriate – the file handling software will then do the rest.

15.9 Record Formats

The file data structure gives access to the required record. Within that record the data has to be formatted in a way that is understandable to the application that uses it. A simple record structure for a product file is shown in *figure 15.8*. An occurrence of one product record is shown in *figure 15.9*.

data item	data name	format
Product Code	prod-code	9(6)
Product Name	prod-name	X(32)
Product Category	prod cat	99
Sales Price	prod-price	9(4).99
Warehouse Location	whse-locn	XX9(4)
Stock Quantity	prod-qty	9(6)
Purchase Stop	prod-p-stop	X (Y or N)
Sales Stop	prod s-stop	X (Y or N)

9 numeric data e.g. 9(6) is a six digit number (numeric data can also be stored in binary format)
X alpha-numeric data e.g. X(32) allows 32 characters

Figure 15.8 Example Product Record Structure

This sort of record structure is reasonably typical of a business system (although for a practical implementation there is likely to be a lot more detail for each product). The data format is specific to the system that uses it and each program must incorporate the same data description. Note that, excepting the textual elements, the data is fairly meaningless without having the record layout (a fact that seems to be ignored when people consider the requirement for data privacy).

```
|1 0 6 0|1 1 S w|e a t  |S h i r|t   ( R|
|e d )                           2 2|
|0 0 1 5|9 9 A A|0 1 0 3|0 0 0 1|6 4 N N|
```

Figure 15.9 Example Product Record

General purpose software packages will have a somewhat different approach to data which, in effect, encodes the usage / formatting data with the user data. This requirement employs a type of 'mark-up' approach. A simple and standardised example of this is HTML. A simple example of (some of) the above product data encoded as HTML is shown in *figure 15.10*.

```
<p>Sweat Shirt (Red):</p>
<ul>
<li>Product Code: 106011
<li>Product Cat.: 22
<li>Sales Price: 15.99
</ul>
```

Figure 15.10 Product Data as HTML
(not a full HTML document)

The mark-up used by packages such as MS Word is both proprietary and much more complex but serves the same purpose; it informs the package of the text, the formatting and control details required by the software.

15.10 Databases

Conventional files, such as those that have been outlined in this chapter, are used for a number of purposes. We use them for:

◆ Software: Source and executable files are used when we write programs. Also, the system uses files for system and application software.
◆ Text files: Word processor data and HTML are examples of text that is stored in conventional files, one for each document.
◆ Data files: Some systems will store data on separate files – one file for each data type. This is not likely to be the most appropriate approach for large or complex systems.

◆ Extract files: Data that is selected from the main database and stored on a conventional file for sorting and further processing.

Most information systems use a number of sets of data and also needs to use relationships between those sets of data. Taking the example of an order processing system, records on the product file are related to the records on an orders file that requires those products. These sorts of relationships between data sets are most conveniently managed by a database management system – these systems are the subject of the next chapter.

Exercises

Just one exercise for this chapter (but it requires a bit of thought):

1. Using the data flow diagram (DFD) of the payroll system, shown in **Chapter 8**, suggest what conventional file type would be most appropriate for each of the datastores shown on the DFD. Assume each datastore is to be implemented as a file. Give reasons for your suggestion.

Further Reading

This chapter is self-sufficient and there is not a lot of other material on conventional files (and some of it that is in the introductory IS textbooks is wrong!). The next chapter is about databases and there is plenty of further reading that can be done there.

Chapter 16
Databases

Summary

A database is a conceptual file that stores most or all the data for an application. The database management software then allows the application to process that data using a variety of paths.

To facilitate access to the data, the database needs to be set up using sophisticated data structures. The most common approach is the relational model but hierarchical, network and object-oriented approaches are also used. Before the database is set up, the data must be analysed and structured to work with the approach taken in the database software.

Database software can be used free standing or be incorporated into an information system. Many database packages come with built-in application generators that can be used for ad-hoc queries or for building operational information systems.

16.1 What is a Database?

A database, in the context of information technology and information systems, is:

> A file management system that collects all (or most) of the system's / organisation's data within one (conceptual) file and provides sophisticated methods to access that data.

Thus, if we take the Order Processing system that was outlined in *Chapter 16*, in place of the several conventional files we had to use for customers, products and orders we could have just one (conceptual) file containing all the data that we required.

We can take the concept further and use a single database to serve all the information system requirements of the organisation. The order processing system has a customer dataset and this could also be used for the customer relations management (CRM) and marketing systems. Similarly, given there is a product dataset, this could be used for any warranty, computer aided manufacturing (CAM) and / or material requirement planning (MRP) systems.

There are considerable theoretical benefits in having all the organisations data on one database, a 'corporate database'. In practice, such an all-embracing system is complex, costly and unwieldy and hence they are not much used. A possibly exception to this is the banks, many of which have integrated systems that link the data on different financial products to a single customer database.

The use of the database should make the development of the system easier and the data more readily accessible (particularly where we need to access related data from more than one dataset). That said, the use of the database comes at a price. The price is in terms of the additional software that has to be purchased (which can be expensive for large systems) and of system performance (if the database is not carefully designed). The data structures used by a database management system (DBMS) are similar to those discussed in the previous chapter. If we want, for example, a way of finding all the orders for a given customer we will have to have a data structure that supports that requirement. Setting that up causes complexity (that may well be hidden from the programmer and the user) and that complexity costs processing time.

There are a number of database paradigms but the one that is normally adopted is the relational approach. This is used by the most popular DBMSs currently in the market place. Currently available DBMSs include:

- Microsoft Access.
- MySQL (a freeware product).
- Oracle.
- DB2 (IBM's relational DBMS).

The DBMS is primarily a file management software provision that can be incorporated in the user's application program. Most database packages now incorporate their own software generators and whole systems can be (and are) developed using these facilities, with little or no need for additional programming.

16.2 Data Structure

With a database, we are attempting to build a data structure that represents and makes accessible the data that belongs to, and is needed by, the information system. These requirements are represented by the entity-relationship diagram (or the class diagram for object-oriented development) produced during the system analysis and design process: see *Part V*. An example of such a entity-relationship diagram, for an order processing system, was given in *Part III* and is reproduced in *figure 16.1* (for simplicity's sake the data requirements of the replenishment sub-system have been omitted). This structure shows the need for:

- customer data,
- product / price data,
- order data (which also covers picking and invoicing requirements).

It also shows the relationships between customers and orders, plus orders and products. The use of a database eases the problems of implementing and using these relationships. We will be using this order processing data as an example and hopefully the advantage of using a DBMS will become apparent.

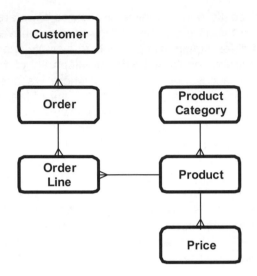

Figure 16.1 Order Processing – ER Diagram

Let us list some attributes for each entity:

- ◆ Customer
  - ◆ Customer Number   cust-no
  - ◆ Customer Name   cust-name
  - ◆ Customer Address   cust-addr
  - ◆ Customer Credit Limit   cust-cred-lim
- ◆ Product Category
  - ◆ Product Category Code   prodcat-code
  - ◆ Product Category Description   prodcat-desc
- ◆ Product
  - ◆ Product Code   prod-code
  - ◆ Product Name   prod-name
  - ◆ Warehouse Location   whse-locn
  - ◆ Stock Total   prod-stock
  - ◆ Product Category Code   prodcat-code
- ◆ Product Price
  - ◆ Product Code   prod-code
  - ◆ Price Start Date   price-s-date
  - ◆ Purchase Price   price-purch
  - ◆ Selling Price   price-sell
- ◆ Order
  - ◆ Order Number   ord-no
  - ◆ Order Date   ord-date
  - ◆ Order Status   ord-sta
  - ◆ Customer Number   cust-no
- ◆ Order Line
  - ◆ Order Number   ord-no
  - ◆ Order Line Number   ordlne-no
  - ◆ Order Line Quantity   ordlne-qty
  - ◆ Product Code   prod-code

And recap on the relationships:

◆ A **customer** *submits* zero, one or many **orders**.
◆ An **order** *contains* one or many **order lines**.
◆ A **products** *is supplied for* zero, one or many **order lines**.
◆ A **product category** *classifies* zero, one or many **products**.
◆ A **product** *is charged at* one or many **prices**.

Some standards for ER-diagrams work these details into the diagram – in this text we will keep the diagram simple but you may learn a more advanced standard at a later stage in your studies. Note also that the attribute lists have been kept short – there is sufficient information to create an order processing system but most order processing systems would be more complex than is implied by this ER-diagram.

16.3 Relational Databases

The relational approach to database design is credited to Edgar Codd who worked in the IBM laboratories in the late 1960s. The relational approach is based on the mathematical concepts of relations and sets. Essentially we convert the data to third normal form (TNF) and then use the resulting relationships as the basis of the database design. The entities and attributes given for the order processing data requirements are in TNF.

The conversion to TNF can be achieved by applying Codd's rules (which tends to be the way it is taught on database courses) or it can be achieved using a table method (which is the approach usually adopted when structured analysis and design is taught). The table driven approach to creating TNF is taught in *Part V*.

Using the order processing system data we can now see how a relational database is described, designed and used.

❖ **Example Relationship**

Taking as an example the product entity we have:

Entity: Attributes:

┌─────────────────┐   ◆ Product Code   prod-code
│   │   ◆ Product Name   prod-name
│   **Product** │   ◆ Warehouse Location   whse-locn
│   │   ◆ Stock Total   prod-stock
└─────────────────┘   ◆ Product Category Code prodcat-code

To document Product entity as a relationship in a relational database we use the following notation:

Product (<u>prod-code</u>, prod-name, whse-locn, prod-stock, prodcat-code*)

For this relationship:

◆ The relationship name is **Product**, it comes first and it is nice to show it in bold if we are typing the database's schema.
◆ The attributes are listed in brackets.
◆ The key of this relationship is <u>prod-code</u>, it is shown underlined.

◆ This relationship includes a 'foreign key', the key to another relationship that 'owns' this relationship. The foreign key is prodcat-code*, denoted by the asterisk that follows it.

Occasionally a relationship will not have a key and in some cases it will have a key made up of more than one attribute: see Order Line and Product Price in the example database below.

❖ **Example Database**

- **Customer** (<u>cust-no</u>, cust-name, cust-addr, cust-cred-lim)

cust-no	cust-name	cust-addr	cust-cred-lim
6213	John Smith	Stockport	10000
6248	Nadia Zar	Dartford	50000
8711	Ann Hunt	Perth	40000

- **Product-Category** (<u>prodcat-code</u>, prodcat-desc)

prodcat-code	prodcat-desc
14	pens
22	fasteners
48	cutters

- **Product** (<u>prod-code</u>, prod-name, whse-locn, prod-stock, prodcat-code*)

prod-code	prod-name	whse-locn	prod-stock	prodcat-code
140101	blue pen	A1061	480	14
140106	staples	A1123	220	22
140107	red pen	A1062	10	14
230231	scissors	B0241	160	48

- **Product-Price** (<u>prod-code</u>, <u>price-s-date</u>, price-purch, price-sell)

prod-code	price-s-date	price-purch	price-sell
140101	01.01.04	0.20	0.40
140101	15.06.04	0.20	0.45
140106	01.01.04	0.80	1.20
140107	01.01.04	0.20	0.45
140107	15.04.04	0.22	0.50
230231	01.01.04	2.00	4.50

- **Order** (<u>ord-no</u>, ord-date, ord-sta, cust-no*)

- **Order-Line** (<u>ord-no</u>, <u>ordlne-no</u>, ordlne-qty, prod-code*)

Figure 16.2 Example Database – Standing Data

Using the format described for documenting the Product relationship we can now document the complete order-processing database, as follows:

> **Customer** (<u>cust-no</u>, cust-name, cust-addr, cust-cred-lim)
> **Product-Category** (<u>prodcat-code</u>, prodcat-desc)
> **Product** (<u>prod-code</u>, prod-name, whse-locn, prod-stock, prodcat-code*)

Product-Price (<u>prod-code*</u>, <u>price-s-date</u>, price-purch, price-sell)
Order (<u>ord-no</u>, ord-date, ord-sta, cust-no*)
Order-Line (<u>ord-no</u>, <u>ordlne-no</u>, ordlne-qty, prod-code*)

Note that all the entities become a database relationship and all the ER-diagram relationships are represented by either a foreign key or a key that forms part of a multiple entity key, e.g. the Order has the foreign key of cust-no that 'links' it to the owning Customer. Check out all the other relations shown on the ER-diagram.

Taking this example database we can populate it with some sample data (as we would if we were setting up test data). I will start with a few standing data records: see *figure 16.2* (fields such as address are abbreviated in order to contain the size of the diagram).

---

* **Customer** (<u>cust-no</u>, cust-name, cust-addr, cust-cred-lim)
  cust-nos: 6213, 6246, 8711

* **Product-Category** (<u>prodcat-code</u>, prodcat-desc)
  prodcat-codes: 14, 22, 48

* **Product** (<u>prod-code</u>, prod-name, whse-locn, prod-stock, prodcat-code*)
  prod-codes: 140101, 140106, 140107, 230231

* **Product-Price** (<u>prod-code</u>, <u>price-s-date</u>, price-purch, price-sell)
  prod-codes: 140101 (15.06.04), 140106 (01.01.04),
  (current prices) 140107 (15.04.04), 230231 (01.01.04)

* **Order** (<u>ord-no</u>, ord-date, cust-no*)

ord-no	ord-date	ord-sta	cust-no
000001	30.06.04	1	6248
000002	01.07.04	1	8711
000003	02.07.04	1	6248

* **Order-Line** (<u>ord-no</u>, <u>ordlne-no</u>, ordlne-qty, prod-code*)

ord-no	ordlne-no	ordlne-qty	prod-code
000001	01	50	140101
000001	02	10	140107
000002	01	10	230231
000003	01	30	140107
000003	02	20	140106
000003	03	20	230231

Figure 16.3 Example Database – Order Data

If we then input some orders, for example:

* Nadia Zar   50 blue pens | 10 red pens
* Ann Hunt   10 scissors
* Nadia Zar   30 red pens | 20 staples | 20 scissors

These can be added to the database and the position then becomes that shown in *figure 16.3*. The orders are put up with a status of '1' indicating that they have been input but no further processing has taken place. Note, the standing data is only represented by keys, see *figure 16.2* for full details.

❖ **SQL**

SQL is the language used to query and process data on relational databases – it is based on relational algebra. SQL stands for Structured Query Language, but the full form is rarely used.

SQL can be used for all the operations we need to perform on a relational database – set-up, updating and queries – and we look at some simple examples of the use of SQL for the third of these applications.

When used for queries, SQL forms a new relationship that contains the data elements that answer the query. The three principal relational algebra functions are restrict, project and join – these are implemented using the SQL select function and are illustrated below using the order processing data that has been set out in *figures 16.2* and *16.3*.

◆ **Restrict**

The restrict function produces a new relationship consisting of a number of rows selected from an existing relationship. For example we could select all customers with a credit limit of greater than 20,000:

> **SELECT** Customer.cust-no, Customer.cust-name
>   Customer.cust-addr, Customer.cust-cred-lim
>   **FROM** Customer
>   **WHERE** Customer.cust-cred-lim >20000

Using the customer data from *figure 16.2* this would produce the new relationship:

cust-no	cust-name	cust-addr	cust-cred-lim
6248	Nadia Zar	Dartford	50000
8711	Ann Hunt	Perth	40000

◆ **Project**

Project produces a new relationship consisting of a number of selected columns (attributes) from an existing relationship. For example we could select just the customer name and credit limit from the Customer relationship:

> **SELECT** Customer.cust-name, Customer.cust-cred-lim
>   **FROM** Customer

Again using the data from *figure 16.2* this would produce the new relationship:

cust-name	cust-cred-lim
John Smith	10000
Nadia Zar	50000
Ann Hunt	40000

◆ **Join**

Join produces a new relationship from two existing relationships 'joined' over a common domain, i.e. a shared key. For example we could join customer data with the corresponding order data – I have also included a project so the resultant table includes just customer names and the corresponding order numbers and order dates:

> **SELECT** Customer.cust-name, Order.ord-no, Order.ord-date
> **FROM** Customer, Order
> WHERE Customer.cust-no = Order.cust-no

Using the data from our example in **figure 16.2** and **16.3** this would produce the new relationship:

cust-name	ord-no	ord-date
Nadia Zar	000001	30.06.04
Ann Hunt	000002	01.07.04
Nadia Zar	000003	02.07.04

SQL can be used when running the DBMS package or it can be incorporated into the user's program. It is, in effect, a functional language (as opposed to a procedural language). SQL specifies the requirement as opposed to how that requirement is to be executed. SQL also produces a table of results (rather than one line / record at a time) and the program will then need to process each data element in turn to produce a report, create totals, or whatever is required.

In principle, SQL should be a standard data manipulation language and hence we could use the same programs to access any database. This could be particularly useful in a distributed system where a client could issue SQL to use any database on any server in the system. In practice, while the basic core of SQL is the same, the various database vendors have included their own enhancements and variations in their implementation.

16.4 Microsoft Access

The most used database on PCs is Microsoft Access and that is the package recommended for use with the exercises at the end of this chapter and in the project in **Part V**.

Access is a relational database and it comes with a wide range of system building features. Access lets you set up and use a database using its basic interface or a wizard (a help guide that takes you through the steps). When using Access I use basic input for some tasks and wizards for others. It is a matter of preference and experience and you are welcome to use the facilities that work best for yourself.

To set up the order processing system, used as the example in this chapter, the following steps are recommended:

◆ Database file:
First we need to open and name a blank file to hold the database we are setting up.

◆ Tables:
The second step is to create a table for each of the six relationships used in the example. We need to indicate the key and, for each data item, we should set appropriate data types, field sizes and whether the data is compulsorily or optional.

◆ Relationships:
The tables we have designed include foreign keys and, in MS Access, we implement these by setting up relationships, e.g. between cust-no on Order and cust-no on Customer. We should also set referential integrity so that we can not set up invalid data such as an order for which there is no customer relationship.

◆ Test data:
MS Access allows data to be input directly into a table, a bit like filling in a spreadsheet – we can set up some test data using this facility.

◆ Forms:
Imputing data directly into tables is not going to be appropriate for a live system – to provide a proper user interface we create input screens using the forms facility.

◆ Queries and reports:
Finally we can generate queries and reports that allow us to select the data we need from the database.

These steps are explained in more detail on the web site (where changes can be made when a new version of the software is issued). The exercises at the end of this chapter require you to set up a MS Access database and it is a skill that you will use in the projects at the end of *Part V*.

16.5   Other Relational Databases

Microsoft Access is the market leader for PC databases. For larger systems there are a number of other database packages on the market. These include:

◆ Oracle
The market leader for database software on mid-size machines but also available for mainframe and PC systems. The software is provided with its own application development system. The latest version is available on more than 80 platforms and now incorporates object-oriented features. Many universities use Oracle as the main software for their intermediate level database courses.

◆ IBM's DB2
DB2 was originally offered on IBM mainframes as a relational database replacement for IBM's IMS, a hierarchical database package. DB2 is available on a number of platforms and this includes a PC version.

- ◆ Microsoft SQL Server
  A Microsoft database package for use on client-server systems. It is based on a product of the same name that was originally developed and marketed by Sybase.

- ◆ MySQL
  A shareware / free software database for use in client-server systems. Often used in Internet applications where the database is accessed using SQL generated by server-side scripts.

PC Packages like Microsoft Access allow a lot of leeway in how they are used and simple systems can be created with little real knowledge of database design principles. The systems listed above are for larger systems and require more careful design. The complexity of the data structures in large systems can cause considerable overheads and performance can be a problem – an issue the database designer needs to be aware of. Oracle and DB2 would be classified as 'industrial strength' database systems and are suitable for the use in large, multi-user corporate information systems.

16.6 Implementing Relational Databases

As we have seen, the relational database is made up of a set of tables; in principle there is one table for each entity on our ER-diagram. To the user or programmer this appears as a single file (and in MS Access it is held as a single file). In practice, each relationship is implemented as a separate file with its own file structure (although these can be sub-files of the overall database for the application). The three basic file / data structures that are used are:

- ◆ Heap – a serial file structure.
- ◆ Index sequential.
- ◆ Hash random.

The database also allows for additional indexes and thus, for example, we might have products with a main key of prod-code but an additional index that allowed access using the prod-name. Variations of the basic indexing and hashing arrangements can be used to improve efficiency, see Connolly and Begg (2002 – Appendix C) for a full discussion.

On a small database system, such as MS Access, the user does not get any say in the way the data is stored (other than what is specified when the tables and relationships are set up). For an industrial strength database such as Oracle the user can have much more control – the successful operation of the system can be dependent on the appropriate tuning of the database and this has to be provided for.

16.7 Other Database Paradigms

The three traditional database paradigms are hierarchical, network and relational. Relational is the newest of the three and has already been discussed.

The hierarchical database structure is, as the name suggests, hierarchical. For our order processing system one hierarchy could be customer, order, and order-line and a second hierarchy product category, product and prices plus order line (with order-line being duplicated so it is represented in both hierarchies). It is not necessarily the best way to implement a data structure but it can be made to work. The most notable implementation of the hierarchical database paradigm was IBM's IMS. As IBM was the predominate supplier of mainframe computers and IMS was its principal database (prior to db2) this ensured that the hierarchical model was widely used.

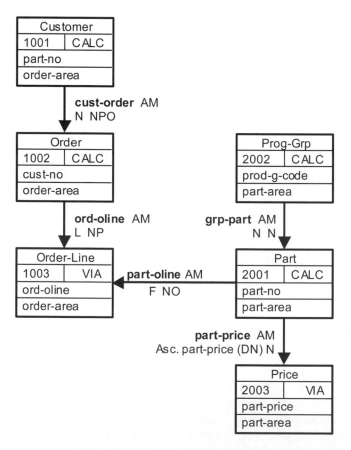

Figure 16.4 Bachman Diagram

The network structure implemented the relationships from the data model as sets. So, for example, the order would have a pointer to the physical location of the first order line and that order line would point to the second and so on – this is a data structure we call a linked-list. Pointers in a set could be to the next record, the previous record and / or the owner of the set (the order in the case just outlined). A record might be a member of more than one set – the order line, for instance, would be linked by two sets, to its owning order and product, respectively. The most used implementation of the network database was IDMS which was available on a number of mainframes including IBM (but not supplied by IBM). IDMS included many features that allowed the data model to be implemented efficiently – storing records via their owner so that they were stored on the same page is one example. A network database is documented using a Bachman diagram. The full Bachman diagram for the IDMS implementation of the order processing data model is shown at *figure 16.4*.

The most recently devised database paradigm is the object-oriented database. An object-oriented database can be used for data with complex relationships that is difficult to model and process with a relational database (Freedman, 1999). The object-oriented database can also store multimedia objects and can invoke processing appropriate to the nature of those objects. Mainstream database systems such as Oracle now come with object-oriented features. Note that object-oriented approaches to IS design are further discussed in *Part V*.

Exercises

1. Set up the order processing system, we have been using as an example in this chapter, as an Access database – use the instructions given on the web page if you are unfamiliar with MS Access. Take care to select appropriate data types for each attribute and make the appropriate key settings (this may not matter for a small example database but it is illustrative of the procedures we would follow if we were setting up a serious facility).

2. Set up some test data on your database, and use the query function. Include queries that interrogate more than one table. Check the SQL that Access has generated for your queries.

Further Reading

A good text for an introductory database course is:

> Beynon-Davies P. (2004) *Database Systems*, 3rd ed, Palgrave Macmillan, Basingstoke.

There are many other database texts, mainly aimed at intermediate database courses that use the Oracle package. Examples of such texts include:

> Connolly T. and Begg C. (2002) *Database Systems: A Practical Approach to Design, Implementation and Management*, 3rd ed., Addison-Wesley, Harlow.
>
> Atzeni P., Ceri S., Paraboschi S. and Torlone R. (1999) *Database Systems: Concepts, Languages and Architectures*, McGraw-Hill, Maidenhead.

A further source of information is the many books aimed at MS Access implementation – I personally use the Norton book. These can help you with any Access assignment / project you may undertake but they are not aimed at providing academic / theoretical material.

Chapter 17
Networks

Summary

The combination of computer systems with network technologies has changed the nature of information systems and has created radical new ways of working, trading and communicating. The use of information and communications technologies is the facilitator of globalisation (with helpful and harmful effects) and the (so called) information age.

Networks serve a number of purposes within organisations and in society. They facilitate:

◆ Access to the organisation's information systems from the desk top.
◆ The sharing of IT resources.
◆ Communications, such as e-Mail, e-Commerce and file transfer.
◆ Information services, most notably the World Wide Web.

Organisations are networked with local and wide area networks. The world, including government, business and many private citizens is networked by the Internet.

The information system designer uses a network to ensure the efficient operation of a system. Designers need to be aware of the networking requirements of their systems, organisation and external stakeholders.

17.1 A Networked World

Most computers are linked into a network (and that is arguably one of the greatest changes in computing in the last decade). Networks are used for a wide variety of purposes by a great diversity of organisations and individuals:

◆ Business computers are linked within the organisation to share computing facilities and to access information systems. Businesses are also linked to networks outside the organisation to transact with trading partners and, in some cases, with retail customers over the Internet.
◆ Academics have been linked to public access networks for longer than most. Academics use the Internet for research but they also use networks for administration and teaching. Modern distance learning is very much dependent on the use of the Internet.

- Individuals (in the developed world) now also get to join in. Many households have at least one home computer and most are joined to the Internet for entertainment, communications, accessing information and for e-Commerce.

Most computer communications are 'hard wired' but the other revolution that has been going on is the wireless / mobile phone revolution. These two technologies are coming together and making business and consumer facilities available from virtually anywhere, 24 x 7 (whether we want it or not!).

17.2 Networks

A computer network is a connection between two or more computer systems that facilitates the interchange of data. A definition provided nearly 20 years ago, when the use of networks was limited, is still applicable in today's networked world:

> A data communications network is used to connect a number of geographically separate computer systems and terminals for the interchange of data. The size of the network can vary from a few metres of connecting cable to a world wide system of inter connected equipment.

For a network we need:

- The connection. At its simplest, this is a wire connecting two computers that allows data to be interchanged. For longer distances and multi-machine networks the connection can involve a range of technologies but the principle is the same: data is sent from one computer, through the connection and is delivered to a second computer.
- A protocol. The data sent over the connection has to be packaged so that it can be checked and correctly interpreted by the receiving computer; the packaging is specified by the protocol.
- Communications equipment. Each computer connected to the network will need to be equipped with a network card (or equivalent) and possibly a modem. This equipment allows for signals to be sent and received. Large networks may also have communications equipment built into the network (in addition to the equipment built into the networked computers).

A simple network is represented in *figure 17.1*.

Figure 17.1 A Simple (Two Computer) Network

Most computers are connected to larger networks and this position is represented in *figure 17.2*. In this diagram the network is represented by a network cloud – showing communication services without being specific about the details of the network architecture. The network may be:

◆ A local area network (LAN). This is a network within the premises of an organisation. It is owned and controlled by the organisation and will, usually, be technically heterogeneous.

◆ A wide area network (WAN). This is a network that reaches out of the building to other branches of the organisation or to cooperating organisations. The network has to be provided by a third party (such as British Telecom in the UK) and may well use a variety of lines and equipment that is shared with other communications users.

◆ The Internet. The worldwide network of networks that uses TCP/IP as its protocol. Most networks are linked into the Internet and the distinction between a private LAN or WAN and the Internet is not always clear.

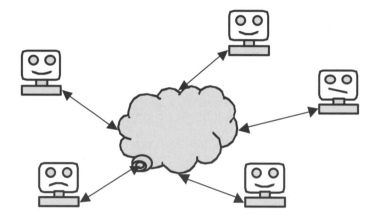

Figure 17.2 A Multi-user Network

This chapter includes a brief look at network architectures but, in general, and as IS practitioners, we rely on technical staff to provide network facilities.

17.3 Uses of Networks

Networks are used for a number of purposes – often a single network will be used for more than one purpose. These purposes can be put into four categories as follows:

◆ Online access to business information systems: For many organisations, the primary purpose of the network is to give staff, at their desks and on the factory floor, access to shared information systems. These systems could include the order processing system, payroll and MIS / DSS systems discussed in *Part III*. Access is normally restricted to members of the organisation and often staff members will only have access to selected systems and facilities within the overall organisational IS. Some business systems include e-Commerce interfaces that allow access to trading partners or consumers.

- ◆ Shared resources: The network can also give access to shared IT resources. Obvious examples are a number of desk top systems sharing a single printer or file-space on the departmental server. The need to share IT resources is decreasing as IT equipment becomes more affordable but there can still be cases where shared resources are advantageous. Shared file-space, that facilitates sharing of data, is one such example.

- ◆ Communications: The provision of networking has facilitated the use of information and communications technology (ICT) for communications (an alternative to telephone or mail). The main technology for inter-personal communications is e-Mail and EDI is the technology for IS to IS communications. Both these technologies have had a massive impact on the way business is done. The integration of computer technology, mobile technology and, in some cases, voice recognition is making ICT facilities accessible and available anywhere, on the move, 24 x 7.

- ◆ Information services: The use of ICT allows access to information that is made available by organisations or members of the public. The Internet and the World Wide Web is the main vehicle, and a unifying infrastructure, for accessing information (or disinformation) from any source and across the world.

The nature of the network being installed will, in part, depend on the intended use of the facility. Networks used for business purposes need to be secure and may well be private. Home and academic networking tends to be less constrained and the (public) Internet is a more applicable solution. Most networks are used for diverse purposes and the network architecture needs to accommodate this.

17.4 Network Technologies

The network has three essential components:

- ◆ The network connection – the wire (or an alternative technology).
- ◆ Network equipment – in the computer and embedded in the network.
- ◆ The protocol – how the data is formatted and controlled.

We will take a brief (and non-technical) look at each of these elements.

❖ The Network Connection

The basic technology for telecommunications is copper wire. This is used for all sorts of electronic communications as it has good conductivity and electrical signals will pass through with relatively little distortion or loss of power. The basic network connection is a twisted pair – two thin copper wires, insulated and twisted together. Higher quality connections can be provided using coaxial cable – a thicker wire with better insulation.

The data is transmitted along the wire as an electrical signal. Computer data is digital (with characters coded using a binary code). In digital transmissions, each binary bit is represented by a current level, e.g. +6 volts for a one and −2 volts for zero. The basic voice connection is analogue and digital data can be converted to analogue if a voice connection is to be used.

A number of alternatives to wire have been developed. These include:

◆ Fibre optics: this uses glass fibre and light as an alternative to copper and electricity. Fibre optics can transmit more data, at higher speeds and with less distortion than wire – the main disadvantage is that they are more difficult to connect than copper. Most new trunk connections and high speed LANs use fibre optic technology, with wire being used for the local connection (where the data volumes and transmission speeds are lower).

◆ Microwave: another alternative to wire for telephone and data transmission is a microwave circuit. The signal is sent, through the air, using microwaves, from one dish to another – there must be a 'line of sight' connection between dishes. An advantage of microwave technology is that companies can use private microwave circuits between separate locations (that are no more than a few miles apart) without having to purchase facilities from a public telecommunications provider.

◆ Satellite: these are used for long-distance links across continents or oceans (in the latter case, as an alternative to laying under-water cables). The system requires a geo-stationary satellite and then microwave transmissions are sent from one station, 'bounced' off the satellite and received at a second station that is hundreds or thousands of miles away.

◆ Radio: not a norm for telecommunication circuits but with the integration of the data communications and mobile telephone technology the mobile phone networks are increasingly used for data transmission.

◆ Infrared: used for (flexible) short distance links in a LAN, say in an open plan office.

The transmission capacity of the network is referred to as bandwidth – measured in bits per second. The term broadband is used for high speed domestic connections. In general fibre optic circuits have a greater capacity than copper wire.

Which network technology is used depends on a number of factors. When an organisation installs a LAN it has a choice – but it is price and performance that really matters, not the technology. When a WAN is used, the customer buys capacity and, very possibly, the data will pass through several different circuit types on its journey to the local exchange, across the trunk network and onwards down local lines to its final destination. A message from a terminal in the UK to another user in (say) the US may well:

◆ Set off as a modulated signal to the local exchange.
◆ Be digitised and sent down a fibre optic link to the satellite station.
◆ Satellite over the Atlantic.
◆ Microwave from the satellite station in the US.
◆ Finally back to copper and a modulated signal for the final leg of its journey.

It could well be more complex than that and, if it is packet switched (we come to that later), parts of the same message could take different routings.

❖ **Network Equipment**

The wires (or equivalent) have to be interfaced into the computer equipment and the computer needs to be set up to format outgoing signals and receive incoming signals. The basic bit of kit is a network board. The board works in conjunction with the software to interface the physical network and the application running in the computer. Other network equipment includes:

◆ Modem: a bit of kit that converts the computer's digital signal into a modulated signal, if an analogue voice circuit is being used. The modem also receives incoming signals that have to be de-modulated to produce a digital signal to be processed in the computer. Typically used for home connection via voice telephone lines whereas most offices will have a LAN circuit that uses digital transmission.

◆ Hubs and switches: device in a network that join communication lines together. Desk top PCs will typically be connected to a LAN via either a hub or a switch. The hub shares the network capacity between devices whereas the switch can devote the full bandwidth to any devices that are active at the time.

◆ Bridges and routers: devices that forward data from one segment of the network to another segment. Bridges are protocol independent whereas routers have to read the protocol to glean routing information.

◆ Multiplexor: a device that merges several low speed transmissions into a single high speed transmission. The multiplexor can use frequency division multiplexing (where several signals are sent down a single link at different frequencies), time division multiplexing (where the signal is interleaved with other signals on the same frequency) or both.

◆ Front end processor: this is a computer that handles computer network processing for a mainframe computer / enterprise server. Sorting out a high volume of network communications is expensive on processing power and using a separate processor for that task leaves the mainframe to get on with the job of running the IS (including messages to and from the network).

A diagram of a simple LAN with a number of clients, one server and network devices is shown in *figure 17.3*. Note that there are a number of ways of configuring a LAN and this diagram does not seek to represent any one specific network topology.

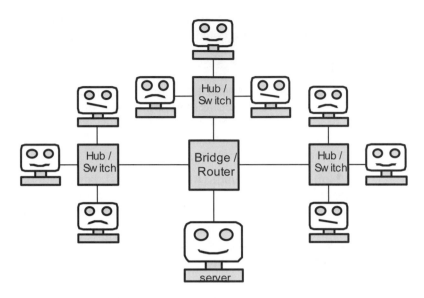

Figure 17.3 LAN with Clients, Servers and Network Devices

❖ **Protocol**

Having established the network, the client and server systems all need to speak the same sort of language and show a bit of courtesy (not speaking until spoken to – or something like that). The way we sort this out on a network is with a set of rules and requirements that are called a network or transmission protocol. The requirements of data transmission and the protocol are:

◆ Data: The data must be in a format that is understandable by both systems. This is the same idea as a record format on a file. There needs to be an agreed way of coding characters and numbers and each application needs to know what to do with each field in the data.

◆ Envelope: In addition to the application data the network needs its own data. For each message there will be a header and a trailer segment that envelope the data. The minimum requirement is for the header to indicate the start of the message and for the trailer to include count / checksum information that allows the network to check that the data has arrived intact. For many protocols the header will also specify the network address of the sending computer and the network address of the destination computer.

Over the years there have been many protocols developed for different network requirements. One of those protocols was TCP/IP (Transmission Control Protocol / Internet Protocol) which was developed for use on the Internet (as an interim measure) and has since become the de-facto global standard.

TCP/IP is a packet switching standard. Using packet switching obviates the need to establish a direct and exclusive network connection between sender and receiver (as would be the case when we make a telephone call). For packet switching a message is divided into packets. Each packet is encased in a digital envelope and the header includes the source address, destination address and sequence number within the message. The packets can then be dynamically routed over the network using any available path. Individual packets within a message may follow different paths. The packages are then reassembled into a message in the receiving station using the sequence number to check the order. The receiving station will request the re-transmission of any corrupted or missing package.

Packet switching allows for the more effective use of bandwidth as it means that trunk connections are shared. Packet switching also gives resilience as if one network connection is unavailable the network will select another path.

Packet switching is a WAN technology. LANs have their own ways of sharing capacity, e.g. Ethernet and Token Ring. These LAN topologies can be used in conjunction with TCP/IP.

TCP/IP can be seen as a two part protocol:

> TCP provides transport functions which ensures that the total amount of bytes sent is received correctly at the other end.

> IP provides the routing mechanism.

> TCP/IP is a routable protocol, which means that all messages contain not only the address of the destination station, but the address of the destination network. This allows TCP/IP messages to be sent to multiple networks within organisations or around the world, hence its use in the worldwide Internet.

(Freedman, 1999)

17.5 Example Network

The network of an organisation will normally be focused on access to business systems with communications as an important additional element (as opposed to the communications and information services focus of most academic and personal users). To illustrate this usage we will imagine an organisation – let's call it Funco plc. This organisation has:

- ◆ A head office that also houses its central IT / IS facilities.
- ◆ A number of regional / branch offices, a manufacturing facility and a warehouse / distribution centre.
- ◆ Mobile staff such as salespeople and teleworkers.
- ◆ Links to trading partners and to members of the public though its e-Shop.

All the staff of the organisation make some use of IT. This includes the use of desk top facilities, e-Mail and accessing end user, functional support and corporate IS. The general picture is illustrated in *figure 17.4*, a picture that is typical of many medium and large organisations (with or without manufacturing and warehouse facilities).

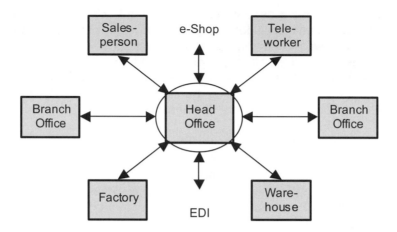

Figure 17.4 Location Chart

Funco needs a network that covers all its locations and its outside links. This will have a number of elements and its design involves a few decisions. The elements are:

♦ LANs in each location. The company can have its own network in each of its premises – the network will be a LAN. There are a number of alternative topologies and the capacity (bandwidth) is largely dependent on how much is spent. The head office will require a high speed network whereas the factory might make less intensive use of IT and a lower capacity network would suffice. The organisation needs to be aware of the options but, normally, it will contract out the instillation of the network to a specialist organisation.

♦ WAN between locations. The LANs in the branches, warehouse and factory need linking together and, in this case, the main linkage is to the central IS / IT at head office. There is going to be substantial traffic over the WAN so some sort of open line connection (a circuit that is permanently available) would seem to be required. This can take the form of an open connection rented from a telecommunications provider or Funco could join a commercial packet switching service (there are a number of such services available – they are like mini Internets but the services are restricted to members – generally they should be faster, more reliable and more secure than the Internet).

♦ Sales people / teleworkers. For these people, network traffic is likely to be relatively low and intermittent. One option is to provide a dial-up to the nearest Funco office. A simpler option would be to use the Internet – the company could pay for these staff members to have broadband internet services installed. The use of the Internet rather assumes that the salespersons will do their order processing and information retrieval from home. Funco could look into mobile communications so that salespersons could use the central IS whilst on the move or from client's premises.

◆ EDI. For EDI Funco will probably join a specialist VADS service: see **Part III**. Funco could use dial-up to connect to the VADS or have an open line connection, depending on the volume of its EDI transactions.

◆ e-Shop. The e-Shop needs to be located on an Internet server. The server is connected to other IS / IT facilities on the head office LAN. The Internet server will need an open line, high speed connection into the Internet and customers will connect to the e-Shop, over the Internet, in the normal way.

Funco's overall network provision is summed up in **figure 17.5**.

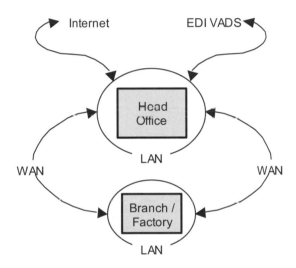

Figure 17.5 The Funco Network

The tendency is for network usage to expand and for technologies to move on. Funco will need to update its network provision at regular intervals if it is to provide an efficient and reliable service to staff and its outside trading partners.

17.6 The Internet

The network of the organisation outlined above is, primarily, a private affair focused on the business IS of the organisation. The Internet, in contrast, is a public access network open to anybody with a computer and a telecommunications link. The Internet is rather a strange phenomena – we tend to expect facilities to be provided by business or public authorities but this is neither of those things. Who owns or controls it is not entirely clear (although there are voluntary committees who give it direction).

The origins of the Internet are commonly traced back to a US military project, the ARPAnet, commissioned in 1969. The aim of the project was to develop a flexible network that could still function if some of the nodes were knocked out in a nuclear attack – hence the development of packet switching. The ARPAnet work was followed by various experimental networks in universities. Significant events in the evolution of the Internet include:

◆ CSNet – the US Computer Science Network was founded in 1981 and split from the ARPAnet in 1984.
◆ TCP/IP was developed in 1982 and put into use on 1 January 1983.
◆ JANET – the UK Joint Academic Network was founded in 1984.
◆ The World Wide Web was developed by the European Laboratory for Particle Physics (CERN) in 1989.
◆ Mosaic, the first web browser (in the way we now understand the term) was developed by the US National Centre for Supercomputing Applications in 1993.
◆ Amazon.com opened its virtual doors in 1995.

So, at the time of writing, the Internet as a public access, information, e-Commerce and communications network is no more than ten years old. It has come from nothing to be the 'information superhighway' and the infrastructure of the information society and a globalised world. The Internet is used by governments, companies, organisations and individuals for a range of activities. These include:

◆ Personal messaging (e-Mail) – for both business and private purposes. The use of e-Mail in the workplace has had a radical effect on the way that business is transacted. e-Mail is asynchronous – the message waits in the recipient's mailbox until it is accessed. More immediate interaction, usually for private purposes, is provided using techniques such as instant messaging and chat rooms.
◆ e-Commerce – for both business-to-business and business-to-consumer exchanges.
◆ Information retrieval – there is a vast library of information, from all sorts of sources, out there on web pages. Most of these information sources are available free.
◆ Teleworking – the use of the Internet makes home to office communications much more available and affordable for those who wish to work from home (on a formal or informal basis).
◆ Distance education – online learning is much more immediate than correspondence courses. ICTs are not just the delivery method for course material but, for many courses, part of the learning process.
◆ Entertainment – the Internet can also be used for entertainment – surfing to see what one can find or playing one of the games that are available online (but jogging round the block is a more healthy option).

The public Internet that I have been describing is public but the Internet (or Internet technology) can also be used for restricted access networks. These are commonly categorised as:

◆ Intranets – a network within the organisation using the web technology for publishing company information and procedures. The intranet may include interactive pages for functions such as booking rooms or registering to attend a meeting.

- ◆ Extranet – similar to the intranet but extending outside the organisation (possibly to include commercial customers). This sort of facility is easily implemented on the Intranet by including a password check before the facilities of the intranet are accessed.

Note that while organisations do use the Internet for commercial purposes, many also use commercial networks for intra and inter organisational transactions: see the Funco example above.

Exercises

The need is for you to be aware of network services and their use in IS (we will not be building a network as part of this course). Check your understanding of networking by running through the following questions:

1. What is a LAN and what is a WAN?

2. Check out the facilities of the computer labs in your university or college. What arc the network facilities and what are they used for? Is the software / data you access on the local drive or on one or more networked servers?

3. Do you have your own PC and Internet connection? What sort of connection do you have and what are the alternatives? What are the advantages and disadvantages of each of the options you have listed?

4. You probably have a mobile phone. Do you use any of the digital (as opposed to voice) services that are provided? The prediction is that mobile access to ISs will increase. What use do you (and your fellow students) see for such services?

Further Reading

There are plenty of books on networking but all of them go into too much detail for this introductory IS course. A good source of further information on specific networking topics is:

Freedman A. (1999) *The Computer Desktop Encyclopaedia*, 2nd ed., Amacon, New York.

For further details of the internet, hopefully explained in a simple and understandable manner, see Chapter 13 of:

Whiteley D. (2000) *e-Commerce: Strategy, Technology and Applications*, McGraw Hill, Maidenhead.

Chapter 18
Transaction and Distributed Processing

Summary

Most information systems, excepting small, free-standing PC systems, are multi-user, networked systems. The configuration of these systems can be described as:

◆ Transaction processing – a system on a central server accessed from terminals on the desktop.

◆ Client–server – a system where the processing and / or data is shared between the desk top system and the central server.

◆ Distributed system – a system that involves processing and / or data located on a number of servers. A distributed system may be a closely coupled system within the organisation or it may be inter-organisational and require a much more open architecture.

In a networked system, requests for processing arrive in from terminals, or other parts of the system, in a random manner. This complicates the design of the IS and is something the IS practitioner needs to take account of when designing a networked information system.

18.1 Interactive Systems

Computer systems, databases and networks can be brought together to create a multi-user, interactive information system. The functional support and corporate IS outlined at the end of **Part III** will usually come in this category. For these types of system we have three (overlapping) classifications of architecture:

◆ The transaction processing (TP) system – the user has a desk top terminal and accesses the IS on a central server.

◆ The client–server system – the user has a workplace PC that runs some of the functionality of the system and is linked to a server that supports shared parts of the IS.

◆ Distributed system – a system where the shared IS function is split across a number of servers.

The configuration of a transaction processing / client–server system is shown in **figure 18.1**.

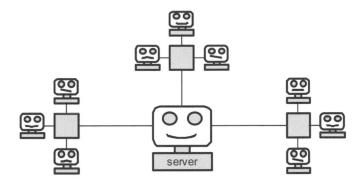

Figure 18.1 Transaction Processing / Client–Server Systems

Distributed systems have a range of configurations. They can be TP or client–server systems that access a second server for a limit functional or data requirement (passing data over to the accounting system could be seen as an example) or they may be truly distributed systems with significant aspects of the system running on different machines (possibly systems and servers that operate in cooperating organisations). The configuration of these systems is shown in *figure 18.2*.

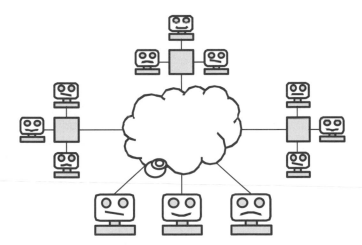

Figure 18.2 Distributed Systems

18.2 Multi-user Systems

The essential reason for an interactive, multi-user system, supported by a networked IT provision, is that several people are working together on the same job and sharing the same database. Examples of business information systems that are likely to be multi-user systems are:

- Order processing in medium and large companies.
- Payroll where there are several staff in the payroll section.

- Student record system where data is required by the university, faculties, departments, administration and academic staff.

For the example of the student record system we can have:

- Faculty staff registering students and checking fees have been paid.
- The university sorting out student numbers, quotas and budgets.
- Course leaders assigning students to tutorial groups, monitoring progress and checking progression.
- Unit leaders updating the system with attendance and marks.

All of this is sensibly done with a shared database of student records (that said, some universities are somewhat lacking in their provision of administrative IS).

18.3 TP Systems

The TP system connects tens or hundreds of terminals to a central information system and its associated database. The users of the system can make use of any of the functions of the system (provided they have privacy authorisation) at any time. This is not like batch processing, where we do one task after another, or a single user system, where only one thing happens at any time. This is a real time situation with messages arriving from the network at any time, often when a previous message is still being processed, and those messages need to be taken and queued until they can be processed. Fortunately for us there is system software, the TP monitor, that looks after the more technical aspects of the system process and we can concentrate on designing the user system.

In a TP system users input their data and then it sends the screen (all the data that has been input). The data that has been sent is then processed and the system responds with the next screen or an error screen (if invalid data has been submitted). This interchange is called an exchange and is illustrated in *figure 18.3*. A number of exchanges may be required to complete a transaction.

The TP monitor handles the technical aspects of the exchange and the application-specific processing has to be designed and written by the user organisation. The application module for this exchange, together with application modules for all the other exchanges in the system, are incorporated into the TP monitor system. The steps involved in processing an exchange, such as that shown in *figure 18.3*, are as follows:

- The arrival of an input message interrupts the TP monitor and the new message is placed on the input message queue.
- When the TP monitor is ready it picks up the next message from the input queue.
- The TP monitor is processing messages from many terminals. To establish the context for this message the TP reads in a 'partial results' record for the terminal. This will contain system data, privacy status and any data the application saved from its last exchange.
- The TP monitor invokes the application module applicable to the message. The application processes the message and accesses the database as required.

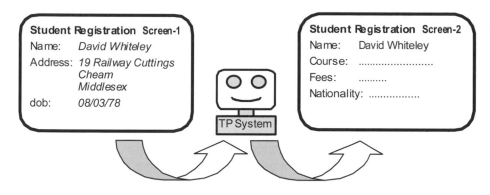

Figure 18.3 The TP Exchange

◆ Once processing is complete the output message is selected (usually the next screen in the transaction or an error screen) and placed in the output message queue.

◆ The partial results will have been updated by the processing of the exchange and these are written back to the partial results file.

◆ The message is taken from the output message queue and sent to the terminal.

The overall TP System is illustrated in *figure 18.4*.

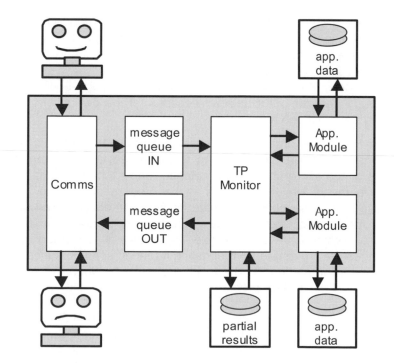

Figure 18.4 The TP System

The system as described is the basic system. The system is made more complex by the requirement for privacy, the need to multi-thread messages, the problem of data integrity and the needs of recovery, should the system crash.

◆ Privacy. With an online system there is an enhanced danger of unauthorised access (it may be possible to provide a physically secure area for the servers but access to desk top systems can not be restricted in the same way). The normal way of restricting access is with a password and user-id – further security such as the need to change passwords at frequent intervals, time-out of unused terminals and the use of swipe cards can be incorporated, if required. The user-id of the current user of any terminal will be held in partial results. A user-id can be associated with a subset of the functions of the TP system so that users can only access the transactions they have authorisation for (e.g. someone could be allowed to enquire about fees but not update them). The designers can also build in an audit trail by recording the user-id on all updates to the database.

◆ Multi-threading. Thus far we have talked about messages been processed one at a time. In a high throughput TP system this will not cope with the traffic and the system has to process more than one exchange at a time – a process known as multi-threading.

Multi-threading uses the ability of the computer to process more than one program at a time, a process known as multi-programming or time sharing. Multi-programming is achieved because the application takes much longer for each disk access than it does running in the processor unit. When a program accesses a file it can be suspended and another program (or in this case a TP application module) can be run. When the disk transfer is complete the operating system is interrupted and the original program can be restarted.

The process of multi-threading is looked after by the operating system and the TP monitor but it has ramifications for the design of the system. We will come to those next.

◆ Record locking. A problem that arises with multi-threading is that more than one application can be trying to make use of the same database records at the same time; if, for instance, one exchange is attempting to update a record while another is in the process of deleting it then the outcome will not be consistent with the users' intentions. The solution to this is lock tables and these are normally incorporated in the DBMS software. When a record is read its identity is recorded and other exchanges are prevented from updating it (and in some instances they are prevented from reading it). The locks are released when the exchange is completed. Two further problems that can arise in the area of record locking are:

• Deadly embrace. This occurs where an exchange has read record A, locked it, and now needs record B. A second exchange has read and locked record B and is now looking for A. Not a common occurrence but one that must be catered for. The TP monitor may have a way of handling this (by abandoning transactions) but standardising access paths to data can help avoid this problem.

- ◆ Cross-phase locking. The lock table sorts out data integrity within an exchange but does not help where a record is read in one exchange and is then processed in the next (as would be the case in an amendment transaction). Here the system designer needs to incorporate a mechanism to check that the data that was presented to the user has not been changed by the time the update phase of the transaction is processed.

- ◆ Screen and record logging. A real problem with any online system is what to do if the system crashes and data is lost (and that could be a lot of data if tens or hundreds of staff members have been using the system for several hours). With a batch system we can run the process again but with a online system the data is not available to be reprocessed (if it is on paper documents it could be typed in again but there is not necessarily a paper trail available). The steps that we can take to ensure data integrity are:
  - ◆ Secure the database at the beginning of the session – the database should be copied to a backup server or to backup files.
  - ◆ Screen logging – each screen that is sent into the system is logged to a file.
  - ◆ Database after-looks – each database record that is updated is written to a log file.
  - ◆ Database before-looks – each database record that is updated has its image before the update written to a log file (the before looks only need to be held for the duration of the transaction).

  The log files should be a facility of the TP monitor. They are preferably on a different disk drive to the database – it will not help if the database disk crashes and the log files are lost as well. Note, there is the more expensive alternative of duplexing the system and applying all updates on both the live and a 'hot standby' server.

- ◆ System recovery. If the system breaks and data is lost the recovery process is as follows:
  - ◆ Restore the database from the security copy.
  - ◆ Roll forward the database by applying the after-looks.
  - ◆ Roll back the database to the start of the current transaction for each terminal by applying before-looks.
  - ◆ Use the screen log to display the first screen of the current transaction for each terminal.

  This process is somewhat complex but, in the case of a failure, it should recover all the processing that has taken place in the session and give a consistent position on the database and to each user of the system.

(The explanation of TP processing in this chapter is largely based on the ICL TPMS TP monitor – the IBM TP monitor system is CICS. The detail that has been included of privacy, multi-threading and recovery is illustrative of the design detail required for multi-user systems – these sort of considerations also have to be taken on board in designing client–server and distributed systems.)

18.4 Client–Server Systems

In the TP system all the application processing is done on the server. This has benefits of conceptual simplicity but might not be the most effective use of the IT infrastructure (where the desk top system will be a powerful PC rather than an old fashioned 'dumb terminal'). By adopting a client–server architecture we can:

♦   Use the desk top for processing and possibly data storage.
♦   Reduce network traffic as less data / fewer messages have to be sent to the server.
♦   Improve formatting of the user interface (screens for TP systems are typically character only).
♦   Possibly increase resilience if the desk top system can run in stand-alone mode should the server be down or inaccessible.

The emphasis between client and server can vary considerably. We use the terms thin and thick client as follows:

♦   Thin client – a system where most of the data and the functionality is provided on the server and the client is limited to (say) screen formatting and some validation of user inputs. Some organisations have started calling their TP systems client–servers systems when the client part is no more than a terminal emulator; it sounds more up-to-date!
♦   Thick client – a system where there is substantial, application specific, local processing and, very probably, local data storage. For a thick client, client–server system the server may be not much more than a shared database.

Probably the most common functionality of client systems is screen formatting and local validation. In the TP system, the user fills in a screen template and only when that is completed is it sent to the server system for processing. It can be useful if the data is validated as it is input and (possibly) if the screen template is adjusted as the data is input, e.g. if an overseas student's details are input the screen template can be changed to include the relevant additional fields.

The design of the system and the distribution of functionality and data has to be assessed in relation to the needs of the system and the organisation. The nature of the data is crucial in this assessment – does it belong to the individual or is it essentially organisational information?

A possible problem of a client–server system is maintenance. If a change is to be made this can require updating both client and server software – the revised client software then has to be installed on tens or hundreds of desk top machines. It may be that the system has to remain operational with different versions of the client software running while the upgrade is completed. It can be that some people's desk tops will be updated with new PCs and later versions of the operating system – the systems team will need to make sure that no incompatibilities are introduced.

18.5 Distributed Systems

Distributed systems take the networking of the IS a step further with the functionality spread over a number of servers. This may be an extension of the TP / client–server architecture with:

- Desktop PC systems, possibly with some client functionality.
- Departmental / branch servers with processing and data appropriate to that level of the business.
- Central server performing the central functions of the IS.

This architecture is illustrated in *figure 18.5*. The shop systems with the EPOS terminals linked to a back-office server and hence to the central stock control / replenishment systems are an example of an application that uses this architecture.

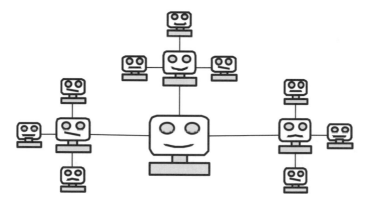

Figure 18.5 Distributed System with Branch and Enterprise Servers

There are obviously more complex configurations of distributed systems (and in part it depends on what you include in the system boundary – an order processing system interfacing with the General Ledger, on a different machine, could be seen as a distributed system as opposed to two separate systems).

An enabling technology of distributed systems has been SQL. Some loosely coupled distributed systems use SQL messages, sent over the network, to retrieve data from separate database servers and will then use that data for the processing function they are performing.

A newer technology is that of web services and service-oriented architectures. Web services are explained, by Power and Acton (2003), as:

> Web services are collections of software functions (behaving in an abstract way similar to 'lego') that allow machines to communicate seamlessly over the Internet in a language, platform and data neutral format. The functionality of web services can range in complexity from a simple information retrieval service, such as up-to-date departure times of flights from a specific airport, to enterprise services such as an automotive rental company's inventory management.

Web services are then integrated over the Internet using XML messaging (providing a software platform communications medium). The idea is that:

> … such services will register themselves in public or private business registries. These services will fully describe their interface structure, business requirements, business processes and terms and conditions for use.
>
> (Power and Acton, 2003)

The combination of the service requestor, the service provider and the service registry creates the (distributed) service-oriented architecture.

This technology is being applied in the travel industry for booking airline seats, reserving hotel rooms and hiring cars. The application is being used by the travel agent, the tour operator (or possibly the customer on the net). The service requestor software enquires, using XML, of the service registry where the required service might be located and how it is to be interrogated. Having identified possible service providers it can then send XML messages to that provider and locate and book the travel services required by the customer. The process is illustrated in *figure 18.6* in a diagram taken from Power and Acton (2003). The scope of the distributed system can be extended with new service requestors and service providers (with new or competitive services) without disturbing the architecture of the existing distributed system. The use of XML is similar to EDI but as XML is a meta language it allows the service provider to define its own message (presumably within prescribed limits).

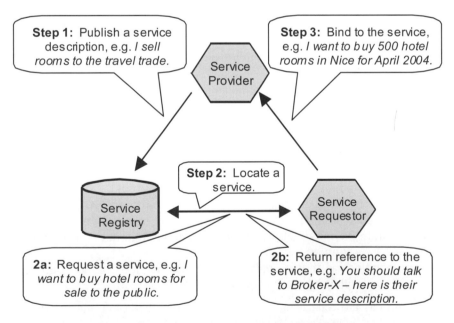

Figure 18.6 Hotel Brokering using Web Services

Sutor (2003) gives the example of Bekins, a major US shipping company with a unit specialising in delivering high-value consumer goods from retailers to the customer's premises. To do this Bekins used a network of agents and had a phone / fax system to allocate jobs to those agents. The system wasn't always fair or efficient. The system has been replaced with a virtual market system, built using web service technologies, where the agents select the jobs they are willing and able to do. The claim is that the system works better for Bekins, the customer and the agents.

Exercises

1. Explain the essential differences between TP systems, client–server systems and distributed systems.

2. The chapter outlines an approach to data recovery on the server in a TP system. What additional data integrity problems arise in a client–server system (I won't ask about distributed systems – that gets too difficult!)?

Further Reading

There is a lack of introductory material on this topic (and the chapter covers the field in sufficient detail for this level of study). Look on the book's web page for links to useful articles.

Part V
System Analysis and Design

In the previous sections of the book we have looked at business, information systems and information technology, and this forms the background knowledge required by the business analyst, the system analyst and the system designer, the people whose job is to analyse user requirements and to design computer based information systems.

The process of system analysis and design (SA&D) is best carried out in using the guidance of some sort of methodology, a sequence of doing things and a set of techniques for documenting the analysis and design:

◆ The sequence of doing things is called the lifecycle. There are a number of differing lifecycles and we have already taken a brief look at one of these in *Part I* – we now look at the main alternatives.

◆ The techniques vary depending upon the methodology, or class of methodology, being used – we will introduce various approaches and look at structured and at object-oriented techniques (courses may wish to adopt one of these approaches and ignore the other).

As well as specifying a lifecycle and including techniques, a methodology will embody a philosophy. The approach to system analysis may be a 'hard', scientific, reductionist approach or it can be a 'soft', human centred approach – I will try to tease out the philosophical differences between the various approaches to SA&D.

Once the system is designed we pass it over to the programmers or the implementers. These tasks are outside the field of our IS course but, for anyone not studying programming, we give an outline of what goes on. That said, we are not letting you off the hook: there is a project for you to design and implement on an MS Access database.

To illustrate the SA&D techniques we will use case studies. Two case studies are included at the end of *Chapter 19* and will be used in the examples and in the exercises.

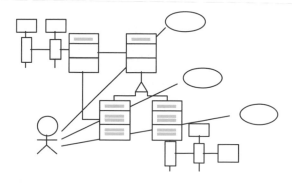

Chapter 19
System Development Lifecycles

Summary

The lifecycle is a sequence of stages, phases and tasks involved in specifying, developing and maintaining an information system. There are many different lifecycles but they are based on one or other of two basic models:

- The waterfall lifecycle – the analysis, design and development phases are carried out sequentially. Each phase is completed and signed off before the next phase is started.
- Iterative / prototype lifecycles – analysis, design and development take place simultaneously using a series of system prototypes. We start with an initial prototype, aimed at discovering requirements, and then iterate it, adding functionality and refining the design, until an acceptable system is produced.

Examples of SA&D methodologies that use these lifecycles are:

- Structured Systems Analysis and Design Method (SSADM). A heavyweight structured method that has a waterfall lifecycle.
- Dynamic System Development Method (DSDM). A rapid application development framework that uses an iterative lifecycle.

19.1   System Analysis and Design Methodologies

A system analysis and design methodology is a package of stages and techniques to help the system analyst (and other members of a project team) in the job of designing an information system. A methodology is defined Maddison (1983) as:

> a recommended collection of philosophies, phases, procedures, techniques, tools documentation, management and training for developers of an information system.

The stages / phases are termed the lifecycle – this is the sequence of stages that the project team go through in analysing, designing and developing a computer application system. The two basic approaches to the lifecycle are waterfall and iterative: these are explained in this chapter. The lifecycle provides a framework for the management of the project.

The methodology defines procedures, tools and techniques that are to be used in each stage. The basic analysis and design techniques for structured and object oriented methods are taught in **Chapter 20** and **Chapter 21**, respectively.

The philosophy of the methodologies can be classified in a number of ways. In this chapter I suggest a four-way classification of methodologies:

◆ A 'hard', structured approach – illustrated by SSADM.
◆ A 'soft', socio-technical approach – e.g. Checkland's SSM.
◆ A rapid application development (RAD) approach – illustrated by DSDM.
◆ Object oriented analysis and design (OOA&D) – illustrated by UML.

Note that UML is an OO modelling language and does not specify a lifecycle – hence it is covered in **Chapter 21** but is not discussed in this chapter.

19.2 The Waterfall Lifecycle

The basic lifecycle is the waterfall lifecycle. This breaks the project down into a sequence of stages and the requirement is that one stage is completed and signed off before the next is started. The waterfall analogy is of a series of pools on a hillside linked by waterfalls. The stages are the pools and we swim around in those pools applying the specified techniques, using tools and producing the required end products before tumbling down the waterfall to start the next stage. Like most analogies it does not bear too close an inspection!

We used the waterfall lifecycle in **Part I** to introduce some of the concepts of IS; we look at it in a bit more detail in this chapter. The basic waterfall lifecycle structure is shown in **figure 19.1**.

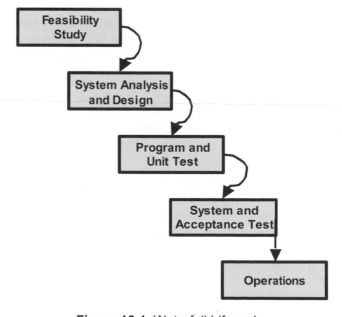

Figure 19.1 Waterfall Lifecycle

The stages of the waterfall lifecycle are:

❖ **Feasibility Study**

The first stage of all methodologies is a feasibility study. Developing an IS can represent a sizable investment and it is obviously a good idea for the organisation to check out what it is letting itself in for, and what it is likely to achieve, before committing to the development and instillation of a system. The feasibility stage seeks to answer three questions:

◆ Is the system technically feasible – will it work?
   The question needs to be not just can it be made to work, but is it appropriate to the organisation and the task? Some systems involve new, unproven technologies and it may well not be appropriate to take the risk of using such techniques.

◆ Is the system financially justified – can we afford it?
   The classic approach to cost justifying a system is a discounted cash flow. We estimate the price of the proposed system and the savings that should be made once the system is installed. We can then factor in an interest charge and calculate the payback that the system will produce, if any. This approach is less appropriate when the system is a 'must have' (e.g. because the current system is reaching the end of its useful life) or where the system is intended to give competitive advantage but there is no accurate way of estimating the benefit.

◆ Is the system ethically acceptable?
   How much ethics comes into business is debatable but any new system, and the uses of that system, should be within the law – the Data Protection Act, see *Part VI*, is one law that could be relevant. The new system also has to be operated by the staff and a system that threatens jobs or makes people's lives more difficult is unlikely to be welcomed by the workforce. These types of issues also need to be evaluated as part of the feasibility study.

To assess the feasibility of the system the business analyst and / or system analyst needs to do a mini version of the systems investigation that will be conducted in the next stage of the lifecycle. From this study the analyst can draw up a feasibility report that includes:

◆ An outline of the proposed systems. The outline must specify what is included in the system and what functions lie outside the system boundary.
◆ A technical summary of the IT equipment and software that is required and the way the system should be implemented.
◆ A high-level plan on how the system should, or could, be implemented.
◆ A costing of the proposed system and of the benefits that are claimed for the system.
◆ The feasibility assessment: will it work? can we afford it? and is it appropriate?

The feasibility study needs to be fairly short and reasonably cheap but it needs to be effective. The intention is to avoid investing a lot of money in a system that will take too long, cost too much, prove ineffective and / or disrupt the organisation. That is worth some time and effort but the investment must not be excessive – there is no usable end product.

❖ **System Analysis and Design**

Given that the project is deemed feasible and development approved, the next stage of the project is systems analysis and design. The task is threefold:

◆   Find out what the business requires: requirements analysis.
◆   Propose a 'logical system' that would meet all or most of the requirements: logical design.
◆   Design a computer system that implements the agreed logical system: technical design.

The single lifecycle stage of system analysis and design can be broken down into these three phases giving the more detailed lifecycle shown in *figure 19.2*.

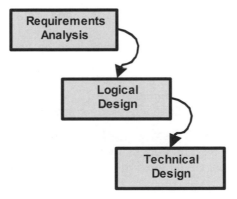

Figure 19.2 SA&D Lifecycle

The first phase, requirements analysis, is concerned with finding out what the users do and how it might be improved. The techniques of requirements analysis are:

◆   Interviews – talking to the managers and staff to find out what is done and how it might be improved. Interviews are likely to be the main tool in a system investigation.
◆   Observation – watch staff using the current system. By observation the analyst can get an idea of what works well and which facilities are inappropriate or difficult to use.
◆   Questionnaires – these might be used where there are a large number of staff and / or where those staff are dispersed in local offices. Questionnaires can be useful but the amount of information that is likely to be obtained is limited.

◆ Current system – the analyst can look at the current system and associated files and documents to see how the job is currently done, the volume of transactions and the data that is used.

From these sources the analyst can document the requirements for the new system. The requirements specification will include diagrams and descriptions that specify the business process and of the objectives for the new system.

The documentation of the requirements leads onto the logical system design. The logical system is a theoretical system that best meets the user's and business's requirements. The logical system is deliberately independent of the IT that might be used. The idea is that, if the design were to be for a pre-defined technical installation, it might not produce the optimum solution – better to first design a theoretical system and then use that to determine the best arrangement and combination of technology for the job. Not all methodologies include a requirement for a logical system design stage.

The final phase of SA&D is the physical / technical design. It is at this stage we determine what the eventual system will look like, the technology that is needed to implement it and the way it will be used by the organisation.

The final end products of the system analysis and design stage will be:

◆ Diagrams summarising the processing and data requirements of the system.
◆ Specifications of the IT equipment that is to be bought and the technical procedures that are to be followed.
◆ Details of the organisational structures and procedures that are to be applied when the new system is in use.
◆ Program / process specifications for the software that is to be developed.

The end products of the SA&D stage need to be reviewed and agreed before the project proceeds. It will also be necessary to review the project plan to check that the costings and timescales, put forward in the feasibility study, are still applicable.

❖ **Program and Unit Test**

This is the stage where the required system is implemented on the IT equipment. The classic way of doing this is to write computer programs but the system may also be implemented using some sort of application generator or a bought-in package (such as the ERP systems discussed in *Part III*):

◆ Programming consists of writing sets of instructions in a tightly defined programming language. The program must be logically correct and cover every eventuality that may occur. Programming is further discussed in *Chapter 23*.
◆ An application generator or fourth generation language cuts down on the amount of work that the programmer must do – the overall framework and some of the logic is provided by the system. For those who are familiar with MS Access, the way that forms and reports can be specified is an example of a simple application generator.

◆ The adoption of a package cuts out much, or all, of the programming stage. There might be modifications or additions and the package will still need the system test – the next stage of the lifecycle.

As each program / module is written it needs to be thoroughly tested. There are many paths through most programs and we can only be confident that it is correct if they are all tested. Normally 100% testing is not possible – the amount of testing is, in part, determined by how crucial is the reliability of the system. Thorough testing of a module can take as long, or longer, than it took to write that module.

❖ **System and Acceptance Test**

The final stage of developing a system is to put it all together and see if it works. A two-stage approach to testing the whole system is a system test and an acceptance test. The requirement is as follows:

◆ The system test is a technical test by the project team. Given thorough testing of all the components in unit testing the system test / link test should just be about ensuring that all the interfaces work (although it never works out to be that simple). In carrying out the system test the development team should be ensuring that the system as developed meets the requirements of the specification.

◆ The acceptance test is a user test. Hopefully the system test has checked out all the bugs and it is the job of the acceptance test to ensure that the system meets the user's requirements and will meet the needs of the organisation in its everyday operation. There is the possibility that the acceptance test will find significant omissions or misunderstandings – but that is not good news when the system is days or weeks away from going live.

As well as checking the functionality of the system, the system and acceptance testing must also make sure that the system will operate successfully under live conditions. There is a world of difference between one programmer testing a single module and an integrated system working with tens or hundreds of online users accessing a multiplicity of functions in the same time frame. Multi-user, online systems need to be volume / robustness tested before they are used in the live environment.

❖ **Operations**

The first event in the operating of a system is going live. This may take place as a big-bang event (switch off the old system on Friday night and start with the new system on Monday morning) or there may be a phased introduction of the new system (with parallel running of the old system for a period of weeks or months). Switching over to a new system is always a fraught affair – however good the preparation there are always things that can (and usually do) go wrong.

The preparation for the system going live must include the system and acceptance testing (or equivalent) but also requires some or all of the following activities:

- Installation of new IT equipment and network facilities.
- Training of maintenance and support staff (who may be the personnel who developed the system).
- Training of user staff.
- Loading of data onto the new system

These preparations for going live, where there is a large system and / or a substantial number of staff involved, can be major activities of themselves. Often these activities will run in parallel with system and acceptance testing and they can be planned as part of that stage.

Once the system has been put live the true operations stage begins. Initially the maintenance / support team will be helping the users and dealing with bugs that got through the testing stage. Over time, new requirements will emerge and the system will need to be enhanced by adding new facilities or amending existing facilities. All changes must be done with care and would normally go through their own design, development and testing stages – we don't want to jeopardise the successful running of the system when some minor enhancement is added in.

Over time, technology and the business will move on. There is only so much that can be done by the maintenance team and eventually it is time to start afresh – back to the feasibility study and start again (but that said, there is some very old software out there in critical business systems – as organisations found out when they had to check out their systems for the millennium bug).

The waterfall lifecycle expects one activity to be finished and signed off before the next activity starts. It allows for clear cut project management – if a stage that should have been finished four weeks ago is not yet finished then you are a month late and counting. Problems with a waterfall lifecycle are that:

- It is assumed that user requirements are captured early in the process but any misunderstandings or omissions may well not come to light until the acceptance test stage – a bit late to be making significant changes.
- It is also assumed that no significant changes will take place after the requirements have been signed off. Business is not always like that and changes can and do come up which then rather upset the carefully drawn up system design and the development plan.
- Projects developed using the waterfall lifecycle and associate methodologies can be bureaucratic, long winded and expensive. The problem of long development timescales is partly down to the lifecycle but is also a consequence of the heavyweight methodologies that are traditionally associated with this lifecycle.

19.3 SSADM

The waterfall lifecycle is most closely associated with structured methods, and the leading structured method in the UK is the Structured Systems Analysis and Design Method (SSADM).

SSADM was created and introduced back in the 1980s by the government Central Computing and Telecommunications Agency (CCTA) in response to problems that had occurred with a number of large government computing projects. The methodology was developed in conjunction with a private sector organisation LBMS. Over the years the method went through a number of iterations and the current (probably final) issue is version 4. The method is public source: that is, it is free for anyone who wants it to use it.

SSADM is a waterfall SA&D methodology that tackles just the feasibility study and SA&D part of the lifecycle. Version 4 has five modules and seven stages which are shown in *figure 19.3*.

```
◆  Module 1          Feasibility Study
   •   Stage 0       Feasibility

◆  Module 2          Requirements Analysis
   •   Stage 1       Investigation of Current Environment
   •   Stage 2       Business System Options

◆  Module 3          Requirements Specification
   •   Stage 3       Definition of Requirements

◆  Module 4          Logical System Specification
   •   Stage 4       Technical System Options
   •   Stage 5       Logical Design

◆  Module 5          Physical Design
   •   Stage 6       Physical Design
```

Figure 19.3 SSADM Modules and Stages

Another way of looking at SSADM, that ties up with the detail we looked at of the waterfall lifecycle, is as three main stages and three smaller transition stages. This view of SSADM is shown in *figure 19.4*. The stages are:

◆ Stage 0: Feasibility – the first of the transition stages. A short sharp study to decide whether to proceed with the project. The end product is the feasibility report which is then assessed by the appropriate managers. If the feasibility study is accepted we make the transition to requirements analysis.

◆ Stage 1: Requirements analysis – where the current system is investigated along with the business and user requirements for the proposed system. One difference with the SSADM approach is that it explicitly acknowledges that investigating the user requirement will include looking at the current system. The documentation from the requirements analysis includes:
   • Data flow diagram (DFD) of the current system.
   • Logical data structure (LDS) of the current system.
   • Problem requirement list.

◆ Stage 2: Business system options – the second of the transition stages. Stage 1 has investigated the current system and there is a real danger that the project could just re-implement that system on newer technology and miss the opportunity for business system improvement. The job of this stage is to think of alternative business approaches that could be included in the new system and choose the optimum way forward. The main end product of the stage is the data flow diagram (DFD) for the proposed logical system.

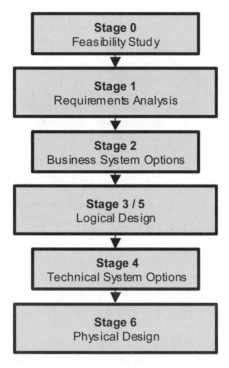

Figure 19.4 The SSADM Lifecycle

◆ Stage 3 / 5: Definition of requirements and logical design where the proposed logical system is specified in some detail. This task is divided into two stages for reasons that will be outlined below. The documentation for the logical design includes:
  • Data flow diagram (DFD) of the proposed system.
  • Logical data structure (LDS) of the proposed system.
  • Relational data analysis (RDA).
  • Entity life histories (ELH).

◆ Stage 4: Technical system options – the third and final transition stage. The task here is to choose the hardware, software and communication provision for the proposed system. The stage is scheduled part way through the logical design because that is the earliest point at which there will be sufficient information to make fully informed technical decisions and (hopefully) there is still time to set up the technical infrastructure before development starts. The major end product of the stage is a document specifying the technical architecture that is proposed for the system.

◆ Stage 6: Physical design – where the logical design is mapped onto the intended technical provision. An important part of physical design is to ensure that the system will give an adequate performance with the intended workload. The Physical Design has to be somewhat iterative as the database and processes designs are tuned to meet performance requirements. The end products for the physical design are:
  ◆ Physical database design.
  ◆ Physical process design.

The main techniques used in SSADM are:

◆ The data flow diagram (DFD) showing the data inputs to the system, the data outputs from the system, the processes and (logical) data stores.
◆ The logical data structure (LDS – also known as an entity relationship (ER) diagram) showing the data used by the system in terms of entity, attributes and the relationships between the entities.
◆ Relational data analysis (RDA – also known as normalisation) where the data is analysed to meet the requirements of database design (third normal form). The results of normalisation are fed back into a revised LDS.
◆ Entity life history (ELH), one diagram for each entity on the LDS. Essentially a cross-reference between the LDS and the DFD showing the events that affect the entity.

SSADM also includes effect correspondence diagrams (ECD) and process and dialogue design using Jackson structures. These are not widely used (or understood) and they are not studied in this text.

The DFD and LDS (or ER diagram) are used across a range of methodologies. The DFD, LDS, ELH and normalisation are described in detail in **Chapter 20**.

SSADM is a 'heavyweight' methodology. There are seven stages and each of them is divided into a series of steps and associated tasks. Applying SSADM in full is likely to be time consuming and many people, who use structured methods, apply an informal / cut-down version of the methodology.

The two principal techniques of DFD and LDS (supported by normalisation) are widely used. Any system that is to be implemented using a database should be subject to full data analysis. The DFD is a good technique for exploring and documenting the functionality of the system. It is not appropriate if the system is to be developed using object-oriented techniques but it is relevant for conventional programming and many application generators.

19.4 Iterative Lifecycles

The main alternative to the waterfall lifecycle is an iterative or prototype lifecycle. With this approach a prototype is used to elucidate the requirements of the system. The project team knock up a 'quick and dirty' version of the main functions of the system and then discuss it with the users. The system can then be modified to incorporate the improvements that the users ask for and to add further functionality. The evolutionary prototyping lifecycle is shown in **figure 19.5**.

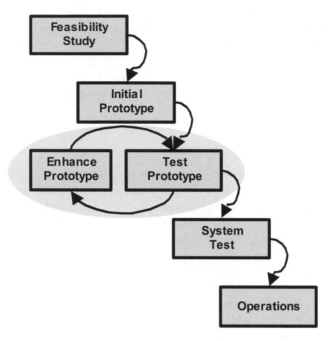

Figure 19.5 Evolutionary Prototype Lifecycle

The stages are:

❖ **Feasibility Study**

As with the waterfall lifecycle, we need to assess the three feasibility questions:

◆ Is the system technically feasible?
◆ Is the system financially justified?
◆ Is the system ethically acceptable?

In the feasibility study we also need to work out what will be in the initial prototype, how we plan the iterations and the timescale for the subsequent stages. See the waterfall lifecycle for a more detailed description of the feasibility report.

❖ **Initial Prototype**

A prototype is a model or mock-up of the system. The first prototype will concentrate on establishing the user requirements for the main functions of the system – it does not need to bother with the many subsidiary functions and the technical structure that will be required for the final system. For an order processing system, like that outlined in *Part III*, we would probably concentrate on functions to maintain customer, maintain product, create order and print picking list, leaving other functions and setting up a full scale database to later. We might also start with a single user system with software needed for multi-user operation also being left for later.

Prototypes need to be put together quickly and need to be changed quickly. The use of a fourth generation language / application generator can greatly assist in this process.

❖ **Test Prototype / Enhance Prototype**

The main two stages of the iterative lifecycle are checking and amending the prototype – this part of the lifecycle is reiterated in *figure 19.6*.

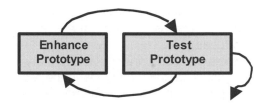

Figure 19.6 Check and Amend Prototype Iteration

Having created the initial prototype members of the project team will sit down with the users and test / evaluate the work than has been done. The questions are:

◆ Does the prototype do what the user requires?
◆ Is the prototype function well designed?
◆ What functions and functionality should be added when the prototype is amended / enhanced for the next iteration?

Small details of the prototype may be changed during the testing process but it is normally better to save up substantial changes and additions to the next iteration. One of the problems with prototyping is keeping control of the process, and planning a limited number of iterations is usually the way to go. Possibly for a medium size project one would plan four or five iterations – the initial iterations establishing the functionality of the major processes and the latter iterations including more facilities but concentrating on adding a fully functional file structure / database and the more technical aspects of the system.

The final iteration of the prototyping loop should produce a fully functional and technically acceptable software system. The system should be accompanied by an agreed level of documentation. Upon completion of these tasks the system can be passed on to system test.

❖ **System Test**

The prototype should have been tested as part of its development process but it needs a thorough test before it can be put live. The prototype process will, presumably, have covered the requirements of the acceptance test but the system still needs to be tested for its technical integrity including any requirement for volume testing.

❖ **Operations**

Once the system test has been completed the process used to develop it is largely irrelevant. Going live is much the same for a system developed using a waterfall lifecycle or an iterative / prototyping lifecycle.

The iterative approach has a number of advantages. These include:

◆ It is easier to work out the user requirement, particularly the user interface requirements using prototypes than using a paper based design process.
◆ Prototyping approaches are generally quicker than waterfall lifecycle methodologies (in part that is because there is generally less design documentation produced).
◆ Changes are more readily incorporated into a prototyping approach than a waterfall based project. That said, changes in the requirements late in the development of a project are always disruptive, whatever approach is used.
◆ The user is involved throughout the process and there should be less likelihood of producing software that does not meet the user's requirements.

The main drawbacks of a prototype approach to system development are:

◆ Project management and progress monitoring are not as easy, or as clear-cut, as when using a waterfall lifecycle. On the prototyping stages the work still to be done is not easily quantified.
◆ The software that emerges from the prototyping process is unlikely to be well designed. It started as a simple system and has been patched, amended and added to over the period of several iterations – not the best way to produce an elegantly engineered system.
◆ There is no formal point where the system should be sized – presumably this increases the likelihood of producing a system that does not perform adequately when used in live conditions.
◆ The prototype approach is probably not appropriate for large scale projects that are producing monolithic software systems.

All that said:

◆ Many modern software development packages lend themselves to a prototyping approach. The technical architecture of the system can be embedded in the package and that limits the damage a somewhat ad-hoc approach to development might cause.
◆ Large scale monolithic system developments are less common than they once were. Many software developments are relatively small scale, possibly on client–server systems and linking with other systems or with legacy systems to provide the required overall functionality.

The prototyping approach forms the basis for the rapid application development (RAD) class of SA&D methodologies. DSDM is one of these methodologies, and it is that method we look at next.

19.5 DSDM

Dynamic System Development Methodology (DSDM) was developed by a consortium of IT industry and IS user organisations. The method is public domain. The consortium is essentially UK based and DSDM has become the de-facto UK RAD standard (just as SSADM had previously become the de-facto UK structured SA&D standard).

The lifecycle of the DSDM is slightly more complex than the generalised evolutionary prototype lifecycle. It is affectionately known as 'three pizzas and a cheese cake' – it is shown in *figure 19.7*.

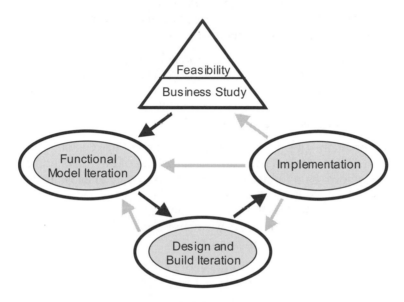

Figure 19.7 The DSDM Lifecycle

The stages of the DSDM lifecycle are:

◆ Feasibility – as with other feasibility studies we need to evaluate what is needed and hence check that the proposed system is technically achievable, affordable and acceptable. For DSDM we also need to check out that a RAD approach is appropriate. To apply RAD / prototyping techniques the system must not be computationally complex – prototypes model the user interfaces and that is not going to sort out a computationally complex system. RAD also requires commitment and compromise and all stakeholders need to be committed for the approach to work.

◆ Business study – a short exercise to elucidate the business requirements and determine the technical constraints. The process normally uses facilitated workshops to gain consensus on the requirements and the way the project is to proceed. The end results of the workshops and the stages include:

- Business area definitions identifying business processes and the users of the proposed system.
  - System architecture definition specifying the IT requirement including equipment, system software and the development software.
  - Outline prototype plan for the next two stages of the lifecycle.

- Functional model iteration – where system models (diagrams) and prototypes are used to work out the details of the system requirements. The stage is iterative. The initial prototype will probably be of just the main functions and these will be refined, and further functionality added, in further iterations. The stage concentrates on interfaces and user requirements; the technical infrastructure and performance of the system is more the responsibility of the next stage.

- Design and build iteration – this continues from the previous stage and prepares the system for implementation. This is the stage where we will complete the IT infrastructure and make sure that the system gives adequate performance and is reasonably robust. The design and build stage, like the previous stage, is iterative and the two stages may overlap.

- Implementation – the final stage is to implement the system. This involves the final set up of the IT infrastructure, training of the users and so on. The stage is shown as a further iteration but this is only to allow installation at a number of different locations (if that is the type of system that is being implemented). It is not the intention that we try to implement the system and if it all goes pear shaped we come back in three weeks for another bash (although that could happen!).

With RAD the emphasis is on early delivery of the system to the users. Getting a computer project delivered on time is not easy and using a DSDM lifecycle may help but it is also going to raise expectations. DSDM adopts a novel approach to delays in the schedule – if you can't complete the required functionality on time, chuck some of it out. One of the principles governing the use of DSDM is:

> Fitness for business purpose is the essential criterion for acceptance of deliverables.

and the assumption is that a system can serve a useful business purpose with far less functionality and exception processing than the user may have originally wanted.

DSDM defines a lifecycle and a number of techniques designed to keep the project on schedule. The method emphasises the importance of system documentation but does not define the techniques that are to be used. We could use structured techniques, see *Chapter 20* or we might opt for an object-oriented design technique, see *Chapter 21*.

DSDM requires commitment of all the stakeholders in the project. It should only be used when that commitment is present, when the project is of an appropriate size and when the functionality is apparent at the interfaces (so that prototyping can be an effective technique).

19.6   Classifying Methodologies

At the start of the chapter we had a definition that indicated that a system analysis and design methodology specified a lifecycle, techniques and a philosophical approach.

In this chapter we have looked at the waterfall and iterative lifecycles. There are many combinations and variations of these two approaches used by various methodologies. Our examples were SSADM, that used a version of the waterfall lifecycle, and DSDM, which gives a way of organising prototyping.

Techniques are looked at in detail in the next two chapters. The main system analysis and design techniques are:

◆ Process diagrams – typified by the data flow diagram used by SSADM and a number of other methods. Covered in detail in *Chapter 20*.
◆ Data analysis diagrams – the core diagram is the entity relationship diagram used by SSADM (where it is called the logical data structure) and by many other methods. Also explained in *Chapter 20*.
◆ Object-oriented techniques – the main technique is the class diagram. Object-oriented analysis, including the class diagram, is explained in *Chapter 21*.
◆ Prototyping – software models that are created in order to identify user requirements and to demonstrate the intended system – used, for example, by DSDM.
◆ Socio-technical techniques – methods that look at the human side of the organisation and its system requirements – Checkland's Rich Picture is one such technique.

The philosophy of a methodology can be difficult to capture but the main classifications (which may overlap) are:

◆ Hard systems – methodologies that assume that there is a problem to solve and take a scientific, reductionist approach to breaking down the requirements and devising a technological solution.
◆ Soft systems – methodologies that recognise that organisations are made up of people and that there are many views on what may be required and why it is needed. The soft system analysis starts with the problem domain and does not assume the need for a specific system.
◆ Structured approach – a method that breaks down (functionally decomposes) the system, using graphical techniques, into its component sub-systems that can then be separately designed and programmed.
◆ Object-oriented (OO) approach – a methodology that interprets the system in terms of objects (self contained modules of data and processing). OO methods relate to OO programming – there is not a lot of point in an OO analysis if the implementation is not going to use OO programming techniques.
◆ Rapid application development – a set of methods that place emphasis on shortening the project development lifecycle. Speed may be at the expense of (traditional) software quality and completeness.

From these various factors we can construct a picture of the possible / likely combinations of lifecycle, techniques and philosophies in a methodology, see *figure 19.8*.

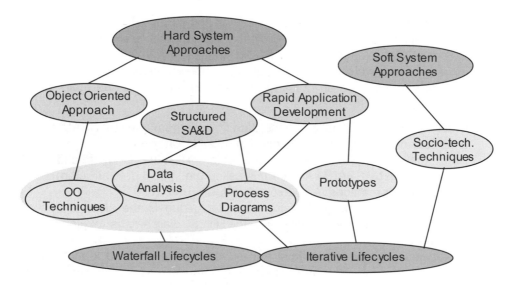

Figure 19.8 Classifying SA&D Methodologies

There are several hundred methodologies that have been produced and more are being produced all the time (this book proposes its own simple approach to applying OO techniques in *Chapter 21*). Which method is appropriate to any particular system requirement could be debated at length (and very possibly such a debate would produce more heat than light). If there is a choice of method (and often the methodology to be used will be determined by the organisation producing or requiring the system) then I suggest:

◆ If the type of IS that could be appropriate is in doubt (possibly we are thinking of applying IS in a new area where the staff / users are not used to IT), then start with a soft system approach.

◆ If the idea is to use a database (with application generator) or get a packaged solution, then start with a requirements analysis using DFDs and ER diagram (some packages come with their own recommended methodology and it makes sense to use this if it is available).

◆ If the organisation is committed to an early delivery then use a RAD approach.

◆ If you intend to use OO development tools (e.g. Java or C++) use UML within an appropriate lifecycle.

19.7 Case Studies

Below are two case studies. The first is the requirement for an IT system in a cycle hire shop – this will be used in *Chapters 20 and 21* to illustrate the application of structured and OO analysis and design techniques. The second is a system for Madcaster University: this case study is used for exercises and the answers are on the web site. Further case studies and exercises are available on the web site.

❖ High Peak Bicycles

Derbyshire County Council have taken over a number of disused railway lines in the Peak District and turned them into cycle paths / hiking trails. There is, at the junction of the High Peak and Tissington Trails, a busy cycle hire shop letting out a wide variety of bicycles, tandems, tricycles and trailers to people who wish to cycle on the trail but do not bring their own machines.

   The shop keeps upwards of 200 machines in stock and on a busy day it is quite a job keeping track of all the rentals. The shop has taken a placement student from MMU and is to ask her to computerise the system. The student has completed her fact finding and these are the notes she has taken:

1. The hire shop stocks some 200 bicycles. Policy is to offer modern machines. Most bicycles are kept for two years and then sold. A register is kept of all machines; details include a registration no, class (all-terrain, mountain, tandem, etc.), make, model, frame size, frame number, date of purchase, purchase price. The register is kept in a loose leaf folder. On purchase, each machine is given a registration number, assigned to a class and the details recorded on a form that is then added into the folder.

2. There is rarely a need to update the forms but occasionally corrections have to be made to the original details. The form is, however, updated with the selling date and price when the machine is sold. The intention is to keep records for five years so that the depreciation rates of the various models can be analysed. In practice record keeping is inconsistent and analysis of depreciation is not available.

3. Rentals are made by the day or half day and in the summer there is a special rate for 'late rentals' that runs from 16:00 to 18:00. Each class of machine has a rental rate for each of these periods, for instance:

	Day	Half Day	Late Rental
Mountain Bicycle (MB)	£10:00	£6:00	£4:00
All Terrain Bicycle (AT)	£12:00	£8:00	£5:00

    (effective 01 June 2003 until further notice)

    The rental rates are displayed on the noticeboard in the shop where staff can see them. When rates are changed the notice is replaced. Superseded rental rates should be retained for use when the accounts are prepared (the tendency is for the old notices to be left lying about and sometimes they become lost).

4. Each rental is recorded on a two part rental agreement form; general details include customer name, tel-no, date, time out, expected time back, expected period, deposit type (cash / credit card) and total prepaid amount. The rental can be for one or more machines (up to a maximum of four); the details for each machine are class, registration no, model and

prepaid amount. When the machine is rented out the customer is given one copy and the second copy is retained within the shop. The customer is also asked to pay in advance for the rental and pay a deposit of £20 (or leave a credit card imprint) for each machine. The deposit is kept clipped to the shop copy of the rental agreement pending the customer's return. An example rental agreement form is shown in **figure 19.9**.

High Peak Bicycles Tel: **01166 434343**	Bicycle Rental Agreement Rental No: *008647*		

Customer: Name: *Tony Blair* Tel No: *0181 643 0101*	Date	01 Sep 97
	Time Out	09:00
	Expected Time Back	12:00
	Expected Period	*Half Day*
	Actual Time Back	13:16
	Actual Period	Day

Deposit: ~~*Cash*~~ / *Credit Card*

Machine Class:		Machine:		Payment:	
Code	Desc.	Reg.No	Model	Pre-paid	Actual
MB	Mountain Bike	001341	Raleigh Max	6.00	10.00
MB	Mountain Bike	001826	Raleigh Max	6.00	10.00
TAN	Tandem	000841	Falcon 2x2	16.00	25.00
TRA	Trailer	000623	Baby Bug	4.00	6.00
			Totals:	32.00	51:00

Figure 19.9 Example Rental Agreement Form
(This is an example of a completed form. Pre-printed elements are in bold and variable entries are in italics)

5. When the customer gets back the shop copy of the rental agreement is found. Hopefully the customer has the top copy with the agreement number on it, otherwise there has to be a search through the pile. Once found, the rental agreement is updated with the time of return and the charges for the actual rental period; the customer is charged for any excess time and the deposit returned.

6. Occasionally a machine is not returned. Sometimes bicycles will be found abandoned and be returned (typically by a park warden) and sometimes the bicycle will never be recovered. In these circumstances the deposit is retained and the rental slip is updated with details of the circumstances. Where the deposit is a credit card imprint the customer will be charged £20 for each abandoned machine or the value or the bicycle for any non-recovered machine. Non-recovered machines are written off after 10 days and this is recorded on the appropriate sheet of the register. (Attempts will

also be made to contact the hirer and / or the matter will be reported to the police – these procedures are outside the scope of any proposed system.)

7. At the end of the day, all rental slips are totted up. Detailed statistics would be useful (e.g. to give a formal basis for deciding what types and quantities of machine to buy) but currently statistics are limited to the number of rentals and the total value.

(Note, this case study is based on observation of a number of bike hire operations and is not a exact representation of any specific bicycle hire operation in the Peak District National Park.)

❖ **Madcaster University**

Madcaster University is a small, traditional university in the market town of the same name in a rural area of Wales.

The recently appointed Vice Chancellor has decided to expand outside the scope of the traditional subjects taught in the university and has set up a School of Business and Computer Studies (B&CS).

B&CS has created a modular scheme where students can choose the units they study from a range of modules. Each student must study six 20-credit modules a year and must achieve 360 credits (120 at each of levels 1, 2 and 3) to achieve an honours degree. The scheme includes three degree titles and students must include the core units for their chosen course of study in their module choices for the year. The three degree titles are:

◆ Business Information Technology (BIT)
◆ e-Commerce Systems (ECS)
◆ Software Engineering (SOE)

In addition to the taught degrees there is a Postgraduate Diploma in IT Research. This is a one-year course; there are no formal taught units but the students are assigned to a staff member who acts as the individual's supervisor.

The B&CS modular scheme is a first for Madcaster University and the current administrative systems do not cope with its structure. It has therefore been decided to set up a new system to register B&CS students and to record their module choices and their progress throughout their chosen course. The requirements of the system are:

◆ The system has to be set up with details of the degree titles (name and reference code). Staff (tutor code and tutor name). Modules (module code, module title, tutor code and core requirements – an indicator for each of the degree titles).

◆ Student registration: each student joining the course has to be registered and associated with a degree / diploma title. The details required are name, address, gender and date of birth. Each student is allocated a unique registration number. The registration form is shown at *figure 19.10*.

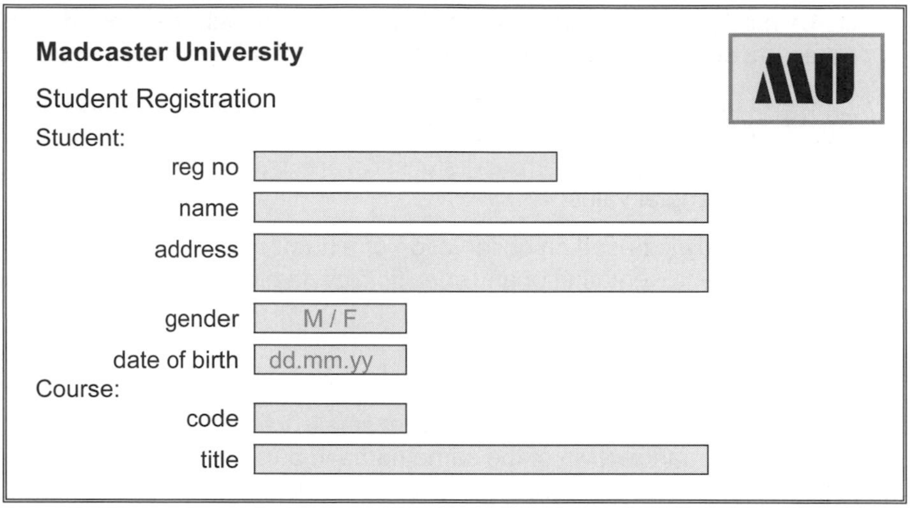

Figure 19.10 Student Registration Form

◆ Student amendment: at any time student details can be amended or corrected. Students can withdraw and this is recorded as an amendment using a status indicator (the details of the withdrawn student are kept on the system). The student registration number can not be amended.

◆ Module choice: at the start of each year all students (excluding research diploma students) choose six modules (including core modules for their chosen title). These choices have to be registered on the system. The module choices form is shown as *figure 19.11*.

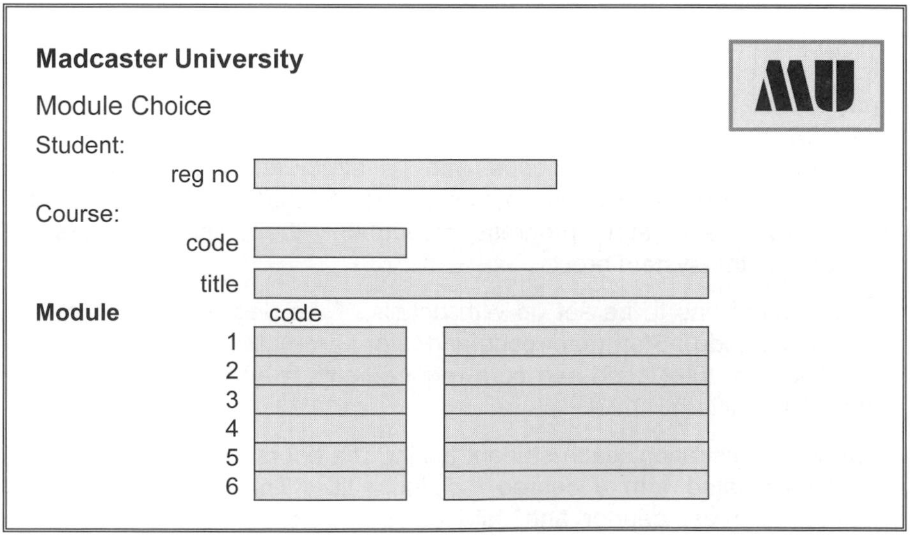

Figure 19.11 Module Choice Form

- Module results: at the end of the year the student's overall mark for each module is recorded together with a pass / fail indicator. To progress students must pass all six modules taken that year; if they fail they are out (and the status indicator is updated to show that). To obtain a degree the student must pass all three years: the student's overall degree grade will be recorded at the end of their final year. Diploma results are also recorded on the system.

Note the Madcaster B&CS system has been kept deliberately simple. There are none of the normal complexities of students joining part way through the course, repeating a year and so on. In a typical university setting there is considerable diversity of course structure and modes of study which can make modelling the system near to impossible.

Exercises

The following questions are designed to reinforce your understanding of the system development lifecycle.

1. List five advantages and five disadvantages of the waterfall lifecycle.

2. List five advantages and five disadvantages of an iterative / prototyping lifecycle.

3. Would you choose a waterfall based methodology of a prototyping methodology to develop an information system for High Peak Bicycles? Justify your answer.

Further Reading

There are a number of books that cover comparative systems analysis and design (and in a lot more detail than is required for an introductory IS course). A good example of such a book is:

> Avison D. and Fitzgerald G. (2003) *Information Systems Development: Methodologies, Techniques and Tools*, 3rd ed., McGraw-Hill, Maidenhead.

Chapter 20
Structured System Analysis and Design

Summary

Structured methods take a system requirement and construct a logical design before moving on to the physical design of the new system. In analysing the requirement, complex problems are decomposed into their component sub-systems for further analysis and design. Structured methods make extensive use of diagramming techniques to represent the requirement and the proposed system. These techniques include:

◆ Data flow diagrams.
◆ Logical data structure / entity relationship diagram.
◆ Relational data analysis.
◆ Entity life histories.

We looked at the lifecycle in the last chapter and, in this chapter (and with a bit of practice) we will learn these four ways of modelling and designing the system. It is noted that most chapters in this book are intended to be covered as a single unit of study (a lecture and a tutorial / self study). This chapter will take considerably longer, say four units of study.

20.1 Structured System Analysis and Design

Structured methods were introduced in *Chapter 19* and SSADM was used as an example methodology. Structured methods make extensive use of diagrams in the design process and to document the system. The two main techniques that are used in this class of methods are:

◆ Data flow diagram / data flow modelling – showing the processing requirements of the system.
◆ Logical data structure / data modelling – showing the underlying data requirement of the system.

These two techniques are used in the documentation of the existing system and then again for the logical design of the proposed system (SSADM also uses them in the feasibility study and the business systems options). These two basic techniques are supplemented by a number of further techniques, including:

♦ Relational data analysis – refining the data model to third normal form.
♦ Entity life history – a technique that cross-references / cross-checks the data model and the processing requirements.

We will now look at these four structured modelling techniques.

20.2 Data Flow Diagrams

The data flow diagram (DFD), in the words of Avison and Fitzgerald (2003):

> enables the system to be partitioned (or structured) into independent units of a desirable size so that they, and thereby the system, can be more easily understood.

The DFD shows the flows of the data from users (externals) into the system, the flows of the data within the system, the processing and the storage of that data, and the flows of information out of the system to the users. The DFD is a hierarchy of diagrams consisting of:

♦ Context diagram (conceptually level zero).
♦ The level-1 DFD.
♦ Level 2 and further levels of functional decomposition, if required.

The context diagram represents the system as a single process and only includes external dataflows. The level-1 diagram then breaks the system down into the main processing requirements. The level-1 diagram is kept relative simple showing, perhaps, five or six (and a maximum of, say, 10) processes. Keeping the diagram simple aids comprehension of the system requirements and ensures the diagram can be presented on a single page (or screen). If processes on the level-1 diagram require breaking down further they can be functionally decomposed as level-2 diagrams, and so on. Each level-2 diagram consists of the detail of a single level-1 process and obeys the same rules on the degree of complexity.

Anyway, enough of words. Let us now look at the symbols we have for externals, processes and dataflows – see *figure 20.1* – and we will use them to draw a DFD.

The system we will use to demonstrate the drawing of a DFD is the High Peak Bicycles case study given in *Chapter 19*. We will start with the context diagram and we need to find any external entities in the case study. The way to do this is to go through the requirement and identify the people who put data into the system or who receive data from the system. For the High Peak Bicycles case study we have:

♦ Staff – mentioned in the paragraph numbered 3 and implicit in all the functions of the system.
♦ Customers – mentioned in the paragraphs numbered 4, 5 and 6 (where the term 'hirer' is used).
♦ Park Warden and Police – mentioned in the paragraph numbered 6.

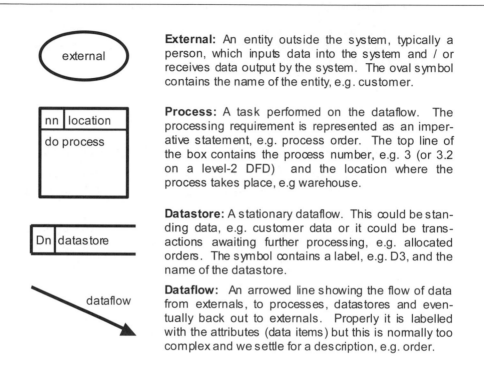

External: An entity outside the system, typically a person, which inputs data into the system and / or receives data output by the system. The oval symbol contains the name of the entity, e.g. customer.

Process: A task performed on the dataflow. The processing requirement is represented as an imperative statement, e.g. process order. The top line of the box contains the process number, e.g. 3 (or 3.2 on a level-2 DFD) and the location where the process takes place, e.g warehouse.

Datastore: A stationary dataflow. This could be standing data, e.g. customer data or it could be transactions awaiting further processing, e.g. allocated orders. The symbol contains a label, e.g. D3, and the name of the datastore.

Dataflow: An arrowed line showing the flow of data from externals, to processes, datastores and eventually back out to externals. Properly it is labelled with the attributes (data items) but this is normally too complex and we settle for a description, e.g. order.

Figure 20.1 DFD Symbols

So having identified (potential) externals we can go through the case study looking for inputs to the system and outputs from the system. Doing that I get:

- Para 1: '*A register is kept of all machines*'.
- Para 2: '*occasionally corrections have to be made*' and '*updated when selling*', both relating to the register of machines.
- Para 3: '(rental) *rates are changed*'.
- Para 4: '*Each rental is recorded*'.
- Para 5: '*the rental agreement is updated with … return*'.
- Para 6: '*In these circumstances* (non return) *the rental slip is updated*'.
- Para 7: '*all rental slips are totted up. Detailed statistics would be useful*'.

Bringing the two lists together and using a bit of common sense, we get:

- Staff, as an external, who will:
    - Input data to maintain the bike register – this includes registering new bikes, (occasional) amendments and recording bike sales.
    - Input data to maintain rental rates.

◆ Extract data in the form of management information – exactly what would be useful here is not made clear and further discussion with the user would seem to be needed.

◆ Customers, as an external, who will:
  ◆ Supply the data required to rent out one or more bikes.
  ◆ Supply the data needed when they return the bikes they have rented.
  ◆ Fail to return the bikes they have rented.
(These are joint activities between the customer and the staff – which external we use is a mater of choice. I think it is helpful to show the customer in preference to the member of staff.)

Using this list we get the context diagram shown at **figure 20.2**. Note that we have not used the Park Wardens or Police as externals – they are people who the staff talk to but they do not directly interface with the system.

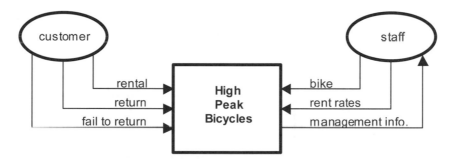

Figure 20.2 Context Diagram – High Peak Bicycles

Moving on from this we can start drawing the level-1 DFD. Checking through the case study we seem to have all of the processing requirements (in this case they correspond to the inputs and outputs). A further check through would then seem to suggest a requirement for the following datastores:

◆ Para 1: 'A register is kept of all machines' – a bike datastore.
◆ Para 3: 'rental rates are displayed' – a rent rate datastore.
◆ Para 4: 'Each rental is recorded' – a rental agreement datastore (although I will abbreviate that to fit on the diagram).

Taking, for example, the rental transaction we have:

◆ The customer as an external.
◆ A dataflow of rental details into the system.
◆ A process to execute that rental. The process would need to:
  ◆ find the required machines by reading bike data,
  ◆ cost the rental by reading rent rate data,
  ◆ store the rental agreement.

This portion of the level-1 DFD is shown in **figure 20.3** and, following similar logic, we can construct the complete diagram as shown in **figure 20.4**.

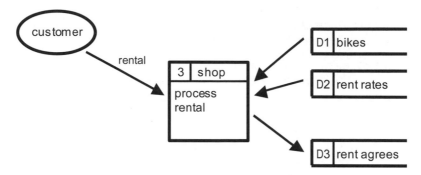

Figure 20.3 Level 1 DFD – Rental Transaction

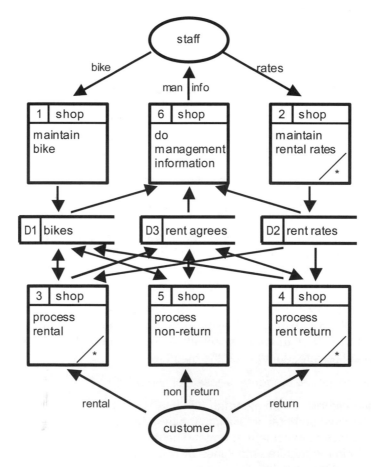

Figure 20.4 Level 1 DFD – High Peak Bicycles

Processes that are fully functionally decomposed are shown with an asterisk in the bottom right hand corner. The first process, maintain bikes, is one where some further details would be useful and a level 2 diagram is shown as *figure 20.5*.

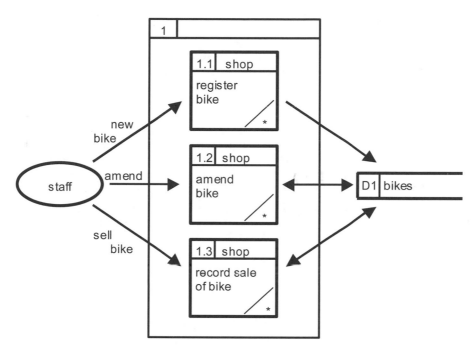

Figure 20.5 Level 2 DFD – Maintain Bike

So that gives you an idea of a DFD. Now practise using exercises 1 and 2 at the end of the chapter, before we look at the next technique.

20.3 Data Modelling

The DFD outlines the processing requirements and we need to supplement this with an analysis of the data. This is particularly true if we are going to use a database management system to hold the data.

The process of analysing the data is generally called data modelling. The diagram we produce is called an entity-relation (ER) diagram – SSADM calls it a logical data structure (LDS).

There are a number of conventions for drawing ER diagrams but we will stick to a basic model that is used by a number of methods including SSADM. It may be that, if you do a database specific unit later in your course, you will be asked to use an enhanced set of conventions. If that is the case, the underlying structure and principles will be the same as you have learnt in this text.

The symbols we need for an ER diagram are entities and relationships: see **figure 20.6**.

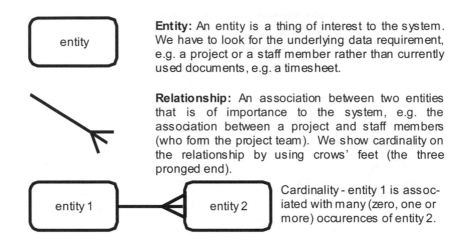

Entity: An entity is a thing of interest to the system. We have to look for the underlying data requirement, e.g. a project or a staff member rather than currently used documents, e.g. a timesheet.

Relationship: An association between two entities that is of importance to the system, e.g. the association between a project and staff members (who form the project team). We show cardinality on the relationship by using crows' feet (the three pronged end).

Cardinality - entity 1 is associated with many (zero, one or more) occurences of entity 2.

Figure 20.6 ER Diagram – Symbols

Continuing with the High Peak Bicycles case study we can start to draw an ER diagram. Again we go through the case study looking for entities, 'things of interest to the system'. For the case study we have:

◆ Bicycle – in para 1 and used throughout the case study.
◆ Bike Class – in para 1.
◆ Rental Rate – in para 3.
◆ Rental Agreement – in para 4.
◆ Customer – in para 4 (presented as an attribute of the rental but could be an entity).

These are our possible entities and we can also use the case study to look for relationships. Looking through the case study we get:

◆ Bicycle – assigned to a Bike Class and associated with all the rental agreements it has been hired out on (we need to keep old rentals for the management information).
◆ Bike Class – see Bicycle.
◆ Rental Rate – for each Bike Class.
◆ Rental Agreement – for up to four Bicycles.
◆ Customer – one for each Rental Agreement.

From this initial list of entities we can construct a first cut ER diagram: see *figure 20.7*. Let us run through the diagram and see what we have got:

◆ Bike Class (e.g. mountain bike) has many Bicycles.
◆ Bike Class has many Rental Rates (we have to keep the old ones when a new one is created).

◆   Bicycle is related to many Rental Agreements (it may or may not be out on hire but we also have to keep details of all the completed Rental Agreements).

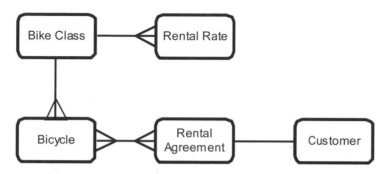

Figure 20.7 ER Diagram – First Cut

◆   The Rental Agreement has many (one to four) Bicycles assigned to it.
◆   The Customer has one Rental Agreement, and the Rental Agreement has one Customer (the case study does not say we reuse the customer details if the same person returns to take out some bikes on another day).
   ('many' is to be interpreted as zero, one or more – zero may not be applicable in every case).

OK, but there are some further 'rules' that we need to take account of:

◆   The Bicycle to Rental Agreement relationship is many-to-many. The Rental Agreement is for up to four Bicycles and the Bicycle is on many Rental Agreements (as we keep details of all current and completed Agreements). Now we could show a many-to-many on the ER diagram but we can not readily implement it on a database. For this reason we normally resolve a many-to-many by introducing a link entity: see **figure 20.8** (link entities are, on some ER conventions, shown as 'weak entities' but not on the basic diagramming convention we are using).

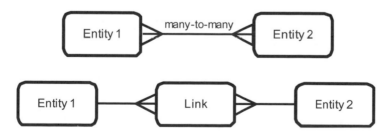

Figure 20.8 ER Diagram – Many to Many Relationships

Using this structure there will be an instance of the link for each valid instance of the relationship. If Entity 1 is the Bicycle then there is an instance of the Link for every Rental Agreement that bike is used by. Following on from that, if Entity 2 is the Rental Agreement there will be one of the link records for each bike used by that agreement. The link elements correspond with the lines on the Rental Agreement: we can call them Rental Lines. The Rental Line entity will be used to store the charges made for each of the bikes that is rented out (it cannot be shown on either the Rental Agreement or the Bicycle – think about it).

♦ The Rental Agreement to Customer is one-to-one. The rental only has one customer (the person paying the bill) and because we are not set up with a customer file the customer is only associated with one rental (if they come back next Sunday we will not look up their previous transactions). There is not a lot of point in a one-to-one – we can merge the customer data onto the rental and that is what we will do.

♦ Most conventions ask for the relationships to be named – SSADM requires two names for each relationship. We could, for instance, say a Bicycle 'belongs to' a Bike Class and that a Bike Class 'owns' zero, one or many Bicycles. I am not sure they serve a lot of useful purpose but for completeness I have included them.

♦ Sometimes people indicate optionality in the relationship. As indicated above, a Bicycle must have a Bike Class but a Bike Class could, conceivably, not own any Bicycles. We can show this by making the 'owns' end of the relationship a dotted line.

These changes then give us our completed version of the ER Diagram, see *figure 20.9*.

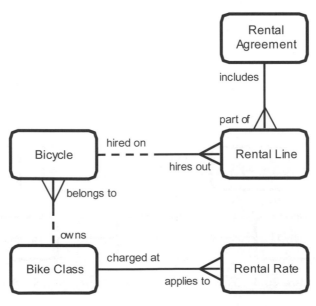

Figure 20.9 ER Diagram – High Peak Bicycles

Now do exercise 3 before continuing with the next section.

20.4 Relational Data Analysis

With data modelling we have done a top down exercise to create an ER diagram. Relational data analysis, in a sense, repeats the exercise but this time using a bottom up technique. The process of relational data analysis uses the input and output documents of the system. Using these documents it makes sure that we have all the attributes for each entity, and then it ensures that the data model is properly structured – a process we call normalisation.

There are four stages in normalisation:

◆ Un-normalised form: We list all the attributes used on the document we are analysing and identify a key.

◆ First normal form: We identify any repeating groups of attributes, separate them as a new entity, and find the key that identifies them.

◆ Second normal form: We identify any attributes that are dependent on only part of their key (where the key is made up of more than one attribute) and again these attributes are split off to make a new entity and the key is identified.

◆ Third normal form (TNF): We identify any attributes that are not dependent on (giving information about) the entity they are currently assigned to – these attributes (or groups of attributes) are separated to form a new entity and we find the key that identifies them.

The result of relational data analysis is a set of entities and their attributes that can be used to cross check the ER diagram. The entities in relational data analysis would normally be termed relationships and they are an appropriate starting point for the design of a database (they fit in directly with the design requirements of a relational database).

Let us now use the rental form from the High Peak Bicycles case study (**Chapter 19**) to illustrate the process. We do relational data analysis using a table with four columns representing the four stages outlined above. This form is shown in **figure 20.9**. The steps are:

◆ Un-normalised form: This is simply a list of attributes. Taking the rental form we get: customer name, customer tel no, rental no, date, time out, and so on. It is that simple: it is just a list. The full list is shown in **figure 20.10** – I have abbreviated some of the attribute names and I have chosen rental-no as the key that identifies the document (the key is underlined and put at the top of the list).

◆ First normal form: For this we look for attributes, or groups of attributes, that repeat. On the rental form there is one such group, the entries for each machine. This group is therefore separated off as a new Rental Line entity and we identify its key as the rental-no plus the reg-no of the bike been rented out.

◆ Second normal form: At this stage we are looking for attributes that are dependent on only part of multiple attribute keys. In our example there is one such key – the rental-no and bike-reg-no of the rental line. The details of the bike, i.e. its model and class are dependent only on the bike-reg-no (these details are the same whatever rental agreement the bike is assigned to). We can therefore separate these details off as a new Bike entity.

◆ Third normal form: At this stage we look for attributes that are not dependent on the key of the group they are in. That may not be very self-explanatory but a couple of examples should clarify it:

   ◆ The rental agreement includes the customer name and telephone number. We need to identify the customer on the rental agreement (and in the absence of a code we will use the name). The telephone number 'belongs' to the customer and we can thus create a separate Customer entity.

   ◆ For each machine on the rental agreement there is a class code and class description. We need to have one of these attributes, presumably the code, but for any given code the description is always the same (as can be seen for the MB code on the form). We can therefore separate off the class code and description as a Bike Class entity with a key of class code.

Having separated off these new entities we then mark their keys (customer name and class code) in the original entities with an asterisk to indicate a foreign key.

We have now completed the relational data analysis of the form: see *figure 20.10*.

Un-Normalised	First Normal	Second Normal	Third Normal
<u>rental-no</u>	<u>rental-no</u>	<u>rental-no</u>	<u>rental-no</u>
cust-name	cust-name	cust-name *	cust-name *
cust-tel	cust-tel	cust-tel	date-out
date-out	date-out	date-out	time-out
time-out	time-out	time-out	exp-time-back
exp-time-back	exp-time-back	exp-time-back	exp-period
exp-period	exp-period	exp-period	act-time-back
act-time-back	act-time-back	act-time-back	act-period
act-period	act-period	act-period	deposit-type
deposit-type	deposit-type	deposit-type	pay-prepaid-tot
class-code	pay-prepaid-tot	pay-prepaid-tot	pay-actual-tot
class-desc	pay-actual-tot	pay-actual-tot	
bike-reg-no			<u>rental-no</u>
bike-model	<u>rental-no</u>	<u>rental-no</u>	<u>bike-reg-no</u>
pay-prepaid	<u>bike-reg-no</u>	<u>bike-reg-no</u>	pay-prepaid
pay-prepaid-tot	class-code	class-code	pay-actual
pay-actual	class-desc	class-desc	
pay-actual-tot	bike-model	bike-model	<u>bike-reg-no</u>
	pay-prepaid	pay-prepaid	class-code *
	pay-actual	pay-actual	bike-model
		<u>bike-reg-no</u>	<u>cust-name</u>
		class-code	cust-tel
		class-desc	
		bike-model	<u>class-code</u>
			class-desc

Figure 20.10 Relational Data Analysis – Bicycle Rental Agreement

To complete the relational data analysis for the system we would go through all the other documents associated with the requirement – for the High Peak Bicycles case study this would include bike registration details and rental rates and the details of a bike sale. The third normal forms of each of these relational data analysis exercises would be merged to produce the overall third normal form for the whole system. To merge we combine all attributes for entities with the same key into a single list. In *figure 20.11* I show the list of Bike attributes from bike registration, bike sale and rental agreement. These are merged into an overall list of attributes in the final column of the table.

Bike Reg	Rent Agreement	Bike Sale	Merged
bike-reg-no	bike-reg-no	bike-reg-no	bike-reg-no
class-code *	class-code *	bike-sell-date	class-code *
bike-make	bike-model	bike-sell-price	bike-make
bike-model			bike-model
bike-frame-size			bike-frame-size
bike-frame-no			bike-frame-no
bike-purch-date			bike-purch-date
bike-purch-price			bike-purch-price
			bike-sell-date
			bike-sell-price

Figure 20.11 Relational Data Analysis – Bicycle

From the merged table of all the relational data analysis exercises we can construct a new ER diagram and compare it with our original ER diagram. In our case we just have the third normal form for the rental agreement (there are further details on the web page). We construct the ER diagram as follows:

◆ The first entity is the Rental Agreement. It has a single attribute key: rental-no, and it is therefore (initially) free standing. We place it on our diagram.

◆ Skipping the second entity we can select the Bicycle. Again it has a single attribute key: reg-no, and it is also (initially) free standing. We place it on our diagram.

◆ Returning to the second entity, Rental Line, we note that it has a two-part key: rental-no and reg-no. This indicates a link element owned by both the Rental Agreement and the Bicycle. We add it to our diagram with many to one relationships with both the Rental Agreement and the Bicycle.

◆ Next we will look at the Bike Class entity. The Bike Class with its key of class-code relates to a number of Bicycles where class-code is a foreign key. Therefore we can put Bike Class onto the diagram with a one to many relationship with Bicycle. The way I remember it is 'crows feet grab asterisks'.

◆ Finally we have the Customer entity. This relates as a one to many to the Rental Agreement where cust-name is a foreign key.

Our new ER diagram derived from the relational data analysis is shown in *figure 20.12*. It is a fair match with our original diagram shown in *figure 20.9*. It does not have Rental Rate but presumably this would appear when we analysed the rental rate transaction. It does have a Customer entity – whether we implement that is another matter (it is relevant if we want to keep a record of all our customers and reuse the data if they come back to make use of our services again – as the case study stands there is no such requirement).

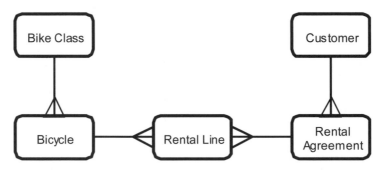

Figure 20.12 Relational Data Analysis – ER Diagram

Now do exercise 4.

20.5 Entity Life History

The entity life history (ELH) cross checks the DFD and the ER diagram. There is an ELH for each entity on ER diagram. The diagram then uses Jackson structures to show all the events, and the sequence of the events, that can affect that entity.

First let us look at Jackson structures. Jackson structures were developed as a way of designing programs. Jackson asserted that there were only three basic programming constructs: sequence, selection and iteration. The diagramming conventions for these three constructs (plus the quit / admit) are shown in *figure 20.13*.

These constructs can then be put together to document the life history of an entity – an abstract example of such a construct is shown in *figure 20.14*. And now we can look at an ELH for our entities, we will start with the Bicycle. Earlier on in the chapter we noted that the Bicycle would be:

◆   Registered when newly acquired.
◆   Amended (occasionally).
◆   Updated to record the sale.

Using these three elements would give us a simple sequence of register, amend and sale. The amendment iterates (and that allows for a zero iteration, i.e. no amendments). This first cut ELH is shown in *figure 20.15*.

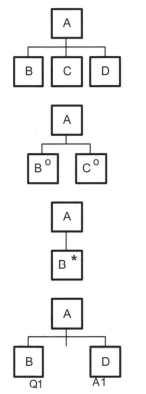

Sequence: A consists of B followed by C and that is followed by D. For instance if A is a waterfall lifecycle project it will have a feasibility stage followed by analysis and then programming stages.

Selection: A consists of B or C. For instance, using the example of a project, the feasibility study could be accepted or rejected.

Iteration: A consists of zero, one or more instances of B. Again using the example of a project, it could be shown as an iteration of stages as opposed to a sequence of named stages.

Quit and Admit: An extra construct added for use in ELHs. It is in effect a go to from Q1 to A1. It is a sort of 'get out of jail card' and should be used very sparingly.

Figure 20.13 ELH – Constructs

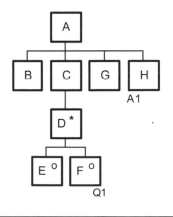

A consists of sequence of B,C, G and H. C is a an iteration of events represented by D (we are not allowed to put an iteration in a sequence). The event D can be either E or F. If the event is F we quit to event H.

Figure 20.14 Combination of Jackson Constructs

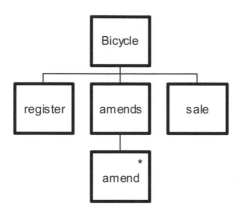

Figure 20.15 ELH – Bicycle – First Cut

I also note that:

◆   For the hire / return process we need to know whether a machine is on hire or available – this could sensibly be implemented by a bike-avail attribute on the Bicycle entity and would then need to appear on the ELH.

◆   When the machine is on hire it may become lost (not returned) and this could be a further value of the bike-avail attribute – after the bike is recorded as lost it could returned and would need to be marked as available.

◆   After a Bicycle is marked as sold it is retained on the system – presumably, eventually, it is no longer required for management information and can be deleted.

Taking the first of these requirements we can update the ELH as shown in *figure 20.16*. As you can see, the process of working out the ELH brings out details of the processing requirement that might otherwise be overlooked. Note the implication that the bike cannot be amended or sold while it is out on hire (work through the diagram till you understand the point). Now it is your turn: do exercises 5 and 6.

20.6   Other Structured SA&D Techniques

The entity life history, in SSADM terms, is only one element of entity-event modelling. The ELH looks at all the events that affect an entity and is matched by the effect correspondence diagram (ECD) that looks at all the entities affected by a process. The ECD was introduced in version 4 and is little used (and often misunderstood). Further techniques used in the logical design process are:

◆   User dialogue design – a somewhat cumbersome process for designing user interfaces. It is usually avoided by using screen prototypes.

◆   Update and enquiry process specification – a Jackson structure chart for each process, annotated with references to conditions and operations.

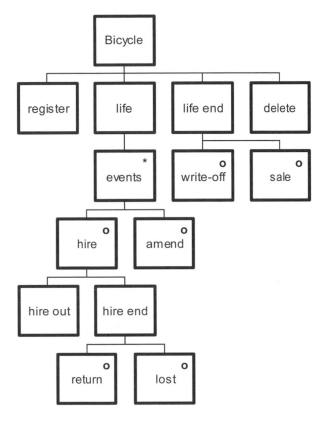

Figure 20.16 ELH – Bicycle – Second Cut

For the final stage or physical design, SSADM is less prescriptive – as it says the approach to physical design will depend on the software and IT infrastructure that has been determined in the technical system options stage. The three end products of the physical design are:

◆ Physical data design – a database schema.
◆ Physical process specification.
◆ Physical data interface.

A vital element of physical design, for large, multi-user systems, is system sizing and tuning design for performance. This is an iterative process that starts with the first cut physical data design, leads on to physical process specifications where timings can be worked out and is then iterated until (hopefully) performance problems are solved.

Exercises

Reading a case study and the author's solution is the easy part. For the novice, drawing your own system diagrams is normally much more difficult. It is a useful skill to have and it only comes with practice – so do the exercises (and only look at the solutions on the web page once you have given them a good go). The High

Peak Bicycles and the Madcaster University case studies are at the end of **Chapter 19**.

1. We have now had a further meeting with the management of High Peak Bicycles and found that they require the following two management reports, for the initial implementation of the system:

   ◆ Daily rental analysis – by machine category, giving numbers and value.

   ◆ Monthly machine analysis – by machine giving age and calculating rental usage.

   Draw a level-2 DFD, for *do management information*, process 6, to show this requirement. Also see if you can work out a level-2 DFD for *process non-returns*, process 5.

2. For the Madcaster University case study draw a context diagram, level-1 DFD and any level-2 DFDs you deem appropriate.

3. For the Madcaster University case study draw an ER diagram.

4. For the Madcaster University case study apply relational data analysis to both the student registration and the module choice forms. Take the third normal form from each analysis, merge them and produce an ER diagram that represents the result. Compare your ER diagram to the one you produced in exercise 3.

5. For High Peak Bicycles, draw an ELH for the Rental Agreement entity.

6. Select a couple of entities from your Madcaster University case study and draw an ELH for each of them.

Further Reading

The Avison and Fitzgerald book recommended at the end of **Chapter 19** includes details of structured techniques. There are numerous IS and SA&D books that cover these techniques – one useful example, with more detailed coverage, is:

Kendall K. and Kendall J. (2002) *Systems Analysis and Design*, 5th ed., Prentice Hall.

Chapter 21
Object-Oriented System Analysis and Design

Summary

An object is a self-contained module of data and its associated processing. The job of object-oriented (OO) systems analysis and design (SA&D) is to interpret user requirements in terms of objects that can then be implemented as software using OO technologies.

The essential technique for OO SA&D is the class diagram (a class being a set of objects with a common definition). Standards for class diagrams are provided by the Unified Modelling Language (UML). UML also includes standards for:

◆ Use cases and use case diagram.
◆ Sequence diagrams.

These are taught, along with the class diagram, to give a basic set of techniques for OO SA&D.

UML is not a methodology. There is no lifecycle and the designer is left to choose which techniques to apply and in what order. To provide a context for the teaching of UML, this chapter proposes a four-stage lifecycle consisting of:

◆ User requirements – expressed in terms of use cases.
◆ Identify objects – using a preliminary (conceptual) class diagram.
◆ Design use cases – using sequence diagrams.
◆ Design objects – the full (design) class diagram.

It is noted that most chapters in this book are intended to be covered as a single unit of study (a lecture and a tutorial / self study). This chapter will take considerably longer, say four units of study.

21.1 Objects

An object, in the context of systems analysis and design and of programming, is:

A self contained module of data and its associated processing.

(Freedman, 1999)

The purpose of objects in system development / software engineering is to produce software components that are self contained and can be used in any system that requires that functionality. The analogy is with engineering where (say) a standard electric motor or a microchip can be taken and plugged into any product that requires that functionality.

Object-oriented (OO) technology started as a programming technique. The first OO programming language was Smalltalk and that has been followed (and superseded) by further programming languages: C++ and Java are the two most used OO programming languages.

Object orientation claims to be a more natural way of viewing software design (although for the many of us brought up on structured analysis and procedural programming, that can be less than obvious – apparently we need to make a paradigm shift). As already indicated, a major aim of OO development is to promote and enable software reuse and this is facilitated by the three major OO concepts of encapsulation, inheritance and polymorphism:

◆ Encapsulation – this is the basic concept that the design and implementation of the object includes the data and the processing that manipulates the data. This creates a self-sufficient module that can be re-used wherever that object is required.
◆ Inheritance allows an object to use the characteristics of a more general object. This is probably best explained by example: if we have objects for 'staff' and 'student' they can inherit a lot of their data and processing from a more general object of 'person'. The person object includes, and processes, name, address, date of birth, etc. These attributes apply to both staff and students, meaning that the staff and student objects only have to deal with the data and processing that is specific to their particular system requirements.
◆ Polymorphism allows objects to be created whose exact type is not known until run time. In designing our system we might find that different groups of students have different characteristics. We could tackle this by specifying further classes or specialist student objects inheriting from the general student object, or we can use polymorphism to have a student object that adapts its behaviour to the requirements of the student type that is being processed.

Where object orientation was used as a programming technology it did not make a lot of sense to analyse the problem in terms of process and data structures that then had to be converted into objects for implementation. Hence object-oriented systems analysis and design (OO-SA&D).

21.2 OO-SA&D

Object-oriented SA&D, as indicated above, grew out of OO programming. Many attempts at OO-SA&D concentrated much more on the later stages of the lifecycle than on the early, user oriented, analysis stages (in contrast to the structured SA&D methods discussed in the previous chapter).

A number of OO-SA&D methodologies have been developed but none of them has achieved general acceptance. The development of OO techniques has been an area of considerable conflict as theorists (with large egos and / or commercial interests) fought out their various ideological positions. What emerged from this process is:

> UML, the Unified Modelling Language – devised by Booch, Jacobson and Rumbaugh.

The surprising thing is that UML seems to have gained general acceptance. Possibly this is because UML uses a toolbox approach – it sets out a number of techniques but it does not say when you use them. It is a modelling language, not a methodology.

So we have general agreement on the techniques and everyone can apply them as they see fit (and deviate from the standard if they feel strongly about it). The compilers of UML have their own approach to methodology called Rational Unified Process (RUP) and many other organisations and practitioners use OO-SA&D in their own different ways. For the purposes of this book, and as a framework for studying UML techniques, we will have our own lifecycle, see *figure 21.1*.

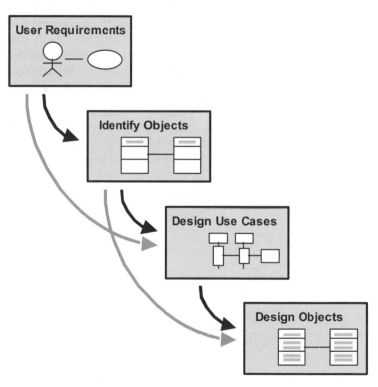

Figure 21.1 Design Method using UML

This simple approach to UML design has the following four stages:

- ◆ Identify user requirements and system boundary.
  Technique: use cases.
- ◆ Identify objects.
  Technique: class diagram (conceptual).

- ◆ Design use cases.
  Technique: sequence diagram.
- ◆ Design objects.
  Technique: class diagram (design).

The UML techniques that we are utilizing are explained in the following sub-sections – with a further sub-section introducing a number of UML techniques which I have not included in the method.

To illustrate the method we will use the High Peak Bicycles case study given in **Chapter 19**. Just reading the sub-sections and looking at my examples is the easy bit. You will only learn when you try out the exercises so, at the end of each sub-section, apply the technique to one of the other case studies that is supplied (and don't look at the answer on the web site until you have given it a good go).

21.3 User Requirements and Use Cases

Before we start making a system it is a good idea to find out what the users want (or what the users need). Actually finding out the user requirement can be a bit of a detective job but, in this chapter, our main concern is to document the requirement using UML. The technique we will use is the use case diagram.

A use case is 'a bit of business done with the system'. An example of a bit of business from the High Peak Bicycles case study would be to make a rental (*rent out*). The use case diagram for this consists of:

- ◆ The actor – the person doing the interaction – shown as a stick person.
- ◆ The use case – the task that is being done – shown as an ellipse containing a couple of words / a phrase summarising the task.
- ◆ A link – a line connecting the actor to the use case.

The use case diagram for *rent out* is shown in **figure 21.2**.

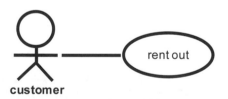

customer

Figure 21.2 Example Use Case

So, to complete a use case diagram, we need to identify all the 'bits of business' that need to occur in our system. How do we do that? Well, it is a bit of a case that I know a use case when I see one – which is not very helpful to someone new to SA&D. To be a bit more helpful let us first go through the requirement (for us that is the case study) and identify the people who use the system. This will give us a preliminary list of actors. For the High Peak case study we have:

- ◆ Staff – mentioned in the paragraphs numbered 3 and implicit in all the functions of the system.

- Customer – mentioned in the paragraphs numbered 4, 5 and 6 (where the term 'hirer' is used).
- Park Warden and Police – mentioned in the paragraph numbered 6.

So having identified (potential) actors we can then go through the case study again, this time looking for 'bits of business'. Doing that (and trying to distinguish the task from the detail) I get:

- Para 1: '*A register is kept of all machines*'.
- Para 2: '*occasionally corrections have to be made*' and '*updated when selling*', both relating to the register of machines.
- Para 3: '(rental) *rates are changed*'.
- Para 4: '*Each rental is recorded*' (there is a lot of detail here but 'the bit of business' is the rental transaction).
- Para 5: '*the rental agreement is updated with … return*'.
- Para 6: '*In these circumstances* (non return) *the rental slip is updated*'.
- Para 7: '*all rental slips are totted up. Detailed statistics would be useful*'.

Bringing the two lists together, and using a bit of common sense, we get:

- Staff, as an actor, who will:
    - Maintain the Bike Register – this includes registering new bikes, (occasional) amendments and recording bike sales (*maintain b. register*) – how much of that detail we should show is something we have to think about.
    - Maintain rental rates (*maintain rent rates*).
    - Do management information – exactly what would be useful here is not made clear and further discussion with the user would seem to be needed (*do mngmnt information*).

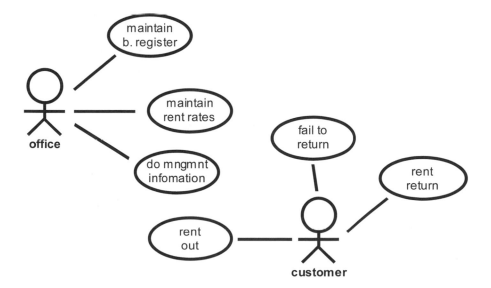

Figure 21.3 Use Case – High Peak Bicycles – First Cut

- Customer, as an actor, who will:
    - Rent out one or more bikes (*rent out*).
    - Return the bikes they have rented (*rent return*).
    - Fail to return the bikes they have rented (*fail to return*).
    (These are joint activities between the customer and the staff – which actor we use is a mater of choice. I think it is helpful to show the customer; there is a further note on this issue below.)

Using this list we get the use case diagram shown as **figure 21.3**. Note that we have not used the Park Wardens or Police as actors – they are people the staff talk to but they do not directly interface with the system.

OK, but we can add to this using a further component of the use case diagram. These are extensions to the use cases used to identify common processing and / or to clarify the diagram. There are three types of these extensions identified in UML:

- Include: a chunk of behaviour that is similar across several use cases – the include is linked to the use cases by dotted arrows.
    There is not a need for an include in the High Peak Bicycles case study. If however we extended the system to include booking of bikes over the Internet we could then say both *rent out* and *book online* would need to *allocate bike* and we could show this common piece of behaviour as an include. See **figure 21.4** (that said, I think that this would be unnecessary detail and I would not show this commonality at this stage).

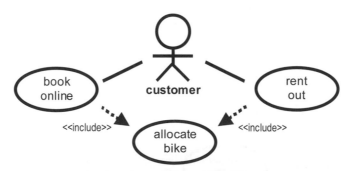

Figure 21.4 Use Case – Example of Includes

- Extend: a variation on normal behaviour to include additional, optional, behaviour – linked to the extended case by a dotted arrow. Some authors say you must define the extension point in the originating use case – in my view it complicates the diagram and I would not do it unless it was needed to make the purpose of the extend clear.
    As with the include, there is not a need for an extend in the High Peak Bicycles case study. However, let us suppose that we intend to get clever and attach a credit card reader to the system and process credit card sales through the system. We could then show *process credit card* as an extension to the *rent return* use case: see **figure 21.5**.

Figure 21.5 Use Case – Example of Extends

◆   Generalisation or 'child use case': Variations on normal behaviour where any one of the child use cases might be invoked – the generalisation points to the parent use case using an arrow.

Generalisation is the one use case extension that I would use in the High Peak Bicycles use case diagram. The *maintain bike register* use case covers *register new bike* and *record bike sale*. It could aid clarity if these were to be shown, and a generalisation seems to be the appropriate format. These generalisations are added to the first cut use case diagram to give us the design stage use case diagram in *figure 21.6*.

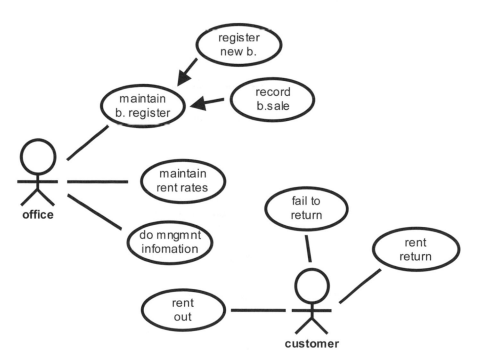

Figure 21.6 Use Case – High Peak Bicycles – User Requirements

Having given examples of each of the three types of use case extension it is noted that it can be difficult to determine which of these extensions to use and when. Remember that our objective is to capture user requirements. We need simplicity. We do not need a complex diagram that captures the minutiae of processing – we will come to that in the design stages. Rosenberg and Scott (1999) say they ignore the specific provisions of UML and just have one form of extension they call 'uses' – sounds a good idea but, for this course, we had better stick to the rules.

Use Case Description: Rent Out (as a narrative)

Basic Course: The member of staff asks the customer for personal details, period of rental and the number, size and types of bikes he / she requires – these details are recorded on the system along with the date and time of the transaction. The system allocates specific machines that fit the customer's specification and calculates the (expected) rental cost and deposit requirement. The customer pays and the transaction is completed by the printing of a rental agreement (two copies).

Alternative Course: The required machines are not available and alternative models are allocated.
Alternative Course: The required machines are not available and no acceptable alternative is available – the transaction is aborted.
Alternative Course: The customer finds the charges unacceptable and the transaction is aborted.

Use Case Description: Rent Out (as a series of steps)

Basic Course:
1. Record customer details, period of rental and the number, size and types of bikes the customer requires.
2. Generate and record date and time of the transaction.
3. The system allocates specific machines that fit the customer's specification.
4. The system calculates the (expected) rental cost and deposit requirement.
5. Record payment.
6. Print rental agreement (two copies).

Alternative Course (1): At step 3 some / all of the required machines are unavailable:
1. Return to step 1 and specify alternatives.
Alternative Course (2): At step 3 some / all of the required machines are unavailable and no acceptable alternatives are available:
1. Abort.
Alternative Course (3): At step 4 the customer finds the charges unacceptable:
1. Abort.

Figure 21.7 Use Case Descriptions for Rent Out

Thus far we have looked at the use case diagram. The use case is actually a description of the 'bit of business' (although the usual focus is on the diagram). The description is required to cover the basic (usual) course of action for the use case and any alternative courses that may occur. Rosenberg and Scott (1999) write their use cases as narrative whereas Fowler and Scott (2000) set them out as a series of steps. The approach you adopt would seem to be optional (unless your team leader or tutor exercises the option for you!). It seems to me that the narrative approach works better for a business system (such as our example) and the step approach would be more appropriate for the design of a piece of system software. The use case description for *rent out* is shown in **figure 21.7** – I have used both formats so you can choose which approach would suit you best.

Use cases are really that simple. There are however a couple of qualifications to be added:

◆ Actors are not always people – they can be other systems. Thus if the High Peak Bicycles system passed financial details of all rental transactions to a separate accounting system then that system would be shown as an actor on our use case diagram.

◆ Sometimes there is more than one actor involved in a use case and it is not clear which should be shown. In our *rent out* example we have the customer who is hiring the bikes but we also have the hire shop staff who enter the transaction into the system. Which of the two actors we show does not matter greatly. Fowler (2000) says he likes *'to show the actor who gets value from the use case'* which, in this instance, is (presumably) the customer. If you think it makes things clearer you can show the customer actor linked to the staff actor which is in turn linked to the use case.

◆ Many authors advocate that the use case is further refined (complicated!) throughout the design process to, among other things, identify elements of processing that are common across a number of use cases. It seems to me that these refinements are best identified by other elements of the design process and there seems to be little merit in feeding them back into the use case diagram. We will keep the use case as a statement of user requirements and we will only update it if those requirements (or our understanding of them) need to be changed.

And before you go on to the next stage it would be a good idea to practise what you have learnt – do exercises 1 and 2 shown at the end of the chapter.

21.4 Identifying Objects and the Initial Class Diagram

The basic / essential diagram for all OO methods is the class diagram. The class diagram shows the (classes of) objects that the system requires. An object is a single occurrence of the component – the class is the set of all objects that have the same definition. Thus, if we have a class called student it will be implemented as a set of objects, one occurrence for each student on the register. The system is defined in terms of classes as each object in the class has the same data and processing requirements.

The class diagram shows classes but it also shows details of:

◆ The attributes (data items) that are required by (or define) each class.
◆ The methods (processing) required for each class.
◆ The associations that exist between classes.

The objects in the class diagram are shown as boxes (including name, attributes and methods) and the associations as lines between them. This basic notation is shown in *figure 21.8*.

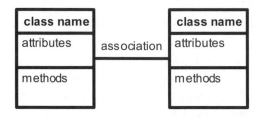

Figure 21.8 Class Diagram – Basic Format

At this stage of the design process we just want to do a draft (or conceptual) class diagram. We want to identify the main classes that are represented in the user requirements. We will add the obvious attributes, the raw processing requirements and the basic associations but we expect these to be substantially revised in the next two stages (the process of OO design is iterative and this stage is to give us a starting point).

For our system we have a case study and, as with the use cases, we can make an initial stab at identifying classes from analysing the text of the case study. Rereading the case study suggests the following (possible) classes:

◆ Bicycle – in para 1 and used throughout the case study.
◆ Bike Class – in para 1 – we will rename it Bike Type or we will get confused between OO classes and Bike Classes.
◆ Rental Rate – in para 3.
◆ Rental Agreement – in para 4.
◆ Customer – in para 4 (presented as an attribute of the rental but could be an object).

As with the entity relation diagram in structured analysis and design we want to identify the underlying objects and not the documentation that is used to represent them – thus I have identified a bicycle as a potential object but not the form that it is recorded on.

Our main purpose is to identify objects but it is also useful to have a first stab at attributes, methods and associations – if nothing else they will help us weed out any bogus objects that turn out to have no attributes and no methods. So, back to the case study to see what we can find:

◆ Bicycle:
  ◆ Attributes: registration no, bike type, make, model, frame size, frame number, date of purchase, purchase price, date of sale, selling price, write-off.
  ◆ Methods: register, update, sell
  ◆ Associations: assigned to a Bike Type.

office

Use Case Description: Maintain Rental Rates

Basic course: The user selects the bike type for which rental rates are to be created and inputs the appropriate start date and rates. Note that start dates can not be retrospective.
Alternative Course: The selected bike type does not exist on the system and the user is invited to correct the selection.

Figure 21.10 Use Case – Maintain Rental Rates

Before we start on the sequence diagram it is probably helpful to mock up a screen for the use case – this is shown in *figure 21.11*.

High Peak Bicycles

Maintain Rental Rates

bike type: ☐

start date: ☐

	Half Day	Day	Late
rates:	☐	☐	☐

Figure 21.11 Screen – Maintain Rental Rates

So let's work out (in terms of objects) what the sequence diagram needs to do:

◆ Read the Bike Type object.
◆ If the Bike Type object is found:
  ◆ Create new Rental Rate object.

And this is represented on the sequence diagram shown as *figure 21.12*.

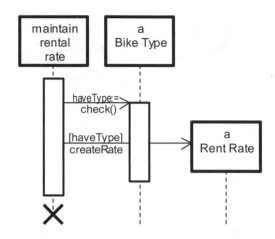

Figure 21.12 Sequence Diagram – Maintain Rental Rates

So let me explain the sequence diagram and hence the notation:

♦ Classes (Objects):
  ◆ Each column represents a class.
  ◆ We are processing one object from that class and we indicate that by the use of the indefinite article, e.g. a Bike Type.
  ◆ The lifeline of the object is indicated by the dotted line – if the object pre-exists the use case then the dotted line starts from the top of the diagram and if the object remains available after the use case the dotted line continues to the bottom of the diagram. The deletion of an object is shown by a cross that terminates its lifeline.
  ◆ The use of the object in the use case is shown by the vertical rectangle on the lifeline.

♦ Interface Object:
  ◆ The first column is the interface object. It comes into existence when the process is invoked and it is deleted at the end of the process – hence the X at the end of its lifeline.

♦ Messages:
  ◆ Objects interact by sending messages to each other. The messages are represented by the horizontal lines on the diagram.
  ◆ The first message we have is invoked from the interface object. It uses a method *haveType* to read the Bike Type object (second column) that the user requires and it returns a result in its argument *check()*.
  ◆ The second message is also invoked from the interface object. It has a guard *[haveType]* and it will only be invoked if the Bike Type was found. If it is invoked it then creates a Rent Rate object (third column) using the method *createRate*.

Working on this use case suggests a couple of enhancements to the initial class diagram:

- ◆ Identifying Bike Class by description would seem rather clumsy and we could use a typeCode as an additional attribute.
- ◆ There is no way to add another Bike Type and it would seem that such a need could arise – we could add that to the requirement.

These two requirements can be saved up for when the class diagram is updated in the next stage of the process.

Let us now look at a more complex use case: *rent out*, see **figure 21.13** (and **figure 21.7** for the use case description).

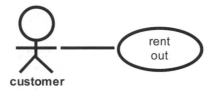

Figure 21.13 Use Case – Rent Out

Again we can start by mocking up a screen (or screens). This interface could be designed in a number of ways – I have chosen to have a basic data input screen with a couple of overlay windows that would confirm the selection of bikes and deal with charges / deposits. The screens are shown in **figure 21.14**.

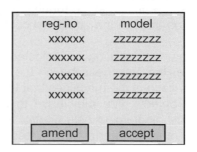

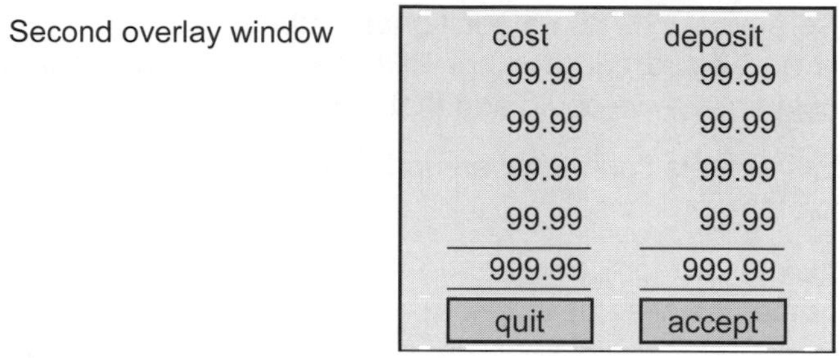

Second overlay window

cost	deposit
99.99	99.99
99.99	99.99
99.99	99.99
99.99	99.99
999.99	999.99
quit	accept

Figure 21.14 Screen – Rent Out

The sequence diagram does not need to worry about the customer details (these are attributes of the Rental we will eventually create, if the deal goes ahead). We start by looking up the bicycles; the processing of objects is as follows:

- For each machine on the rental request:
  - Read Bike Type.
  - If Bike Type found, then:
    - Until available bike found:
      - Read Bike (if no available Bike found – reg-no displayed as n/a).

(First overlay can now be displayed).

- If accept, then:
  - For each machine on rental request:
    - Read Bike Type.
      - Until current Rent Rate (latest start date <= today) found:
        - Read Rent Rate

(Calculate totals and second overlay can now be displayed).

- If accept, then:
  - Create Rental
  - For each machine on rental request:
    - Read Bike.
    - Update Bike to be unavailable.
    - Link Rental and Bike (many-to-many – could need a link object?).

(Print rental agreement and transaction complete).

And from these notes we can draw the sequence diagram: see *figure 21.15*. It was not entirely easy – but then writing software is not always easy and if we check it out at the design stage then we should hit fewer problems when we code it. Let us first go through the additional constructs and notation we have used:

- Iterations: An iteration is indicated by an * on the message line. For example, the first message on the diagram is an iteration – we need to process each of the machines that the user has selected.
- Control objects: We may have to introduce additional objects onto the sequence diagram to help control the processing. I have used one such object: machine iter(ation). These can be called control objects, as

opposed to the interface objects and the entity objects (that come from our class diagram).

◆ Returns: We can add a return message as a dotted line showing an action (or series of actions) has been completed. These are most helpful for indicating the end of a iteration.

◆ Self Call: this is where an object sends a message to itself. I have used this on the Bike object to show when the availability entity is updated to show that the bike is on hire.

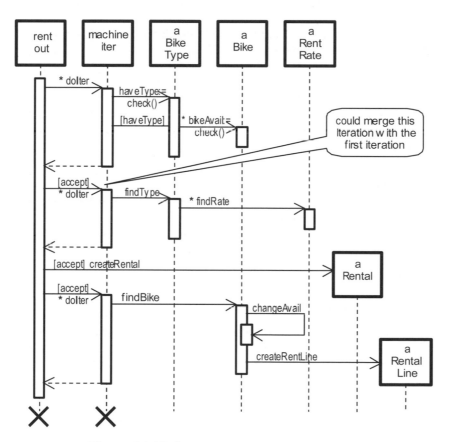

Figure 21.15 Sequence Diagram – Rent Out

And finally we need to note any changes we need to make to the initial class diagram:

◆ As we noted earlier on, we need to associate the Rental with the Bikes that are included in the rental agreement. On the initial class diagram we showed a simple association but, thinking about this during the design process, this seems likely to prove inadequate. The Rental is for one to four bikes but the Bike will have been on a number of previous rentals (and we want to keep that information for future analysis). This gives us, as we would say in data modelling terms, a many-to-many relationship. The way we can solve this is by introducing an additional entity (or for OO design a object / class): we will call it Rental Line. This new class also allows us to record the charges for each bike (arguably a duplication of data but it will simplify things when the Bike is returned). It also seems likely to be required when we do the sequence diagram for the fail to return use case.

♦ We need a way of knowing if a bicycle is for hire or already hired out. An availability indicator should be added to Bike – the indicator can also have settings for sold, lost and written-off.

These changes will be applied in the next stage of the design process, to the class diagram.

So, while you are suitably confused, let's do some practice – do exercises 4 and 5 shown at the end of the chapter.

21.6   Design Objects and the Full Class Diagram

The final stage of our method is design objects. In this stage we need to complete the class diagram so that development can begin. There are three interconnected elements to the task:

♦ Incorporate additional features of class diagram design that we ignored at the identify object stage.
♦ Make the changes and corrections that we noted when drawing the sequence diagrams in the design use case stage.
♦ Make any changes that are appropriate to achieve an efficient and economical design for our chosen development environment.

We look at each of these in turn.

❖ **Additional Class Diagram Notation**

At the identify object stage I deliberately (and reluctantly) kept the class diagram very simple – we did the essential job of identifying objects, associations and obvious attributes and methods. We now need to add three more constructs to our repertoire for drawing class diagrams:

Generalisation: This is the class diagram convention for documenting inheritance. At the beginning of this chapter we used the example of an OO design where Staff and Student had been identified as objects and it was recognised that these objects had much in common. On the class diagram we document this as a generalisation. The common attributes, methods and associations of these objects can be assigned to a supertype of Person and the characteristics that are different are assigned to the subtypes of Student and Staff. The documentation of this generalisation construct is shown at *figure 21.16*.

Identifying generalisations is an important part of OO design, not least because it facilitates the re-use of code. In our example we only code the methods required for Person once whereas, without identifying generalisation, we may well have included the same functionality in the routines used for both Students and Staff.

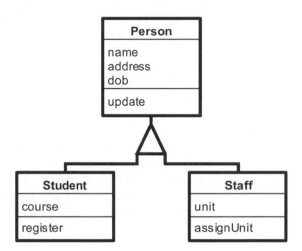

Figure 21.16 Class Diagram – Generalisation

◆ Aggregation and composition: The aggregation construct is a special case of association between two classes. Fowler and Scott (1999) describe aggregation as '*the part of relationship*' and say it is '*like saying that a car has an engine and wheels as its parts*'. The analogy with components of a machine is probably a good one. Aggregation is a strong form of association and should be used sparingly. I would not, for example, use aggregation to show that a student was 'part of' a course – after all, the course would still be an object in our system even if no students chose to study it.

UML provides for two forms of aggregation: these are aggregation and composition. Composition is a stronger form of aggregation where the part object can belong to only one whole and its lifespan, creation and deletion, is the same as the object which it is part of. The construct for aggregation is a hollow diamond and for composition is a solid diamond; in both cases on the 'owning' end of the association. These are shown by the example in *figure 21.17*.

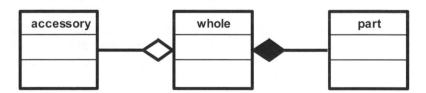

Figure 21.17 Class Diagram – Aggregation and Composition

For the High Peak Bicycles case study we will use composition for the association between Rental and Rental Line (although, in my view, it would not be a problem if we did not include it).

◆ Cardinality of associations: Finally we need to add the cardinality to each association, i.e. how many objects are associated. If we take, as an example, the High Peak Bicycles associations between Rental, Rental Line and Bike, we have:

   ◆ A Rental is associated with from one to four Rental Lines (up to four bicycles can be hired on one rental agreement).
   ◆ A Rental Line belongs to just one Rental.
   ◆ A Rental Line is for just one Bike.
   ◆ A Bike can be on zero, one or many rental lines (zero would be for a new bicycle that has not yet been rented – many is because all the old rentals are retained on the system).

These details are shown in **figure 21.18** and will be added to the final class diagram for High Peak Bicycles. Note that a range from n to m is shown as 'n..m' and that many is shown as '*'; one to many would then be '1..*'.

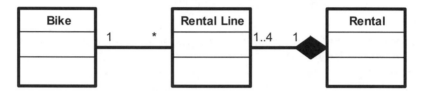

Figure 21.18 Class Diagram – Cardinality of Association

❖ **Update Class Diagram from Design Use Case Stage**

The drawing of the sequence diagrams in the previous stage has updated our understanding of the system and we now need to add this detail into the class diagram. The main change is to the methods. We started with requirement oriented methods (relating to the use cases) on the conceptual class diagram and we now need to replace these with methods that we are going to implement with our OO technology (and the methods we will implement will depend, to some extent, upon the OO development environment that is selected). The methods we will show on our design class diagram are those from the sequence diagrams in **figures 21.12** and **21.15**.

   The design use case stage had also updated our understanding of the data requirements and we now need to add those changes to the class diagram. The changes we discovered in drawing just two of the sequence diagrams were:

◆ Add the key typeCode to Bike Type.
◆ Add a function (and method) to create a Bike Type.
◆ Add a new Rental Line class to implement the many-to-many between Rental and Bike.
◆ Add an availability indicator to Bike.

❖ **Tuning the Design**

A major point of OO technology is code reuse. A method written and tested for one function can then be used for other functions and in other systems. Such reuse would presumably save time, create consistency and hopefully increase reliability (as the code would have already been proved). In practice, and in general, the levels of code reuse achieved by users of OO methods have been less than expected – creating reusable code requires careful analysis and design and OO users have not always paid as much attention to the SA&D process as they should.

The obvious area for code reuse is where we are able to identify a generalisation (and use the inheritance concept of OO). In the explanation of generalisation we used the example of Staff and Student classes and identified a supertype Person class. Obviously this should then cut down on coding as processing for Person would be common to functions that processed either Student or Staff objects. This is also the area where the concept of polymorphism might be applicable.

We also achieve code reuse because the methods are associated with the object as opposed to being included in the function. Thus if we have a method to find the current rental rates (findRate) it can be used in both the rent out use case (see sequence diagram) and in rent return (to calculate the final cost).

As we finalise our design we need to check it for cases where code can be reused. Looking at my sequence diagram for Rent Out (*figure 21.15*) I see that:

◆ I have two methods to read the Bike Type object – haveType (to read it and check if it exists) and findType (to read it in again). These seem to serve much the same function and I have taken only the findType name forward to the design class diagram. (I should also update the sequence diagram but I have left it unchanged to illustrate the point.)

A second way that we might improve our OO design is to break down some of the larger objects into more than one object, particularly where some of the attributes and methods work together and are not used on every instance of the object. Our two largest objects are Bike and Rental and this treatment could be applied in both cases:

◆ Bike – this object has a number of attributes and methods that are only used when the bicycle is sold or written off. These attributes and methods can be used to create a new object, and hence a new class, of Gone Bike. This is included in the design view class diagram.
◆ Rental – this object has a number of attributes and methods associated with the return of the bicycle. These attributes and methods could also be put on a new Rental Return object – that said, most rentals in the system will have been returned and the advantage is (perhaps) not as clear cut. This change is not included in the design new class diagram.

Our class diagram from the design objects stage is now shown at *figure 21.19*. There is more work to be done: specifically we have only drawn two sequence diagrams and there are six more use cases to be worked through. I have shown the methods that remain from conceptual class diagram in italics. A fully updated class diagram is shown on the web site – don't peek until you have done the relevant exercises. Note that there is a convention that we do not need to show create methods (it is rather assumed that there will need to be one) but I have included them anyway.

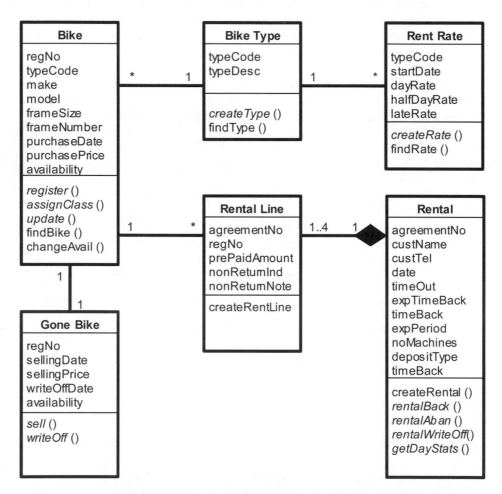

Figure 21.19 Class Diagram – Design Version

You should now tackle exercises 6 and 7.

21.7 Other UML Techniques

UML is a toolbox method and includes a number of techniques we have not studied in this chapter. The way Rosenberg and Scott (1999) put it is:

> The UML is an inclusive superset of almost everything that was in Booch's, Rambaugh's and Jacobson's original methodologies. ... Just as you don't need every word in the dictionary you don't need every element of the UML.

The techniques we have studied have been carefully chosen to give a coherent and usable subset of UML. Further techniques that are included in UML and might be studied as part of a more advanced course include:

♦ Package diagrams: The package diagram is a way of dividing a large system up into component parts. Using them with the class diagram we can divide the overall system up into a number of sub-systems and allocate them to different teams or implement them as stages. The package diagram needs to identify dependencies between packages and ideally these dependencies are be kept to a minimum – you can not implement a packet that is dependent on other packages that are not yet available.

    The package diagram concept can also be used to divide up the use case diagram of a large system.

♦ Deployment diagrams: The deployment shows how the software components are allocated in a distributed system – in a client–server system it would show the functionality assigned to the client and the functionality allocated to the server. It would be tidy if each class could be allocated to just one component, but often this is not the case.

♦ Collaboration diagrams: The collaboration diagram is similar to the sequence diagram. It documents a use case, shows the objects used and the messages that are passed between them. The basic flow is vertical rather than horizontal and the messages are numbered. Most writers on UML seem to prefer the sequence diagram and that is a judgement we will accept in this book.

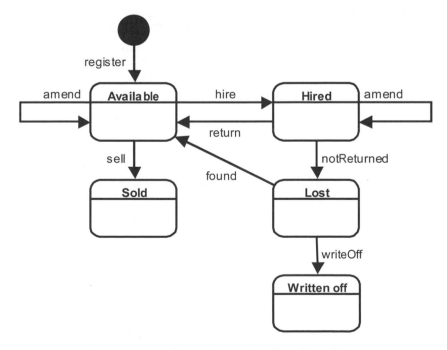

Figure 21.20 State Diagram – The Bike Object

◆ State diagrams: The state diagram takes an individual object and shows the activities that can affect it during its lifecycle. It is in many ways the inverse of the sequence diagram in that the activities are all the methods that have been planned for that object. Drawing the state diagrams is a cross-check of all the sequence diagrams (and the use cases they represent) as it should identify any activity that should have been included in the system that has been overlooked. A state diagram for the bike class is shown in *figure 21.19*. Note that I have only had to use about half the features available for a state diagram to construct this example.

◆ Activity diagrams: The activity diagram is related to the state diagram but it can show parallel behaviours (where two sets of activities can take place over the same time frame). It is also related to the flowchart (a diagramming technique that went out of fashion some 30 years ago) – the sequence will normally be from a start at the top of the page to an end at the bottom.

21.8 Object-Oriented Analysis and Design

After analysis and design comes implementation and that is a job for the programmers (or analyst-programmers wearing their programming hats). We outline the programming role in *Chapter 23* but it is outside the normal scope of the IS discipline and not something that this text is going to try to teach you.

OO analysis and design sensibly lead onto OO programming – and the way that relates to the design is, in part at least, dependent on the OO technology that is used. The advantages of an OO approach to system development, according to Bocij et al. (1999) are:

◆ It is easier to explain object concepts to end users since they are based on real world objects (possibly, but I suspect that users more easily relate to the tasks / processes that they are responsible for).
◆ There is more reuse of code – standard, tested business objects (objects can be specifically written for the user system or they may be general purpose objects that are imported).
◆ Faster, cheaper development of more robust code.

OO analysis, design and implementation should be seen as a complete package. You will not get the advantages of the OO approach if you use OO programming with inadequate design. Similarly there is little point in producing an OO design if you are not using an OO approach to implementation. *Chapter 23* sets out an analysis, design and implementation project using an MS Access database. Using MS Access's built in application generators is not an OO approach and some of the UML documentation we have looked at in this chapter would not be ideal for these projects.

Exercises

Looking at, and understanding, someone else's system diagrams is usually simple enough – learning to draw your own takes practice. These exercises will give you a start:

1. For the High Peak Bicycles case study I have written a use case description (in two formats) for *rent out*. Select the approach you feel comfortable with and write your own use case description for the *rent return* use case.

2. For the Madcaster University case study (**Chapter 19**), draw a use case diagram and supplement it with use case descriptions for a couple of the main processes.

3. Following on from exercise 2, draw a preliminary class diagram for the Madcaster University case study.

4. You have written the use case for the *rent return* in exercise 1 – now draw the sequence diagram for that use case (it is easier than *rent out*, I promise!).

5. Using your class diagram from exercise 3, draw sequence diagrams for the use case descriptions you wrote in exercise 2.

6. Update the High Peak Bicycles design class diagram for the sequence diagram you drew in exercise 4.

7. Revise the Madcaster University preliminary class diagram you drew in exercise 3 to be a design class diagram. This should include any of the additional class diagram features that are appropriate to the requirement and the outcomes of the sequence diagrams you produced in exercise 5.

Further Reading

There are many books on OO-SA&D / UML. Addison-Wesley has an excellent series of slim volumes, edited by Booch, Jacobson and Rumbauch, by experienced OO practitioners. My favourite is:

> Fowler M. and Scott K. (2000) *UML Distilled: A Brief Guide to the Standard Object Modelling Language*, 2nd ed., Addison-Wesley, Reading Mass.

Other titles in the series that I have found useful are;

> Rosenberg D. and Scott K. (1999) *Use Case Driven Object Modelling with UML: A Practical Approach*, Addison-Wesley, Reading, Mass.
> Stevens P and Pooley R (2000) *Using UML: Software Engineering with Objects and Components*, Addison-Wesley, Reading, Mass.

These books, while generally very good, are slim (which is not necessarily a bad thing) and expensive. For the same sort of money you can get a text book that is at least double the length (and probably very worthy). Whether you will understand an OO concept explained over 20 pages better than the same concept explained in five pages is doubtful. None of these textbooks are specifically recommended – there is a level at which, if you need more (or better!) explanation of a UML technique, then any of these books can be helpful .

The final book to mention is the reference guide written by the 'three amigos' who devised UML:

> Booch G., Rumbaugh J. and Jacobson I. (1999) *Unified Modelling Language: Reference Manual*, Addison-Wesley, Reading, Mass.

Note that this is a reference book – it is not bedtime reading except for real anoraks.

Chapter 22
Interfaces

Summary

A business information system takes in transaction data and outputs business transactions and management information.

The basic way of inputting information into a computer system is by typing on a keyboard that is used in conjunction with a template displayed on the screen. This process is slow, costly and error prone. Any improvement that can be achieved by good design is to be welcomed. For some systems the screen and keyboard can be substituted by devices such as barcode readers and mark sensing devices – these, and other available technologies, need to be considered by the system designer.

The main way of outputting business transactions and management information is to print them. Output documents need to be timely and informative and it is the job of the system designer to ensure these aims are achieved. Some outputs are to devices other than the printer, for example display screens or electronic transmissions to other systems.

The science and art of interface design is human computer interaction (HCI). This chapter include some of the basic concepts and design principles from that subject area.

22.1 Data In and Information Out

However fascinated you, and I, may get about what goes on inside a computer, the essential requirement is that we put data in and get information out:

- ◆ Keying data into a computer system is a slow, laborious and error prone process. Anything we can do, when selecting the technology to be used in the interface, to help the process is to be welcomed.
- ◆ Information can be displayed on the screen but most output business transactions and management information reports are printed. Part of the job of the system designer is to make sure that reports are timely, relevant and understandable.

See *figure 22.1*. The essential mechanism of typing data in and printing out information has not changed for many years (arguably since computers were first used commercially and data was keyed on punched cards). That said, modern IT equipment gives us the ability to design screens and reports that are more attractive, understandable and usable than their predecessors. The science and art of designing interfaces is human computer interaction (HCI). As system designers we need to be aware of the principles of HCI and then apply them in the systems we produce.

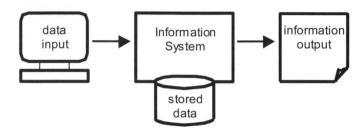

Figure 22.1 Data In and Information Out

22.2 Data Input

Data is input to the system from a variety of sources and there are data input devices other than the keyboard. The following list of examples of data capture requirements illustrates some of this diversity:

- ◆ Students registering when they join the university.
- ◆ A supervisor filling in timesheets for the payroll system.
- ◆ A customer completing an order for a supplier.
- ◆ A supermarket registering a customer's purchases at the checkout.
- ◆ A meter reader recording domestic electricity consumption.
- ◆ A weather station that automatically records meteorological data.
- ◆ A secretary using a word processor to type the minutes of a meeting.

For all these requirements, and any other requirement we may have, the need is to make the data capture process as quick, efficient and accurate as possible. To achieve this we must:

- ◆ Organise the data capture activity.
- ◆ Use appropriate technology.
- ◆ Design the user interface in accordance with good HCI principles.

We will now look at each of these aspects in turn.

❖ Data Capture

The first requirement is to get the data that is needed, from the people who have it and in a form that can be input to the system. Often this is a two-stage process, such as when the student fills in a registration form that is subsequently keyed into the system by a member of the university staff. For such a process we need to design a form that is:

- ◆ Readily understood by the data provider.
- ◆ Convenient for the member of staff that has to key it into the system.

To achieve this the form needs to be logical, contain clear instructions (or even better, be self explanatory), provide adequate space for the user to fill it in and be as simple as it can be (consistent with capturing the necessary data). It should also be matched to the input process, with the order and format of the data on the form being the same as that on the screen.

For many situations it is possible to dispense with a separate data capture process and input the data directly into the computer. This can be achieved by networking the system to the end user or applying a technology other than the keyboard and the screen. Direct data input can save time, cost and hopefully reduce the number of errors.

❖ **Data Capture Technology**

The usual technology for data capture is a keyboard and a screen. This may be part of the computer that is processing the data (as with desktop productivity software such as word processors) or be networked to a business information system on a server. The network may be the Internet and the user can be a member of the public. Other data capture devices that may be used include:

◆ Barcode readers: This is a technology we are all familiar with in its retail application. The barcode represents a product code; in Europe it is usually a 13 digit EAN code. The use of a barcode speeds up data capture and cuts down errors as all the operator has to do is wave the product at the scanner. The barcode is convenient in retail applications as it can be printed on the packaging of the product at no extra cost – except for items such as self-select fresh products where there is no appropriate packaging to print the barcode onto.

A product code is not a lot of data to capture. Its power is that it ties up with the product record in the EPOS / stock control system and hence gives access to price data and enables the update of stock and sales totals. Barcodes are used in many other product handling situations. Examples of this are:

  • Organisations that send delivery notes by EDI and then print a barcode on the consignment. This allows the physical delivery to be matched up with the electronic notification.

  • Parcel delivery services where the barcode on the packet allows for the parcels to be automatically sorted and recorded in the branch offices and hubs. The use of barcodes also means that the system records the stage the packet has reached in its journey from sender to its eventual destination.

◆ Mark Sensing: For mark sensing, the data provider marks a small box on a form that represents a simple code such as a number or the answer to a multiple-choice question. Mark sensing technology has had a number of applications, such as recording meter readings, but some of these have been replaced by hand held devices. Two common uses of mark sensing technology are:

  • The lottery – punters record the numbers they have selected by marking the appropriate boxes and the retail operator reads the card into the lottery system terminal.

  • Multiple choice tests – where the test requires the student to chose one out of several answers. The mark sensing device then records the selected answers in a computer system that works out the score that the student has achieved.

◆ Voice recognition: This has been the subject of much research but it has only recently come into use. There is voice recognition software available for PC users – it has to be trained to work with a specific user. The uptake of these system has, to date, been limited. Another application is to use the technology for a strictly limited set of responses in, for example, call centre applications (as an alternative to asking the customer to respond to simple questions through the telephone keypad).

◆ Magnetic ink character reading: This is extensively used on financial documents such cheques and paying in slips. The documents are standardised (to an extent) and a machine can read the account information while an operator types in the written information.

◆ Magnetic strips: These are used on credit, debit and loyalty cards, and on ID cards for security systems – they provide a machine-readable version of the account and personal identification. Magnetic strips can also be used in ticketing systems and, in these cases, the strip can be updated with details of the use of the ticket or of payments that have been made.

◆ Scanners: Another way of getting a document into a system is to scan it. Some organisations scan documents, such as claim forms, and then use that image of the working version of the document. Scanned documents can be used in conjunction with a workflow management system that controls the path of the document through the various departments that have to action it. An alternative use of a scanner is with character recognition software which converts the written words to electronic form. This is not an entirely reliable process. It works best with printed documents and it is mainly used to digitise textual information where there is no electronic source available.

◆ Automatic recording devices: These are used in process control systems such as at a power station or an oil refinery. Data logging is a form of automatic recording and can be used, for example, for weather readings, fault logging and counting traffic. The results of data logging can then be input to an IS for further processing.

◆ Hand held devices: The final device in this list is the hand held device – a small, special purpose computer that can be used to prompt the user on the next task and then to record the results. Applications of hand held devices include ticket sales (e.g. on trains), stock take, stock picking in a warehouse and meter reading. The data collected in the hand held device might be transmitted to the server by an infrared or radio network or it can be downloaded by plugging the device into a special purpose terminal at the end of the day.

◆ EDI and Internet forms: The smart way of doing data capture is to let someone else do the job. With EDI or Internet forms the customers, or trading partners, send the transaction data in an electronic format. It may be that the data has had to be keyed in but we did not have to pay for it and we are not (ultimately) responsible for any mistakes. If we get real smart we may persuade our trading partners that we are doing them a favour by getting them to do the job of data capture!

As can be seen from the above list (which is not exhaustive), there is a wide variety of alternatives to the keyboard for data capture. These devices are, however, only suited to a limited range of applications. Where they are appropriate they can make a real difference to the speed, cost and accuracy of data collection. In some cases, such as barcodes and EPOS, they have altered the way that businesses operate. For most applications we are left with a screen and a keyboard, and it is designing for these systems that we concentrate on.

❖ **Designing the Interface**

Designing a user interface requires close consultation with the users, usability testing and a good dose of common sense. Clifton et al., (2000) says about data entry / HCI:

> The main point to bear in mind is that a clear, consistent structure should be designed for the data entry sequence. The system should behave consistently and give feedback so that operators can tell where they are in the sequence and whether anything has gone wrong.

The data input screen is, essentially, an electronic form and designing and using it is similar to the paper equivalent. A screen to, for example, register a student would require much the same layout and most of the same information as the paper version. A simple input screen for registering a student is shown in *figure 22.2* (an adapted version of the form in the Madcaster University case study).

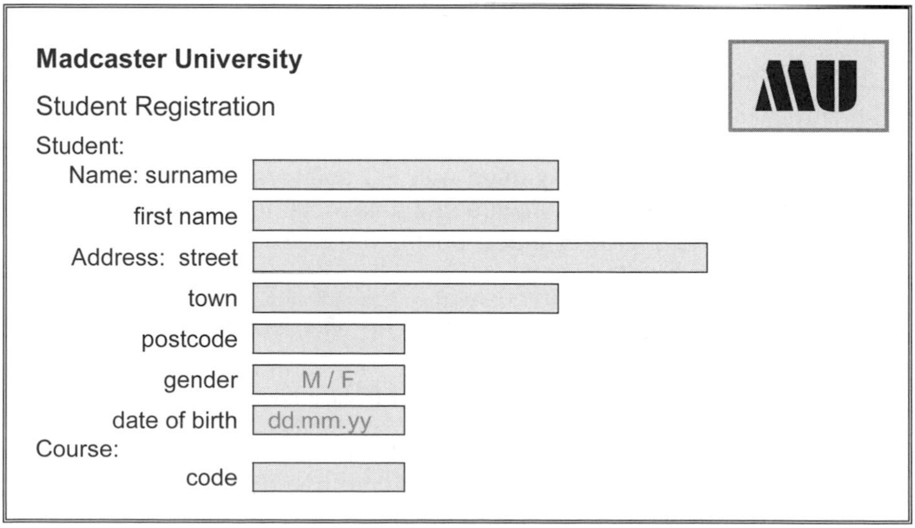

Figure 22.2 Student Registration Form

As well as, or in conjunction with, electronic forms we can use the following types of data / command input:

◆ Command Line: This consists of a line of characters that convey an instruction to the system. Normally very cryptic – easy enough for those who know the codes but difficult for the novice user. The most obvious example was the DOS command line (for those of you who can remember that far back). I have also seen it used for complex transactions in an airline reservation / ticketing system. Not an approach we are likely to incorporate into a user application.

◆ Menu / radio buttons: This is where there is a limited set of options and we can get the user to select one of them by clicking on it or by typing in its code. The obvious use of the menu is a list of system facilities and the user selects the one that he / she wants to access. Menus can also be used for data input. For instance, on the student registration form, we could have:
  ◆ Radio buttons for gender. This seems to be neat, self explanatory and proof against errors. The drawback is that the user has to move from keyboard to mouse and then back again and, for a regular user, typing in 'M' or 'F' could be a better option.
  ◆ A drop-down menu for course codes. This helps by reminding the users what course codes are available and avoids erroneous input. Possibly an experienced operator would find it quicker to type in the course code.
  What we will do on the student registration screen is to make gender and course code the last two items on the screen – the user then only has to switch from typing to the mouse once during the process of filling the screen. An updated version of the student registration screen is included later on.

◆ Objects / icons: Here (possibly instead of a menu entry) we have a small picture (icon) that represents an instruction, selection or data item – the idea is that the icon is self explanatory (an ideal that is not always achieved). These are widely used with PC software but are normally less appropriate to application software and data input. Icons are more complex to program than character input, unless the development system makes specific provision for their use.

◆ Natural Languages: The ultimate is to be able to communicate with the computer in natural language:

  'Hi, I am John, come from Sheffield and I think it could be cool to give your business IT course a bit of a go, OK?'

to which the computer replies, in a distinct, machine generated monotone 'john of sheffield - naff-off'. It can be done for simple instructions that conform to an accepted vocabulary, but it is not yet ready for John.

Here are some design guidelines for designing data input screens:

◆ Screen headings: Include appropriate headings on each screen, including the transaction name and a screen-id. The user (and the help desk, if required) then knows which function is being used.

◆ Identifying data: If there are several screens in a transaction then include identifying data on second and subsequent screens. If, in our example, there was a second screen to the student registration process we could repeat the student's name on that second screen.

◆ Visual verification: Where it is available, give back a description of an input code. In the example, where the user selects the course code we could come back with the course title and possibly avoid an incorrect selection.

◆ Cursor position and cursor sequence: The cursor should be in the first field ready to type and the sequence of input boxes (and the cursor sequence) need to be logical. The sequence should also tie up with any paper documents we intend to transcribe.

◆ Standard position for data: If the same data is to be output on two or more screens then, if possible, keep it in the same place and format. On screen error messages should also appear in a standard position.

◆ Confirmation screen: For something like a delete the system can output details of the record to be deleted and require confirmation. Don't overdo it: for instance, confirming an amend would normally be a waste or time.

◆ Keep the screen tidy and uncluttered.

Updating our original student registration screen with these techniques and guidelines we can now register John from Sheffield: see *figure 22.3*.

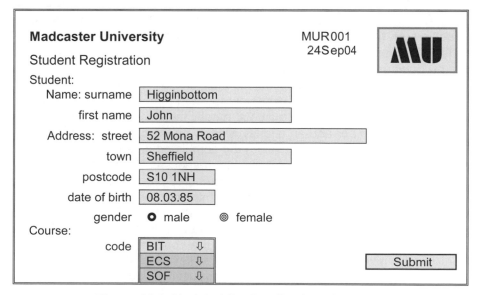

Figure 22.3 Updated Student Registration Form

22.3 Transaction Design

Many business transactions require more than one screen to complete. In the case of the student registration form we will need, at the very least, a confirmation screen giving the student registration number allocated by the system: see *figure 22.4*.

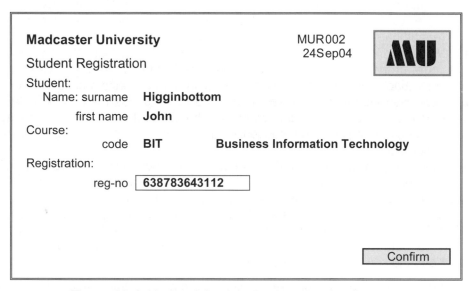

Figure 22.4 Updated Student Registration Confirmation

Just as the separate screens need to be well designed, so does the transaction. The design of the transaction should be consistent throughout and use the minimum number of screens that is necessary for the processing requirements and to produce an attractive design.

The way we design a transaction depends, in part at least, on whether the processing is local (as on a PC) or remote (as with a multi-user TP system). With local processing we can validate the data, modify the screen design, output details from the system and / or add an overlay window as the data input proceeds. With a TP system (with no client processing) the completed screen template has to be submitted before the system makes any response. These differences were explained in *Part IV* when transaction and distributed processing was discussed.

A further issue in transaction design is controlling the navigation through the system – we need to let the user select the next step without imposing more options than are likely to be useful. In the case of the student system, the valid registration screen needs to be followed by the confirmation screen so that the student can be given the registration number. However, what the system should do after the transaction is confirmed is another question. It could:

◆ Return to a system menu where the user can select the next transaction. OK but a bit annoying if there is a queue of 50 students waiting to be registered.

- Continue to the next student registration transaction. OK but there needs to be 'a get out of jail' route back to the main menu, possibly cntrl+M.
- For a PC or client server system there can be some sort of menu included in the screen design that, optionally, gives paths other than the default.

22.4 Information Output

Just as data is input to information systems from a variety of sources, the outputs from the system must meet a diverse set of requirements. The following list of transaction and output requirements illustrates some of this diversity:

- A monthly sales report giving sales totals for each regional office.
- A report on student performance and marks for the exam board.
- An invoice.
- A cheque printed out by the accounting system.
- Electronic orders in EDI format.
- Details of a customer account in response to a specific enquiry.
- A display of train times including information on delays and cancellations.
- The text of this book in camera-ready copy.

For each of these requirements we must design the output to be timely, relevant and understandable. These information output requirements can be classified as:

- Management information.
- Business transactions.
- Other information requirements.

We will look at the design and technology for each of these in turn.

❖ Management Information

Management information is typically a set of printed reports that are scheduled on a weekly, monthly and / or annual basis and distributed round the organisation. Often the reports are voluminous and the requirement and distribution lists date back many years. A lot of management information is not looked at but just filed away. It does not meet the tests of timeliness, relevance and understandability.

How the situation should be addressed is another question. It may be true that a lot of management information is not looked at but the recipients would, very probably, feel vulnerable without it. The appropriate approach is probably to provide a fairly small set of management information that lists key statistics and performance indicators and then let individual users pull off their own more detailed reports, as they require them.

The main types of management report are:

- Analysis report.
- Exception report.
- Key target report.
- Ad-hoc report.
- Data enquiry.

These types of report have already been discussed in *Part III*, in the chapter on Management Information. The management information can be printed or displayed on the screen – for complex reports, where the user needs to make a detail inspection of the figures, there is still a lot to be said for paper. Management information on key performance indicators can also be put on the company intranet and be accessed by all staff members (possibly a bit radical for some organisations where management like to keep information secret – or at least they try to!).

The principles of good design and of HCI apply to information out as much as to data in. Many of the pointers to good design given for screen design also apply to report design. The choice between using tables of figures or some form of graphical representation has already been addressed in *Part III*.

❖ Business Transactions

The underlying purpose of many information systems is the processing of business transactions; the result is the output of documents such as delivery notes, invoices, pay slips or cheques.

These documents need to be designed to perform their function effectively and efficiently. Often these documents are sent outside the organisation and they also need to create the right image and, if possible, promote the interests of the organisation.

To design these documents we need to consider:

◆ The needs of both the sending and receiving organisations. An invoice, for example, needs to readily tie up with both the customer's and the supplier's internal transactions. The customer will probably be receiving invoices from a number of organisations. Processing all the different formats quickly and accurately is not easy. Good layout and sticking to generally accepted conventions will help.

◆ The production process. Often these transactions are produced in large numbers and sometimes on pre-printed documents. The system needs to allow for paper line-up, restarts in the event of a system crash and an industrial-type process to fold, envelope and despatch the documents.

The interchange of electronic transactions is an alternative to paper documents – EDI has already been examined in *Part III*.

❖ Other Information Requirements

Information technology is being applied in an ever increasing range of application areas, many of them outside the more traditional area of business administration. With these new application areas come new requirements for information dissemination. Examples of such applications are:

◆ Public information displays. These have long been a feature of the railway station and the airport lounge and now they are appearing, for example, on the motorway to indicate any traffic problems that lie ahead. Some of these displays seem to be aimed at staff, or the informed traveller, rather than the less informed users – possibly an area where the design needs to be revisited. See notes on railway travel information below.

◆ Electronic information services. Some information is made available to staff, trading partners and / or the public in electronic format – the Internet is the most obvious example of this. On the Internet, information is set up using HTML but this is a static form – it can be made dynamic by generating web pages 'on the fly', from data held on a database. There is a lot of scope for designing good web pages – some information providers achieve it and some do not.

Railway travel information displays at railway stations come in various shapes and sizes. Taking the electronic displays (and leaving aside poster displays, announcements and asking staff – all of which can be problematic), we have:

* At most city terminal stations a large departure board listing all the trains about to depart. These displays are generally easily visible. They are easiest to follow if your intended destination is the final destination of the train – If you want an intermediate station, and you are unfamiliar with the service pattern, they can be more problematic. The board is frequently updated and these changes often take place while the customer is trying to read the information.
* Smaller stations tend to use a video monitor to display a summary of services. Typically this shows the start and end point of the service. This does not necessarily help a traveller who is looking for an intermediate station and who is not familiar with the service, e.g. a display at Sheffield station listing the 07:33 Norwich to Liverpool on platform 2a is only useful to someone going to Manchester if they know that the train passes through Manchester.
* Most stations also have a video monitor on the platform giving the next train due at that platform. This display gives the destination and all intermediate stations, but you have to find the right platform before you can consult this display.

A new type of display is being installed at some large stations. It lists all available destinations, in alphabetic order, and the time and platform for the next train. There is one of these at Manchester Piccadilly but, as there are too many stations to be listed, it switches between two list of stations – often before one has found the information one is looking for.

Passenger information is a demanding environment. There is a lot of information; it has to be displayed so people can view it from a distance; some customers have special needs and each customer only requires only a small subset of the information that is available. Whatever the difficulties, it is apparent that the train companies have not yet come up with an ideal solution.

22.5 Human–Computer Interaction

Human–computer interaction or human–computer interface design, both referred to by the acronym HCI, is the study of effective person-to-machine and machine-to-person interface design. The science of HCI involves the disciplines of psychology, sociology, linguistics, graphic design and ergonomics.

Pressman R. (2000) bases his discussion of HCI on Mandel's (1997) three golden rules:

- Place the user in control.
- Reduce the user's memory load.
- Make the interface consistent.

The first point, place the user in control, is the opposite of the system being in control. Users should be able to use the system in a way they feel comfortable with, that fits in with what they are doing and that is appropriate to their level of experience. The user should be able to interrupt the task that is underway and, if necessary, undo the actions already taken. The technicalities of how the system operates should be hidden from the user.

The more the user is required to remember, the more stressful and error prone the system becomes. We can reduce the user's memory load by reminding the user of past actions on the current screen – I have already made the point that the screen design should include appropriate heading information and repeat key data that has already been established in the transaction. We can also help user understanding by disclosing (or asking for) information in a logical sequence.

The final point is that the interface should be consistent. A user who has learnt to use one transaction in a system should not have to start the learning process again when he or she takes on further transactions. This is helped by adopting a consistent design style to both the layout of screens and the way the system is operated. If, for example, the system uses control keys then they should have the same, or a consistent effect, wherever they are used.

In designing a user interface we need to cater for all sorts of users. Users might be classified as:

- Novice or expert user of IT.
- Casual or regular users of any given transaction or facility.

Two possible user types (derived from the four parameters given above) are:

- Expert regular users who usually just want to get on with the job. They do not need a screen that is cluttered with explanations of what should be done, contains facilities for looking up simple codes or navigation paths that require several steps before the next transaction is started. They may, for example, prefer a hot key system (cntrl+n) rather than a menu system to select the next, or an additional, function.

- The novice or casual user of the system needs a lot more help. Menu systems, on screen instructions, code selection and help facilities can all help the person who is new to the system (or a part of the system).

The novice or casual user will, very probably, soon become something of an expert and the facilities that one were a great help then, if not cleverly designed, become a hindrance. General purpose software, such as a Microsoft package, can obviously attempt to cater for all levels of user experience. A more modest application, developed for a limited user population, has to balance the cost of facilities and options against their likely use. Nevertheless the underlying points on levels of experience and on good HCI design are valid and should be born in mind.

Exercises

Now it is your turn to see what you have remembered and what you have learnt:

1. Consider the screen designs suggested for student registration at Madcaster University. Accepting the data requirements shown on the sample screens, have you any suggestions for improving on the design?

2. The Madcaster University case study in *Chapter 19* includes a module choices form. Convert this into a screen design / electronic form. Don't just copy the paper document – you need to think a bit harder than that!

3. In this chapter I set out what seems to be the less than ideal state of train information available on railway stations. How could this situation be improved? Are there any alternative technologies that could be utilised to make sure that individual passengers have easy access to the information they need?

Further Reading

There are numerous texts on HCI. Many of the points made are now part of the norm for system design and the emphasis of academic study has tended to move on to multi-media computing and design for multimedia. One very useful source of information on a variety of topics is:

Pressman R. (2000) *Software Engineering: A Practitioner's Approach*, 5th ed., McGraw Hill, Maidenhead.

The chapter on User Interface Design is useful additional reading.

Chapter 23
Projects, Programming and Implementation

Summary

System analysis and design (SA&D) is only one aspect of the creation of an information system. SA&D is key to achieving a well designed system that is efficient and meets the user's requirements. The process of SA&D leads on to the production (or purchase) of software and takes place within the overall structure of a project team.

Information systems projects are notorious for running late and costing a great deal more than the originally planned budget. To minimise these problems it is essential that the project is thoroughly planned and actively managed.

The information system also needs to be fit for purpose, it needs to be reliable and to meet the business requirement. This aspect of the project requires close user involvement, thorough testing and quality management.

These aspects of developing a information system are summarised in this chapter.

23.1 Implementing the Information System

This section of the book has concentrated on the design of the information system. However the process of system analysis and design (SA&D) is only one part of the process of developing an information system. Other tasks to be performed in the development and deployment of an IS project include:

- ◆ Project management and quality control.
- ◆ Production or procurement of the software (programming).
- ◆ Procurement and instillation of the IT equipment.
- ◆ Testing within the project team and with the users.
- ◆ Implementation.
- ◆ Maintenance.

The creation (or enhancement) of an information system is normally organised as a project. The size of the project team and the duration of the project will obviously depend on the size of the task that is to be done.

Assuming it is a fair sized project there will be a project manager assigned to the task. He or she has the responsibility of ensuring that a quality product is delivered on time and to budget. Producing an information system is a complex task involving analysis and design, programming, installation of IT equipment, training of users and so on. Ensuring that all aspects of the project fit together requires careful planning and strong management. The task of the project manager is to focus on the needs of the project to the virtual exclusion of other priorities of the organisation. The project team, as an organisational form, has been discussed in *Part II*.

As well as the project manager, the project team will require a number of other specialist staff. These can include:

- ◆ System analysts.
- ◆ Database designers.
- ◆ Programmers.
- ◆ System testers.
- ◆ Implementators.

A general organisational chart for a project team is show in *figure 23.1*.

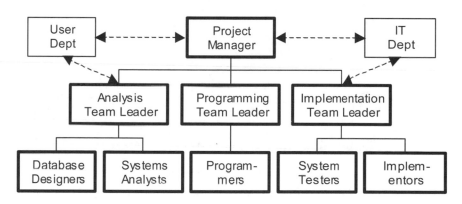

Figure 23.1 An IS Project Team

23.2 Project Management

Projects, particularly large projects, need careful planning. Planning would normally be the prime responsibility of the project manager. It is the project manager's job to draw up the plan and then to deliver on time, to budget and in accordance with the plan.

A standard approach to project planning is to draw up a critical path analysis / PERT network (PERT stands for programme evaluation and review technique). This technique charts each activity in relationship to other activities taking into account the dependencies between those activities. This approach can be illustrated using a very much simplified example project that requires the following activities:

- ◆ a1 Install IT for development – 1 person for 8 weeks,
    start anytime.

◆ a2 System analysis – 3 people for 12 weeks,
   start anytime.
◆ a3 Database design – 1 person for 6 weeks,
   start anytime.
◆ a4 Install live IT – 2 people for 6 weeks,
   start after a1, a2 and a3.
◆ a5 Programming – 4 people for 12 weeks,
   start after a1, a2 and a3.
◆ a6 Test and implement – 2 people for 8 weeks,
   start after a4 and a5.

The PERT technique requires that these activities are plotted on a chart showing dependencies, i.e. that activities 4 and 5 can't start until a1, a2 and a3 are finished and that activity 6 can't start until a4 and a5 are complete. See *figure 23.2*.

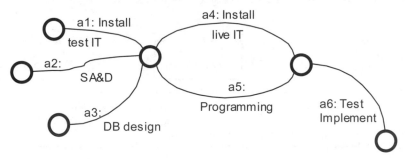

Figure 23.2 PERT Chart Showing Dependencies

This chart can then be developed to show a start and end event for each activity. These events then have:

◆ Event label.
◆ Earliest time for event (et).
◆ Latest time for the event (lt).
◆ Slack / float time (st)

Our network is redrawn to include this detail in *figure 23.3*. This enhanced diagram allows us to identify the critical path and the minimum overall elapse time. The critical path is the sequence of activities where the slack times are zero – marked in bold on *figure 23.3* (there may be more than one critical path). The minimum overall elapse time is 32 weeks – the sum total of the elapse times on the critical path.

Having done the planning the project manager then needs to plot progress. This can be done using the PERT chart but is more easily seen if that chart is converted to a bar or Gantt chart. *Figure 23.4* shows our example project converted into a Gantt chart.

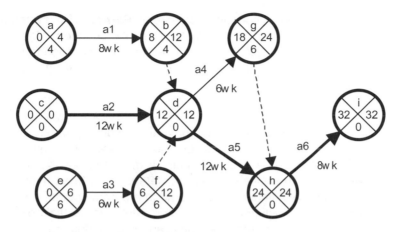

Figure 23.3 PERT Chart Showing Critical Path

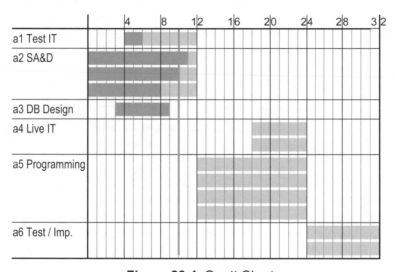

Figure 23.4 Gantt Chart

The Gantt chart shows the activities planned for the project and, in this case, I have shown the number of staff. The project manager has recorded the progress of each person, up to week 10, in a darker grey. The updated chart makes it clear that while the DB design activity is complete and the SA&D is a little behind schedule there is a real problem with activity 1: installing the test IT equipment – this activity is four weeks behind with only two weeks to run.

23.3 Programming

The paper design produced by the system analyst may be a vital step in the production of an information system but it is the software that is the real end product. The software for the system can be:

◆ Bought-in. We looked at sourcing software in *Part III*. ERP systems were one example of the type of system that can be obtained 'off the shelf'. Quite often a bought-in system will require some modification to make it fit the requirements of a particular organisation – installing an ERP is normally a major project.

◆ Created using an application generator. This is a package that allows users to specify their requirements and then the package will generate the application – complex requirements may need to be separately coded and slotted in. Application generators tend to be associated with database packages and Oracle is a good example. A more familiar example will be MS Access where the user sets up the database and can then generate forms and reports with little or no recourse to program coding.

◆ Programmed. The requirement is interpreted as a set of detailed instructions in an appropriate programming language and those instructions are then used to generate the executable software.

We have already taken a brief look at machine code instructions, the code the computer operates with, in *Part IV*. It is unusual for modern systems to be written in machine code and we normally write in a high-level language that is then translated (compiled or interpreted) into machine code for use on the computer system.

Many programming languages have been developed over the years, for differing purposes, and many of these still have to be used when the software they were used for is maintained. One of these programming languages is COBOL, used for commercial systems on mainframes – there is still a lot of it about. Programming languages that are used for the writing of new software include:

◆ C and C++. The language of the UNIX operating system and available across a wide range of systems. A detailed (low level) language that tends to be used for system software and real time applications.

◆ Java. A language derived from C and generally associated with Internet applications (although it can be used for almost any programming job).

◆ Visual Basic (VB). A visual programming language that gives the user facility to paint the user interface and then generates code shells for those interfaces (a bit of a cross between a programming language and an application generator). VB is a PC language from Microsoft and can be used to add functionality in many of its desk top products.

◆ Delphi. A similar product to Visual Basic but in this case from Borland. It was developed before VB and has been widely used by small software companies to develop specialist PC applications.

Some example Java code is shown in *figure 23.5*. The function of this code is to calculate how long it takes to pay back a loan. You put in the value of the loan, that annual interest rate and the monthly repayments – the program then tells you how long the loan takes to repay, the final month's payment and the total amount repaid (including interest). The program assumes that interest is charged on a monthly basis. If you want to cheer yourself up, type it into a Java development environment and see how much damage your debts could cause you.

```java
import java.io.*;
public class Payments {

public static void main(String [] args) {
double cap=0.0, capo=0.0, capt=0.0, interest=0.0, rpay=0.0, fpay=0.0;
int mths=0, i;
char ch;
String instring = "              ";
BufferedReader in
          = new BufferedReader(new InputStreamReader(System.in));

  System.out.print("Value of loan? : ");
   i =0;
   try{
          instring = in.readLine();
          cap = Float.parseFloat(instring);
          }
   catch (Exception e){System.out.println(e);};

  System.out.print("Annual interest? : ");
   try{
          instring = in.readLine();
          interest = Float.parseFloat(instring);
          }
   catch (Exception e){System.out.println(e);};

  System.out.print("Monthly repayments? : ");
   try{
          instring = in.readLine();
          rpay = Float.parseFloat(instring);
          }
   catch (Exception e){System.out.println(e);};

  mths = 0;
  capo = cap;

  while ((capo > 0.0) && (capo <= cap)) {
          capo = capo + (capo * interest/100.0/12.0) - rpay;
          mths++;
          }

  if (capo <= 0.0) {
          fpay = rpay + capo;
          capt = rpay * mths + capo;
          System.out.println("Repayment period " + mths + " months");
          System.out.println("Final month's payment " + fpay);
          System.out.println("Total amount paid " + capt);
          }
   else {
          System.out.println("Interest exceeds monthly payments");
          }

}
}
```

Figure 23.5 Example Java Code

When you run the program it will ask you to type in:

- ◆ Value of loan? :   e.g. 2000
- ◆ Annual interest? :   e.g. 10
- ◆ Monthly repayments? :   e.g. 100

The program then does the calculations and, using the above example figures, gives the answers (we could cut the excessive decimal places but it would require extra coding):

- ◆ Repayment period 22 months
- ◆ Final month's payment 96.97435707392518
- ◆ Total amount paid 2196.974357073925

The code example is no more than a snippet. To be useful in an information system it would need, for example, to take data from a formatted screen, validate that data, update a database and then present the user with another formatted screen for the next stage in the processing. The system may be a free-standing package on a PC, software on the client within a client server system or part of a multi-user server system. For the latter two cases, the modules will have to fit within an overall architecture that includes network handling and multi-user provision. Most information system consist of many modules and very often many thousands of lines of code. All of this software should be carefully planned, designed and tested.

It is not the purpose of this book to teach programming – many of you will be undertaking a separate, introductory, programming module and there will be a separate recommended text for that unit.

23.4 IT Equipment

To develop and install an information system we need the IT infrastructure. This can be a single PC or the system may require central servers, an extensive network and a large number of desk top and workplace terminals. The system will also require system software for both development and live running. Sometimes the new IS can be installed on the existing infrastructure but often that infrastructure will have to be enhanced or replaced. The types of IT provision we might require for an information system have been discussed in *Part IV*.

Where extensive enhancement to existing equipment and / or new equipment is required the IT aspect of the development may become a separate project in itself. The equipment must be purchased, installed and tested. The installation of the IT equipment has to be coordinated with the SA&D and development aspects of the project. Appropriate computer systems need to be available to the project team before programming can start. The full IT infrastructure needs to be installed before the implementation (and preferably for acceptance test). It may be necessary to maintain the existing IT infrastructure while the new infrastructure is tested and implemented.

23.5 Testing

Once the software has been written, generated or bought it must be tested, and some of that testing is likely to be the province of the IS specialist. Testing can take a number of forms but a basic classification would be:

◆ Module testing. This is where the basic unit of programming, the module, is tested to check it does the task expected of it. The test is normally the responsibility of the programmer who wrote the code. Once the module is thoroughly tested we should be able to assume it to be internally correct, a 'black box', when we use it in later stages of testing.

◆ Link testing. Having checked all the separate modules we can put them together as a program (or sub-system) and check that they work together. This test is likely to be done within the programming team. Given the modules have already been tested the focus of this stage is the interfaces between the modules.

◆ System testing. This requires that the whole system be put together and tested in a live environment. At one level this is a scaled up link test but it is also required to test that the data meets the requirements of all sub-systems and that the system will cope with the volumes that will occur in live operations.

◆ Acceptance testing. The first three stages of testing are within the project team. The final stage of testing is for the users of the system; it is a final check that the system is an effective business tool. With general purpose software, e.g. a Microsoft product, the acceptance test is carried out by pre-release of the package to selected users; this is commonly referred to as the 'Beta test' (with the internal testing being called the 'Alpha test').

The stages in testing a system can be matched to the stages of the design process; this is called the 'V' model and is shown in *figure 23.6*.

Testing, done properly, is a time consuming business. Programs are (generally) complex pieces of logic and to test most / every path requires careful planning and extensive preparation. It is only by thorough testing of software that we can be confident that it is 'fit for purpose'. The extent of the testing is dependent on the complexity of the system and the degree of importance placed on reliability. The requirement for reliability of (say) a student registration system is rather less than a banking system and a lot less than for an operating system or the software control systems in a aircraft. The amount of project time spent testing can range from (say) 20% up to as much as 60% where reliability is of crucial importance (which is several orders of magnitude greater than the time spent by most students testing any programming assignment that they might undertake).

It is to be noted that while testing needs to be rigorous it does not prove that the software is correct. In the words of Dijkstra (1972), one of the early programming gurus:

Testing proves the presence of bugs, not their absence.

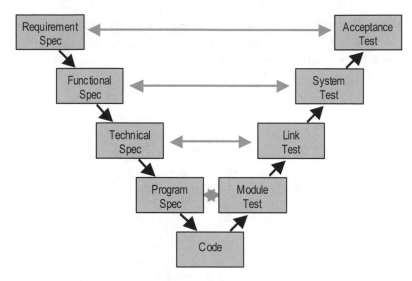

Figure 23.6 Specification and Testing – the V Model

23.6 Implementation

Once the system is tested it is time to start reaping the benefit from all the time, money and effort that has been put into developing the system – the system has to be made live.

Making a system live will often be a mini project in itself. Tasks that are involved in putting the system live (some of which will have been started during earlier stages of the project) include:

◆ Installation of new IT equipment. Discussed earlier in this chapter.

◆ Data capture and data cutover. The data from the existing system (manual or IT) needs to be typed into, or converted over to, the new system. For a large organisation this can involve many thousands of records and special software may have to be written to make the conversion. It may also need to be a last-minute job as existing data will be changing in the current system.

◆ Training. The users and technical staff, who will be operating and supporting the new system, need to be trained on that system. The training needs to be thorough if the new system is to operate efficiently but the training also needs to be fitted in with minimum disruption to existing operations. Training needs to be supplemented with appropriate documentation and / or help facilities that are built into the software.

The way the system is to be put live also needs to be considered. There are a number of approaches and these can be summarised as follows:

◆ Big bang. This is where the organisation switches off the old system on (say) Friday night and the new system starts on Monday morning. The weekend is spent doing the data conversions, setting up the system and some final confidence tests. For a large system it can be a very full weekend and the smooth operation of all aspects of the process is crucial.

◆ Staged roll-out. Sometimes it is possible to implement a new system in stages. This may involve implementing it in one department or branch at a time or it can involve implementing one sub-system at a time. Such an approach is obviously less risky than the big bang approach but it may not suit the nature of the system and / or the operation. The staged approach would, for example, require that the standing data (customers, products or whatever) to be maintained on both the old and new system and this may not be practical.

◆ Parallel running. This is the safest option but, in most cases, it is not a practical option. Parallel running involves running both the old system and the new system for a few weeks. Data has to be updated and transactions processed through both systems. The outputs from both systems can be compared and when the new system is demonstrated to be functioning correctly and reliably it takes over the operation and the old system is switched off.

As well as an implementation strategy there is normally a fall-back strategy. If things go disastrously wrong, and there is no way to fix the problems quickly, then the organisation needs to go back to the existing system to keep the business running. Some implementations are so complex that there is no way back (keep your fingers crossed!).

Whatever approach (or combination of approaches) is used to the implementation of a system it is likely to be a somewhat fraught process. Careful planning and appropriate rehearsals will minimise the risks involved.

23.7 Maintenance

Implementing the system is not the end of the story. Once the system is in use it will need to be maintained, enhanced and the users will need support. Many medium to large organisations have a help desk system where users can raise problems. The help desk answer simple queries and pass on those it can not handle:

◆ First level support sorts out problems with the desk top environment and queries about the system.
◆ Second level support takes over where the problem is more complex – all problems that require changes to the application software are the province of second level support. Large application systems have their own dedicated maintenance teams.
◆ Third level support becomes involved if the problem is more technical involving the system architecture of the IT installation.

Maintenance also includes enhancements to the system. Business requirements are not set in concrete and the information systems need to evolve with business requirements and business expectations. Enhancements normally involve a request for change procedure where each proposal is costed, evaluated and prioritised. Where possible, enhancements will be batched and included in a new release of the system.

Exercises

Having read the chapter, try these exercises to consolidate what you have learnt:

1. The department is intending to build a new computer lab. The following jobs have been identified.
   * a1   Build stud walls to form the new lab – 10 days.
   * a2   Decorate – 5 days.
   * a3   Install power supply and network cables (after the walls but before the room is decorated) – 5 days.
   * a4   Order / delivery period for computer equipment – 20 days.
   * a5   Order / delivery period for power and network materials – 15 days.
   * a6   Install and test computer equipment – 10 days.

   Work out the dependencies (they should be fairly obvious) and draw a PERT chart. Identify the critical path and the minimum elapse time (people only do a five day working week). We have six weeks before the start of term – can we do it?

2. In *Chapter 23* you are to be asked to do a team project to analyse, design and implement a small database system. List the major activities involved in this assignment. Assuming a team of three and four weeks to do the project, draw a project plan.

3. The chapter includes a sample Java program. If you are not studying programming elsewhere then try dry running it with some simple test data:
   * Capital   = £100.
   * Interest   = 12%.
   * Monthly Payment   = £20.

Further Reading

This chapter is not seen as a core part of the course but more as background reading to complete the picture. If you wish to follow up on any of the areas covered, useful sources are:

Pressman R. (2000) *Software Engineering: A Practitioner's Approach*, 5th ed., McGraw-Hill, Maidenhead.

Cadle J. and Yates D. (2001) *Project Management for Information Systems*, 3rd ed., Financial Times / Pitman, London.

Chapter 24
Student Project

Summary

This chapter presents two small case studies and the suggestion is that you take one of them and implement it as a computer based information system. The exercise requires that you:

◆ Design the system using the design techniques that you have learnt in earlier sessions.
◆ Design forms and reports applying the HCI principles that have been outlined.
◆ Implement the system using a MS Access database.
◆ Test and demonstrate the system using appropriate test data.

It is envisaged that the Student Project will be a marked assignment.

24.1 Implementing the Information System

Thus far, in this book, we have looked at business, the business use of IS, the IT that is used in IS and the way we analyse and design an information system. Now you have the chance to use that knowledge and those skills in creating a small information system of your own.

This chapter contains two case studies and there are more on the web site. Select one of the case studies (or take the case study given to you by your tutor) and create an information system. The steps you need to take are:

◆ Examine the case study and document the system requirement using the system analysis and design techniques that you have studied in either **Chapter 20** or **Chapter 21**.
◆ Design an MS Access database for the requirement. Databases were discussed at length in **Chapter 16** and the normalisation of data is explained in **Chapter 20**.
◆ Design the screens and reports you require for the system. **Chapter 22** can help you with this.
◆ Implement the system as an MS Access database.
◆ Load test data and check all the input forms and output reports of your system work correctly.

The intention is that you use MS Access for the project. MS Access is a database package that contains an application generator. It does not require programming (although MS Visual Basic routines can be included where calculations or data transformations are required). The implementation process is not object oriented. It is arguable that for a small system, in this sort of development environment, that the design process can be cut down. However dispensing with the design process can lead to mistakes (and part of the intention is that you demonstrate your understanding of design techniques). The design process should include:

◆ An exploration of the user requirements – this should be documented as either a context diagram and a level 1 data flow diagram (DFD) (structured design) or a use case diagram (OO design).
◆ A design for the database. This is most appropriately done using the structured techniques of an ER diagram and relational data analysis. If you have been studying OO design, then you should produce a conceptual class diagram (assigning design version methods to objects will not be relevant to a MS Access implementation).

More detailed design using entity life histories or sequence diagrams is probably not strictly necessary for a project of this size and nature, but your tutor may direct that you include some of this documentation in your project submission.

The implementation should include:

◆ Forms for all the major inputs.
◆ Reports as indicated in the case study requirements.

The case studies are designed for implementation using the facilities included in MS Access. It should not be necessary to include any additional program code (although you may do so if you wish to and know how). An outline of how to use MS Access is included in *Chapter 16* and further details are given on the web site.

24.2 Case Studies

The two case studies included in the book are:

◆ Dave's Database.
◆ Library System.

Both these case studies can be used for groups of up to four students. Further case studies are given on the web site (my practice is to give different groups in a class their own case study – it encourages the groups to work independently).

❖ Dave's Database

Assignments are sometimes set as group work but with a class size of between 250 and 350 students it becomes a bit of a task keeping track of what is going on. You, as a sympathetic group of students, appreciating the difficulties your lecturer has to work with, have agreed to set up Dave's Database to help keep the books straight.

First job is to set up a list of the students. The identity of the student is the student number and we also need their surname, forename, e-Mail address and tutorial group.

The tutorial groups are allocated to one of the lecturers and that lecturer is responsible for putting students into assignment groups – students can request which other students they will be grouped with and this will be taken into account. The process of setting up a group consists of identifying three or four students and assigning them to a group. The group has a four-letter code and the case study the group is working also needs to be recorded. The lecturer setting up the groups needs the following reports:

- A report that identifies all the students in the tutorial group that have not yet been put into groups for the assignment.
- A report that lists all the assignment groups, within the tutorial group, and can be put onto the notice board.

One of the problems with group work can be that some group members do most of the work and other group members contribute little or nothing but still get credit. To help overcome this each group member is asked to assess all other group members' contribution on a scale of 1 (done nothing) to 4 (excellent). These ratings are to be recorded on the system and there needs to be a report that allows the lecturer marking the assignment to see these student assessments and decide how to take them into account in awarding the group work marks.

The final task is to input the marks for the students and to produce a report listing the students and their marks, within the tutorial group; if possible the report should be in alphabetic order and / or in mark rank order.

❖ **Library System**

A library system requires a list of registered borrowers and a list of books. Each borrower has a registration number, name, address and telephone number and is assigned to a course. Each book has a catalogue number, title, author, date published and classification. The system requires facilities to update both borrowers and books. The courses (course code and name) and classification (code and name) need to be set up prior to the input of borrowers and books.

Once the borrower has been set up he or she can take out books – an interface is required to register a loan. Once the book has been used it is returned and a further interface is then required to cancel the loan.

To help the library staff administer the system the following enquiries are needed:

- Borrower Enquiry – for a specified registration number, give full details of the borrower and the catalogue number + title for each book he or she has on loan.
- Book Enquiry – for a specified catalogue number give full details of the book and the registration number and name of any borrower.
- Catalogue List – list all books in a specified classification.
- Borrower List – list all borrowers in a specified class.

These systems have been kept simple for use in this assignment – if you are able to improve on the functioning of the system that can be noted when your work is marked. In general the input processes specify the data to be included but the data appropriate to the reporting requirements is left to your judgement. It may be that you wish to add to the data specified, or to codify it, to facilitate some of the reporting requirements.

Further Reading

The further reading is as specified on the chapters on databases and system analysis and design. The Beynon-Davies book on databases can be particularly helpful when working on this project:

Beynon-Davies P. (2004) *Database Systems*, 3rd ed, Palgrave Macmillan, Basingstoke.

Assignments

The suggested assignment is to design and develop a MS Access database system for one of the case studies given in the chapter or on the web site. The assignment is suitable for a group project (which is the way I do it). The deliverables are:

◆ Analysis and design documentation – handed in for marking. This should consist of:
  • Requirements documentation – either a context diagram plus level 1 DFD or a use case diagram.
  • Data design – an ER diagram plus relational data analysis. For students who have studied only OO design a class diagram should be submitted.
  These submissions should be group work. Further documentation requirements can be included – these can be individual submissions.

◆ The MS Access system demonstrated in the lab. The system can be marked as a group effort (with all members of the group getting the same mark) or each group member can be assigned one input function (form) and one report and be assessed individually.

Part VI
Legal, Social and Ethical Implications of IS and IT

Information systems and information technology have a part to play in just about everything we do. We use IS at work and when we go shopping. There are records about us at the university, the doctor's, the bank and in government departments. IT is embedded in transport systems and is an essential part of telecommunications services. And, very probably, we have our own computer equipment at home.

The widespread use of IS and IT is changing the way society functions and the way we live. The use of IS and IT affects:

- The jobs we do and how we do them (and possibly whether we have a job at all).
- Our safety – many complex services rely on IT for their delivery and, if that IT malfunctions, there is the potential for a disaster.
- Civil liberties – many organisations hold information on us. The information is not always accurate and, if aggregated together, could be used in ways that would be unhelpful to individuals and, possibly, to society at large.

As a society we have a choice (or should have a choice). Do we accept any and all applications of IS and IT that organisations and governments choose to impose on us or are there uses of technology that are not acceptable?

As IT professionals and members of society we should be mindful for the future and thoughtful of the consequences of our actions.

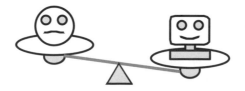

Chapter 25
IT and Society

Summary

The widespread availability and use of IT is changing the way we work, the way we organise our lives and the way we are governed. We are, it is suggested, moving from the industrial age to become an information society.

The use of IT impacts all areas of life. This includes:

◆   Employment – the availability of jobs and the nature of work.

◆   Safety – systems that used to be controlled by people are now controlled electronically. Can we rely on such systems? Are working conditions for IT workers as safe as they should be?

◆   Civil liberties – does the widespread use of IT by government (and other organisations) simply enhance the quality of administration or does it have implications for our freedom and democracy?

As IT / IT professionals we are part of this transformation – what are our duties and responsibilities? We look at the role of professional organisations and, in particular, the British Computer Society.

25.1   The Information Society

The study of information systems grew up when the main application of computer systems was administrative processes in organisations. Initially the information system was a way of automating processes that had previously been carried out by clerical staff. Over time the scope of the processing expanded (the computer systems could handle complexity that would not have been practical in a clerical process) and the provision of management information became more important. We were able to change the way business was done using the information system (a process sometimes termed business process re-engineering). The scope of the information systems was dramatically expanded by:

◆   The development of the personal computer.
◆   The availability of network facilities, now including the Internet.

Information systems and information and communications technology (ICT) can be applied to tasks of all sizes and these systems may interface with one another, with systems in other organisations, with systems embedded in machinery and with people at home and on the move. In a few short years we have moved from a society where the scope of information processing was limited by what could be processed clerically and communicated by post to a society where almost any collection, communication and dissemination of information is possible. The change is dramatic. It has been compared with the industrial revolution where people moved from the land and from cottage industries to the cities and to work in factories. It has been called the information revolution. It heralds the post industrial, information society. It can, or so it is claimed, reverse the process of industrialisation as instead of taking people to the factory to work, the information can be delivered to the workers, wherever they are. It should, or so it is suggested, bring in an age of prosperity and leisure where short working hours and economic prosperity foster personal fulfilment. It might change the notion of production and service delivery so we can all have what we want, when we want it and have it customised to our own specific requirements. It has changed the nature of communications – data, in vast quantities, can be delivered anywhere across the globe, virtually instantaneously.

The information society is changing our lives (and don't count on Utopia just yet!). The process has its own momentum and it is not clear how, and to what extent, governments and society can control and direct it. Galbraith (the American liberal economist) writing in 1972 in his book *The New Industrial State*, commented on the dangers:

> A society propelled by imperatives of technology is increasingly closed, inertial, inflexible and isolated from any true conception of human needs.

More recently, Portillo (a Conservative politician and then a government minister) also recognised the problems and risks but seemed to suggest we had little choice:

> The Employment Secretary (Portillo) admitted yesterday that the labour market was beset by job insecurity and resentment, but said that Britain had to embrace the technological revolution rather than attempt to turn the clock back.

> (*Guardian* 23 Feb 1995)

It is to some of these problems and risks that we now turn our attention.

25.2 Employment

The nature of employment has been and is changing rapidly. In the first half of the 20th century the big employers, in industrial countries, were coal mining, steel making, railways, manufacturing and farming. When I left school, most of my friends took up an apprenticeship in one of the three local large engineering works. Now those three factories are all gone and there are very few apprenticeships on offer anywhere.

The decline in employment in manufacturing (and in primary industries) has a number of causes. One aspect of that is the incorporation of electronics into the production process (globalisation is another significant factor and this process is also facilitated by the use of ICTs). The changes in the production process have also reduced the requirement for skilled workers and many of the jobs that remain in manufacture are simple assembly jobs.

As employment declined in manufacture there was a corresponding rise in employment is administration and in service industries – the banks, insurance companies and in administration in central and local government. Administrative jobs could be assisted by the use of IT and it is rare to find a office worker who does not have a computer on his / her desk. For a long time the use of IS did not seem to affect the level of employment – the investment in IT increased but so did the office headcount. More recently this has changed. Many large organisations have cut staff but the process has been typified by top down target setting rather than any bottom up assessment of the level of workload and the number of staff that are properly required to get the job done. Whatever the use of IS did to administrative procedures there does not seem to be any general rule that it made them more efficient in terms of the number of staff required.

The application of IT to administration also changed (or was part of a change in) the way that office work was done. There are two (very different) tendencies that can be detected:

◆ Empowerment. In some offices staff are being given more responsibility for individual cases (as opposed to a task being passed through a number of departments and being referred to supervisors for sign-off). The use of desk top computing plays an important part in this process. Staff members can readily access the system for the information they need and update the system with the details of the cases in hand and the decisions that are made.

◆ Taylorism. The opposite tendency is to break down a job into component parts that can be processed simply and without much knowledge or skill being required – a process known as Taylorism when applied to manufacturing processes. This tendency is exhibited in the increasing adoption of call centres where the expectation is that all transactions can be dealt with in accordance with a predefined script and using a limited set of IT facilities.

The use of IT in call centres facilitates a very regimented approach to work. The IT records every task that each operator does and the performance of the operator can be assessed at the end of each shift. Some call centres have very regimented employment and supervision practices and this is often coupled with fairly low levels of pay. These types of employment practice, facilitated by IT, are reflected in the 'job insecurity' and 'resentment' remarks quoted earlier in this chapter.

The use of IT has also created an industry supplying the IT equipment, developing the systems and supporting the users of the systems. The manufacture of IT equipment is in many ways like other manufacture but technology changes rapidly and suppliers have had to be quick to adopt technological advances and incorporate them in their products. Employment in the software side has also changed with many of the skilled jobs moving to the software companies and consultancies – jobs in user departments are now more concerned with end user support. In the IS service industry we have the help desk – the IT industry's own version of the call centre.

25.3 Reliability and Safety

IT is an integral part of many procedures and systems. The benefits are that we can control systems with less labour and, in some cases, have systems that would not be possible with manual control. This includes systems that we rely on in our everyday lives, for example:

◆ Our weekly social security payment or monthly pay cheque.
◆ The bank system and ATM machines.
◆ The integrated EPOS systems in the shops we use.

Failure of any of these systems would be an inconvenience or an embarrassment – a prolonged period of failure would cause many people real hardship. Examples of the disruption that can occur when technological systems break down or are not effectively implemented include:

◆ Air Canada. In August 2003 there were problems in the power systems in the north east of North America and the power failed in a large area of Canada and the USA. Major cities that were affected by the blackout included New York and Toronto. The power-outage lasted a number of hours and in some areas for several days. All aspects of life were affected and that included computer systems. The Air Canada Flight System Operations Control Centre in Mississauga, Ontario was one of the affected systems. It appears that it had a secondary power system but that also failed. Without the system Air Canada was unable to calculate flight loadings, crew schedules and the like and, as a consequence, all flights were cancelled for a day with schedules being disrupted for several further days.

◆ The Child Credit Scheme. In 2003 the UK government introduced a new child credit scheme designed to better help families on low income – the scheme replaced the previous support system. In the event the workload of taking on the new scheme proved too much for the new system and many vulnerable families were left without the support they needed for extended periods. The scheme relied on information systems that were not able to cope with the volume of transactions and the number of queries that occurred when things started to go wrong.

These problems are not an everyday occurrence but when they do happen they cause widespread disruption, inconvenience and, in the worst case, loss of life. All organisations need to plan for these, and other, eventualities. This process is known as disaster recovery planning. The plans need to be thorough but also need to be in proportion to the problems that would be caused (to the organisation, client groups and society) by a loss of the system. All organisations, whatever their systems and the implications of failure, must make sure that they keep secure backups of their system. In addition the disaster recovery plan can / should include:

◆ Provision of a standby generator. This is an expensive facility and is only justified for systems where continuous operation is essential. The standby generator needs to be properly maintained, have an adequate supply of fuel and be tested at regular intervals. The Air Canada example shows the importance of a reliable, secondary, power supply.

◆ Alternative facilities. Should the system fail, or be hit by a disaster, the organisation needs to have plans to re-create the system and get back into operation. One approach is to engage the services of a disaster recovery organisation that has standby facilities ready for such eventualities (provided all its clients don't have problems at the same time!).

◆ Duplicate systems. Some large organisations, such as banks where reliability is seen as vital, will have duplicate facilities. One approach is to have two data centres at different locations. The system will be running at one of the data centres but all updates are done in parallel on the second system. Should the first system fail the network is automatically switched to the second system – a procedure known as 'hot standby'.

These arrangements are just examples of what can be done to ensure that the service is adequately protected. Disaster recovery planning needs to fit the circumstances of the organisation and match likely threats with a proportionate response. The essential point is that with organisations and society so dependent on IT and IS systems there needs to be appropriate provision to ensure adequate and continuous service.

In additional to the administrative systems we have been discussing, there are some IT systems that are classified as 'safety critical' – the failure of any of these systems can create a disaster. Examples of these systems include:

◆ Intensive care systems in hospitals.
◆ Railway signalling systems and the control systems for driverless trains.
◆ The avionics systems of fly-by-wire aircraft.
◆ The control systems of nuclear power stations.

Fortunately, cases of failures in such systems that have caused real disasters are rare. Examples of systems that have had problems include:

◆ London Ambulance Service (LAS). In June 1991 the London Ambulance Service contracted for a new command and control system that was to be used in the control room to assist in the handling of emergency calls and the allocation of ambulances to those calls. The system went live in October 1992 and the control room rapidly became overloaded as it failed to operate effectively with the new system. The result was that many people suffered long delays waiting for ambulances and a number of deaths were attributed to the delays. After a couple of days the new system was switched off and the control room reverted to its previous procedures. There was a public enquiry that revealed a number of problems with the project. The project had been commissioned from a provider that had limited experience in the field on the basis of a very low tender price. The project was inadequately managed, the software was incomplete and unstable and the emergency back-up system was untested.

- The Big One at Blackpool Pleasure Beach. This was a new roller-coaster system and as with all such systems it was trying to push the sense of thrill and excitement to the limits. The Big One was designed to run with two 'trains' and had a computer control system to ensure that they did not collide. In testing the software protection mechanism did not work and the safety margins could not be adhered to. The problem was attributed to software but finding the problem proved elusive. In the event the roller-coaster had to open with only one train running at any one time.

The importance of safety critical systems requires that appropriate procedures be followed to ensure that the systems are error free and reliable in their operation. These provisions can include:

- Duplicated systems. Many safety critical systems have duplicated IT facilities – if one system fails the other is on hot standby to take over. In some cases the systems are programmed independently and they have to agree on a course of action before it is implemented (this tries to avoid the problem of failures being caused by errors in the software).

- Fail safe procedures. This is nicely illustrated in railway signalling systems – if there is a system failure the signals default to stop and hopefully that avoids any problem that might otherwise have occurred. Fail safe seems a good principle for the railway and a number of other process control requirements but is rather more difficult to apply in avionics.

- Special design procedures. Special analysis procedures are needed to identify circumstances (and combinations of circumstances) that can affect the control system – techniques include fault tree analysis and Petri nets. The design of the software must also be rigorous and can employ procedures, such as formal specifications, which introduce a degree of mathematical control to the design process.

A final area of concern is that of the health and safety of people who operate computer systems. Before we start, let us be clear, computing is not a dangerous manual task such a building or being a firefighter and the risks are not as dramatic as in many other professions. That said, there are problem areas involved in working with computers and it is proper that staff who use computers are adequately trained and protected (and home users could also do well to take the risks into account). The problems that can arise from computer usage include:

- Eyestrain. Usage of visual displays can lead to eyestrain and that in turn exacerbates visual defects. The problem arises from prolonged periods of usage and is exacerbated by poor screen quality.
- Upper limb disorders / repetitive strain injury (RSI). Usage of the keyboard and mouse can lead to a number of aches and pains and eventually to permanent disabilities. This can affect the neck and shoulders but is most common in the wrist, where an inflamed tendon causes carpal tunnel syndrome.

◆   General safety problems include dropped equipment, electrical dangers, and people falling over cables that have not been properly secured and covered.

The basic requirement is for all equipment to be electrically safe, properly secured and for cables to be safely routed away from where people walk. The prevention of conditions such as eyestrain and RSI requires:

◆   Quality computer equipment. Staff need good quality VDUs with minimum flicker and keyboards where the angle can be adjusted. The VDU should be positioned at the right height and distance for the user.
◆   Ergonomic workstations. Staff must have a comfortable position that is suited to their stature. This requires a good size desk at an appropriate height, a seat with adjustable height and backrest and possibly a footrest.
◆   Good lighting. The lighting, and if necessary blinds, should be arranged to provide good illumination but also to avoid glare on the screen.

It is also necessary for staff who make extensive use of computer equipment to take frequent breaks – to do another task or to have a coffee break away from the machine. There are EU health and safety standards for habitual users of computer workstations.

25.4   Civil Liberties

George Orwell in his book *1984* painted a picture of a squalid society where Big Brother was always watching you – and now we have the technology.

Big Brother watches us on CCTV when we walk down the high street and go into shops. Big Sister knows where we are, within a few metres, if we move about with a mobile phone switched on. Uncle government could well be intercepting our phone calls and our e-Mails. And very possibly, quite soon, all cars will have electronic equipment that allows their location to be monitored and recorded.

Big Brother is on our side. This technology can help prevent traffic congestion, fight crime and could even give us directions to the nearest McDonald's! As with all technology it can have wider effects than intended. It could:

◆   Catch out the husband who has told his spouse he is working late but is out with a colleague doing something other than work – possibly he deserved to be caught?
◆   Record the identities of all the students taking part in an anti-tuition fees demonstration. Possibly there is no harm done but the authorities have a rather ambivalent attitude to the right to protest and to those who take part in demonstrations.

Big Brother did not just watch, he remembered – and computers are good at remembering. As individuals there will be data on us at the university – it needs a list of its students, what course they are doing, where they live, have they paid and how they are progressing. There will also be data on us:

◆   At the bank – each bank account, building society account and credit card company keeps personal details of each of its customers.

- With the insurance company – the system needs details of each policy holder. The insurance industry also pools information between insurance companies to help them track down fraudulent claims.
- At the doctor's – the doctor wants a record of past problems and previous treatments as they can affect the current diagnosis.
- With our employers – they need details on who they employ and what to pay us. The personnel file can also include reports from our supervisor and details of our sick record – possibly it won't all be complimentary.
- At the supermarket – if we have a loyalty card it can look up everything we bought each time we went shopping – if anybody wants to know (there are cases where the Inland Revenue has asked).
- With government – there are records at the tax office and with the Department of Social Security. If we have a car we are with the DVLA. If we commit an offence (and a third of young males do) we will be on the police computer, and the internal intelligence services (MI5) keep some sort of record on millions of law-abiding citizens. When we fill in a census form that goes onto a computer as well – they are not supposed to use the data to identify individuals but I guess they could.

All (or at least most) of this data is there for good reason. Organisations need data to conduct business on behalf of their clients and the government needs to administer its social and public order programs. This plethora of information can be a problem:

- When it is wrong. People have been refused credit, turned down for jobs or, in a few cases, arrested on the basis of wrong information held on a computer. To make it worse these mistakes can be very hard to correct: organisations seem to be more likely to believe their computer records than clients who claim they have acted on the basis of misinformation.
- When the information gets into the wrong hands. It may be that there is information on individuals that they are entitled to keep private (e.g. an offence that has expired or a medical test that revealed a genetic vulnerability to some disease). If this information is revealed to an employer or an insurance company they could be severely disadvantaged when they should not have been.

The area of how the availability of information affects civil liberties is a difficult one. At a first look it would seem that the more information that is available the better. That said, all of us have aspects of our past that we would not be happy to publicise and other aspects that we would rather downplay – when we fill in a job application we emphasise the positive and it might act to our disadvantage if all aspects of our past, however trivial, were available to the potential employer. The Data Protection Act attempts to keep a balance between the use of personal information and our right to privacy. This is further discussed in the next chapter.

Finally, I note that this discussion of personal data and civil liberties has been in the context of a democratically governed liberal democracy. Out of that context, the availability of information is a powerful tool in the hands of an authoritarian government or in a society that chooses to discriminate against some minority groups. In the Second World War the Germans, when they took over France, made use of a list of all Lyons' Jews that was held at the city hall.

25.5 Professional Societies and Codes of Conduct

The way IT and IS are applied in society is a responsibility of government and the organisations who use IT but it is also a responsibility of the professionals who plan, create and operate computer systems.

It is a responsibility of professionals to adhere to appropriate standards, and their responsibility to society is enshrined in the codes of conduct of professional societies. The best known example are doctors with their Hippocratic Oath – a doctor who behaves in an inappropriate way can be suspended or 'struck off' by the British Medical Association (and there are similar organisations for the medical profession in other countries). The activities of professional societies include:

◆ Controlling entry to the profession. To become a member of a professional society a candidate has to demonstrate a certain level of knowledge – typically there are a number of levels of membership determined by qualification and experience. Entry normally requires that the candidate passes the society's exams, is nominated by an existing member and that a satisfactory level of experience can be demonstrated. Exemption from (some of) the exams can be achieved by passing an accredited course, typically a degree.

◆ Enforcing standards. Professional societies have codes of conduct and their members are expected to adhere to those standards. A breach of the standards is a disciplinary offence and the member can be suspended or struck off. Where membership is a condition of practice (as is the case for doctors), being suspended or struck off means that the person can no longer practise his or her profession.

◆ Statutory duty. Professional societies are set up by Royal Charter or statute (Act of Parliament). In some cases the process imposes a number of duties and responsibilities on the society.

For computing the professional association is the British Computer Society (BCS). The Institute of Electrical Engineers (IEE) also represents some of the more technical areas of computing.

The BCS was formed in 1957 and was granted a Royal Charter in 1984. Computing is recognised as an engineering profession by the Engineering Council. The BCS accredit courses for exemption from its exams – your course might have exemption. Ask your tutor if you are interested in joining the BCS. Members of the BCS are entitled to add their grade as a qualification after their name – members have the designation MBCS and fellows can use FBCS. It is not necessary to be a member of the BCS to practise computing – the fact of membership does however imply a high level of competence and membership can be helpful to the individual in gaining employment (possibly it is most relevant overseas).

The BCS has its own code of conduct. This conduct sets out the responsibility of members in the areas of:

- The public interest.
- Duty to employers and clients.
- Duty to the profession.
- Professional competence and integrity.

Its effect is somewhat limited compared with, for example, doctors and lawyers where membership of the society is a condition of practice or compared with other engineering professions where some tasks are reserved to chartered engineers. There is also a problem of how an employee should apply professional standards when, possibly, to apply them would go against the instructions given by the employer. Bott et al. (2000) give a number of examples of possible ethical conflicts. Example include where an organisation is contracted to provide IT systems for a totalitarian regime or where a safety-critical system is behind schedule and staff are urged to cut corners to ensure on-time delivery.

Exercises

Ethical issues at work and in computing are a difficult area. Hopefully this chapter has created some awareness of the issues involved and the exercises are intended to reinforce that awareness.

1. Think about the systems that (probably) hold your personal details. Are there any systems you can think of in addition to those indicated in this chapter? Use a tutorial session to compare notes and find out if any of your colleagues have been inconvenienced by personal data held on computers.

2. The police use finger prints in their detective work and there is increasing use of DNA analysis. Finger prints and DNA details are kept on a computer system that can be used for matching when fresh evidence is found. Currently data is held for people who have a conviction but there have been proposals to include additional groups such as immigrants or the whole population. Discuss what is appropriate.

3. Computer systems are used for a wide variety of applications and in countries with differing degrees of democracy, corruption and / or repression. Are there any computer applications you would not be prepared to work on? Are there any applications or types of data that should not be computerised? These questions could also be discussed in a tutorial.

Note, there are no exercises given for **chapter 26** – it could be helpful to study both this chapter and the next chapter before attempting the exercises.

Further Reading

More detailed coverage of professional societies (including the full text of the BCS code of conduct) is given in:

Bott F., Coleman A., Eaton J. and Rowland D. (2000) *Professional Issues in Software Engineering* ,3rd ed., Taylor and Francis, London.

The web site of the BCS can be found at:

http://www1.bcs.org.uk

If you are doing a computing course there is, very probably, a staff member who deals with liaison with the BCS (or equivalent society for students studying in other countries). You can ask them for further details – the BCS has a student membership programme.

Chapter 26
IS and the Law

Summary

The use of IS and IT permeates nearly all aspects of economic and social activity. As with all such activity there is a legal angle. The law is used to regulate legitimate activity, for example contracts, and it is used to outlaw inappropriate activities, for example malicious damage and theft.

In most cases the use of computers is a new way of doing tasks that have been done for many years using other means. Areas where computers have been extensively used are banking, trade exchanges, publishing, etc. and, in general, it has been found that existing law is still applicable. The computer has also provided dishonest people with a new way of committing acts, such as theft, fraud and damage to other people's property – again existing law has been generally applicable in these changed circumstances. That said, there are two areas where new laws have been seen as necessary. These are:

- Computer Misuse Act (1990) – this applies to the unauthorised use of computing facilities. The offence is aggravated where there is an intent of committing a serious criminal offence or making unauthorised changes to data or programs.
- Data Protection Act (1998) – this regulates who can store what personal data and the uses that data can be put to.

In this chapter we take a brief look at the legal implications of IS and IT and then summarise the provisions of the Computer Misuse Act and the Data Protection Act.

26.1   Computing and the Law

The use of IS and IT is extensive in administration, commerce and in people's private lives. As with all other areas of human activity the law can come in when things go wrong and it can be appropriate to take legal precautions before things get to that stage. Much of the law that applies to the provision of IT services and the use of IS is the same law that applies where IT is not explicitly involved. Examples of areas where the law has had to be interpreted and / or applied for an electronic age include:

- Electronic Contracts. The traditional way of making a contract is on paper and, in some cases, it will be signed by the contracting parties. However, with EDI and Internet e-Commerce the transaction and hence the contract is electronic. The question then arises as to whether the contract is legally enforceable and at what stage in the exchanges the contract came into force.

The answer is complex. It depends, in part, on what the contract was for and hence which pieces of legislation apply. Many types of trade transaction can be carried out electronically but some exchanges specify paper documentation.

The general form of an exchange of contract has three steps:

- An invitation to treat: I will sell my secondhand Bob Dylan CD for £2. This is, in effect, an advert. It has no legal status and I can put the price up, sell the CD to someone else or withdraw it from sale.
- An offer: Susan says, OK Dave, sounds good, I will give you £2 for your Bob Dylan CD.
- Acceptance (of the offer unmodified): I say, Done. You Susan will have my Bob Dylan CD for £2.

These three stages are neatly demonstrated in an e-shop. The invitation is the goods displayed on the screen; the offer is the order form (for retail transactions that is accompanied by payment) and the acceptance is the confirmation screen. Other forms of electronic ordering, such as EDI, seem to (generally) miss out the acceptance stage, but the way transactions are to be conducted is generally covered by an interchange agreement. Generally standard electronic trade exchanges, such as these, will not result in disputes (although there have been cases of goods offered online at mistakenly low prices and customers rushing to take advantage of the mistake). Electronic exchanges (e-Mails and electronic document transfers) can also be used for more complex transactions and, in these exchanges, problems and delays in sending and receiving the documents could cause problems.

- Contracts for computer equipment and computer services. Contracts are also applicable to the purchase of computer hardware, software and the employment of IT staff. This can be an area of great difficulty as IT and IS systems are complex and the outcomes of computer projects frequently fail to meet the expectations of the parties involved. Obviously the best way to avoid disputes is for the parties involved to draw up a comprehensive and explicit contract before work is started or goods are delivered. That said, IT contracts are not different from other commercial transactions and the same laws apply. The sale of computer hardware is subject to the Sale of Goods Act 1979 and the writing of bespoke software to the Supply of Goods and Services Act 1982. The legal position of contracts for 'off-the-shelf' software is far from clear (Bainbridge, 2000). Contracts for goods and services work within the legal framework and that can mean that conditions within the contract are invalid or that conditions that are not stated apply. The Sale of Goods Act, for example, requires that goods must be of satisfactory quality, and a piece of IT equipment that failed to operate effectively or continually broke down would seem to fail that test.

◆ Intellectual property. Intellectual property rights (IPRs) include copyright and patent law. The intention is that an inventor of a new device or the author of a document can benefit from his or her work without others making unauthorised use of the material. Legal protection has existed in these areas for many years but the use of computers raises the questions of how to apply patents and copyright law to something as essentially intangible as software and to material that exists, or is to be reproduced, in electronic form. The answer seems to be that patents apply to hardware and that software, and other forms of original work that are electronically recorded, are subject to copyright protection. The applicability of copyright law to software has been made explicit in the Copyright, Designs and Patents Act 1988.

◆ Theft and forgery. Computers are used for many financial transactions and, arguably, the smart way to rob a bank is electronically (rather than with a pick-axe handle and a stocking mask). Many computer crimes are inside jobs – done by an employee of the company or the bank. An example in the news as I write this passage is an employee of Lloyds TSB who stole more than GB£ 2 million from 38 accounts – he used the money to set up, house and maintain the country's biggest collection of exotic birds (Alison, 2003). A more subtle way of using the computer for theft is a technique known as 'salami-slicing' where small amounts are taken from many accounts using procedures written into the banking or accounting software. One such fraud rounded all calculations down to the nearest penny and then transferred the fractions of a penny to the perpetrator's own account – in the course of thousands of transactions a tidy sum was accumulated. The vehicle for the crime can be a computer but the crime is still theft or forgery – the issue is detection, not which law is to be used for prosecution.

Two areas where legal provision has been made that is specific to the application and use of computers are:

◆ Computer misuse with the Computer Misuse Act of 1990.
◆ Data protection with the Data Protection Acts of 1984 and 1998.

These two IS / IT specific provisions are discussed below.

26.2 Computer Misuse Act

The Computer Misuse Act 1990 was designed to deal with a number of 'inappropriate' uses of computers that could not be effectively dealt with under existing law. The Computer Misuse Act is fairly limited in its scope; it makes it an offence to:

◆ Obtain unauthorised access to computer material. The intention here is to deter hacking. It is the unauthorised access that is the offence and there does not need to be any damage done. Unauthorised access is only an offence if there was intent involved – if I am working on the university computer or on a web site and I stumble across something by accident then there is no offence.

◆ Obtain unauthorised access to a computer with the intent to commit or facilitate a serious crime. This is an extension of the first offence; Bainbridge (2000) suggests it can be summed up as 'aggravated hacking'. The offence still applies whether or not the crime is committed (and even if it would not have been possible for the crime to be committed). The example most often quoted is blackmail. If someone hacks into another person's computer with the intent of finding material that could be used for blackmail then it is an offence. It is still an offence if the blackmail is not committed and it is also an offence if the expected blackmail material did not exist or could not be found. If the blackmail did take place then this could (also) be tried under the relevant statute.

◆ Deliberately make unauthorised changes to the content of a computer. This offence could include deliberately deleting files, creating and distributing a virus that causes damage or creating a time bomb (a program, or section of a program, that is loaded onto a computer and is designed to cause damage at a certain time or in certain circumstances, e.g. after a member of staff has left or if a contractor is not paid). The provision requires intent and knowledge – accidentally deleting a file or leaving bugs in a program are not offences.

   Bainbridge (2000) gives, as an example, the case of a nurse who was successfully prosecuted under section 3. The nurse hacked into the hospital computer and changed a patient's prescription in a way that was potential lethal – fortunately no harm was done to the patient and prosecution was limited to an offence under the Computer Misuse Act.

One problem that arises with computer crime is the question of where the offence was committed. I could (in theory at least) from my office in the university, hack into a computer in America and transfer funds to an account in Switzerland. The Computer Misuse Act tries to cover this by making its provisions applicable to acts that originate from the home country or are directed at a computer within a home country (i.e. the UK).

Sources used for the section on the Computer Misuse Act include Bainbridge (2000) and Bott et al., (2000). Note that the intention is to give an outline of the Computer Misuse Act and this summary should not be seen as constituting legal advice.

26.3 Data Protection Act

Computers allow the creation of large databanks of information. We have discussed how they can be created using an information system and then used for management information. It is not necessary to have a computer to create and access information but the use of IT increases the ease with which the data can be stored, searched, correlated and distributed.

The availability of information can be of great advantage in the administration of businesses and services. That said, where personal information is involved it can be seen as an infringement of personal privacy, it can cause the individual inconvenience or distress and ultimately, if misused, it is a threat to civil liberties.

In order to regulate the collection and use of personal data by organisations we have data protection legislation. The first UK Data Protection Act was passed in 1984 and this was superseded by a second Act in 1998. The 1998 Act was passed to harmonise UK data protection legislation with the provision in other members of the European Union. Data protection legislation applies only to personal data on living individuals. The act has the underlying objective of protecting the individual from three potential dangers (Bott et al., 2000):

◆ The use of personal information that is inaccurate, incomplete or irrelevant.
◆ The possibility of personal information being accessed by unauthorised persons.
◆ The use of personal information in a context, or for a purpose, other than that for which the information was collected.

The problems of incorrect information and the misuse of information have been illustrated by a number of cases – many of them more of a case of 'cock-up' than intentional damage. Bainbridge (2000) quotes the case of a man who was charged with driving while disqualified because of convictions wrongly recorded on the police national computer. Another problem area is credit reference agencies that hold incorrect data or use data inappropriately – the result is that people are denied access to the credit, loans or mortgages for which they would otherwise qualify. A new area of concern relates to the increasing availability of genetic information and the possibility that people with 'genetic abnormalities' could be denied jobs and facilities such as insurance.

It should be noted that English law, including the Data Protection Act, does not give a general right to privacy. However the Human Rights Act 1998, incorporating the European Convention on Human Rights into UK law, does include, in Article 8, a provision that everyone has the right to respect for his private family life, his home and his correspondence. The Human Rights Act is not specific to data protection and requires interpretation by the courts. However its interpretation so far has tended to reinforce and extend a right to privacy.

Enforcement of the Data Protection Act (1998) is presided over by the Information Commissioner (replacing the Data Protection Commissioner of the 1984 Act). The act provides a number of definitions which include:

◆ Data controller – a person within the organisation that holds the data, who determines the purpose and processing of the data. Organisations must designate a person as being responsible for personal data when they register with the Information Commissioner.
◆ Data subject – a person who is the subject of personal data.

Under the Act data controllers are required to notify the Information Commissioner of the purpose for which they will hold personal data and processing they intend will take place on that data (there are exemptions to the requirement for notification). The Act also provides the Information Commissioner with powers to investigate the use of personal data by organisations. The investigation may be triggered by a request received from a data subject. The Information Commissioner can make rulings that may include, for example, a requirement to rectify or destroy inaccurate data. The Information Commissioner can issue enforcement notices or bring a prosecution.

The Data Protection Act requires that anyone processing personal data must comply with eight principles of good practice. The principles require:

- Personal data shall be processed fairly and lawfully. The Act specifies the conditions under which it is lawful to process personal data. For 'ordinary personal data', such as names, addresses and telephone numbers at least one of the conditions set out in Schedule 2 must be met. There is then a more stringent additional test for the processing of 'sensitive personal data' where at least one of the conditions set out in Schedule 3 must be met. Sensitive personal data includes information relating to racial or ethnic origin, political opinions, religious beliefs, trade union membership, health, sex life and criminal convictions. One of the conditions set out in Schedule 2 is consent; the corresponding requirement in Schedule 3 is explicit consent. Schedule 2 includes several alternative conditions such as the data is being used to perform a contract between the parties or data that is necessary in order to comply with a legal obligation. For sensitive personal data, Schedule 3 alternative conditions include the meeting of legal requirements, medical reasons or to ensure / promote equal treatment of racial / ethnic groups.

- Personal data shall be processed for limited purposes. The requirement of the Act is that: '*Personal data shall be obtained only for one or more specified and lawful purpose, and shall not be further processed in any manner incompatible with that purpose or those purposes*'. The purpose for which the data is collected must have been specified to the Information Commissioner and the data can not then be used for other purposes.

- Personal data shall be adequate, relevant and not excessive. Put simply, this means that you shouldn't collect more data than you need for the purpose specified. Before you start asking people for their date of birth, religion or even their gender – think whether it is necessary for the declared purpose.

- Personal data shall be accurate and up-to-date. This requires that the data collection process is conducted with care and that, where necessary, it is updated. A common practice with, for example, staff records is to send out a print of the data on the system and to ask staff to update it or to sign that it is correct.

- Personal data shall not be kept longer than necessary. This requirement is a difficult one (and one that many sources avoid commenting on). If we take for example your university student record, how long should the university keep those details? Arguably once the student has left the details can be erased but what if the student asks for a reference a year later or a duplicate degree certificate after ten years?

◆ Personal data shall be processed in accordance with the rights of the data subject. There are provisions in the Act that prohibit processing that is likely to cause damage or distress; limit the circumstances where personal data can be used for direct marketing; and relate to automatic decision making.

   This principle also requires that the data subject is given access, on request, to his or her data and details of why it is held and to whom it may be disclosed. This provision is subject to a reasonable administrative charge. A problem with this provision is it is only useful if you know that an organisation is holding your personal data.

◆ Personal data must be kept secure. The requirements of the act are that: '*Appropriate technical and organisational measures shall be taken against unauthorised or unlawful processing of personal data and against accidental loss or destruction of, or damage to, personal data*'. This requirement is met by making the type of privacy and security provision that would be expected in IS / IT systems. These typically include appropriate virus checking, password protected access (with access to systems and functions restricted to those staff who have a proper need to use the data) and regular backups of the data (and the backups need to be subject to an appropriate privacy and security regime). These provisions are sensible precautions for all business systems – under the Data Protection Act they become a statutory requirement for systems that store and process personal data.

◆ Personal data must not be transferred to countries without adequate data protection. The Data Protection Act derives from the Data Protection Directive of the European Community (now the European Union (EU)) and this ensures that all EU countries have a similar level of protection for personal data. There are, however, many other countries in the world that have less stringent (or minimal) data protection requirements and there is an obvious loophole if personal data can be transferred to a jurisdiction where it would not be protected – hence this final principle. This principle is particularly important where personal data is held by a multinational organisation. It is to be noted that the US is one country with fairly minimal data protection provisions and this can cause problems as many multinationals are US based. The use of e-Commerce and the Internet adds a further complication as it is not necessarily clear cut as to which country's laws apply to an online operation. Note there are exceptions to this principle that include consent to transfer and data used in the performance of a contract.

The operation of two of these principles was illustrated by cases that came up in connection with the poll tax (community charge – subsequently replaced by the council tax). The legislation in effect at that time was the 1984 Act but the data protection principles were similar. The cases that came up stopped councils from:

◆ Cross-checking the poll tax register with the electoral register. Obviously there was a disincentive to fill in the forms to register to pay poll tax and the idea was that a cross-check with the list of voters might flush out some of the people who had failed to register. The ruling was that the purpose of the electoral register was to provide a list of voters and using it for the poll tax was outside that specified purpose.

◆ Collecting extensive details on the poll tax register. Councils were left to devise their own poll tax registers and many of them asked for quite extensive personal details on the registration form. The ruling was that the personal details that could be collected were to be limited to those that were strictly necessary for the administration of the poll tax.

There are exemptions to the requirements of the Data Protection Act and the eight principles. These exemptions include national security and crime prevention. Exemptions are qualified and usages of data and refusal to disclose data can be appealed.

Sources used for the section on the Data Protection Act include Bainbridge (2000), Becta (2003), Bott et al., (2000) and Keith Millar's lecture notes (MMU). Note that the intention is to give an outline of the Data Protection Act and this summary should not be seen as constituting legal advice.

Further Reading

Two books that give a more detailed coverage on IS and the law are:

Bainbridge D. (2000) *Introduction to Computer Law*, 4th ed., Longman, Harlow.

Bott F., Coleman A., Eaton J. and Rowland D. (2000) *Professional Issues in Software Engineering* ,3rd ed., Taylor and Francis, London.

The full text of the Data Protection Act 1998 is available from the HMSO web site and there is extensive information on the site of the Information Commissioner. The web addresses are:

http://www.legislation.hmso.gov.uk/acts/acts1998/19980029.htm
http://www.dataprotection.gov.uk

Part VII
Conclusions

There is a wide variety of information systems (IS) and an ever increasing availability of information and communications technologies (ICTs). To be beneficial, the IS must be appropriate to the task and it is the job of the IS specialist to ensure that is the case. To fulfil that function the IS specialist must:

- Be aware of the way the business is organised and of its objectives.
- Understand how IS can be applied to business requirements.
- Be knowledgeable of the IT facilities that could be used for IS applications.
- Be competent in the use of system analysis and design (SA&D) methods and techniques.
- Understand the social, ethical and legal implications of IS and IT.

ICTs and their applications are developing all the time. In that developing field the role of the IS specialist remains the same – to design and deliver IS systems that fulfil the needs of the organisation and help it to play its proper role within society. This book is an introductory course that provides a basic education and training for the IS specialists of the future.

Chapter 27
Conclusions

27.1 Data In and Information Out

The essential function of an information system (IS) is to take in data and process it to produce information. Computer based information systems are implemented using computers, data storage and communications networks – a set of facilities that we call information and communications technologies (ICTs).

The classic application of IS is to the large administrative processes within organisations. The data input is the business transactions received by the organisation or generated by the activities of the organisation. The information produced consists of output business transactions and of management information.

The use of networks has linked the IS to members of staff at their desks, to other systems within the overall IS infrastructure of the organisation, and to trading partners, administrative organisations and to members of the public. The development and widespread adoption of ICTs has produced other types of application. These include:

- ◆ Desk top productivity aids – such as word processing, spreadsheets and desk top publishing.
- ◆ Communications – e-Mail, EDI and web based communication systems.
- ◆ End user systems – small information systems used by small numbers of staff – possibly developed by the staff themselves using facilities such as MS Access.
- ◆ Public information and access systems – for example, information for travellers and the bank's automated teller machines.
- ◆ Embedded systems – in machinery, transport equipment and consumer products.
- ◆ e-Commerce and online information – accessed via the Internet or with the use of mobile telephony.
- ◆ Entertainment systems – computer games and the use of the Internet as a recreational tool.

This widespread use of ICTs is affecting not just the workplace but virtually all other aspects of life: People can now:

- ◆ Work from home or on the move – a process know as teleworking.
- ◆ Study a distance-learning course that uses the Internet and their home PC as the main delivery tool.
- ◆ Book their holiday, order groceries and file their tax return online.

And as they go on holiday the plane will be controlled by computer systems for much of its journey (think about that one when your next programming exercise falls over in a heap).

27.2 The IS Practitioner

Whatever the IS application and the technologies that are used, there remain the basic requirements that the system should meet user needs and user requirements – and ensuring that is the case is the role of the information system discipline.

To ensure that the system is fit for the intended purpose, the system designer must:

- ◆ Be aware of the way the business is organised and of its objectives. The IS specialist needs to understand business and how it operates. Any new IS should contribute to the efficiency of the organisation, the quality of its service to clients / customers and to its competitive advantage. Many organisations have a strategy and IS developments will often be an important component of its delivery. An introduction to business was the subject of *Part II*.

- ◆ Understand how IS can be applied to business requirements. ICTs are a tool and, as with any tool, there are appropriate ways of using it. Technology is developing all the time and the applications we can use ICTs for, and the ways we use the technology, are changing with those developments. We need to understand how ICTs are used in business and the sort of considerations that need to be taken into account when they are introduced. In *Part III* we looked at a number of IS systems and facilities that contribute to an understanding of the IS infrastructure of an organisation.

- ◆ Be knowledgeable about the IT that could be used for IS applications. There is a range of IT facilities available to the system designer. This includes the computer systems, data storage facilities, networks and a range of peripheral devices. These can be configured in a variety of ways with processing and data distributed across a network of devices to suit the needs of the organisation and the requirements of the application. The IS practitioner needs to be aware of what IT is available and what it is sensibly used for. An introduction to IT facilities was the subject of *Part IV*.

- ◆ Be competent in the use of system analysis and design (SA&D) methods. The standard way of designing a computer system is to find out what the user needs, design an IT system that meets that requirement, write (or obtain) software to implement the requirement, test the system and then, finally, we are in business. The process of designing and implementing useful information systems is fraught with difficulty and many (or most!) IS / IT systems do not achieve the expected benefit. Appropriate design procedures are a way of eliminating some of the risk. In *Part V* we studied

lifecycles, methodologies and either structured or object-oriented techniques for system design.

◆ Understand the social, ethical and legal implications of IS and IT. ICTs
give authorities and organisations powerful tools to automate processes,
collect data and to correlate information. The use of ICTs can make
processes efficient and provide facilities that would otherwise not be
possible. However there are risks: to the health and safety of workers, to
the quality of life and to the civil liberties of the citizen. In *Part VI* we took a
brief look at the social, legal and ethical implications of IS and IT.

IS is a diverse subject area. The opportunities presented by the use of ICTs and
the aspirations of the users are constantly changing. To be an effective IS
specialist requires an education across a range of topics and this must be
supplemented by a process of lifelong learning. I have been an IS practitioner
since 1967 and an IS educator since 1991. The field is constantly changing but, in
many ways, the fundamentals remain the same. Knowledge and skills must be
constantly updated as new techniques and technologies are introduced. The field
of IS and IT is stimulating and ever changing. We have to learn to distinguish the
useful from the fanciful. Above all we must give primacy to the (real) user
requirement. Any IS we are involved in developing should be appropriate,
effective, efficient and, above all, useful.

Bibliography

Alison R. (2003) 'Doing bird, the parrot loving conman', *Guardian*, 3 Sept 2003. p. 2.

Andrews K. (1971) *The Concept of Corporate Strategy*, Urwin, Homewood, Ill.

Atzeni P., Ceri S., Paraboschi S. and Torlone R. (1999) *Database Systems: Concepts, Languages and Architectures*, McGraw-Hill, Maidenhead.

Avison D. and Fitzgerald G. (2003) *Information Systems Development: Methodologies, Techniques and Tools*, 3rd ed., McGraw-Hill, Maidenhead.

Bainbridge D. I. (2000) *Introduction to Computer Law*, 4th ed., Longman, Harlow.

Becta (2003) *The Data Protection Act*, http://dataprotection,ngfl.gov.uk/schools.

Benjamin R. I., de Long D. W. and Scott Morton M. S. (1990) 'Electronic Data Interchange: How Much Competitive Advantage', *Long Range Planning*, Vol 23, No 1, pp. 29-40.

Bennett S., McRobb S. and Farmer R. (1999) *Object Oriented Systems Analysis and Design using UML*, McGraw-Hill, Maidenhead.

Beynon-Davies P. (1991) *Expert Database Systems: A Gentle Introduction*, McGraw-Hill, London.

Beynon-Davies P. (2004) *Database Systems*, 3rd ed., Palgrave Macmillan, Basingstoke.

Berge J (1991) *The EDIFACT Standard*, NCC – Blackwell, Oxford.

Bhs (1994) *The Role of Computers within Bhs*, Bhs, London.

Bocij P., Chaffey D., Greasley A. and Hickie S. (1999) *Business Information Systems: Technology, Development and Management*, Financial Times – Pitman, London.

Booch G., Rumbaugh J. and Jacobson I. (1999) *Unified Modelling Language: Reference Manual,* Addison Wesley, Reading, Mass.

Bray P. (1992) 'Web or Wheel', *Which Computer*, January 1992, pp. 50–58.

Cadle J. and Yates D. (2001) *Project Management for Information Systems*, 3rd ed., Financial Times / Pitman, London.

Cassidy J. (2002) *dot.con: the greatest story ever sold*, Penguin, London

Ciborra C. and Jelassi T. (1994) *Strategic Information Systems: A European Perspective*, Wiley, Chichester.

Clark A (2002) 'Tail of woe', *Guardian 2*, 10 Sept 02, pp. 2–3.

Clifton H. D. Ince D. C. and Sutcliffe A. G. (2000) *Business Information Systems*, 6th ed., Prentice Hall, Hemel Hempstead.

Code P. and Yourdon E. (1991) *Object Oriented Design*, Yordon Press, Englewood Cliffs, NJ.

Connolly T. and Begg C. (2002) *Database Systems: A Practical Approach to Design, Implementation and Management*, 3rd ed., Addison-Wesley, Harlow.

Cope N. (1996) *Retail in the Digital Age*, Bowerdean, London.

Crinnion J. (1991) *Evolutionary System Development: A Practical Guide to the Use of Prototyping within a Structured System Methodology*, Pitman, London.

Curtis G. (1998) *Business Information Systems: Analysis. Design and Practice*, 3nd ed., Prentice Hall, Harlow.

Daniels A. and Yeates D (1988) *Basic System Analysis*, Pitman, London.

De Kare-Silver M. (2000) *e-shock 2000: The electronic shopping revolution: strategies for retailers and manufacturers*, Palgrave Macmillan, Basingstoke.

Dijkstra E. W. (1972) 'Notes on Structured Programming', in Dahl J., Dijkstra E. W. and C. A. R. Hore (ed.) *Structured Programming*, Academic Press, London, p. 182.

Doganis. R (2001) *The airline business in the 21st century*, Routledge, London.

Downs E., Clare P. and Coe I. (1992) *Structured System Analysis and Design: Application and Context*, 2nd ed., Prentice Hall, Hemel Hempstead.

Earl M. J. (1989) *Management Strategies for Information Technology*, Prentice Hall, Hemel Hempstead.

Edwards C., Ward, J. and Bytheway A. (1995) *The Essence of Information Systems*, 2nd ed., Prentice Hall, London.

Esprit (1997) *ESPRIT and Acts projects related to Electronic Commerce*, http://www2.cordis.lu/esprit/src/ecomproj.htm.

Eva M. (1992) *SSADM Version 4: A User's Guide*, McGraw-Hill, London.

Fazlollahi B. ed. (2002) *Strategies for eCommerce Success*, IRM Press, Hershey.

Fowler M. and Scott K. (1999) *UML Distilled*, 2nd ed., Addison Wesley, Reading, Mass.

Freedman A. (1999) *The Computer Desktop Encyclopaedia*, 2nd ed., Amacon, New York.

Galbraith J. K. (1972) *The New Industrial State*, 2nd ed, Penguin, Harmondsworth.

GE Global eXchange Services (2002) *Tesco: Collaboration on the Supply Chain 'TIEs' Tesco Closely to the Needs of the 21st Century Customer*, www.gsx.com.

Globalisation Guide (2002) 'What is globalisation?', *Globalisation Guide.org*, www.globalisationguide.org.

Goodland M. and Slater C. (1995) *SSADM Version 4: A Practical Approach*, McGraw-Hill, London.

Handy C. (1993) *Understanding Organisations*, 4th ed., Penguin, London.

Huff S. L., Wade M. and Schneberger S (2002) *Cases in Electronic Commerce, McGraw-Hill*, New York.

Huws U., Korte W. B. and Robinson S. (1990) *Telework: Towards the Elusive Office*, Wiley, Chichester.

Jelassi T. (1994) 'Binding the Customer through IT', *Competing through Information Technology*, Prentice Hall, Hemel Hempstead, pp. 84–106.

Jennings F. (1986) *Practical Data Communications*, Blackwell, Oxford.

Johnston H. R and Vitel M. R. (1988) 'Creating Competitive Advantage With Interorganizational Information Systems', *MIS Quarterly*, June 1988.

Kalakota R. and Whinston A. B., eds. (1997) *Readings in Electronic Commerce*, Addison Wesley, Reading, Mass.

Kalakota R. and Robinson M. (1999) *e-Business: Roadmap for Success*, Addison Wesley, Reading, Mass.

Kewill (2000) 'Tesco, the Largest UK Food Retailer, Adopts Kewill.NetSM to Bring Efficiency and Visibility to its Supply Chain', *Kewill News*, Vol 1, Issue 2, Dec 2000, www.kewill.com/news/knews/knews1200.htm.

Krcmar H., Bjorn-Anderson N. and O'Callaghan R., eds. (1995) *EDI in Europe: How it Works in Practice*, Wiley, Chichester.

Kuo J. D. (2001) *dot.bomb: Inside an Internet Goliath – from Lunatic Optimism to Panic and Crash*, Little Brown, London

Lane G. (1990) *Communication for Progress: A Guide to International e-Mail*, CIIR, London.

Lehrer D. and Whelan J. (2003) *3G Revenue Generating Applications: Briefing Paper*, Alatto Technologies Ltd. Dublin.

Lynch R. (1997) *Corporate Strategy*, Pitman, London.

Maddison R. N. (1983) *Information System Methodologies*, Wiley Heyden, Chichester.

Mandel T. (1997) *The Elements of User Interface Design*, Wiley.

Mathews R. (2003) 'Supercomputers: top of the Teraflops', *Focus*, No 127, June 2003, pp. 27–31.

Meldrum M., Lejk M. and Guy P. (1993) *SSADM Techniques: an introduction to Version 4*, Chartwell Bratt, Bromley.

Metzgen F. (1990) *Killing the Paper Dragon*, Heinemann Newnes, Oxford.

Morton R. and Chester M. (1997) *Transforming the Business: The IT Contribution*, McGraw-Hill, London.

Needle D. (2004) *Business in Context: An introduction to business and its environment*, 4th ed., Thomson, London.

Norton P. and Anderson V. (2000) *Guide to Microsoft Access 2000 Programming*, SAMS, Indianapolis.

Negroponte N. (1995) *Being Digital*, Hodder and Stoughton, London.

Parfett M. (1992) *What is EDI? A Guide to Electronic Data Interchange*, NCC Blackwell, Manchester – Oxford.

Porter M. E. (1998a) *Competitive Strategy: Techniques for Analysing Industries and Competitors*, Simon & Schuster, London.

Porter M. E. (1998b) *Competitive Advantage: Creating and Sustaining Superior Performance*, Simon and Schuster, London.

Power and Acton (2003) 'The Application of Emerging Technologies in the Travel Industry: Perspectives on Web Services and Service Oriented Architecture, in *CoLLecteR (Europe)*, Galway, 24 June 2003, pp. 9–14.

Pressman R. (2000) *Software Engineering: A Practitioner's Approach*, 5th ed., McGraw Hill, Maidenhead.

Romm C. T and Sudweeks F., eds (1998) *Doing Business Electronically: A Global Perspective of Electronic Commerce*, Springer, London.

Rosenberg D. and Scott K. (1999) *Use Case Driven Object Modelling with UML: A Practical Approach*, Addison Wesley, Reading, Mass.

Scott J. P. (1979) *Corporations, Classes and Capitalism*, Hutchinson, London.

Sokol P. K. (1989) *EDI: The Competitive Edge*, McGraw-Hill, New York.

Spector R. (2002) *amazon.com: Get Big Fast*, Harper Business, New York.

Stapleton J (1997) *DSDM: Dynamic System Development Method*, Addison Wesley, Reading, Mass.

Stevens P and Pooley R (2000) *Using UML: Software Engineering with Objects and Components*, Addison Wesley, Reading, Mass.

Sudweeks F. and Romm C. T. (1999) *Doing Business on the Internet: Opportunities and Pitfalls*, Springer, London.

Sutor B. (2003) 'Plumbing Web Connections', *Harvard Business Review*, Sept 2003, pp. 18–19.

Wheatley (1997) 'Minding the Stores', *CIO Magazine*, 01 Oct 97, www.cio.com/archive/100197_stores_content.htm.

Whiteley D. (1998) 'Would you buy an ice-cream cone over the Internet?, *Eleventh International Bled Electronic Commerce Conference*, June 1998, Bled, Slovenia.

Whiteley D., Hersey I., Miller K. and Quick P. (1999) 'Internet e-Commerce: buying the book and catching the plane', *BIT'99*, November 1999, Manchester

Whiteley D. (2000) *e-Commerce: Strategy, Technology and Applications*, McGraw Hill, Maidenhead.

Whiteley D. (2002) *The Complete e-Shop*, Chandos, Oxford.

Wigland R. T. (1997) 'Electronic Commerce: Definition, Theory and Context', *The Information Society*, Vol. 13, No. 1, pp. 1–16.

Wild R. (1985) *The Essentials of Productions and Operations Management*, Holt Rinehart & Winston, London.

Winfield I. (1991) *Organisations and Information Technology: Systems Power and Job Design*, Blackwell, Oxford.

Index